THE ANNUAL OF PSYCHOANALYSIS

THE ANNUAL OF PSYCHOANALYSIS

A Publication of the Chicago Institute for Psychoanalysis

Volume XVI

International Universities Press, Inc.
Madison Connecticut

Library of Congress Catalog Number: 72–91376
ISBN: 0–8236–0375–X
Published annually and available in print:
Vol. I, 1973; Vol. II, 1974; Vol. III, 1975; Vol. IV, 1976; Vol. V, 1977; Vol. VI, 1978; Vol. VII, 1979; Vol. VIII, 1980; Vol. IX, 1981; Vol. X, 1982; Vol. XI, 1983; Vols. XII/XIII, 1984/1985; Vol. XIV; 1986; Vol. XV, 1987.

Manufactured in the United States of America

With continuing appreciation to Fred M. Hellman, whose interest and generosity make possible the publication of *The Annual of Psychoanalysis*.

CONTENTS

CONTRIBUTORS

Benjamin Garber, M.D.
Training and Supervising Analyst, Institute for Psychoanalysis, Chicago; Clinical Assistant Professor, University of Chicago Medical School; Attending Psychiatrist, Institute for Psychosomatic and Psychiatric Research, Michael Reese Hospital.

Merton Gill, M.D.
Supervising Analyst and Member of the Faculty, Institute for Psychoanalysis, Chicago; Professor of Psychiatry, University of Illinois Medical School, Chicago.

Jules Glenn, M.D.
Clinical Professor of Psychiatry, New York University Medical Center; Training and Supervising Analyst, New York University Medical Center.

Charles M. Jaffe, M.D.
Professor of Psychiatry, Rush Medical College; Member of the Committee for Postgraduate Education, Institute for Psychoanalysis, Chicago.

Daniel S. Jaffe, M.D.
Former Training and Supervising Analyst, Washington Psychoanalytic Institute, Pittsburgh Psychoanalytic Institute, Washington Association for Psychoanalytic Education; Clinical Professor of Psychiatry, Georgetown University School of Medicine.

Charles Kligerman, M.D.
Faculty Member Emeritus and Consultant to the Psychoanalytic Education Council, Institute for Psychoanalysis, Chicago.

Hans W. Loewald, M.D.
Faculty, Western New England Institute for Psychoanalysis; Clinical Professor of Psychiatry Emeritus, Yale University School of Medicine.

George Moraitis, M.D.
Training and Supervising Analyst and Member of the Faculty, Institute for Psychoanalysis, Chicago.

Kenneth M. Newman, M.D.
Training and Supervising Analyst and Member of the Faculty, Institute for Psychoanalysis, Chicago.

George H. Pollock, M.D., Ph.D.
President, Institute for Psychoanalysis, Chicago; Professor of Psychiatry, Northwestern University; President, Center for Psychosocial Studies.

Philip Rubovits-Seitz, M.D.
Clinical Professor, Department of Psychiatry and the Behavioral Sciences, George Washington University Medical Center.

Margret Schaefer, Ph.D.
Research Associate, Institute for Psychosomatic Research and Training, Michael Reese Hospital.

Victoria Shahly, M.A.
Doctoral Candidate, Clinical Psychology, University of California Berkeley; Intern, Psychological Clinic, University of Michigan.

David S. Spira, M.D.
Faculty, Postgraduate Education Program, Institute for Psychoanalysis, Chicago; Faculty, The University of Chicago.

Bhaskar Sripada, M.D.
Medical Director, Illinois State Psychiatric Institute; Candidate, Institute for Psychoanalysis, Chicago.

David M. Terman, M.D.
Training and Supervising Analyst, Institute for Psychoanalysis, Chicago.

Harry Trosman, M.D.
Training and Supervising Analyst, Member of the Psychoanalytic Education Council, and of the Faculty, Institute for Psychoanalysis, Chicago.

Robert S. Wallerstein, M.D.
President, International Psycho-Analytical Association, 1985-1989; Training and Supervising Analyst, San Francisco Psychoanalytic Society and Institute; Professor, Department of Psychiatry, University of California San Francisco School of Medicine.

I

MEMORIAL

Dedication to Samuel D. Lipton, M.D.

For the Chicago psychoanalytic community, Sam Lipton always performed an important function. It was his job to cut through obfuscation, whether in the clinical, the educational, or the administrative realm and reveal fundamental issues in order to arrive at clarity and understanding. In the clinical area, this often took the form of highlighting the importance of the psychoanalytic clinical situation, deemphasizing abstract theory or conventional ways of thinking. For Sam, the writings of Freud were often the touchstone, and it was Freud the clinician—Freud who was best revealed in his work with the Rat Man—rather than Freud the metapsychologist or system-builder whom he treasured. Sam saw the essential script of psychoanalysis in Freud's notes to the Rat Man, and these notes served as a continuing source of inspiration for his solid clinical work. For others, this position of Sam's seemed reactionary, obstructing a view of psychoanalysis as a developing and progressive scientific enterprise. And, indeed, there was a quality of intransigence about Sam's defense of Freud's technical interventions in 1907, as if nothing of consequence has happened since. But Sam believed that if anyone was in a position to lay claim to fundamentals of method, surely it was Freud himself at the height of his powers.

It was not that Sam was impatient with innovation. Rather, he had a "show-me" attitude with regard to new developments. He was fundamentally a pragmatist, a practical man. If it worked, it was all right. The clinical crucible was the testing ground. If it was done merely to advance the elegant or the clever, it was never enough and thus suspect.

In the realm of psychoanalytic politics, Sam was impatient with cant, grandiose and flowery exposition, and specious rationalizations. He was an iconoclast, highly distrustful of public displays and ostentation. To a large extent, he was above and outside the fray. His essential nature was not that of a joiner, not that of a participant. He always remained an outsider even in his own immediate community, and yet he was an outsider who was highly respected and often turned to because of his passionate honesty, his absolute morality, his lack of self-interest or personal ambition. He was totally trustworthy. His motives were never governed by self-gain or personal aggrandizement. Without being highly visible or seeking power, he was an imposing and decisive influence.

Although as an analyst he was committed and serious, his humor was boundless. He often used wit and jokes as a way of making a point when a more ponderous approach would have been fruitless. For him, the contrary and dynamic unconscious was a pure delight, a source of continuous excitement and refreshment. His clinical anecdotes were frequently sprinkled with the pleasure that he took in describing a witty remark of his own, often followed by an even wittier riposte by a patient.

The same tendency which allowed Sam to get so much joy from his work allowed him to be a frequent and spontaneous discussant at Psychoanalytic Society meetings. He commented readily on numerous occasions when a paper would recall a vignette from his own practice. In these situations, Sam was always eminently precise, empirical, and deflating of pomposity.

It can genuinely be stated of colleagues such as Sam that they are irreplaceable. Our profession needs curmudgeons, men and women of singular and individualized opinion. Sam belongs in the tradition of those who think for themselves, speak out, and believe that the courage to do so is the most important attribute an analyst can have. We miss him.

Harry Trosman, M.D.

Samuel David Lipton, M.D.

October 30, 1915–July 13, 1984

When Samuel Lipton died on July 13 our Society and the psychoanalytic community lost a unique and irreplaceable member.

Sam was born in Detroit on October 30, 1915. Thus, he would have been 69 one week from today. His father was a physician; he lost his mother in his boyhood. I believe these two circumstances played a decisive role in his choice of profession and in the development of a deep idealizing devotion which underlay an often deceptively cryptic exterior. Always an outstanding student, Sam received an A.B. at the University of Michigan in 1936 and an M.D. in 1939, close to the top of his class. Following internships at the U.S. Marine Hospital in Staten Island and the Detroit Receiving Hospital, he was a psychiatric resident at the Cincinnati General Hospital 1941–1942. Like so many residents of Maurice Levine, he was inspired to pursue the study of psychoanalysis, an interest that was further fueled by his subsequent experience with analysts in the army. Also during this year, he undertook the treatment of a woman with a classical case of dissociated personality. He saw her one hour a day from July to May, then wrote a paper which was published in the *Psychiatric Quarterly* in 1943. The article was promptly included by Fenichel in his discussion of the syndrome in *The Psychoanalytic Theory of Neurosis.* This was awesome to us who began our training when Sam was still a candidate. Rereading this article recently, I was struck by the thoroughness and maturity of style of a first-year psychiatric resident. Sam always radiated maturity and competence. He never seemed like a student.

Cincinnati was followed by three war years in the army in neuropsychiatric installations, where he attained his captaincy. He served overseas eighteen months in the South Pacific in Bora Bora and Guadalcanal. In

This eulogy was delivered on October 23, 1984, by Charles Kligerman, M.D.

the spring of 1946, now a civilian, Sam entered the Chicago Institute and simultaneously began a neurology residency at the University of Chicago; I believe he was Richter's second resident, succeeding Heinz Kohut with whom he developed a long friendship. He also married at this time.

Sam's first analytic experience was with Edoardo Weiss, who had been the first analyst in Italy and a disciple of Paul Federn. This was a relatively brief experience, as was often the case in the era of Alexander and French. Although disaffected with the brief-analytic philosophy, Sam never lost his personal regard for Weiss, and I believe absorbed much of the psychoanalytic approach to psychosis that had been the hallmark of Federn's thinking. Sam later went to Max Gitelson, with whom he did his major analytic work. He remained warmly attached to Gitelson, both theoretically and personally, for the remainder of Gitelson's life.

During his student years at the Institute and beyond, Sam was very highly regarded even though his misgivings about the Institute's approach were very clear. He was even given a research job while a student, from which he resigned because of critical feelings about the project.

Although his ideological leanings were toward the so-called Blitzsten group, he was never an ardent member there either, because Sam could never be a dyed-in-the-wool partisan; he was always too fiercely independent, thoughtful, and rational to be an emotional adherent of any faction. He was always his own man. This is not to say that he did not idealize certain admired and respected figures. Undoubtedly, the most important of these was Paul Kramer. In his own eulogy to Paul two years ago on this podium, Sam told how he consulted four different analysts without telling each about the others, on a perplexing problem with a patient, and how Paul was the only one who clearly understood the problem and offered effective help. This led ultimately to a lifelong friendship in which I believe Sam really took Paul as his psychoanalytic ego ideal.

After the turmoil of the Alexander era, Sam went on to become, in his own right, one of the most respected analysts in the city, indeed in the country. He became a training analyst in 1955, and a supervisor in 1957. For reasons earlier mentioned, Sam never became an integral member of the Institute structure, but from time to time he was a valuable teacher in the program, particularly in courses on dreams and in advanced clinical seminars. He also did much outside teaching and supervision and became a Professorial Lecturer at the University of Chicago as well as a Clinical Professor of Psychiatry at the University of Illinois.

He was always very active in the affairs of this Society, and his clear vision and animated participation often sparked otherwise lackluster meetings. In 1966 he was elected president of the Chicago Psychoanalytic Society, and promptly endeared himself to that body by setting a reasonable time limit on the duration of business meetings and urging that papers be delivered extempore, not read.

On the national scene he participated in many functions of the American Psychoanalytic Association, often as chairman of panels, and he served many years on the important membership committee. In the early sixties he was asked to join the first group of the Center for Advanced Psychoanalytic Studies (CAPS) which meets twice a year at Princeton. His group included such recognized national leaders as Arlow, Brenner, Martin Stein, Heinz Kohut, Calef, and many others. He formed a warm and close association with the members, especially with Samuel Guttman, which I know meant a great deal to him.

Sam was not a prolific writer, but he wrote several extremely original and interesting papers on a wide variety of subjects. I will mention a few:

1. "The Last Hour" (1961), an interesting study advocating that the standard technique be followed throughout the termination.

2. "On the Psychology of Childhood Tonsillectomy" (1962), highlighting the medical irrationality and the psychological dangers of this common practice.

3. "The Manifest Content of the Dream" (Panel, 1966).

Most recently, his papers have dealt with his thesis that psychoanalytic technique was fully developed in Freud's Rat Man case and that further emendations were either unjustified or already implicit in Freud. Exactly one year ago on this platform, Sam gave a paper on "Further observations on the Advantages of Freud's Technique" [see pp. 19–32 of this volume], in which he stressed that Freud did not make such a sharp distinction between psychoanalysis proper and psychoanalytic psychotherapy.

But the real area in which Sam excelled was in his dedication and skill as an analyst. Apparently, the acerbic manner that sometimes crept into his supervision, because he had strong convictions, high standards, and did not tolerate fools easily, was entirely absent in his clinical work. It is not easy to know what transpires in an analytic chamber, but there seems to have been a common understanding that Sam was a superb analytic clinician. To him that was the most meaningful activity, far above anything else. While adhering to the basic Freudian paradigm, he was able to impart a warmth and sense of care to his patients that was out of the ordinary and growth-promoting. He did not think much of a sanitary situation with a silent or unresponsive analyst. Yet I never had any question about his core analytic stance.

The above achievements were carried out during years of increasing personal difficulty, and this personal side requires at least brief mention.

At the time of their marriage, Sam and Annetta were one of the most attractive, happy, and sought-after couples in the psychoanalytic community. When Mark, their son, was born, they seemed the ideal young analytic family. They always lived in large, tasteful, Hyde Park apartments where Annetta's dinners were famous. She was one of the earliest French gourmet cooks in the Midwest. They had a wide circle of friends and entertained in a warm, gracious manner. Sam himself was a very gregarious man, combining charm with an outstanding wit. He also had an uncompromising honesty that sometimes seemed blunt and testy, but he was essentially a man of kindness and decency. He loved jokes and could indulge in boyish enthusiasm. On my first trip to Detroit for a meeting of the "American," Sam exultantly drove me off to a favorite soda-parlor to sample the hometown pride—unknown in Chicago—Vernor's cream soda! It was ambrosial.

Although not at all addicted, on rare occasions he showed a zest for gambling. At a convention in Cincinnati, he proved his prowess at the crap table across the river at Beverly Hills, a Kentucky resort that later met disaster.

He was a first-rate tennis player, pursuing this sport for years until a recurrent back problem forced a withdrawal. From Paul Kramer he learned to love hiking in the mountains, and when he described Paul's conquest of Long's Peak in Colorado, he should have added his own, as well as many others.

But most of his sports were intellectual. He and Annetta were fervent duplicate-bridge players, attaining many master points; Sam was a whiz at crossword puzzles, and a *New York Times* version started on the train at Randolph was usually done long before 57th Street, where he got off.

Sam was not particularly musical, nor was he interested in visual arts, but he loved literature and the theater. He and Annetta were discriminating and devoted playgoers and developed a practice which became almost legendary: if they decided a play was not worthwhile (which was not seldom) they would march out in the middle. Many feel that way, but few have the courage to so express their disapproval. That was the Lipton style of living up to one's convictions. Sam was never one to flinch from a position of truth.

As the years went by, the happy times became more and more constricted, as Annetta's neurological illness ran its course, and she was progressively invalided, finally bedridden. Gradually, as the world goes, they became more isolated—although the warm and close relation with the Kramers persisted. Always an unusually solicitous and caring husband, Sam became as devoted in his care of his wife as any man I have ever known—not in a sentimental or masochistic way, but with a kind, mature simplicity. On a very rare occasion he would make an ironic reference to the neglect of friends, for he learned from bitter experience that the world, including psychoanalysts, has a phobic avoidance of illness.

Paul Kramer's illness and subsequent move to Palo Alto were a deep deprivation for Sam. He himself traveled little—the trips to Princeton were, I think, very sustaining. Sam also derived deep satisfaction from his son Mark who became a lawyer, married, and fathered Joshua, a grandchild in whom Sam took great delight.

Ultimately, Annetta died. Sam mourned and began his adaptation to a new way of life. One day, while at work, he learned that an accidental fire had gutted his home, destroying almost every tangible link to the memories of the past. It was at that point I believe that his spirit was finally broken. I think it was then that his heart succumbed.

Before closing I would like to mention one more trait of Sam's that may not be widely known—his generosity. Sam believed and followed the old Jewish tradition that it is more blessed to give anonymously than to donate for honor. I knew that he gave generously to many just causes, but there were so many more that no one knew about. I think this aspect of his character, which he chose to reveal in a letter to the rabbi who presided at his funeral, again highlights the inner decency and sense of integrity of this man, and—justly—he will be long remembered.

In retrospect, Sam's life was a combination of great promise and high achievement mingled with deep misfortune. Not many have coped with life's blows with the fortitude, consistency of self, and spirit that he showed. The events took their toll, but in the end he richly fulfilled his life in the area that was most precious to him: he was first, last, and always, a superlative analyst.

Charles Kligerman, M.D.

REFERENCES

Lipton, S. D. (1961), The last hour. *J. Amer. Psychoanal. Assn.*, 9:325–330.

——— (1962), On the psychology of childhood tonsillectomy. *The Psychoanalytic Study of the Child*, 17:363–417. New York: International Universities Press.

Panel (1966), The manifest content of the dream; presented by S. D. Lipton, C. G. Babcock, reporter. *J. Amer. Psychoanal. Assn.*, 14:154–171.

An Argument in Favor of Making Training Analysis Voluntary Rather Than Mandatory

SAMUEL D. LIPTON, M.D.

I have not attempted to review the extensive literature on training analysis. The views I express are in general agreement with those of Siegfried Bernfeld as reported in his paper presented in 1952 and published posthumously in 1962 (Bernfeld, 1962).

Before the 1920s and the 1930s—that is, before the time when psychoanalytic institutes were first organized and then proliferated—psychoanalytic training, as we know it now, did not exist. Instead of undertaking training at an accredited school, the student had the responsibility of learning analysis as best he could. Of course even with the organized training now available the student still has the problem of learning analysis. The extent to which analysis can be taught, as compared to the extent to which it must be learned, is a difficult question to decide. Although students do go through institutes, graduate, and become psychoanalysts, it is difficult to be certain how much the outcome was the result of training, how much it was unrelated to training, and how much it was in spite of training. However, there is no question that the organization of training decreased the responsibility of the student in learning.

This decrease in the student's responsibility took a particularly striking form in connection with his personal analysis. This was one method of learning that was recommended by Freud and followed by many students voluntarily. It is important to recognize that this recommendation for personal analysis, or didactic analysis as it was called then, was not defined according to its duration and that the analysis might have lasted only a

Presented at the October 24, 1972, meeting of the Chicago Psychoanalytic Society.

short time, much less than what we now think of as the minimum duration. Freud used this broader definition all his life.

In 1937, he discussed what we now know was Ferenczi's analysis, simply as an analysis, without making any reference to the fact that its total duration was six weeks (Freud, 1937, p. 221). Others used the same broad definition. For example, Bernfeld (1962) refers to an analysis which he had carried out which had lasted fifty hours. An additional confirmation of Freud's meaning is evident in his recommendation that the analyst return to analysis every five years. Obviously, with that interval, he was conceptualizing the duration of the analysis as short.

Even after institutes had been organized, Freud still continued to carry out short, didactic analyses despite the disapproval of colleagues whom he referred to as "the authorities" (Bernfeld, 1962, p. 463), and he did not even insist on this as a prerequisite to practice. When Bernfeld consulted Freud about starting practice in Vienna in 1922 and asked about a didactic analysis, Freud told him that it was not necessary. He said that Bernfeld should just go ahead, that he would be sure to get into trouble, and that they would see what should be done then. Freud soon referred a patient to Bernfeld, a man who had only a month to spend in Vienna. Bernfeld consulted Freud about what to do, and Freud told him to do as much as he could in a month.

I stress the fact that the definition of analysis included such short periods of time because it was while this definition was considered acceptable, in the 1920s, that training analysis was made a prerequisite. With the duration potentially short, I think the analysis must have been conceptualized as relatively unintrusive and as demanding no more of analytic students than of those who had undertaken it voluntarily. Even so, the issue was argued, and objections were stated then which have remained and have been repeated ever since, despite the tendency to accept the requirement as part of reality. That is, there were those who said that the personal analysis should be left to the individual and that it should have no connection with an institute (Lorand, 1969). It seems likely that the objections were advanced as a matter of principle alone and that the specific complications could not be foreseen.

One might ask why those who had undertaken personal analysis voluntarily felt constrained to insist that students who followed them had to be forced to undertake it. Evidently, their purpose was to protect both the public and the psychoanalytic movement from unqualified practitioners. The timing of the action may have been connected with Freud's illness (Bernfeld, 1962). It could hardly be true that they thought that it was the only possible way to begin the study of psychoanalysis since presumably many of them had not begun that way. Even now it would be surprising if any candidate had failed to learn something about analysis before he began his own analysis. An example of how common the view has been that a training analysis was not an essential prerequisite to training is the fact that it was not until 1937 that the New York Society made personal analysis a requirement (Lorand, 1969). Even at that, the timing of this step makes it seem as if it had been aimed at the European analysts then fleeing Hitler, rather than being motivated by a belated concern about the qualifications of analysts already practicing in New York. In summary, both history and current experience demonstrate the fact, if it is not self-evident, that the learning of psychoanalysis does not have to be initiated with a personal analysis.

Still, even if preliminary personal analysis is not essential, is it so clearly desirable that it should be mandatory? This can hardly be true generally. Many analysts know from their own experience how limited the value of the preliminary personal analysis may be, especially in regard to their work. Bernfeld (1962, p. 469) believed that the preliminary analysis afforded little knowledge and no skill, that it was overrated as a remedy for blind spots (p. 477), and that it was not essential in order to recognize transference reactions (p. 478). This is not to imply that the preliminary, personal analysis may not be of value but that its value does not usually lie in the area of psychoanalytic knowledge and skill. In contrast, a personal analysis after the analyst has had experience is often a great value in his work.

Then, if no educational reason demands that the personal analysis be timed to precede any other learning, what is left of its value as a prerequisite? Its only essential value is that it serves as a means of selection. That is, the main reason why the training analysis was made a prerequisite to training, and the main reason why it has been kept as a prerequisite to training, is that it serves as a screening method. It is true that it may also have personal value, and it may have some educational value, but neither of these facts can explain why it must be timed as it is or why it must be mandatory.

The elements of coercion, judgment, and selection cannot be of any advantage in an analysis and can be serious obstacles. It is true that such obstacles become subject to analysis just as other obstacles are in other analyses, but the fact that obstacles can be overcome does not argue in favor of their introduction into an analysis. These obstacles within the analysis are not the only difficulties that have followed the introduction of the mandatory training analysis. Other difficulties have been troublesome, if not insoluble, administrative problems that have followed the attempt to *enforce* the requirement.

Simply stating that a preliminary training analysis is mandatory is one thing; enforcing that rule is quite another. How can one *prove* that a candidate had an analysis? It would be difficult even if the content could be disclosed, and with the content secret it becomes impossible. For that reason emphasis had to be placed not on what was essential, but on what could be disclosed and documented: frequency of sessions and duration. These peripheral elements of analysis have been elevated to the position of standards even though everyone knows that they are valueless in themselves.

The only other way in which the candidate can prove he had an analysis is to get the implicit, or explicit, endorsement of the analyst. This necessity tends to interfere with optimal secrecy. Disclosures of unfavorable information are rare, but they do occur. In the ones that I know of, the training analyst felt that his obligation to the public, or to an institute, superseded his obligation of secrecy to the patient. Disclosures of favorable information are not unusual. Some training analysts write quite enthusiastic letters of recommendation to the membership committee of the American Psychoanalytic Association, and, if they write what they do to a national committee, one can only surmise what they say in conversations with colleagues whom they know well, when they would be even less concerned about such disclosures. One cannot help wondering if a candidate, analyzed by an analyst who followed that practice, would have an advantage over one whose analyst disclosed nothing except the fact of the analysis.

In addition to the obstacles introduced into the candidate's analysis by making it mandatory, and in addition to the administrative problems that have arisen from trying to enforce this requirement, there has been another far-reaching repercussion. That is that psychoanalysis itself has been unintentionally redefined in an expedient but unscientific way as a treatment that takes a certain length of time.

As you know, many scientific definitions of psychoanalysis have been advanced. They range from Freud's broad view that it might be any treatment that dealt with transference and resistance, to the more restricted views that would specify the development and resolution of a transference neurosis, the reconstruction of the infantile neurosis, reliance on interpretation rather than suggestion, and so on; but I cannot recall a single definition which adds the explicit qualification that it is also a treatment that must last for 300 hours, for four years, or for any other specified time.

Of course the purpose of setting time standards was not to redefine analysis but to try to enforce the aim of making the personal analysis adequate. It was for that reason that a minimum duration was established, and it has been for the same reason that this minimum duration has been increased. In 1925, the Berlin Institute required a minimum of six months of personal analysis (Bernfeld, 1962). In the late 1940s training analyses in Chicago were of comparable length; some of them continued for a year or so, at a frequency of three times a week. It was not until controversy had arisen about this that the current standards were formulated.

With this reformulation the requirement that the candidate have a preliminary personal analysis was changed, in fact, even though the words used were the same. The original, relatively minor intrusion became a major demand for a commitment of years of time, forced on everyone, to prevent any individual from sneaking through the training system without adequate personal analysis, a goal that remains as unenforceable by external authority as it ever was.

However, the broader repercussion of this expedient definition of analysis by means of frequency of sessions and duration is that short periods of analysis have been relegated to limbo or erroneously categorized as psychotherapy. In my own experience, and I presume in that of others, I have found consistently that patients may benefit from short periods of analysis conducted in the same way that any other analysis is conducted. Two typical situations are when the life situation of the patient requires a time limit, and when the patient has already had analysis.

It is misleading to designate such treatment as psychotherapy merely because it is short, because it then becomes confused with brief psychotherapy in which various psychotherapeutic measures other than interpretation are relied on. It is restrictive because it tends to narrow the use of psychoanalysis to patients who can meet the optimal criteria. It is also restrictive because it tends to discourage those who are learning psychoanalysis from using all the knowledge they can muster for the benefit of the patient. At times it has seemed to me that psychoanalysis has taken on a mystique, as if someone attempting to use psychoanalytic information might endanger the patient. At a time when tame psychoanalysis seems to be more of a danger than wild psychoanalysis, we might recall that Freud wrote that the latter, wild psychoanalysis, would do more harm to the psychoanalytic movement than to individual patients, and that the individual patient he wrote of was still better off than she would have been at the hands of some highly respected authority (Freud, 1910, p. 227).

Finally, still another difficult problem has followed the attempt to enforce the mandatory training analysis—that is, the appointment of training analysts. Of course, originally there was no such designation of status, and as far as I know Freud never referred to it. Then, for some time, the need for experienced analysts made the issue of appointment academic. Now we have passed the point where there is any shortage of potential, or actual, training analysts in the big cities, and the appointment has become a late additional accreditation, rather than a commitment to fulfill a task. Calling the training analysis part of the curriculum and calling training analysts teachers are just transparent evasions. The training analysis is as much the same as any other analysis as the analyst and patient can make it, and the training analyst does nothing of any consequence that is different from what he does in any other analysis.

Now that the appointment to training-analyst status has come to mean that the training analyst has the right to analyze candidates, but not that he necessarily will analyze candidates, it involves two separate questions. One is the policy of referral by an institute, since candidates will naturally seek recommendations from institute members. Even if the training-analyst appointment were abolished, the candidates' requests for referrals, and the recommendations of institute members, would probably suffice to maintain the status quo on an informal basis. Ultimately, this question depends on the definition of the broad issue of the relation of an institute to a society and the recognition that the responsibility of an institute is to all the members of a society.

The second question—in addition to that of actual referrals—is one of accreditation, or of status. I believe that this problem would be mitigated if we took the position that institutes have the same obligation to graduates in relation to accreditation as training analysts as they have to students in relation to graduation. We would not expect a student to just wait around until he could conclude from the inaction of his teachers that he had not been "selected" for graduation, and we should not expect a graduate to just wait around until he could decide from the inaction of the institute that he had not been selected as a training analyst. If an institute does not wish to accredit him, then it should be obligated to explain its reasons. Insofar as there are requisites in addition to graduation, they should be openly formulated. Secret information should not both be used against an individual, on the one hand, and withheld from him, on the other.

The present policy of selection of training analysts leaves exclusion as an unmentioned repercussion. By changing the policy to an explicit one of exclusion, with selection as a repercussion, I would hope to shift the burdensome and potentially traumatic effect of this process from the individual to the institute. If an institute were given the right of exclusion, like the right to flunk a student, it could not duck the problem in convenient silence leaving the individual analyst to adapt to the situation as best he could. I would also hope that more analysts would be accredited for training and that they would also carry out analyses of candidates, but, as I have said, I think that the latter is more a matter of administration than of policy.

During the same period in which preliminary personal analysis was first made mandatory and then defined in terms of duration, other prerequisites to training were established and the curriculum was organized. While originally the preliminary personal analysis was the only effective method of screening, there are now other methods which can take its place. Work under supervision is required now, and it can serve as one of the means of selection. It should be the task of an institute to find out whether a candidate can learn to conduct an analysis, not whether he has been analyzed himself. It is paradoxical that, although other methods of selection have been developed in the organization of training, we have still maintained our reliance on the preliminary personal analysis.

In summary, I maintain that the mandatory, preliminary personal analysis has outlived its usefulness as a means of selection and should be abandoned. With his analysis voluntary, the candidate would be free to undertake it at a time of his own choice, under optimal conditions. Selection could be carried out by other elements in the educational system. The administrative difficulties that have arisen from the impossible task of attempting to enforce the adequacy of an analysis would be eliminated. Finally, we might then free ourselves from the misleading and restrictive definition of analysis as a treatment that necessarily has a predetermined duration and return to Freud's broader and more practical definition which included short periods of analysis.

REFERENCES

Bernfeld, S. (1962), On psychoanalytic training. *Psychoanal. Quart.*, 31:453–582.

Freud, S. (1910), "Wild" psycho-analysis. *Standard Edition*, 11:221–227. London: Hogarth Press, 1957.

——— (1937), Analysis terminable and interminable. *Standard Edition*, 23:211–253. London: Hogarth Press, 1964.

Lorand, S. (1969), Reflections on the development of psychoanalysis in New York from 1925. *Internat. J. Psycho-Anal.*, 50:589–595.

October 1972

Further Observations on the Advantages of Freud's Technique

SAMUEL D. LIPTON, M.D.

In designating these observations as "further," I am alluding to prior papers on the same subject (Lipton, 1977a, 1977b, 1979, 1982, and 1983). In a nutshell, I have been attempting to demonstrate that important and valuable elements of Freud's technique have been repudiated. I maintain that a trend in technique, now called Freudian, classical, or standard, is, in fact, a post-Freudian development.

In understanding Freud's technique, I think that it is important to know something about the history of the currently accepted distinction between psychoanalysis proper and psychoanalytic psychotherapy. By psychoanalysis proper, I mean what is generally understood by the term as a treatment in agreement with Freud's definition, with the current emphasis on formal requirements: duration, frequency of sessions, and the use of the couch. The best definition, or perhaps description, I have found of psychoanalytic psychotherapy is that it is a form of psychotherapy based on the theoretical and technical principles of psychoanalysis "without, however, fulfilling the requirements of a psychoanalytic treatment as strictly understood" (LaPlanche and Pontalis, 1973, p. 373). I think this statement captures the dilemma that has arisen in trying to reach a consensus on the distinction.

The point which is relevant to my thesis is that Freud never made this distinction at all. I do not know if this fact is generally known. In my sampling of the literature, I found only a single explicit reference to it (Thompson, 1977, p. 202). In the earliest papers I found (Knight, 1937;

Prepared for presentation to the Chicago Psychoanalytic Society on October 26, 1983.

Crank, 1940; and Berliner, 1941), the authors reported on the application of psychoanalytic concepts to treatment of short duration. They did not take up the history of such efforts, and did not consider the possibility that what they were doing was no different from what analysts had been doing all the time. Nor did they distinguish the procedure from psychoanalysis by giving it a different name. They did seem to wish to preserve the name, psychoanalysis, for a more thorough procedure. By the time that the controversy over Alexander's proposals (Alexander and French, 1946) arose, the distinction seemed to be taken for granted and even attributed to Freud (Stone, 1954, p. 573; Gill, 1954, p. 771). In subsequent years, many other papers do not take up the historical question at all.

As we know, Freud distinguished psychoanalytic treatment from suggestion. By psychoanalytic treatment he meant, as I understand it, simply a form of psychotherapy based on psychoanalytic theory. It recognized the importance of transference and resistance, of the drives, and of childhood sexuality. The purpose of the treatment was not to influence the symptoms directly, but to demonstrate to the patient the unconscious motives of his symptoms by means of interpretation. The cure of the patient's disorder remained the goal of the treatment, but it came about as a byproduct of interpretation.

In contrast to psychoanalytic therapy, suggestion was aimed at relieving the patient's symptoms by some sort of direct influence: hypnosis, medication, various sorts of encouragement and injunctions, and so on. The symptom was combatted directly, as it usually is in the practice of medicine.

The two forms of psychotherapy are thus distinguished according to their purpose, and the formal arrangements become secondary. I still find this distinction valid. I concur with Fenichel's opinion that the formalities of a treatment situation, particularly the couch, are not definitive (Fenichel, 1941, pp. 23–24; 1945, p. 573), and with Hoffer's opinion that the frequency of sessions and the duration of the treatment are important, but also not definitive (Hoffer, 1950, p. 194). It is true that occasions arise in analysis when the analyst may exert some direct influence on the patient, such as Freud recommended in "Lines of Advance . . ." (Freud, 1919, p. 162), but such measures are secondary to the main purpose of the treatment.

We know that, according to the definition he used, Freud reported on analyses which would be relegated to psychotherapy according to current standards, mainly because their duration is now considered too short (such as the cases of Dora and the Rat Man) and for other reasons as well. It is important to note that as late as 1937, in "Analysis Terminable and Interminable," Freud chose as illustrations patients whom he had treated for short periods: Ferenczi, whom he analyzed for two three-week periods in 1914 and 1916 (Freud, 1937, p. 221, n. 1) and a woman whom he had treated for nine months (p. 222).

Other analysts were presumably treating patients according to the same definition, making such expedient arrangements as they found necessary. For example, in 1910, J. J. Putnam had written to Ernest Jones that he could not find patients who would attend sessions frequently. Jones replied that he was pessimistic about a frequency of once a week, but that he had had some very good results at a frequency of three times a week. He also cited cases whom he had treated for four to eight months, with good results (Hale, 1971, pp. 241–242). In 1911, David Eder reported on a case which he said he had treated by Freud's psychoanalytic method. He saw the patient twice a week for three months (Glover, 1945, p. 251).

It is in the context of Freud's distinction between psychoanalysis and suggestion that his emphasis on the exclusive value of a trial of analysis for diagnostic evaluation must be understood. Usually, it requires only a screening interview to decide whether a patient is best treated psychoanalytically or by suggestion, and, as often as not, the patient has already decided this for himself. Then, since one plans to use the same treatment anyway, there is no hurry in reaching a definitive diagnosis. Only the new dilemma, the choice between psychoanalysis proper and psychotherapy, makes it necessary to engage in exhaustive diagnostic evaluations even though everyone knows how unreliable they are.

It is in the same context that one must understand the way Freud conducted his analyses which, by current standards, seem so easygoing and informal. It shocks analysts now to find that Freud referred to analysis as a conversation on a number of occasions, and shocks them even more to read of the conversations which he reported. However, he was guided by the principle which governed the treatment, not by the interchanges, sometimes incidental, of a particular session.

In the ambience I am referring to, one of Abraham's papers is of interest (Abraham, 1919). He reports on the analysis of patients of an advanced age, by which he meant forty to fifty, and older. He found that some of these patients found it difficult to begin an hour, and that therefore he had to begin it with "a little stimulus," perhaps an allusion to a previous session (p. 317). What is pertinent here is that he simply incorporates this measure into analysis with, of course, no concern about what we might now think of as psychotherapy.

To summarize, Freud's technique incorporated various procedures which were later excluded from psychoanalysis proper and relegated to psychotherapy. Of course, even if you concur with this statement, you might consider the current division an advantage. However, the question of whether it is an advantage or not is tangential to my thesis. I have discussed the issue only to offer a hypothesis to explain the development of modern technique. I think that it may be one of the reasons why modern technique tends to be unduly cautious and restricted, at least in my opinion. It seems to overemphasize the behavior of the analyst, instead of his purpose, and attempts to prescribe and codify his conduct excessively. It seems to me that modern technique has the purpose not only of conducting analysis but also of guarding against its contamination by psychotherapy.

However, such general statements are of limited value. I can advance my argument better by discussing a specific example in detail. In a paper on the subject of the concept of alliances, Brenner (1979) states,

> If, for example a patient suffers a catastrophe or a success in life, it is not the best for him and his analysis for his analyst to express sympathy or congratulations before "going on to analyze." It is true enough that it often does no harm for an analyst to be thus conventionally "human." Still, there are times when his being "human" under such circumstances can be harmful, and one cannot always know in advance when those times will be. As an example, for his analyst to express sympathy for a patient who has just lost a close relative may make it more difficult than it would otherwise be for the patient to express pleasure or spite or exhibitionistic satisfaction over the loss. As another example, it is difficult for me to imagine instructing an adult patient to have a physical examination or to go for contraceptive information. I can easily imagine saying to a patient that there must be a reason why he is neglecting his health and that I wonder what his thoughts are about it, or to another that there must be some reason why she is inviting or risking pregnancy and that I wonder what she thinks about it. Either such statement, however phrased, is perfectly in keeping with an analytic attitude on the part of an analyst. Either is quite as analytic, i.e., quite as appropriate to an analytic situation, as it would be to point out to a patient that he invariably tells his dreams at the end of an hour or that he is consistently late in paying his bill—to choose two everyday examples. I cannot imagine circumstances that would justify telling an analytic patient to get a physical examination or to be fitted for a diaphragm any more than I can imagine telling an analytic patient to please tell his dreams early in the hour and to be prompt in paying his bill [pp. 153–154].

Even though the statement is brief, and even though it is taken out of context, I believe it can serve as a paradigm which illustrates a number of points about modern technique, and I will therefore discuss it in detail.

First, I shall take up three general points. The first point is what I construe as a misunderstanding of the effect of silence. While Brenner does not use the term explicitly, it is obvious from his criticism of various possible interventions, either altogether or in their timing, that he implies that silence facilitates the progress of the analysis, while various statements may impede it.

In fact the situation is more complex. It is important to distinguish the silence which simply accompanies listening from the silence which is a decision not to say something which the listener has thought of saying. Outside of analysis, the effect on the speaker is obviously and drastically different, so much so that listeners conventionally interpolate phrases intended to confirm the fact that they are listening. There are situations in which a statement is mandatory conventionally, and the failure to make one may be construed as a rebuff, or an insult. One such situation is one of those referred to by Brenner, a death in the family. Another is simply the conventional greeting when one meets someone one knows. At one time, snubbing someone by refusing to greet him was taken so seriously that it was considered a valid reason for a challenge to a duel.

The analytic situation is different, both because the analyst often offers some introductory explanation about his not speaking, and also because so many patients expect him to be silent. However, it is not so different that silence has either no effect at all, or merely facilitates free association. On the contrary, it sometimes has a powerful effect and also one that may be hard to recognize. One effect is the idealization of the analyst's understanding. I have discovered this mainly when I asked about it. It is less often the subject of spontaneous association.

A second effect is the inference by the patient that he is not supposed to mention something. I have had an experience repeatedly which confirms this. If I am significantly late, I always acknowledge it to the patient. However, if my tardiness is insignificant, say two or three minutes, I have sometimes acknowledged it and sometimes not. Often, in response to my acknowledgment, whether the tardiness was significant or not, the patient will report on some fantasy he had while waiting, for example, that there was something wrong with me, or that he had come at the wrong time. However, when I do not acknowledge it, the patient almost always says nothing. If I ask about it, it sometimes turns out that the patient did have some fantasy in the waiting room, of the sort I have mentioned.

A third effect is unnecessary discouragement and frustration. I know of only two instances in which the patient quit the treatment because of the analyst's silence, but I have seen several who had remained resentful of the analyst's silence. Analysts all know that they should avoid giving the patient such gratifications as may make analysis simply a happy interlude without necessarily accomplishing anything. However, it will not accomplish something just because it is a miserable interlude, either.

I have found that the point I am making about silence is misunderstood by some with a regularity which is quite impressive. They respond to the word conversation, as if its only important meaning were the fourth one given in the Webster's Second Edition, sexual intercourse. I do not mean that conversation in analysis is reciprocal, as it is socially. I have compared the frequency of my statements in analysis with what they would be socially and found that I was listening most of the time. Especially during the first half of a session, I found that, socially, there would have been five or ten occasions when a response would have been appropriate, but that in analysis none was appropriate. What I do mean by conversation is the necessary component of questioning, clarifying, explaining, elaborating, rephrasing, and hypothesizing, which I think is simply the natural accompaniment of analysis.

Returning to my general comments about the excerpt from Brenner's paper, I think it not only distorts the effect of silence but also exaggerates the effect of precise phraseology. One would think that the analyst had some authority to order the patient about and that the patient would either obey or perhaps become extremely guilty. Conversely, one might assume that if the analyst merely pointed out something in formally neutral phraseology, such as wondering what the patient's thoughts were about neglecting his health, or pointing out that the patient was paying his bills late, that the patient might indeed assume that the analyst was neutral about the issues.

My third objection to the implications of Brenner's statement is that it expands the concept of technique beyond its optimal scope. It implies that such exceptional events as a death in the family, which may not even occur during an analysis, should be covered by the same rules which cover common situations in analysis.

To summarize my objections to the implications of Brenner's statement:

1. It distorts the effect of the analyst's silence.
2. It overestimates the importance of the analyst's statements, in general, and their phraseology, in particular.
3. It expands the scope of technique unduly.

I turn now from criticism of Brenner's statement to a positive statement. I shall attempt to demonstrate how the contingencies cited by Brenner are dealt with according to Freudian technique, as I understand it.

To begin with, technique is applicable only during the psychoanalytic session when the patient is associating. During that period, the patient knows that the analyst is listening with evenly hovering attention and is occupying himself with his understanding of the material. In other situations, technique is neither applicable nor appropriate. Then, simply the rules of civility apply, in accord with the personal relationship which always exists between the patient and analyst. I shall mention, but not elaborate on, a point which everyone knows, that is, that sometimes patients will try to exclude from analysis some comment before the session begins, or after it is over, and that it is often an advantage to bring such comments into the analysis. While I have encountered this, I have never found that it was a problem of any consequence.

What I am referring to are the statements which a patient makes which are not associations, are not part of the analysis at the time, and for that matter may never become part of it, although I suppose that I must add the analytic shibboleth that nothing is excluded from the analysis potentially. The most common statements of the type I am referring to are about arrangements. A patient may have to cancel an hour, ask for a change in time, make some statement about insurance, or make some other similar statements. The analyst simply acknowledges such statements and makes whatever civil response is appropriate.

Sometimes it is necessary for the patient to telephone the analyst. The occasion may be the necessity to make some factual announcement which may be unexpected: some accident or injury which will prevent him from attending his session, or illness, or, rarely, a death. Here again, I do not see that the interchange is best incorporated into technique. The patient's statement may be surprising, or even shocking, and it seems to me that it is both unnecessary and stilted for the analyst to confine himself within technical restrictions. To cite a few examples of what I mean: a patient called to cancel his session because his grandson, an apparently healthy four-month-old infant, had been found dead in his crib; another called to cancel because her son had been hit by a bus and she was in the emergency room at the university hospital with him; another called to cancel because he had had a perforated appendix operated on over the weekend. I have never found that the response I made to announcements like that interfered with the patients' later thoughts about the incidents.

During the two crippling blizzards we have had during the past fifteen years, there were many occasions when telephone calls were necessary. I have not thought of such interchanges as governed by technique, and I have never found any interference with the analysis as the result of the interchanges.

I know that a patient may telephone for some reason connected with the content of the treatment. I am not referring to such calls. I think that the distinction is obvious.

Aside from telephone calls, and aside from statements about arrangements, there are occasions at the outset of sessions, or even during the session, when the patient has something to say which is not an association subject to analysis at the time. It may be some special event, like a birth, or some special success, like getting a job, a contract, or a grant. Here, again, there is no need to clutter up technique with prescribed responses. I must disclaim one implication of Brenner's view explicitly. When I say that there is no codified response, I most certainly do not mean that the analyst is confined to some conventional banality or that he is supposed to act some odd role which is called, by that astounding word, human.

There is another exception to the technical principle that the analyst listens to all the material and interprets it: when it becomes evident that the patient is confronted with a danger which he does not recognize, and when it becomes advisable for the analyst to abandon the search for latent meaning long enough to inform the patient of the danger.

This is a rare occurrence, and, for that reason, I shall spend little time on it. What happens, though, is not a matter of "instructing" a patient to have a physical examination. What I have run across are some incidents in which the patient was exposed to mistreatment by an incompetent physician, a fact which was obvious to me, but not to him or her. One patient consulted an orthopedist for a minor tennis elbow and was scheduled for surgery, immediately. Another was scheduled for a dilation and curettage by telephone for some minor spotting. In both instances the patient had displaced a transference wish onto the physician she consulted. Each was demonstrating, unconsciously, that she would agree to anything a doctor said and implying that she would agree with me, too. However, the elucidation of this content was not interfered with at all by my statements of skepticism about the validity of the medical management. I have also encountered a few situations in which the patient maintained that some complaint was psychogenic when I did not think it was. For example, a patient said that he was anxious. The only evidence, he said, was a manual tremor. I asked him to show me the tremor, and it turned out to be unilateral, as far as I could see; he said that it was just much worse on one side. My action did not prevent us from taking up the question of why he had ignored such obvious evidence that the tremor was organic.

I turn now to another implication of Brenner's statement, that if the patient does not say something, the analyst does not either, even if he knows that the idea that the patient is not mentioning is either conscious, or, at most, preconscious. While this comes up in Brenner's statement in relation to the minor matter of bills, it holds true generally for modern technique. Eissler (1974) states the principle more clearly when he states, "To take the lead in calling the patient's attention to his slowness in paying has its hazards, since one is thereby interfering with the patient's spontaneous and ego-syntonic flow of free associations" (p. 93). Brenner seems to agree with this idea since he states that he makes no comment until the patient has been consistently late, presumably a matter of months. Eissler does add that he brings up the matter if he finds evidence of it in dreams.

This principle, that of not interfering with what is called the flow of associations, is one that I have encountered often outside the literature, and, to me, it is the most astonishing single element of modern technique. It seems to me to deny important principles of analysis that I thought, at one time, were well established. We all know, I presume, that the analyst has to stay on the surface of the material. In regard to this, Fenichel (1941) stated that the patient determines the subject matter of the analytic session, not only by what he says, but also by what he does not talk about (p. 44). This is just another way of stating that the interpretation of resistance is the business of analysis, and that one of the most obvious indications of resistance is the patient's silence about something which the analyst knows perfectly well that he is aware of. It seems to me that the failure of the analyst to bring such an exclusion to the attention of the patient will tend to slow down the analysis, and, if he never brings it up, lose material altogether. The idea that there is some advantage to a protracted flow of associations with a continuing glaring exclusion, seems quite strange to me.

Taking bills as an example, my own practice is different. The matter does not come up often, and only at the beginning of the analysis. Occasionally, a patient neither pays his first bill promptly nor says anything about it. Sometimes I find some evidence about the matter in associations or dreams, but whether I do or not, I ask him his thoughts about it. In fact, I am actually interested in his thinking, but I grant that the patient will take my inquiry as an indication that I want to be paid promptly. That is true, too. Occasionally, I run across some interesting material. For example, one patient told me that he had been trying to figure out what the correct time to pay was, not too fast and not too slow. Very rarely has there been an objection to my inquiry. This proved to be most informative, too.

I said that material could simply be lost, and I shall cite one example of what I mean. I once undertook the analysis of a patient who had already had two analyses of several years' duration. After a brief initial interview, we began. He lay down on the couch, and, to my surprise, took off his thick glasses, put them on his chest, and only then began to talk. It soon became clear that he was not going to say anything about this, and so I asked him about it. It turned out that throughout his two periods of analysis that was what he had done, and neither analyst had mentioned it, nor had he. He explained that since he was so myopic, removing his glasses prevented him from seeing anything clearly and made it certain that his associations were generated internally. I said that his perceptions had an internal motive, too. The first thing he said after he put his glasses on was that the pictures in front of him were no good. Then, more negative feelings emerged, and later, important material about his defense against hatred.

In regard to dreams, Brenner cites what he calls an everyday example, a patient who invariably tells his dreams at the end of the hour. I have never encountered this even once. I assume that the reason for the different experience is that Brenner says nothing about the late report, while I inquire about it or comment on it. Saying nothing would be in accord with the modern principle of not interfering with the flow of the patient's associations. It may also be connected with the modern assumption that the dream is not a special communication, but is just like any other association. Disagreeing with the assumptions, and following Freud's recommendation, I often use the first dream to tell the patient something about the method we will use to analyze dreams. Of course, this entails taking time with them and makes it necessary that they be reported early in the session.

So much for the consideration here of the difference between modern technique and Freud's technique, as I understand it. I have already commented on one objection to the latter, that is that there is an interference, as it is thought of, with the flow of associations. A second objection is the cryptic, but common and important one that the analyst will become too real (Erle and Goldberg, 1979, p. 51). The idea seems to be that if the analyst becomes too real, then the transference cannot be analyzed. Even the recommendation that the patient confront a phobia is supposed to make the analyst a real object, rather than a transference object. I think that it is reasonable to infer that, from this standpoint, when I brought up the matter of the glasses, I became too real and thereby destroyed the purity of the analysis. This view seems to assume that optimally the transference is so pure that nothing of the reality of the analyst enters into it. In fact, that never happens, and it cannot happen. The transference can attach itself only to something which is real to the patient, even if it is nothing more than what the patient is convinced the analyst is thinking, and, even at that, the patient usually has some clue to go on. It is the task of the analyst to unearth this clue so that the patient can understand that a transference reaction has not been just dragged in from the past as if it were a pure repetition, but has a connection with current actuality. The analyst is invariably both a real and a transference figure, granting only that a transference develops and that it does not become overwhelming.

It is true that there are patients who develop such an intense conviction of the importance of the analyst that the transference becomes unresolvable. However, this development depends on the nature of the patient's disorder and not on some nuance of the behavior of the analyst. I have seen in several occasions in reanalyses that major important elements of the transference were repeated even though the circumstances of the analysis and the management of the case were quite different. I will illustrate the point with a brief case report.

A man had an extended period of analysis when he was in his twenties and early thirties. The analyst was supportive, free with advice, and realistically helpful. To cite one example, he secretly countersigned a note at a bank so that the patient could get a loan. The patient discovered this by accident. By the time he repaid the loan, the bank officer who had made the original arrangement was dead, and the new officer simply returned his note to him. No doubt, the first officer would have found some excuse for concealing it. He became attached to the analyst, and, while he stopped at times, he always returned. The analyst called him an albatross, and finally insisted that he transfer to another analyst.

Years went by, and he undertook analysis with me. By this time he had come to think of the first analyst's helpfulness as not being good in the long run, and he told me, using the word that a consultant had used, that now what he wanted was pure analysis. That suited me, and I carried out a pure analysis, and I brought it to a successful conclusion in five years, with clear relief of a phobia which had plagued him all through his previous experience.

However, as you have guessed, he returned. There were new problems, and now it turned out that he still could not manage without analysis. The nature of his neurosis has reminded me of one of the Wolf Man's characteristics. You all know how his transference to Freud defied resolution and how later he was treated by analysts all his life. I think that this result came about because of his own disturbance, not because of any mismanagement by Freud. An important clue to the nature of this disturbance is documented in a footnote (Freud, 1918, p. 37, n. 5). Freud notes that the patient said that he had witnessed his parents having intercourse three times, but he claimed that Freud had discovered this number by means of interpretation. In fact Freud had not done so at all. Freud said that it was a spontaneous association, but "in his usual way he passed it off on me, and by this projection tried to make it trustworthy." (Mahoney [1982] has pointed out that Strachey has altered Freud's statement by qualifying it and writing that Freud wrote, "tried to make it seem more trustworthy.")

One incident from this protracted treatment will illustrate the similarity I am referring to. At one session the patient came in extremely distraught because there had been a fire in one of his buildings. He said that this was unbearable and that there was nothing left but suicide. He had already made a serious attempt for no better reason. As was usual when he was disturbed, he was almost incoherent because he would keep interrupting any narrative statement with repetitive complaints about his agony. Thus it was only with difficulty that I could find out what the facts were, and whether the damage had wiped him out or was something less. It turned out that it had been an extensive fire and that the damage might be one or two hundred thousand dollars. However, he was insured and would suffer little out-of-pocket loss. He would lose some rental income, but he could stand that. I asked him how long it would take to make repairs. He said it was very hard to say, but that it might be two or four months, or even six months. So I said that suppose we said six months, what was there to do except wait? Then we went on to the material which I thought was of psychological importance, his mother's histrionic exaggeration of every misfortune in his life, and his repeated attempts to get me to respond like his mother.

Some five years passed, and I was commenting on the fact that he so consistently exaggerated my importance to him. He said that I did not seem to understand that I had saved his life. I asked him to explain, and it turned out to be the incident of the fire. He said that I had told him that he would have to wait six months for the repairs to be completed. He said that if I had not told him that he would have remained in such intolerable distress that he would have killed himself, but that once I had told him, he was able to relax. I said that I had not told him six months at all, that I had simply used his own estimate, and that indeed it would have been ridiculous for me to make my own estimate since I had never even seen the damage. He said, "I know that, but that makes no difference. Who am I? An ignorant Jew. When I say six months, it means absolutely nothing. But when you say six months, that means six months. I relaxed immediately, and the panic was over." I asked him about my interpretation about his mother. He had forgotten it completely.

I suspect that the patient had identified himself with my calmness about the fire, as unremarkable as that was. However, regardless of the mechanism, the patient had endowed my statement with such importance that it relieved his anxiety. It does not have to be a statement which the patient uses for his own purposes. I recall once a patient said, after a few sessions, that she was relieved to find out that I was liberal. I had no idea how she formed this conclusion and asked her about it. She said she had inferred it because when she told me that she had smoked marijuana, I had said nothing. I asked what I would have said if I had not been liberal. She replied that I would have asked her for her associations on smoking marijuana. I could give other examples, but I assume that these suffice.

Possibly the concern about formal correctness in analysis has kept alive the anachronistic concept of wild analysis. We might recall that even in 1910 Freud noted that wild analysts he cited did less harm than some respected authority would have done (Freud, 1910, p. 227). If there is any danger now, I think that it is more from tame analysis than from wild analysis. I have treated patients who had been treated by therapists who had engaged in what might be called wild analysis and also in misconduct. I saw no patient who suffered any lasting injury, and, as a rule, it was possible to determine the element of the patient's collusion. One mitigating factor was that the treatments were relatively short. On the other hand, I have seen patients who suffered more severe traumas from a protracted, ostensibly correct, but unproductive analysis.

In conclusion, I have attempted to show that modern analytic technique suffers from an undue formalism, which is quite different from Freud's technique. I have presented a few illustrations to illustrate this broad subject. I have suggested that one reason for the modern formalism may be the post-Freudian division of psychoanalytic treatment into psychoanalysis proper and psychoanalytic therapy.

REFERENCES

Abraham, K. (1919), The applicability of psychoanalytic treatment to patients at an advanced age. In: *Selected Papers of Karl Abraham.* London: Hogarth Press, 1948, pp. 312–317.

Alexander, F. & French, T. (1946), *Psychoanalytic Therapy.* New York: Ronald Press.

Berliner, B. (1941), Short psychoanalytic therapy: Its possibilities and limitations. *Bull. Menn. Clin.,* 5:204–213.

Brenner, C. (1979), Working alliance, therapeutic alliance and transference. *J. Amer. Psychoanal. Assn.,* 27 (Supplement):137–158.

Crank, H. (1940), The use of psychoanalytic principles in outpatient therapy. *Bull. Menn. Clin.,* 4:35–40.

Eissler, K. R. (1974), On some theoretical and technical problems regarding the payment of fees for psychoanalytic treatment. *Internat. Rev. Psycho-Anal.,* 1:73–101.

Erle, J. B. & Goldberg, D. A. (1979), Problems in the assessment of analyzability. *Psychoanal. Quart.,* 48:48–84.

Fenichel, O. (1941), *Problems of Psychoanalytic Technique.* New York: Psychoanal. Quart. Publishing Co.

——— (1945), *The Psychoanalytic Theory of Neurosis.* New York: Norton.

Freud, S. (1910), Wild psychoanalysis. *Standard Edition,* 11:219–227. London: Hogarth Press, 1957.

——— (1918), From the history of an infantile neurosis. *Standard Edition,* 17:3–122. London: Hogarth Press, 1955.

——— (1919[1918]), Lines of advance in psychoanalytic therapy. *Standard Edition,* 17:158–168. London: Hogarth Press, 1955.

——— (1937), Analysis terminable and interminable. *Standard Edition,* 23:211–269. London: Hogarth Press, 1964.

Gill, M. (1954), Psychoanalysis and exploratory psychotherapy. *J. Amer. Psychoanal. Assn.,* 2:771–797.

Glover, E. (1945), Eder as psychoanalyst. In: *The Yearbook of Psychoanalysis,* ed. S. Lorand. New York: International Universities Press, 1946, pp. 251–278.

Hale, N. G., Jr. (ed.) (1971), *Jones Jackson Putnam and Psychoanalysis.* Cambridge: Harvard University Press.

Hoffer, W. (1950), Three psychological criteria for the termination of treatment. *Internat. J. Psycho-Anal.,* 31:194–195.

Knight, R. P. (1937), Application of psychoanalytic concepts in psychotherapy: Report of clinical trials at a mental hygiene service. *Bull. Menn. Clin.,* 1:99–109.

LaPlanche, J. & Pontalis, J.-B. (1973), *The Language of Psychoanalysis.* New York: Norton.

Lipton, S. D. (1977a), The advantages of Freud's technique as shown in his analysis of the Rat Man. *Internat. J. Psycho-Anal.,* 58:255–273.

——— (1977b), Clinical observations on resistance to the transference. *Internat. J. Psycho-Anal.,* 58:463–472.

——— (1979), An addendum to "The advantages of Freud's technique as shown in his analysis of the Rat Man." *Internat. J. Psycho-Anal.,* 60:215–216.

——— (1982), A critical review of Dewald's "The Psychoanalytic Process." *Contemp. Psychoanal.,* 18:349–365.

——— (1983), A critique of so-called standard psychoanalytic technique. *Contemp. Psychoanal.,* 19:35–46.

Mahoney, P. J. (1982), Unpublished lecture on Freud's writing presented at the Institute for Psychoanalysis, Chicago, October.

Stone, L. (1954), The widening scope of indications for psychoanalysis. *J. Amer. Psychoanal. Assn.,* 2:567–594.

Thompson, W. C. (1977), In: *The International Encyclopedia of Psychiatry, Psychology, Psychoanalysis, and Neurology,* ed. B. Wolman. New York: Van Nostrand, Reinhold, 9:202–209.

October 1983

II

THEORETICAL STUDIES

Metapsychology Revisited

MERTON M. GILL, M.D. (Chicago)

Definition of Metapsychology

This essay is based on the concept of metapsychology in the sense in which it was introduced into psychoanalysis by Freud. It has been said that the term *metapsychology* should properly mean an examination of what branch of human knowledge psychoanalysis is part of, in particular whether it is a natural science or a hermeneutic discipline. But the term metapsychology as used in psychoanalysis ordinarily refers not to such an epistemological discussion but to the particular position on the issue taken by Freud, namely, that psychoanalysis is a natural science.

Metapsychology is a term which figures centrally in psychoanalytic theory but has no generally agreed-upon definition. That is one of the important reasons why the proper role of metapsychology in psychoanalytic theory is much disputed among analysts.

Freud used the term metapsychology in two significantly different senses, one use occasional and the other by far the prevalent one. The occasional use distinguishes theory from the psychology of consciousness. Metapsychology in this usage means depth psychology, defined as the psychology which takes unconscious processes into account.

Many psychoanalysts do use the term metapsychology in this way. To them, therefore, an analyst who rejects metapsychology is rejecting the unconscious, undoubtedly a shibboleth of psychoanalysis.

The concept of unconscious mental processes is so central in psychoanalysis that Freud's first proposal for dividing up the systems of the

This paper originally appeared in 1985 as "Un nouveau regard sur la metapsychologie," *Revue Française de Psychanalyse,* 49:1237–1252.

mind—called the topographic theory—was in terms of the relation to consciousness. The systems were the Conscious, Preconscious, and Unconscious. If one considers psychoanalytic theory to be that theory which developed through the study of unconscious processes but includes preconscious and conscious processes as well, metapsychology becomes equivalent to psychoanalytic theory and in effect, a superfluous term (Brenner, 1980). To an analyst who equates metapsychology with psychoanalytic theory, someone who rejects metapsychology is at best atheoretical and at worst is rejecting some central psychoanalytic concept, whether that be the unconscious, drive, or whatever.

The second use of the term and the usual one in Freud's writings, was not formally introduced and defined until 1915 in the paper "The Unconscious." That definition is so central that it should be quoted in full: "I propose that when we have succeeded in describing a psychical process in its dynamic, topographical, and economic aspects, we should speak of it as a *metapsychological* presentation" (1915a, p. 181). These three points of view refer respectively to the forces, structures, and energies involved in a psychical process.

One might readily conclude that Freud's definition does indeed take in all of psychoanalytic theory. That conclusion is subject to two important specifications, however. The first and most important specification is that Freud considered the forces, structures, and energies in natural-science terms, despite some ambiguities and disavowals. The forces are the instinctual drives, the structures include the id, the repository of the drives, and the energies are defined as psychic energies but they are conceptually manipulated without any clear distinction from somatic energies. It is for this reason that I stated that on the epistemological question Freud takes the stand that psychoanalysis is a natural science.

The second, less important specification is where metapsychology stands in the hierarchy of psychoanalytic conceptualization, a hierarchy defined in terms of level of generalization. The literature includes two major suggestions for this hierarchical classification. Rapaport and Gill (1959) propose in ascending order of generalization: empirical proposition, general psychoanalytic proposition, and metapsychological proposition. Waelder (1962), dividing empirical proposition into observation and interpretation, similarly proposed: clinical observation and data, clinical interpretation, clinical generalization or theory, and metapsychology.

This placing of metapsychology at the highest level of generalization would seem to be consistent with Freud's (1917, p. 222) reference to metapsychology as "the theoretical assumptions on which a psychoanalytic system could be founded," although Brenner (1980) reads this reference not to mean the assumptions, but rather to equate metapsychology with the psychoanalytic system. Brenner further points out that Waelder described the successive levels as more abstract rather than more generalized, and he objects to the invidious implication—one which a number of analysts have clearly accepted—that metapsychology is theory formation at the most speculative level and the furthest distant from data. True though it be that many psychoanalysts have difficulty in seeing the relevance of metapsychology to their clinical work, and hence presumably to the data, the fault may lie in their inability to recognize the role which metapsychological propositions are in fact playing in their work. I have attempted elsewhere (Gill, 1976) to show how intertwined natural-science and hermeneutic considerations are in many psychoanalytic propositions.

I distinguish four major and two minor positions on the epistemological status of psychoanalysis. The major ones are psychoanalysis as natural science, hermeneutic discipline, bridge between mind and body, and information theory. The minor ones, which I shall not discuss further, are *sui generis* (Rycroft, 1966) and metapsychology as metaphor (Wurmser, 1977), in effect a hermeneutic position.

NATURAL SCIENCE

Most psychoanalysts accept Freud's view that psychoanalysis is a natural science, although metapsychological discussions of forces, structures, and energies which are based on this assumption do not often make their natural-science status explicit as I did above.

HERMENEUTIC DISCIPLINE

A hermeneutic discipline is one concerned with interpretation and meaning, terms not easy to define (see Palmer, 1969).

Those who hold that psychoanalysis is not a natural science but a hermeneutic one believe that Freudian metapsychology employs natural-science dimensions, that these are not the dimensions of clinical theory, and that therefore metapsychology is not a generalization from the clinical theory but rather is in a different universe of discourse. This position has been taken by G. Klein (1976) whose formulation is that psychoanalysis does not need a theory to explain a theory, that is, a metapsychology to explain the psychology. He says, therefore, that psychoanalysis needs one theory, not two. It is important to recognize that this position is not atheoretical but rather holds that the clinical theory suffices. At the same time, if this position is accepted, the intricate intertwining of metapsychological and hermeneutic considerations in many psychoanalytic propositions is such that the discipline is confronted with the major task of disentangling the two kinds of considerations.

As an illustration I take the so-called U-tube theory (Freud, 1914) which alleges a reciprocal relationship between self love and love of others. The natural-science law of conservation of energy would indeed call for a diminution in one as the other rises. Yet many clinical phenomena seem contradictory to such a reciprocity. Self love and love of others may in fact rise and fall together. Only a detailed examination of the qualitative psychological meanings obscured by global references to self love and love of others and a recognition of the inapplicability of natural-science considerations of more or less (or different qualities of) energy will illuminate the issue.

In attempting to resolve the controversy as to whether metapsychology, and indeed psychoanalysis altogether, should be a natural-science or a hermeneutic discipline, it must first be pointed out that there is a disagreement as to whether natural science is the only kind of science. Brenner (1980) says that is so. He argues that the data of every branch of science are unique, that meaning is the unique province of psychoanalysis, and that science is defined by its approach to data rather than by the data with which it deals. Others (Gill, 1976) argue that there are hermeneutic sciences, too, which do, or at least can, employ the same canons of empirical investigation in dealing with data as the natural sciences, which are defined as the sciences dealing with material objects, whether inorganic or organic.

The impression that a hermeneutic discipline cannot be a science may stem from two sources. One is the origin of the term in the exegesis of religious texts. The other is its use in literary criticism which may imply to some that it is confined to texts or, somewhat more broadly, to verbal productions. The psychoanalyst who espouses the conception of psychoanalysis as a hermeneutic science emphasizes that the patient does much more than speak and, even more important, that he responds in an interpersonal dialogic exchange to the analyst's interventions as a text cannot.

Those who believe a hermeneutic discipline cannot be a science point to the fact that hermeneuticists use the concept of reasons in their explanations rather than causes, as in natural science. They point to the distinction advanced by hermeneuticists between understanding and explanation (*verstehen* in the *Geisteswissenschaften* and *erklären* in *Naturwissenschaften*, Hartmann, 1927) as implying that a hermeneutic discipline cannot employ the canons of natural science. Those who believe there can be a hermeneutic science, even if the major extant systems of philosophical hermeneutics reject that possibility, argue on the contrary that a hermeneutic investigation in psychoanalysis can employ such canons, albeit in dimensions other than those of the natural sciences. Yet a third group argues that hermeneutic data require canons of investigation which differ from those of natural science, and which are admittedly only in the process of development. They argue that hermeneutic thought has so far been primarily philosophical and applied only to theological, juridical, and literary productions essentially in the interpretation of texts but that they need be no less empirical and oriented toward explicating the nature of reality than the canons of natural science. Those who hold this position stress that hermeneutic canons must not be bound by the Cartesian split between subject and object which is the hallmark of the canons of investigation in the natural sciences (Barratt, 1984).

Those who argue that psychoanalysis must be more than a hermeneutic discipline point to the havoc which they believe is being wrought in psychoanalysis by concepts being brought into it by hermeneuticists and which they believe demonstrate that hermeneuticists in fact do not obey canons of empirical investigation. They point to such concepts as psychoanalytic explanation as narration (Schafer, 1981), the relativity of conceptions of reality, and the questioning of the possibility of reconstructing an individual's past in a veridical sense (Spence, 1982). They see hermeneutics as leading to a reliance on empathy as a criterion of validity with a dethroning of observation, logic, and reason (Eagle, 1984).

Schafer (1976) has proposed an "action language" as a feature of a hermeneutic position to supplant metapsychology. He argues that action language is free of two of the major faults of metapsychology as well as possessing the advantages of hermeneutics. One fault is the reification of psychological processes in metapsychological theory. The other is the manner in which metapsychological theory abets the analyst in an unwitting collusion with the patient's abdication of personal responsibility for his behavior, ascribing it to alien internal forces. Schafer further suggests that metapsychology is "congruent with the archaic body language of infancy" (1975, p. 42). The idea of energy discharge, for example, may be unconsciously congruent with infantile excretory fantasy.

The debate involves strong emotional currents so that each side has a tendency to view the other as a global, undifferentiated position. Individual hermeneuticists espouse particular theories which are unthinkingly considered by others to be inevitable concomitants of any hermeneutic position, so that an argument against one contention is considered to be an argument against the entire hermeneutic position. Schafer's emphasis on language in the development of his scheme, for example, lends fuel to those who see in the hermeneutic position the elevation of language to an unwarranted centrality in psychoanalytic conceptualization. Despite his obvious sophistication as a clinician, his alleged equation of responsibility with conscious volition leads some to the accusation that he denies the unconscious and perverts psychoanalysis into a superficial manipulative therapy which ignores the power of involuntary forces and inhibits the regression alleged to be necessary in the psychoanalytic process (Barratt, 1978).

BRIDGE BETWEEN MIND AND BODY

A third epistemological position on the role of metapsychology, one which has been relatively little discussed as such in our literature, is metapsychology as a bridge between mind and body. It is in fact so defined in the International Scientific Vocabulary, cited by the Merriam-Webster and Random House dictionaries.

Brenner (1980), a staunch supporter of the definition of metapsychology in both the simpler sense which equates it with depth psychology and the more complex sense which equates it with psychoanalytic theory, explicitly suggests the more specific meaning that metapsychology means the study of the relation between mind and body. In doing so, however, Brenner uses only the neurophysiological, natural-science, Freudian metapsychological language when in fact there is also the more general bodily Freudian, natural-science metapsychological language. The psychic energy of the economic point of view is in the neurophysiological language while the drive forces of the dynamic point of view are stated in general bodily language.

Consistent with the fact that the mind-body problem is ordinarily discussed as the relation between mind and brain, Brenner (1980) writes that psychoanalysis is obviously a natural science because "mind is but an aspect of brain functioning . . . mind has no 'existence' no meaning, apart from brain" (p. 206). Rubinstein (1974) considers that metapsychology must be consistent with what is known of neurophysiology. He objects to Freud's energy concepts, not because they are in natural-science terms but because they are wrong according to current neurophysiology.

Ricoeur (1970) argues for an epistemological position related to metapsychology as a bridge between mind and body by holding that a great merit of psychoanalysis is that it is a "mixed discourse" including force and meaning, a "semantics of desire."

The more significant locus of the metapsychology-versus-hermeneutics controversy for psychoanalysis seems to me to reside in the general bodily propositions of psychoanalysis—that is, how to take account of the role of the body in psychological functioning—rather than in the neurological mind-body propositions, because both force and energy considerations are primarily dealt with in terms of the drives.

The hermeneutic position appears to many analysts to amount to giving up the psychoanalytic discovery of the crucial role in man's functioning of the drives in general and sexuality and aggression in particular. The psychoanalytic hermeneuticists deny that they are doing so and argue that they do deal with man's biological nature as it is mediated in psychologically meaningful terms. They deny that they neglect infantile sexuality and its derivatives, for example, and argue that they deal with these matters in terms of their psychological meaningfulness rather than as biological matters. They believe they are defining psychology in relation to its organic substrate in the same way Freud does in this illuminating passage, which deserves to be quoted not only for what it says on this topic but also for its definition of psychological meaningfulness:

> Anything that is observable in mental life may occasionally be described as a mental phenomenon. The question will then be whether the particular mental phenomenon has arisen immediately from somatic, organic, and material influences—in which case its investigation will not be part of psychology—or whether it is derived in the first instance from other mental processes, somewhere behind which the series of organic influences begins. It is this latter situation that we have in view when we describe a phenomenon as a mental process, and for that reason it is more expedient to clothe our assertion in the form: "the phenomenon has a sense." By "sense" we understand "meaning," "intention," "purpose," and "position in a continuous psychical context [Freud, 1916–1917, pp. 60–61].

Freud's primary basis for inferring unconscious processes is to fill the gaps in consciousness which interrupt a continuous psychical context. Rapaport (1944) also defined meaning in terms of continuity of psychical context.

Two principal problems appear with regard to this explication of how a hermeneutic psychoanalysis deals with man as a biological organism by way of mediating meanings.

One has to do with how one accounts for motivational urge, that is, the energy and force with which a motive seems endowed. In the Freudian metapsychological scheme this urge is dealt with in the dynamic and economic propositions of force and energy. It is these propositions which are the principal focus of attack by hermeneuticists. Though metapsychologists insist this energy is not to be equated with physical energy, its derivation from somatic urges seems inescapable, and indeed Freud did define a drive "as a concept on the frontier between the mental and the somatic, as the psychical representative of the stimuli originating from within the organism and reaching the mind, as a measure of the demand made upon the mind for work in consequence of its connection with the body" (1915b, pp. 121–122). This passage also supports the view presented above that metapsychology deals with the bridge between mind and body.

A second problem confronting hermeneutic explanation is that, while it leans heavily on mental representation as psychic coin, there is an important preverbal, presymbolic period in human development in which such representations cannot yet be presumed to exist. Gedo (1979) has based his conclusion that psychoanalysis must be a natural science as well as hermeneutic on this fact and has built upon it a theory of motivation in terms of his view of the repetition compulsion which sharply divides the presymbolic from the symbolic explanations of behavior. The presymbolic is "beyond the pleasure principle," a manifestation of the "principle of self initiated active reversal of passive experience" (p. 204) and, consistent with Gedo's understanding of this period in natural-science terms, "a natural reflection of the general propensity of the human nervous system to create order" (p. 181). The symbolic, under the sway of the pleasure principle, is the familiar theory of subjectively represented motivation in the domain of hermeneutics.

While a shift from the idea that metapsychology is conceptualized in natural-science terms to seeing it as a bridge between mind and body may not at first seem like a very important change, I believe it could be quite clarifying in a number of directions. It would help explain why metapsychology can be seen as natural science by the proponents of psychoanalysis as a hermeneutic discipline and as dealing with psychological meanings by the proponents of psychoanalysis as a natural science. That is, it would help explain why the adherents of metapsychology insist that they are defining psychological force, energy, and structure without reference to an organic substrate (Rapaport and Gill, 1959), while those who reject metapsychology insist that force, energy, and structure are in fact being used as natural-science concepts, despite the disavowal (Gill, 1976).

For example, despite insisting that they were dealing with the concept of psychic energy without reference to its somatic substrate, Rapaport and Gill (1959) postulated that psychological energies follow a law of conservation, are subject to a law of entropy and to transformations which increase or decrease their entropic tendency. They suggested that the assumption of conservation underlies propositions concerning displacement of cathexis (the term used by Strachey to translate *bezetsung*, that is, investment). The law of entropy is an economic principle which adds a directional tendency to the quantities of energy involved in psychological processes. It underlies propositions concerning mobile cathexis and primary process while the transformation of energies underlies propositions concerning binding, neutralization, and deneutralization of cathexes. The decrease of the entropic tendency is the assumption underlying the explanation of the transition from the primary to the secondary process and the relationship between energy and structure in psychological phenomena.

A major argument advanced to show that Freudian metapsychology is indeed natural science is that the first major metapsychological document—Freud's "Project" of 1895—employs force, energy, and structure explicitly as natural-science concepts. Their natural-science status has been obscured because it becomes usually implicit, although no less important, in Freud's subsequent metapsychological writings. It was often even explicitly disavowed (Gill, 1976; Pribram and Gill, 1976).

The debate as to whether Freudian metapsychology is natural science or hermeneutics would be resolved by concluding that it is neither but rather a bridge between the two, that is, an effort to solve the mind-body problem.

With the resolution of the debate by considering metapsychology to be neither natural science nor hermeneutics but the bridge between the two, the questions for psychoanalysis become these: Is it possible to develop a self-contained science of psychological functioning without reference to the organic substrate of mind? Should psychoanalysis be such a science? How would such a science deal with man as a biological organism? Does metapsychology indeed offer a solution to, or even illuminate, the mind-body problem, or is it essentially an ambiguity which permits a theorist to see it as on the body or mind side of the line, as the occasion demands?

Hermeneuticists, of course, accept the necessity for a biological science of man, too, but argue that psychoanalysis does not have the data required to build such a science and does not purport to be a total science of man. While they agree in principle with the idea that psychoanalytic concepts should be consistent with the findings of other sciences, they believe that hermeneutic propositions are in a different realm of discourse from natural science so that the issue of compatibility does not even arise.

INFORMATION THEORY

Although a natural-science motivational theory in terms of force and energy seems to most analysts an inevitable conclusion from the role of drives in psychic life, alternative conceptualizations of motivational phenomena are beginning to appear. Schafer (1975), for example, has attempted to demonstrate that his action language is consistent with "psychoanalysis without psychodynamics" without sacrificing the clinical insights of psychoanalysis into motivation.

A detailed effort to develop a model which accounts for the dynamic propositions of psychoanalysis and the subjective sense of urgency without employing force and energy concepts but rather by a hierarchy of goals whose priorities are determined through information processing has been made by Rosenblatt and Thickstun (1977). They, as well as Peterfreund (1971), have attempted to recast psychoanalytic theory into information-theory language, which, they argue, is consistent with modern neurophysiology. The force-and-energy paradigm is thus replaced by an information-theory paradigm.

It has been objected (Gill, 1977) that these reformulations seem to use information in a common-sense fashion rather than in the technical sense of information theory. Whether these reformulations are in natural-science terms and/or represent a bridge between mind and body is by no means clear. Rapaport (1950) has written that even if information-theory reformulations of psychoanalytic propositions are more than an analogy, a bridge for the mind-body problem requires not only the communication-engineering concepts of cybernetics and information theory but their integration with power engineering, that is, in psychoanalytic terms, with the dynamic and economic propositions of the Freudian pleasure principle and primary process. Rosenblatt and Thickstun believe that the clinical propositions of psychoanalysis, shorn of their metapsychology, are in fact already stated essentially in information-processing terms.

TWO ADDITIONAL POINTS OF VIEW

The three points of view proposed by Freud remained the only explicitly agreed-upon metapsychological points of view until a paper by Rapaport and Gill in 1959 proposed adding the genetic and adaptive points of view as formalization of what they regarded to be already informally accepted points of view among analysts. The speed with which the two new points of view were generally accepted among analysts suggests that they were indeed only a formalization and not new concepts.

Abrams (1977) has pointed out that the genetic point of view includes two somewhat different, albeit interrelated, kinds of propositions—those relating to antecedents and those relating to transformations, both progressive and regressive. Regressive transformations need not be solely repetitions of the past nor need progressive transformations be entirely explicable by the past.

The adaptive point of view refers to the relation between the person and the external world. Psychoanalysis is often criticized for an alleged disregard of the external world. The fact that Freud defined the metapsychological points of view in terms of mental processes, for example, is sometimes taken to mean that the system is solipsistic and solely intrapsychic. In fact Freud included consideration of the external environment from the very beginning. His complemental series (1914) refers to the codetermination of mental life by the innate and the experiential. He defined the distinction between ego and the external world as one of the three great polarities that dominate mental life. The other two are the biological, activity-passivity, and the economic, pleasure-unpleasure (Freud, 1915b, p. 140).

An important reason that psychoanalysis is sometimes misunderstood to ignore the external world is that Freud's first major exploration was of the id, that is, of the epigenetic unfolding of the life of the drives. It may well be that this was connected to his disillusionment on discovering that the tales of seduction his patients told him turned out to have been mainly fantasies. Even the initial development of ego psychology related primarily to the defenses against drive rather than relations to the outside world. The first detailed and influential formalization of consideration of the external world was in Hartmann's (1939) monograph, *Ego Psychology and the Problem of Adaptation.* Erikson's (1950) development of an epigenetic theory of ego development marks another major contribution to a theory of adaptation. With the detailed consideration of the environment, psychoanalysis aspires to become a general psychology. As adaptive considerations became prominent many analysts feared the loss or at least dilution of the unique contribution of psychoanalysis, the discovery of the unconscious and the drives. The concern remains an active one, and revisionist movements in analysis commonly deemphasize the role of the id. Analysts also warn that one must guard against the degeneration of adaptation into adjustment with a loss of the revolutionary, nonconformist spirit of psychoanalysis.

Questions have also been raised as to whether the genetic and adaptive points of view are on the same level as the other three or are subsumable by them. Both Glover (1961) and Schafer (1970) argue that genetic and adaptive propositions are reducible to the other three. Glover refers to genetic and adaptive propositions as complex serial measures rather than irreducible postulates, while Schafer also argues that genetic propositions are explainable in terms of the original three propositions. He considers adaptational propositions in a narrow sense to articulate and amplify the structural, specifically, ego-psychological point of view. He further suggests that adaptation in a broad sense is a biological vantage point, outside of and prior to psychology. Schafer is among those who do not regard natural-science considerations, biological in this instance, to be appropriately included among psychoanalytic propositions. Both Glover and Schafer, of course, are in no way calling into question the relevance and importance of genetic and adaptive considerations in psychoanalysis.

My Own Views

I believe that Freudian natural-science metapsychology is a serious obstacle to the development of psychoanalysis. It purports to provide explanations which are only pseudoscientific apings of natural science. Psychoanalysis needs to develop in its own terms as a self-contained hermeneutic science. The usual canons of empirical research are applicable to variables in hermeneutic dimensions.

The disputes about metapsychology obscure crucial controversies in psychoanalysis because it is presumed that certain basic psychoanalytic findings can be maintained only if natural-science metapsychology is retained. These include the following:

1. There are innate givens which codetermine how a human being responds to experience. The abandonment of natural-science metapsychology is mistakenly considered to mean a concept of the human being as a blank slate on which experience writes.

2. The natural-science metapsychological concept which carries these innate givens is the concept of drive. But there are other innate givens as well as drives, and the innate drives need not be restricted to sex and aggression.

3. The abandonment of a natural-science conception of drives in psychoanalytic theorizing is mistakenly considered to be the abandonment of the importance in psychological functioning of the fact that a human being is a biological organism as well as a person. But, as I suggested above, psychoanalysis deals with biology as it is psychologically experienced, not in somatic terms.

4. The rejection of the natural-science concept of drives is considered to be the abandonment of the importance of sexuality and aggression in human psychological functioning. It is true that serious questions are being raised as to whether sexuality and aggression are either the source of all motivation or superordinate in the motivational hierarchy. I believe they are not—that is, that there are other independent motivations, too, and that sexuality and aggression occupy different positions in the motivational hierarchy in different people. I am inclined to believe that a superordinate self concept will become increasingly recognized as clarifying the nature of human motivation, though I do not mean thereby to ally myself necessarily with Kohutian psychology (1977) which has more or less preempted

the self as a term in psychoanalytic theory. For recent valuable discussions in psychoanalysis of self concepts and motivation I cite in addition to Kohut, Gedo (1979), Eagle (1984), and Pine (1985). I (Gill, 1983) have also recently published a related essay.

REFERENCES

Abrams, S. (1977), Genetic point of view. *J. Amer. Psychoanal. Assn.*, 25:417–426.

Barratt, B. (1978), Critical notes on Schafer's action language. *This Annual*, 6:287–303. New York: International Universities Press.

——— (1984), *Psychic Reality and Psychoanalytic Knowing*. Hillsdale, N.J.: Erlbaum.

Brenner, C. (1980), Metapsychology and psychoanalytic theory. *Psychoanal. Quart.*, 49:189–214.

Eagle, M. (1984), *Recent Developments in Psychoanalysis*. New York: McGraw-Hill.

Erikson, E. (1950), *Childhood and Society*. New York: Norton.

Fairbairn, W. (1952), *An Object-Relations Theory of the Personality*. New York: Basic Books, 1954.

Freud, S. (1914), On narcissism. *Standard Edition*, 14:73–102. London: Hogarth Press, 1957.

——— (1915a), The unconscious. *Standard Edition*, 14:166–204. London: Hogarth Press, 1957.

——— (1915b), Instincts and their vicissitudes. *Standard Edition*, 14:117–140. London: Hogarth Press, 1957.

——— (1916–1917), Introductory lectures on psychoanalysis. *Standard Edition*, 5:60–79. London: Hogarth Press, 1953.

——— (1917), A metapsychological supplement to the theory of dreams. *Standard Edition*, 14:219–236. London: Hogarth Press, 1957.

——— (1923), The ego and the id. *Standard Edition*, 19:12–59. London: Hogarth Press, 1961.

——— (1924), The economic problem of masochism. *Standard Edition*, 19:157–172. London: Hogarth Press, 1961.

Gedo, J. (1979), *Beyond Interpretation*. New York: International Universities Press.

Gill, M. (1976), Metapsychology is not psychology. In: *Psychology vs. Metapsychology*, ed. M. Gill & P. Holzman. New York: International Universities Press, pp. 71–105.

——— (1977), Psychic energy reconsidered: Discussion. *J. Amer. Psychoanal. Assn.*, 25:581–598.

——— (1983), The point of view of psychoanalysis: Energy discharge or person? *Psychoanal. & Contemp. Thought*, 6:513–551.

Glover, E. (1961), Some recent trends in psychoanalytic theory. *Psychoanal. Quart.*, 30:86–107.

Hartmann, H. (1927), Understanding and explanation. In: *Essays on Ego Psychology*. New York: International Universities Press, 1964, pp. 369–403.

——— (1939), *Ego Psychology and the Problem of Adaptation*. New York: International Universities Press, 1958.

Klein, G. (1976), Two theories or one? In: *Psychoanalytic Theory*. New York: International Universities Press, pp. 41–71.

Kohut, H. (1977), *The Restoration of the Self*. New York: International Universities Press.

Palmer, R. (1969), *Hermeneutics*. Evanston: Northwestern University Press.

Peterfreund, E. (1971), *Information Systems and Psychoanalysis*. [*Psychological Issues*, Monogr. 25/26]. New York: International Universities Press.

Pine, F. (1985), *Developmental Theory and Clinical Process*. New Haven: Yale University Press.

Pribram, K., & Gill, M. (1976), *Freud's Project Reassessed*. London: Hutchinson.

Rapaport, D. (1944), The scientific methodology of psychoanalysis. In: *The Collected Papers of David Rapaport*, ed. M. Gill. New York: Basic Books, 1967.

——— (1950), Book review. Norbert Wiener, Cybernetics or control and communication in the animal and the machine, in *The Collected Papers of David Rapaport*. London: Basic Books, 1967.

——— & Gill, M. (1959), The points of view and assumptions of metapsychology. In: *The Collected Papers of David Rapaport*, ed. M. Gill. New York: Basic Books, 1967.

Ricoeur, P. (1970), *Freud and Philosophy.* New Haven: Yale U. Press.

Rosenblatt, A., & Thickstun, J. (1977), Modern psychoanalytic concepts in a general psychology—Parts 1 and 2. *Psychological Issues* Monogr. 42/43. New York: International Universities Press.

Rubinstein, B. (1974), On the role of classificatory processes in mental functioning: Aspects of a psychoanalytic theoretical model. *Psychoanalysis and Contemporary Science,* 3:101–185. New York: International Universities Press.

Rycroft, C. (ed.) (1966), *Psychoanalysis Observed.* New York: Coward-McCann.

Schafer, R. (1970), An overview of Heinz Hartmann's contributions to psychoanalysis. *Internat. J. Psycho-Anal.,* 51:425–446.

——— (1975), Psychoanalysis without psychodynamics. *Internat. J. Psycho-Anal.,* 56:41–55.

——— (1976), *A New Language for Psychoanalysis.* New Haven: Yale University Press.

——— (1981), *Narrative Actions in Psychoanalysis.* Worcester, Mass.: Clark University Press.

Spence, D. (1982), *Narrative Truth and Historical Truth.* New York: Norton.

Waelder, R. (1962), Psychoanalysis, scientific method and philosophy. *J. Amer. Psychoanal. Assn.,* 10:617–637.

Wurmser, L. (1977), A defense of the use of metaphor in analytic theory formation. *Psychoanal. Quart.,* 46:466–498.

February 1987

Psychoanalysis in Search of Nature
Thoughts on Metapsychology, "Metaphysics," Projection

HANS W. LOEWALD, M.D. (New Haven)

I

With the psychoanalytic conception of the unconscious and of psychic reality psychoanalysis is stepping outside the bounds of nineteenth-century natural science and its interpretation (a hermeneutic construction) of nature as objective material reality. In the course of the development of psychoanalytic thought, the id—uniting unconscious and instincts under one roof—became the concept for human nature as unconscious activity. Ego and superego represent individual developments of that activity, and human consciousness is a sporadic resultant of its further evolution.

With Freud's theory of life and death instincts, as pertaining to universal nature no less than to human nature, psychic reality has swallowed up, as it were, material objective reality. With that "projection," psyche in its unconscious aspect has become the title for nature as living, as creative-destructive activity. Cosmic life evolves and contains human life, and human life as a microcosm can, in the mirroring of *conscire,* of consciousness, grasp something of the dynamics—the psyche—of nature. Psychoanalysis as a distinct discipline is concerned with the detailed exploration of the human microcosm, its permutations and mirrorings, the vicissitudes, disturbances, and conflicts peculiar to it. But psychoanalytic theory, having developed basic general concepts, must not lose its moorings in a theory of nature.

This essay is offered to honor the memory of Samuel Lipton, whom I came to know as a man of independent mind, dedicated to both psychoanalytic tradition and innovation.

The traditional theory of nature is changing, and with that change the theory of knowledge of nature is changing. Nature is no longer simply an object of observation and domination by a human conscious mind, a subject, but an all-embracing activity of which man, and the human mind in its unconscious and sometimes conscious aspects, is one element or configuration, albeit of uttermost importance to that human mind. By virtue of the unison and reverberation with the rest of nature we gain what understanding of nature, including our own, we possess. Rather than descending, as happened in the initial phase of psychoanalysis, from the objectivity of subjective consciousness to the unconscious, we now ascend from id to ego. Unison and reverberation, as regards other human beings, is called empathy. But it would be erroneous to assume that this empathic resonance stops at the frontier of human mentality. Our knowledge of organic and so-called inorganic nature is likely to derive from similar attunements; these are in themselves not defensive projections, but they most often have been altered by the model of consciousness to conform to its structure. It may indeed be claimed that in traditional natural science, too, the objectivity achieved in human consciousness was *projected* onto the universe and to what we call, then, physical material reality, and that this nature, so structured by us was now perceived as ultimate reality, in the same vein as the "ultimate reality" of metaphysics, mythology, and religion.

Older philosophers distinguished *natura naturans* (nature as active process) from *natura naturata* (nature as the assembly of created objective entities); and Descartes distinguished *res cogitans* from *res extensa* (the germ of psychic and material reality). They struggled with similar problems but were still able, in the last resort, to appeal to God as universal consciousness, being the origin and model of human consciousness. Postmodern science appears to convey a new insight: we understand something about nature and reality, know something about them, by being open to their workings in us and the rest of nature as unconscious life, the openness being what we call consciousness. This insight—also very ancient—transcends, subsumes into itself the antagonism of "ego" and "reality" which ultimately derives from the equation of psyche and consciousness.

We must further briefly consider the emergence of individuation and the interpretation of "psychical" as *endopsychic*. Equating the two takes its cue from consciousness, which is individualistic. Unconscious and instincts assume decidedly individual features, as the human id, in the rise of consciousness, and this is the main concern of psychoanalysis. The origin of individual psychic life, however, is a transindividual field, represented by the mother/infant matrix, not an individual unconscious and instincts residing in an individual. The objectivity of traditional modern science is an outcome of the gradual differentiation of this field culminating in individual consciousness. Yet it disregards (represses) the transindividual matrix which continues to actively originate, in ever-widening spirals, the various transformative internalizations of individual psychic life, i.e., endopsychic life. In other words, an earlier form of "infantile amnesia" is at work in traditional natural science. The introduction of the concepts of narcissistic libido and of identification/internalization represented an explicit shift away from the traditional perspective. What is needed is a natural science that realizes that the interpretation of nature in terms of (individualistic) consciousness limits our view, granted that it has pragmatical validity for human conscious thought and action and appears to enhance man's domination of the world. But a deeper understanding of nature will widen the horizons of a science of nature and increase, one may hope, its power of mastery, a mastery that involves yielding no less than dominion. Such deeper understanding subordinates the traditional view to a more comprehensive perspective on nature as unconscious activity *("natura naturans")*. Psychoanalytic theory is on that path, and so are the physical sciences themselves (Freud remarked on the parallels). Indeed, "classical" psychoanalysis fights a rearguard action against such a wider framework, a battle in which theoretical physics is no longer immobilized.

Freud's formulation of the distinction between psychic reality and material reality (psychic reality as "a particular form of existence not to be confused with material reality"; 1900, p. 620) is superseded in a fully developed conception of the unconscious. Superseded also is the notion of a fundamental antagonism, as opposed to a developmental differentiation, of unconscious and consciousness and of id and ego. This developmental differentiation leads to the heights of human mentation as awareness, and to the actualities of developmental arrest and of normal and pathological conflict.

II

In "The Psychopathology of Everyday Life" Freud (1901) writes:

> In point of fact I believe that a large part of the mythological view of the world, which extends a long way into the most modern religions, is *nothing but psychology projected into the external world.* The obscure recognition (the endopsychic perception, as it were) of psychical factors and relations in the unconscious is mirrored—it is difficult to express it in other terms, and here the analogy with paranoia must come to our aid—in the con-

> struction of *a supernatural reality*, which is destined to be changed back once more by science into the *psychology of the unconscious*. One could venture to explain in this way the myths of paradise and the fall of man, of God, of good and evil, of immortality, and so on, and to translate *metaphysics* into *metapsychology* [pp. 258–259; Freud's italics].

This is "the first published appearance of the word" 'metapsychology' according to Strachey (Freud, 1901, p. 259, n. 1). As Freud wrote in a letter to Fliess in 1898, 'metapsychology' would be the name "for my psychology that leads behind consciousness" (1985, pp. 301–302). From the beginning it was meant as a term for a scientific theory of unconscious mentation, of "psychical factors and relations in the unconscious." This basic meaning is preserved throughout all of Freud's writings, also in the seemingly narrow so-called definition of the term in the paper on "The Unconscious" (1915, p. 181) which has sidetracked many authors. Nowadays the word *meta*-psychology seems redundant, since psychology is no longer viewed as simply the science of human *conscious* life and its underdeveloped forms in animal life. When Freud invented the term, he had to fight a battle.

Projection, according to Freud, gives us the key for understanding the mythological world view. If "metaphysics" is a projection of the psychology of the individual's unconscious life into the external world, then Freud's life and death instincts, in their Empedocledian version applying to the universe which Freud explicitly adopts (1937, pp. 244–247; 1940, p. 149), would be nothing but a reprojection of psychical forces or processes into the external world, a bare-bones mythology or metaphysics. Most analysts' objections to his last instinct theory (as distinguished from an accepted theory of sexual and aggressive drives) are based on just that view of the matter: Freud now appears to have left the firm ground of empirical investigation of unconscious processes, coming full circle by postulating a new metaphysics. The human unconscious, elucidated by his lifework, now seems to be mirrored in the construction of cosmic life and death forces or principles of ultimate import, granted that this construction has done away with gods, demons, angels, original sin, good and evil, etc. I don't deny the force of this argument. It is valid within the confines of nineteenth-century natural science, for which psychoanalysis is destined to remain, at best, an illegitimate child and troublesome outcast.

But there is more to projection than meets the eye, more than its being a mechanism of defense against recognition of unconscious currents within oneself: it bespeaks an obscure unconscious recognition of the deep sameness of instinctual driving forces in the inner and the external world. In his paper on "Some Neurotic Mechanisms in Jealousy, Paranoia and Homosexuality" Freud (1922) wrote:

> We begin to see that we describe the behaviour of both jealous and persecutory paranoics very inadequately by saying that they project outwards on to others what they do not wish to recognize in themselves. Certainly they do this; but they do not project it into the blue, so to speak, where there is nothing of the sort already. They let themselves be guided by their knowledge of the unconscious, and displace to the unconscious minds of others the attention which they have withdrawn from their own [p. 226].

In other words, projection is based on an obscure knowledge—which turns out to be different from a purely "endopsychic" perception—of the correspondence, the resonance, between endopsychic unconscious processes and unconscious processes of other individuals. It is indicated to apply this deeper understanding of projection to that projection of which Freud speaks in my quotation from "The Psychopathology of Everyday Life." Thus the following conclusion suggests itself: the projection of psychology into the external world—the earmark, according to Freud, of the mythological/religious world view or "metaphysics"—takes place because there are unconscious forces operating in the external world no less than in the internal world of the individual. These are called by Freud life and death instincts. It is a defensive use of projection to ignore our own unconscious and to pay, instead, attention to the unconscious forces of nature and make them into conscious motivations of supernatural personages. It is an egocentric view, in the sense that the human ego, and its evolutionary culmination in consciousness, have become the model of nature. To declare or postulate that there is a dynamic unconscious is to remove man, as Freud has seen, from the center. In a way similar to paranoid defensive projections, in a "metaphysical" view the universe is thought of as governed by powers that are egocentrically seen in the image of human consciousness, and not by unconscious powers. On the other hand, there is anthropocentrism of another kind at play when the concept of the unconscious is limited, as "classical" theory would have it, to the human unconscious uncovered by psychoanalysis. It amounts to a defense against acknowledging live, driving forces beyond and encompassing those operating in individual existence. It would be fruitful to work out the connections between these lines of thought and the conception of instinct as a border-concept straddling the somatic and psychical realms.

But particularly also the connections, of the contemporary shift in interest and emphasis to preoedipal issues with the foregoing theoretical considerations, need to be articulated: the changing views on nature and the instincts turn to a more "archaic" core of being, and so does present-day clinical work.

Summary

An attempt is made to understand Freud's last instinct theory, in conjunction with his revised view on projection, as pieces of a philosophy of nature inspired by psychoanalysis as science of the unconscious. Sexuality and aggression, in this philosophical shift harking back to presocratic philosophy, are projected into nature—not a projection "into the blue" but the rediscovery of an original concordance and lasting affinity. I am aware that Jung's thoughts on the unconscious have in some respects moved in a similar direction, although his emphases have been quite different.

REFERENCES

Freud, S. (1900), The interpretation of dreams. *Standard Edition*, 4 & 5. London: Hogarth Press, 1953.

——— (1901), The psychopathology of everyday life. *Standard Edition*, 6. London: Hogarth Press, 1960.

——— (1915), The unconscious. *Standard Edition*, 14:159–218. London: Hogarth Press, 1957.

——— (1922), Some neurotic mechanisms in jealousy, paranoia, and homosexuality. *Standard Edition*, 18:221–233. London: Hogarth Press, 1955.

——— (1937), Analysis terminable and interminable. *Standard Edition*, 23:209–254. London: Hogarth Press, 1964.

——— (1940), An outline of psycho-analysis. *Standard Edition*, 23:141–208. London: Hogarth Press, 1964.

——— (1985), *The Complete Letters of Sigmund Freud to Wilhelm Fliess*. Trans. and ed. by J. M. Masson. Cambridge & London: Harvard University Press.

January 1987

Psychoanalytic Principles and Principle Deviations

DANIEL S. JAFFE, M.D. (Washington)

Introduction

Mankind's resistance to change being what it is, great innovators have to expect that their new ideas will be met with skepticism, rejection, and even outrage. Freud was a striking example of this phenomenon, largely on account of the shock effect produced by his sexual theories, but also because of opposition to his thesis of psychic determinism and the role of the unconscious. Thus, academic psychology long rejected his contributions, though this attitude eventually changed. As noted by Boring (1950): "So Freud. Psychologists long refused him admission to their numbers, yet now he is seen as the greatest originator of all, the agent of the *Zeitgeist* who accomplished the invasion of psychology by the principle of the unconscious process" (p. 743). (See also Klein, 1970, p. 775.)

From the earliest days of the development of psychoanalysis as a theory and as a therapy, in addition to the critics outside the movement, there have been many within it who have attempted to demonstrate the advantages of altering some of its fundamental propositions. In the sections to follow, a brief summary will be given of the basic principles of psychoanalytic theory and practice, with a description then of some of the schools of thought that have set up alternative assumptions. Finally, there will be a discussion of contributions by those who have remained within the psychoanalytic fold but who have altered the formulations of Freud and the mainstream in some significant respect.

It may be appropriate to note here that the incentive for my addressing these issues at the present time came from three main sources. The first was the dramatization of the life of Sigmund Freud, produced by the BBC-Hearst/ABC and presented by the Arts and Entertainment Network of Cable Television in a six-part series, during the past year. As a theatrical production, the series was very impressive. For historical accuracy, the thorough and convincing portrayal of career and life development was marred by the presentation of Freud's personal relationship with his sister-in-law Minna in a version that was based on speculations which have never been substantiated by any known facts. As reporter Janet Malcolm (1983) pointed out, it "was all wrong." Another flaw was the inclusion in the intermission commentaries of the slanted viewpoint by Jeffrey Masson to the effect that Freud's abandonment of the seduction theory was intentionally deceptive. Such an ignoring of one of Freud's premier discoveries, namely, that wishes (as the functional units of instinctual drives) can produce illness, needs no further comment. But more importantly for the purposes of the present paper, Freud's concepts could not be given an adequate hearing or carried sufficiently far along in their development, so that a fuller explication seems desirable.

The second stimulus for this paper has come from the increasing number of contributions to the analytic literature that have reflected the expanding indications for analysis and the developing of new paradigms and techniques. This has been an ongoing process through the years, but has gained new vigor. A reevaluation of principles is thus a timely undertaking.

Thirdly, the announcement of the publication of a volume to honor the memory of Samuel Lipton has reminded me of the valued contribution which he made in his paper evaluating and comparing Freud's technique with that often advocated in modern times as an improvement and replacement (Lipton, 1977). A restatement and review of principles of technique, then, may also be of timely interest. The fact that the centenary of the beginnings of psychoanalysis is approaching is another indication for a review.

Major Hypotheses of Psychoanalysis

It is a simple matter to state in a summary fashion the basic theories of psychoanalysis: within the framework of a thoroughgoing psychic determinism were the concepts of infantile sexuality subsumed under the theory of instinctual drives; a dynamic unconscious, in which the role of intrapsychic conflict was central; and the theory of transference, in which the concept of a molding of the psyche by the subjective experiences of the individual's early-life relationships reached a position of importance never before recognized.

However, to paint some picture of the richness which characterized the development of these ideas is not so simple a task. Because Freud framed his theories in the light of his clinical experience, a review of the topics that evolved in his case histories may be a useful way to begin. As familiar as this ground may be, a review will serve to highlight the themes. In briefest summary we can observe the following sequence.

"Studies on Hysteria" (1893–1895, with Breuer). The first formulation of the theory of a dynamic unconscious was given here: *pathogenic ideas* (those that produce shame, guilt, psychic pain, feeling of injury) lead to defense (repression, symptom formation, conversion, resistance). Related to this were the concepts of cathexis, primary and secondary process, bound and unbound energy, the principle of constancy, and overdetermination in symptom formation. As therapeutic process the associative method was used to achieve abreaction and catharsis: the "talking cure." The phenomenon of transference was recognized in its interfering role as a "false connection," providing clues to resistances.

"Fragment of an Analysis of a Case of Hysteria" (1905a). The Dora case was presented in large part to show the role of dream analysis in psychoanalytic work, as well as the role of infantile sexuality and incestuous wishes in pathogenesis. Thus, a clinical study was used to illustrate the nature of the psychic apparatus that had been presented in "The Interpretation of Dreams" (1900); and to supplement the theses in "Three Essays on Sexuality" (1905b). The role of bisexuality in conflictual processes was demonstrated, and the notion of neurosis as the negative of perversion was suggested. There were formulations of primary and secondary gains of illness, supervalence (repression as reactive reinforcement in establishing defense); and secondary resistance was touched on (a concept later to be elaborated upon as the basis for ego alteration). The concept of transference was broadened with recognition of its usefulness as a therapeutic tool, beyond its just operating as a pitfall. Acting out instead of remembering or reproducing was described, and considerations of destiny versus therapy as a means of resolution of conflict were taken up.

"Analysis of a Phobia in a Five-Year-Old Boy" (1909a). Here the experience of Little Hans was probed to offer conclusive evidence of the importance of the Oedipus complex and of sibling rivalry with its death wish and fear, alongside of the castration complex, and castration anxiety in the context of the anal-birth theory of children (a note on the role of fantasies in pathogenesis). Phobia was understood in its function as a displacement, and the role of screen memories was noted. Derepression was seen as the task of analysis, with the aim of treatment being one of achieving conscious control and sublimation.

"Notes upon a Case of Obsessional Neurosis" (1909b). In the case of the Rat Man there was a recognition of the role of anal erotism in obsessional neurosis, and an elaboration on the characteristics of obsessional thinking (omnipotence, doubting, undoing, isolation, compulsion). Further, the role of ambivalence in pathogenesis was emphasized, with a discussion of regression, autoerotism, and what was stated to be the nuclear complex of neuroses: the conflict between object love and infantile autoerotism, with fantasy rather than events producing pathology. Here was a statement of the specific role of infantile sexuality in psychic life, and of the sexualization of infantile memories.

"Psychoanalytic Notes on an Autobiographical Account of a Case of Paranoia" (1911). In the Schreber case, Freud's study of the writings of that paranoid man led to his development of a theory of the pathogenesis of psychosis, which he saw as centrally involving the intrapsychic struggle between object cathexis and narcissistic regression, with the dread of world destruction accompanying the latter movement. Freud considered homosexuality to constitute a phase of the narcissistic regression, with paranoid delusion constituting an attempt at restitution. The mechanism of projection in its various forms was studied, with formulation of the concepts of primal repression and repression proper, fixation points, and return of the repressed as specific for each illness.

"From the History of an Infantile Neurosis" (1918). The case of the Wolf Man provided an opportunity for a recapitulation of the primary role of infantile sexual drives in psychic development and conflict, as distinct from other influences (phylogenetic; power motives). The importance of the unconscious organizing pathogenic fantasy in neurosogenesis was emphasized, as was the role of primal-scene experience or fantasy in this regard. The concept of the negative Oedipus complex with castration anxiety from passive wishes was developed, bearing on the relationship between choice of neurosis and genetic level of fixation. There was a consideration of pregenital stages and genital organization; activity and passivity; and sadism and masochism. The links between object cathexis and mechanisms in the process of identification were studied. (The latter were more fully discussed in "Mourning and Melancholia," 1917a.) New milestones were set in regard to psychoanalytic technique, with respect to the role of reconstruction of early experience. As the therapeutic process worked, the contrast between the constricting effects of repression and the freeing up brought about by sublimation could be observed.

As comprehensive as such themes were, the psychoanalytic theory that Freud developed was enriched by the additional organization of concepts embodied in the metapsychological papers (1914, 1915); the formulation of the dual-instinct theory (1920); and beyond these, three landmark contributions that blazed still more new trails: Structural theory (1923) established the basis for the further development of ego psychology. The signal theory of anxiety (1926) provided the conceptual underpinnings for the understanding of all motivation and symptom formation in terms of the hierarchies of danger situations confronting each successive phase in individual development. And finally, in defining the limiting factors in the application of the analytic process (1937), further guiding principles were provided.

The past half century has seen an expansion of conceptualization and a refinement of theoretical constructs, notably in the development of ego psychology. To list just a few of the contributions, we should include A. Freud (1936) on mechanisms of ego defenses, Hartmann (1939) on adaptation, including ego autonomy, Waelder (1936) on multiple function, Nunberg (1930) on synthetic function. Erikson (1950), Jacobson (1964), Mahler and coworkers (1968, 1975) have all added to our knowledge of developmental processes, adaptation, and psychic structuring. Hartmann (1948) and Hartmann, Kris, and Loewenstein (1949) provided further understanding of the aggressive drive beyond that of Freud's problematic death instinct.

With reference to technique, we will again state familiar precepts. Freud's technique papers (1911–1915), augmented by structural considerations, defined the procedures for achieving analytic goals: ego growth comes through facing what was warded off defensively. Unconscious anxieties of ego and impulses of id produce derivatives. Through free association, derivatives come more clearly to the surface. Interpretation of resistance, then of id impulse, provides the ego with evidence of the derivatives. The development of transference neurosis, and interpretation of resistance in the transference, were seen as constituting the essential means by which the therapeutic goal was to be accomplished. Analysis, in contradistinction to other therapies, was not to exploit transference as a therapeutic device, but was to analyze it. This would permit integration of previously excluded aspects of the personality, and would promote discharge of instinctual energies that had been bound in defensive conflict. Repressed tendencies which had retained their infantile character would, as defenses were removed, become integrated into the more mature personality. Working through would serve to assure insight and resolution of the pathogenic mechanisms.

This statement of the classical viewpoint (see Fenichel, 1945) will be discussed further as we explore the varying efforts to apply it, by practitioners who have inevitably brought their own attitudes and formulations into their work. Much of this variance has occurred within the framework of the traditional model. Before considering that aspect, we need first to note the deviations that were clearly away from the mainstream. At this point, suffice it to say that the principles guiding classical technique may be regarded as including the instituting of controlled regression (use of couch, promoting sensory deprivation); adhering to a position of abstinence (withholding transference gratifications); interpreting resistance in order to block defenses so that drive derivatives may emerge; clarifying the organizing unconscious fantasy; and using reconstruction in genetic and transferential terms. A therapeutic alliance is of course considered to be essential in all of this.

Deviant Schools

Alfred Adler was the first among the early group to secede from psychoanalysis, during the period 1910–1911. His theory, known as "Individual Psychology," had three elements, of which Freud (1914b) gave the following account. Initially, a useful contribution to the psychology of the ego had been made, regarding the egoistic component of the libidinal instinctual impulses. But Adler denied the libidinal impulses, and by this rationalization concealed the unconscious motive. This led to the construing of man's motive in sex to be that of being on top; thus, a secondary gain had a primary gain imputed to it. This resulted in analytic facts being translated into a new jargon. For example, "protective measure" became "safeguarding"; "phantasy" became something "feigned." Then, unwelcome analytic facts were distorted by the new jargon: so, the "inferiority complex," "overcompensation," "will to power," "masculine protest," which became *the* motive force for Adler, was actually repression detached from its psychological mechanism and then sexualized. The aggressive instinct was taken to be all there is, without a libidinal or love instinct. "Organ inferiority" replaced infantile instinctual impulse and conflict. The distinction between conscious and unconscious became unimportant, and hence, repression also.

In a word, Adler abandoned the theory of infantile sexuality, and the theory of a dynamic unconscious, with its concept of intrapsychic, intersystemic conflict. The therapeutic endeavor became simplified to that of seeking a creative self. (See Adler, 1917; Ansbacher and Ansbacher, 1956.)

Carl G. Jung was the next to renounce Freud's concepts, beginning as early as 1911 and completing his removal from the mainstream in 1914. His "Analytic Psychology" centered around the denial of sexual instincts, which were replaced by a higher ethical and religious principle. The Oedipus and family complex came to occupy a symbolic role, through a process of sublimation. The conflict, then, no longer became one between erotic wishes and the ego's self-preservative trends (Freud's view at that time), but one between the "life task" and "psychical inertia." The investigation of individuals was replaced by a study of the anthropological sources, the "collective" or "racial unconscious," and "archetypes." (See Jung, 1915, 1953.)

Here again, the abandonment of the theory of infantile sexuality, of a dynamic unconscious and of any concept of intrapsychic conflict, marks the course taken by that colleague who had ironically been chosen by Freud to be his successor. Refutations of the theories of Adler and Jung were expounded on by Freud in the paper on the Wolf Man (written in 1914 though not published until 1918), in the paper "On Narcissism" (1914a), and in that entitled "On the History of the Psycho-analytic Movement" (1914b).

Wilhelm Stekel was another member of the early circle of psychoanalysts who was unable to continue in the mainstream. A gifted psychologist with a deep capacity for understanding repressed material and symbolism, even surpassing Freud in this respect, he was apparently so lacking in scientific integrity that his data could not be relied upon as factual. His approach was one of a direct interpretation of symptoms rather than that of recognizing the importance of the central task of analysis, namely, overcoming resistances (see W. Reich, 1928).

Otto Rank had been a mainstay of the original group until his final break in 1924. His major work, on the trauma of birth (1923), proposed that all mental conflicts were based on the child's relation to its mother, originating in the traumatic experience of birth. Whatever seemed to relate to the father, including the Oedipus complex, were to be considered a mask. Psychoanalytic treatment should consist of a repetition in the transference, of the drama of birth, with the resulting rebirth constituting the cure. A few months would be sufficient for this process. Freud raised questions (see Jones, 1957) as to how the incest taboo became accounted for without the father figure to repeat the phylogenetic source, and the explanation of birth anxiety as causing incest anxiety was regarded as contradictory. An instinct, Freud pointed out, is not subject to inhibition by association, as Rank claimed the instinct to return to mother must be, on account of birth terror.

Rank was evidently subject to manic-depressive illness. He wrote on the birth trauma during a hypomanic episode, and recanted when depressed, but later reasserted his thesis. For a far more comprehensive concept of the effects of the birth experience in constituting the prototype for subsequent danger situations, Freud (1926) developed the signal theory of anxiety, which still provides the criteria for measuring the validity of any psychodynamic theory.

Sandor Ferenczi was the colleague in the original circle and throughout the early years who had been the closest friend to Freud, and the most steadfast adherent. The development of an alienation between them was difficult to conceive of, but it did occur and gradually grew, between the years from 1923 to 1933, until it became irretrievable. The beginnings, with the publication of the book by Ferenczi and Rank (1923), *The Development of Psychoanalysis,* dealt with the topic of acting out and the use that could be made of it in analysis. But the possibility of introducing a note of neglect of childhood sources was there, as noted by Jones (1957, p. 56).

Ferenczi's "active therapy" stemmed from his ideas about the role of infantile trauma, especially that of parental unkindness. He undertook in the analyses to act the part of a loving parent, in order to compensate (a forerunner of some subsequent techniques). The role of the mother was emphasized, that of the father minimized. Objectivity was lost as Ferenczi permitted the patient to analyze him, as well. His deviation from Freud increased, and particularly with the brain complications from pernicious anemia that he suffered, mental aberrations and delusions further alienated him from Freud.

Wilhelm Reich was another early contributor to psychoanalysis who moved from providing significant ideas on character resistances in analytic work (1928) to a deviation from the mainstream of psychoanalysis. He proceeded to develop bizarre ideas about biophysics, fear of contact, orgone fields, vegetative excitability, and the like. His approach became more and more one involving physical procedures (Reich, 1945).

Melanie Klein was undoubtedly the most influential and controversial innovator on the psychoanalytic scene during the decades between 1921 and 1955, with her impact continuing in some places to the present time. Her contributions have been considerable, particularly in the beginning with pioneer work with children and the introduction of play therapy, and with the stimulation of interest in the earliest phases of mental development. The aspect of Kleinian theory that has elicited most criticism was that in relation to the formulation of the "paranoid-schizoid position" during the first three to four months of life, and the "depressive position" during the second half of the first year: the first dealing with part-objects, splitting processes (good and bad internal and external objects), and paranoid anxieties; the second with whole objects, ambivalence, depressive anxieties, and guilt (Klein, 1948). This presupposes a higher degree of ego organization and capacity for fantasy formation than Freud had postulated; and superego formation in the earliest phases, requiring retrojection of the oedipal phase to the first year of life.

Conflict was seen as one between life and death instincts, from the beginning; the mental apparatus was indistinguishable from mental content, all mental activity was reduced to fantasy with one fantasy fighting against another in a never-ending defense; anxiety was referred to depression or persecution, from the operation of the death instinct with no contribution from libido. In the analytic situation, id content became subject to direct interpretation, symbols became primary in emphasis, transference neurosis or psychosis was present from the beginning of the analysis, and reality factors were given little recognition. The opportunities for suggestion to come into play, and for a special language to be learned by the patient, became evident as pitfalls. (For a critique, see paper by Yorke, 1972, and its bibliography citing other critical appraisals.)

Kleinian theory is an instance both of the genetic fallacy and the adultomorphic fallacy. Intersystemic conflict is underemphasized in the sense of a sequential development as aims and drives evolve, and as a result the signal theory of anxiety is all but abandoned. In the area of technique, the drive derivatives and evolving transference emerging from a controlled regression, as a therapeutic alliance develops, are nowhere described.

Karen Horney (1937, 1946, 1950) developed a viewpoint based on a concept of tension stemming from an unrealistic, idealized image of the self. Anxiety was seen as arising from the frustration, hostility, and helplessness that ensued, with secondary anxieties evolving from the defensive processes incident to the pursuit of false values. The therapeutic goal became one of clarifying the current problems based on the neurotic trends, with little emphasis on or interest in the developmental history, and with the aim of restoring a more realistic and authentic self.

It is clear that this approach abandons the concepts of a dynamic unconscious, of instinctual drives, of transference, and of all the structural, genetic, and economic frames of reference that characterize psychoanalytic metapsychology.

Erich Fromm (1941, 1947) was a psychoanalyst who abandoned the view of individual development as being determined by instincts, and held that human adaptation and character were molded by cultural forces. Needs were seen as being created by society and the individual's responses to his society. Neurotic problems were thought to be the product of needs created by a man's culture, along with the frustrations of those needs. The individual's ways of relating to the group were seen as being dictated by escape mechanisms; and even destructive patterns were said to be attempts to protect against isolation and loneliness. Therapy became a matter of finding the essential inner health and integrity. The departure from the principles of psychoanalysis is evident.

Harry Stack Sullivan (1947, 1953) presented his theory as belonging to psychoanalysis, but referred to it as a theory of interpersonal relations. His also was a concept of man as being molded by his culture. The major motivating force was held to be that of "security operations," central to which was the securing of approval from the mothering person. Anxiety was considered to be empathically transmitted from mother to child, and was held to be largely responsible for those aspects of the self that one dissociates from awareness ("not me"), dealt with by selective inattention; or may be dealt with as "bad me," in contrast to aspects that were met with approval, hence considered "good me." Thus, the individual was seen to be made up of reflected appraisals. The concepts of a self-dynamism, its relation to anxiety, and its subjection to "parataxic distortions," were woven into the theoretical framework. The distinction between reality and what has been distorted had to be made by comparing one's views with those of others, with the aid of consensual validation. The therapist was considered to be a participant-observer in the process of correcting distortions, clarifying the interactions with others, and thereby achieving insight.

The major problem with this approach is its lack of comprehensiveness in trying to give an account of human development, and its neglect of instinctual drives, hence of dynamic and structural considerations.

Other so-called *Neo-Freudian Schools* have had contributors with varied viewpoints. For a critique of Sandor Rado and others, see Zetzel (1963) and Levine (1967). The abandonment of the dynamic framework and of instinct theory were well described by these reviewers.

Variant Techniques

Aside from those deviations in theory and hence technique that have been aimed at extending psychoanalytic understanding and therapy to a broader population base, many variations in technique have been proposed as a means of expediting the analytic process or of shortening its duration.

Franz Alexander was fully aware of the value of Freud's recommendations on technique and was an early champion of them (Alexander, 1935), just as he sounded a cautionary note about any efforts to revise psychoanalytic theory (Alexander, 1940). But he extended the viewpoint that analysis exerted a curative effect through its modifying the superego as a result of transference interpretations (Strachey, 1934; see also Alexander, 1925), and he introduced the concept of the corrective emotional experience in terms of a "consciously planned regulation of the therapist's own emotional responses to the patient's material (countertransference) in such a way as to counteract the harmful effects of the parental attitudes" (Alexander, 1948, p. 287; Alexander and French, 1946). There followed a considerable criticism about this dilution of the analytic process, and the element of artificiality.

Leon J. Saul recommended an approach which is also allied to that of the corrective emotional experience. He advocated an evaluation of the patient's early life experience, in the first interviews, in order to use this predetermined insight to persuade the patient to change and mature, to correct the patient's "central emotional forces." The theoretic base has been amended so that anxiety and psychopathology are alleged to stem mainly from hostility; libidinal development is relegated to a defensive, regressive role. Technique was altered in order to avoid regression, so that the analyst may then "analyze out" the infantile tendencies, to correct the effects of parental blunders (Saul, 1972).

Two fundamental deviations are evident in this viewpoint. One has to do with theory, since symptom formation is not simply a matter of guilt resulting from aggression, but also involves the repression of libidinal elements. The other is in regard to the role of analysis as an "after-education." Instead of a careful utilization of the transference as a means of step by step reconstruction that can clarify the drive derivatives, through interpretation of resistances and defenses, the analyst was to use his knowledge to substitute for the patient's task of gaining his own knowledge. This cannot help but perpetuate the patient's dependence. (See Jaffe, 1975.)

Edmund Bergler was a most original thinker and prolific writer, contributing nearly 300 papers and over two dozen books to the analytic literature. He proposed (Bergler, 1948, 1949, 1952) that the starting point for psychic development and for neurosogenesis was the stage of infantile omnipotence. The fury produced by its frustration had to be inhibited, leading to a triad of retribution: punishment, moral reproach, guilt. Persistence in the original aims and objectives could result in psychic masochism, with unconscious love of humiliation, defeat, refusal. The superego would object to the latter, resulting in another triad: repetition of the refusals of wish gratification, a reactive indignation (pseudo-aggression), and self-pity with further "injustice collecting." Bergler regarded the phallic and oedipal regression as the most superficial part of neurosis. He considered every neurosis to represent a rescue attempt from the dangers of oral rage and sadism.

The main shortcomings of "Berglerian" theory and technique stem from the genetic fallacy: everything in psychic life is attributed to an original flaw. Ongoing development is neglected; there is no recognition of the fact that the central role of the oedipal phase in neurosogenesis rests on a sufficient development of psychic structure, incomplete until that period, in order to form the basis for intersystemic conflict. As a consequence of this conceptual weakness, the therapeutic technique fails to systematically explore and reconstruct past experience; the analytic role becomes one of exhortation and persuasion, a controlled regression is avoided, the use of the couch is immaterial, the analyst's silence is to be avoided. The features of the corrective emotional experience are again in evidence here. (See Jaffe, 1986a.)

Variations in Classical Technique

Numerous papers and panels have been devoted to discussions of differences among analysts who have adhered to a classical viewpoint, as well as those who have advanced divergent concepts. In the latter category, in a 1952 panel, Waelder (1953) noted the difference between the traditional view which stresses the central role of repression, and that represented by Alexander's viewpoint which attributed neurosogenesis to "faulty interpersonal adaptation in childhood" (p. 532). Similarly, in a 1953 panel, conceptual differences prevailed, along lines already discussed, between proponents of the classical view versus those supporting the views of Alexander, and Sullivan.

Among analysts who remained within the classical framework, differences of emphasis and, at times, of conceptualization have also appeared. In the panel on variations in classical technique, Loewenstein (1958) pointed out that there are occasions when the analyst may have to forgo the rule of abstinence and supply some gratification, or interrupt the flow of associations, and certainly to discriminate between the tactical and the strategic values in making interpretations. In the same panel, and on a similar note, Eissler (1958) emphasized the usefulness of flexibility in the use of tools that could be designated as pseudo-parameters (such as jokes); but added that empathy is not necessarily a reliable tool if, for example, it becomes based on reaction formation. (See also Eissler, 1953.)

Lipton's paper (1977) provided a comprehensive discussion of differences in conceptualizations among classical analysts, with regard to technique. This will be elaborated on in some detail in a section to follow.

Specific preferences for one attitude or another in the matter of technique are detailed in a Supplement of the *Journal of the American Psychoan-*

alytic Association devoted to "Psychoanalytic Technique and Theory of Therapy" (1979).

In a book essay, Kanzer (1979) noted that among classical analysts there has been a focus on one central idea or another. Thus, Menninger and Holzman (1973) emphasized the principle of optimal tension; for Greenson (1967) a central concern was that of the working alliance; Brenner (1976) advocated a principal attention to conflict as constituting the proper analytic attitude; and Sandler, Dare, and Holder (1973) incorporated many viewpoints but selected the matter of feeling states as one of great importance.

Among many pertinent papers, Rangell (1979) firmly advocated that the reconstruction of past roots is just as important as the analysis of transference. Leites (1977) had been in agreement with this position; whereas Gill (1979) gave priority rather exclusively to analysis of transference. Valenstein (1979) traced the trend toward a watering down of the genetic point of view to Strachey's (1934) influence, countered by Lampl-de Groot (1976) who cautioned against such an overemphasis.

The reminders by Valenstein (1979) and Rangell (1979) of the need for even-handedness between what Fenichel (1941) had referred to as the Scylla and Charybdis, between knowing and feeling, is generally agreed to; though the present-day emphasis on the use of empathy (see Lichtenberg et al. 1984) may tend to weight the scales in the direction of a heavy reliance on feelings. The boundary between empathy and countertransference has to be carefully marked (Jaffe, 1986b).

Of fundamental importance in the matter of cognitive and affective admixtures is the balance between scientific and humanistic influences that have always been inherent in psychoanalysis. There have been many attempts to modify psychoanalytic theory in the course of "the science versus humanism debate" (Meissner, 1985). Among these have been the contributions of the information-processing theorists (Holt, 1965; Peterfreund, 1971); the object-relations theorists, including Winnicott (1960); Fairbairn (1954); Guntrip (1971); as well as some with differing emphases (Bowlby, 1960a, b; Balint, 1953; Bion, 1963); Schafer (1976) and his advocacy of an action language; and Lacan (1977) with a rather exclusive attention to linguistics. It would be too labored to explore here the problems associated with all of these movements. Suffice it to say that most of them depart from the metapsychology that has unified psychoanalytic theory, either in respect to the role of instinctual drives and the defenses against them, or in regard to the quantitative factors that underlie the signal theory of anxiety and the implications of the latter for sequential psychic development.

With reference to the humanistic aspect as it contributes to psychoanalytic technique, the argument advanced by Lipton (1977) in his paper on Freud's technique with the Rat Man was at some variance with the position taken by some other writers who had raised questions about that technique (Kris, 1951; Kanzer, 1952; Grunberger, 1966; Zetzel, 1966; Weiner, 1973; Beigler, 1977). Lipton's opinion was that the therapeutic alliance involves a personal relationship of the sort that Freud formed with his patients, which was based on "unobjectionable" aspects of the transference, not to be considered an element in technique. (For cautions, however, see Stein, 1981; Bird, 1972.) Lipton had indeed recognized the necessity of analyzing the repercussions of such acts as the giving of food, or gifts, or compliments, or engaging in conversation, or correcting erroneous information—all of which entered into Freud's handling of the case of the Rat Man and other patients, and which Lipton considered to be part of ordinary courtesy and considerateness. The absence of the latter attitudes, Lipton argued, would be equally complicating, and should be just as much subject to analytic scrutiny.

Lipton believed that modern technique developed as ego psychology gained in prominence, and he suggested that the analysts' avoidance of interventions other than the making of interpretations was promoted by Eissler's (1953) paper on parameters, an effect not at all intended in that contribution. Once more, Alexander's sponsoring of the corrective emotional experience was seen as the source of such overcompensating reactions.

The position taken by Lipton that Freud's technique with the Rat Man was not modified later was questioned by Muslin (1979), who referred to Freud's later paper on technique (Freud, 1914a), in which the here-and-now transference seemed to have been given greater emphasis. Muslin (1979, p. 575) acknowledged the multiple aspects of transference with respect to resistance and to genetic reconstruction, and pointed out that although there are no clinical data to demonstrate a change in Freud's technique after the Rat Man paper, there were transitions in contributions to theory which indicated a further development in Freud's focus on the analysis of transference (Freud, 1914a, 1917b).

The concept of a model technique, and the necessity of introducing parameters (interventions beyond interpretation) but ideally to limit these to a minimum, brought the problems of technique into the difficult area of the limitations of the psychoanalytic method with respect to patients with severe pathology based on ego alterations (e.g., borderline or narcissistic disorders).

Contrasting approaches to these conditions have been evident in the conceptualizations offered by Kernberg (1970, 1974, 1975) and by Kohut (1966, 1971, 1972, 1977, 1978). The former has adhered to a drive-conflict model, albeit based on one which highlights the predominant role of primitive aggression, with splitting and projective identification as the most prominent defenses: a concept that was challenged by Rangell (1981). Further, the vicissitudes of the internal object relations as postulated by Kernberg (1970) were framed in the context of conflicting good and bad self and object images, derived essentially from the love on the one hand versus the frustration on the other, experienced at the hands of the mother. Thus, "fear of attack from the mother represents a projection of his own aggression, linked to the rage caused by his frustration by mother" (1970, p. 81). (Parenthetically, it should be noted that frustration is not the only factor that promotes pathologic development. Overstimulation, overprotection, inconsistency, and many other influences have been described.) But beyond this, if aggression gets attributed to the actual experience with the mother, does not this overlook the innate nature and quality of the drive itself, in determining anxiety and conflict?

In any event, Kernberg (1974) described his technical approach as one which interpreted narcissistic manifestations as defenses against object-instinctual conflicts, particularly those arising from envy and devaluation of the object as consequences of primitive rage.

Kohut proceeded along entirely different lines, moving from an initial adherence to instinct theory, to an eventual downgrading of it in what he offered as a new paradigm, namely, that of self psychology.

Self Psychology

The following brief sketch of Kohut's theory is excerpted from his 1971 book and from a paper by P. Ornstein (1978). (For later contributions which have extended these views, see Kohut [1977, 1978]; and Ornstein [1978].)

Preliminarily, it may be noted that it had long been thought that the so-called narcissistic neuroses were not amenable to psychoanalysis because of the unavailability of object-instinctual cathexis, such as was able to become mobilized in the formation of a transference neurosis. Kohut described the transference and transferencelike features that he observed in his clinical work with narcissistic patients, and designated them as mirror transferences and idealizing transferences. From these phenomena, he hypothesized a line of development in the narcissistic personality that pursued a separate path from that of the object-instinctual development.

From this point of view, the normal developmental sequence was described as one in which autoerotism with its fragmented self or self-nuclei proceeds to primary narcissism with some cohesiveness being achieved. Shortcomings in maternal care leads to the child's attempt to regain perfection through a *grandiose self.* Optimally, this is tamed and integrated into the personality, and provides the basis for ambition and self esteem. Interferences lead to narcissistic disturbances, and to the perpetuation of the grandiosity, as seen in the clinical phenomenon of *mirror transference.*

Another alternative in this process is that the child attempts to gain the perfection through formation of an idealized parent imago, an omnipotent *selfobject.* Optimally, this gets integrated into the personality as an idealized superego, building up an ego-ideal, and making possible the development of empathy, creativeness, humor, wisdom. Again, interferences lead to narcissistic disturbances, and the process can be reconstructed from *idealizing transferences* characterized by selfobjects. The *"bipolar self"* is referable to the ambition and self esteem derived from working through of mirroring; and the acquiring of guiding ideals and values derived from working through of the idealizing imagoes.

In normal development, gradual dosed frustrations lead to the formation of psychic structure, through a *transmuting internalization.* This is promoted by the mother's pleasurable responses to the child, holding him, calling his name, smiling, praising. The process becomes pathological when *lack of maternal empathy* leads either to excessive frustration or insufficient frustration, experienced by the preoedipal child as a trauma in the form of grandiose, omnipotent strivings and fantasies that are excessively exciting because no stimulus barrier has yet been formed. The excitation is experienced as narcissistic rage, or as a disruption of the cohesive self (which we have to consider to be in the nature of an actual neurosis). This sector of the personality is walled off by a *vertical split in the ego,* which then follows a separate line of development from that of the object-instinctual strivings which go on in another sector, subject to a repression barrier, and constituting a *horizontal split in the ego.*

"Ego" is an abstraction, referring to the *functions* by which the individual adapts. Such functions are improved by feelings of greater self-cohesiveness. "Self" is a clinical referent: the "experience of a physical and mental unit which has cohesiveness in space and continuity in time" (Kohut, 1971, p. 118).

The aims in analysis are the same in narcissistic disorders as in the transference neuroses based on object-instinctual conflicts: to remobilize the repressed instinctual wishes, keeping them alive through nongratification and preventing evasion or denial, by interpretation. The result should be an increasing, gradual integration into the more mature psyche, with new structure formation then available to master the drives. In narcissistic disorders, the analyst must permit the mirroring and idealization, in order to foster analyzing. Introspection and empathy are all-important in this process.

There may have been some tendency to accept a kind of complementarity in the new viewpoint, though with general skepticism about the untestability of a separate line of development, during the early period of debate about the theory. But with further elaborations and theory-building, the differences in concepts and aims became more and more striking. The contrast between Guilty Man and Tragic Man, as Kohut had termed the respective views of conflict theory versus deficit theory, led to an increasing polarization of opinions. It is not possible here even to list all of the arguments in the literature that have appeared, particularly during the past decade. A sampling will have to suffice.

Loewald (1973) found the concepts valuable, though he questioned how useful it is to see two lines of development, and wondered how independent they could be. He felt that there must be reciprocity between the two. Also, the neglect of defenses and resistances was noted, leaving too many unanswered questions about how an integration of the narcissistic sectors with the more mature sectors comes about. The possibility of seductive elements in the therapy was noted.

Hanly and Masson (1976) criticized the concept of a separate line of development and particularly that of a higher form of narcissism, seeing the latter as quasi-religious. They preferred the traditional formulation of narcissism as a fixation or regression to pregenital stages, opposed to progressive movement toward object love. The element of transference gratification in the therapy was commented on here, too.

Slap and Levine (1978) were critical of the hybrid character of Kohut's theory, feeling that he mixed different levels of data and theory and used metapsychological terms as referable to substantial phenomena.

Kohut's (1977) book was met with reviews that were even more sharply critical of the new paradigm which was now being presented as one that superseded the whole of metapsychology and clinical theory. The concept of two separate lines of development was again challenged as unprovable and at variance with clinical experience; oedipal phenomena being accounted for on the basis of parents' unempathic attitudes toward the child's growth was held to be an inadequate viewpoint; the fact that traditional analysis relies on an introspective-empathic approach in addition to bringing objectivity to bear seemed to have been ignored in the new formulations; fragmentation of the self is too limited a concept to account for anxieties from a wide variety of sources, it was stated; and as a result of these considerations, the contribution of a valuable new way to explore clinical issues was weakened by the one-sided presentation and the claims of a new world view (Schwartz, 1978).

The reductive nature of the theory, particularly the replacing of complex developmental factors by a single etiology (defect in maternal empathy, to be compensated for by an empathic analyst), was seen as ignoring the principle of multiple function; the theory was considered to be solipsistic, with neglect of varieties of observation beyond the empathic-introspective; it was held to be appealing through its simplification of the complex aspects of sexual and aggressive drives, of ego and superego development, of the Oedipus complex with associated phenomena of castration anxiety and penis envy, and the intricacy of dream work; and the inspirational and revelatory quality of the thinking was seen as a problem (Stein, 1979).

The view of the self as supraordinate, with drives and defenses subsumed as constituents; the departure from the view of oedipal conflict as central to normal human development; and the either/or character of the view of conflict versus deficiency, were questioned by Wallerstein (1981).

Another challenge to the concept of deficit in contrast to conflict held that the role of defense in the selfobject concept had been neglected, that the multiple functions of selfobjects had been overlooked, and that the distinction between selfobjects and preoedipal objects in general was unnecessary (Coen, 1981).

Treurniet (1983) presented a strong argument for the primary role of oedipal conflict, rather than as a secondary manifestation, with the attendant corrosion of the prevailing concepts of conflict, defense, and resistance. The predominant reliance on empathy and introspection was considered to lead to an epistemological fallacy, weakening an explanatory power and confusing the realms of content and function.

London (1985) presented a balanced appraisal, seeing strengths in the technical advances that offered a broadened application of therapeutic efforts to the more archaic mental levels of functioning, but weaknesses in a reductionistic theory that places such heavy emphasis on failures in empathy. This estimate of the excessive emphasis on failures in empathy was shared by Rothstein (1980), Friedman (1980), and Segel (1981).

Richards (1982) reviewed the work of three theorists who have attempted to revise psychoanalytic theory by utilizing a superordinate self-concept. He viewed *Kohut's* theory as taking only a part, or manifest content, rather than the whole, with multiple, latent meanings. Of *George Klein's* (1976) criticism of psychoanalytic metapsychology and attempts to replace it with a "self-schema" that would have more human qualities, Richards saw his results as having the very features he had criticized. He believed it to be overly abstract and no less biological. *Gedo* (1979), as Richards pointed out, conceptualized a self-organization based on a hierarchy of values involving biological as well as psychological determinants; and a technique that advocated what he called pacification, reunification, and optimal disillusionment. A shortcoming here was the neglect of the role of drives and defenses.

In his subsequent work, Gedo (1981) further explicated the theory and focused on clinical issues. Still there were many problems with the theoretical and technical formulations. (For a critique, see Jaffe, 1984.) In the clinical illustrations, psychopathogenesis was attributed to patients' dread of helplessness and destruction in the symbiotic bondage with the mother. There was no convincing evidence that the anxiety attributed to the presymbolic stage was in fact derived from that era. To explain the repetition compulsion on that basis is unconvincing, and prone to genetic fallacy. Gedo's abandonment of drive theory put him on the difficult ground of accounting for anxiety on the basis of threats to self-cohesion; and though he renounced the quantitative factor, along with metapsychology (which includes psychoeconomics), the factor of intensity in his patients' dread of extermination, can be clearly discerned.

Gedo's theoretical structure, like those of many other revisionists, lacks an adequate theory of anxiety such as was provided in Freud's signal theory, defined in an earlier section of this paper: need tension in the absence of the need-satisfying object, with its precedent of traumatic undischargeable overload in the birth experience, subsequently structured hierarchically through each developmental stage with its specific dangers, and forming the basis for intersystemic conflict. In Gedo's account, anxiety is either that of an actual neurosis, as in his patient with a dread of destruction through symbiotic bondage; or intrasystemic, as in the presence of mutually exclusive goals; or conflict is with reality, as in the pursuit of magical aims.

Regarding the analytic process, the question of transference cure has to be raised, in view of the many influences that seem to have been brought to bear: that of soothing, providing judgments about courses of action, exhibiting preferences, with considerable charisma and erudition in evidence.

Concluding Comments

In light of all of the proposals for new paradigms and of the various critiques of them, I am reminded here of some guidelines suggested by Arlow, several years ago, and again recently (1963, 1981). In the earlier contribution (Arlow, 1963) he suggested that the earliest identifications and preoedipal patterns of drive discharge determine later libidinal development as well as the ego and superego patterns for dealing with them. It is in the unconscious organizing pathogenic fantasy that the drive derivative and the danger it represents gets portrayed, and there is a condensation in the organizing fantasy of elements from antecedent phases. Any attempt to push the pathogenic fantasy back to the earliest phase can result in the obscuring of the precise mental content of the wish and of the danger, in the nuclear conflict.

In the later paper, on theories of pathogenesis, Arlow (1981) warned about the pitfalls in the many variations on the theme of *specificity* (among other things, of the assumption of inadequate early caretaking); and he further challenged the corollary thesis that the analyst's curative role rests on a capacity to provide better parenting than the patient originally received.

In closing, I wish to bring some historical perspective to the matter of efforts toward new model-making in psychoanalysis. I repeat here what I have said in earlier discussions evaluating some trends in object-relations theory and in the development of self psychology (Jaffe, 1971, 1979). In the advances made by psychology as a science, many of the issues carried over from its earlier philosophical foundations are evident in present-day theorizing. Aristotelian entelechy and particularly the concept of final cause had special influence on Brentano, whose act psychology with its transcendent intentionalism found echoes in the motivational psychology of Freud. British empiricism and associationism, though also drawing on Aristotelian principle, took another direction in advancing the thesis of experience as predominant in contradistinction to inherent endowment, and thereby revived the old rationalist-empiricist controversy of philosophy in the more current guise of the nature-nurture problem. It seems that current ego psychology, and some of its offshoots like object-relations theory, may represent a shift away from the transcendent motivational principle implicit in drive theory, back toward the empiricism which places superordinate emphasis on the experiential. (Loewald [1971] may be cited as one who proposed that the drives are not givens, but are determined by the earliest object relations.)

Self psychology goes further in its basic revision of a fundamental Freudian position, and although it may be maintained that there is a complementarity between drive psychology and self psychology, the latter is given an applicability and opportunity for encroachment on the former that requires the sounding of a note of caution and the maintenance of a degree of skepticism. I say this because the formulations of self psychology do not lend themselves to the kind of convincing validation that we have achieved through those of drive psychology. As between the innate and the experiential, we must be careful that the pendulum of our theories does not swing too far in either direction.

REFERENCES

Adler, A. (1917), *The Neurotic Constitution.* New York: Moffat, Yard.

Alexander, F. (1925), A metapsychological description of the process of cure. *Internat. J. Psycho-Anal.*, 6:13–34.

——— (1935), The problem of psychoanalytic technique. *Psychoanal. Quart.*, 4:588–611.

——— (1940), Psychoanalysis revised. *Psychoanal. Quart.*, 9:1–36.

——— (1948), *Fundamentals of Psychoanalysis.* New York: Norton.

——— & French, T. M. (1946), *Psychoanalytic Therapy, Principles and Application.* New York: Ronald Press.

Ansbacher, H. & Ansbacher, R. R., eds. (1956), *The Individual Psychology of Alfred Adler.* New York: Basic Books.

Arlow, J. A. (1963), Conflict, regression, and symptom formation. *Internat. J. Psycho-Anal.*, 44:12–22.

——— (1981), Theories of pathogenesis. *Psychoanal. Quart.*, 50:488–514.

Arts & Entertainment Network (1985), *Freud: The Drama of a Life.* Cable Television, BBC-Hearst/ABC Production.

Balint, M. (1953), *Primary Love and Psychoanalytic Technique.* New York: Liveright.

Beigler, J. S. (1977), A commentary on Freud's treatment of the Rat Man. (Presented to the Chicago Psychoanalytic Society, February 1974; unpublished paper.)

Bergler, E. (1948), *The Battle of the Conscience.* Washington, D.C.: Washington Institute of Medicine.

——— (1949), *The Basic Neurosis.* New York: Grune & Stratton.

——— (1952), *The Superego.* New York: Grune & Stratton.

Bion, W. R. (1963), *Elements of Psycho-Analysis.* London: Heinemann.

Bird, B. (1972), Notes on transference: Universal phenomenon and hardest part of analysis. *J. Amer. Psychoanal. Assn.*, 20:267–301.

Boring, E. G. (1950), *A History of Experimental Psychology.* New York: Appleton-Century-Crofts.

Bowlby, J. (1960a), Separation anxiety. *Internat. J. Psycho-Anal.*, 41:89–113.

——— (1960b), Grief and mourning in infancy. *The Psychoanalytic Study of the Child,* 15:9–52. New York: International Universities Press.

Brenner, C. (1976), *Psychoanalytic Technique and Psychic Conflict.* New York: International Universities Press.

Breuer, J. & Freud, S. (1893–1895), Studies on hysteria. *Standard Edition,* 2:3–319. London: Hogarth Press, 1955.

Coen, S. J. (1981), Notes on the concepts of selfobject and preoedipal object. *J. Amer. Psychoanal. Assn.*, 29:395–411.

Eissler, K. R. (1953), The effect of the structure of the ego on psychoanalytic technique. *J. Amer. Psychoanal. Assn.*, 1:104–143.

——— (1958), Remarks on some variations in psycho-analytical technique. *Internat. J. Psycho-Anal.*, 39:222–229.

Erikson, E. H. (1950), *Childhood and Society.* New York: Norton.

Fairbairn, W. R. D. (1954), *An Object Relations Theory of the Personality.* New York: Basic Books.

Fenichel, O. (1941), *Problems of Psychoanalytic Technique.* New York: The Psychoanalytic Quarterly.

——— (1945), *The Psychoanalytic Theory of Neurosis.* New York: Norton.

Ferenczi, S. & Rank, O. (1923), *The Development of Psychoanalysis.* New York/Washington, D.C.: Nervous and Mental Disease Publishing Co., 1925.

Freud, A. (1936), *The Ego and the Mechanisms of Defense.* New York: International Universities Press, 1946.
Freud, S. (1893–1895), Studies on hysteria (with J. Breuer). *Standard Edition,* 2:3–319. London: Hogarth Press, 1955.
——— (1900), The interpretation of dreams. *Standard Edition,* 4 & 5. London: Hogarth Press, 1953.
——— (1905a), Fragment of an analysis of a case of hysteria. *Standard Edition,* 7:7–122. London: Hogarth Press, 1953.
——— (1905b), Three essays on the theory of sexuality. *Standard Edition,* 7:130–243. London: Hogarth Press, 1953.
——— (1909a), Analysis of a phobia in a five-year-old boy. *Standard Edition,* 10:3–149. London: Hogarth Press, 1955.
——— (1909b), Notes upon a case of obsessional neurosis. *Standard Edition,* 10:155–318. London: Hogarth Press, 1955.
——— (1911), Psycho-analytic notes on an autobiographical account of a case of paranoia (dementia paranoides). *Standard Edition,* 12:9–82. London: Hogarth Press, 1958.
——— (1911–1915), Papers on technique. *Standard Edition,* 12:85–171. London: Hogarth Press, 1958.
——— (1914a), Remembering, repeating and working through. *Standard Edition,* 12:145–156. London: Hogarth Press, 1958.
——— (1914b), On the history of the psycho-analytic movement. *Standard Edition,* 14:7–66. London: Hogarth Press, 1957.
——— (1914c), On narcissism: an introduction. *Standard Edition,* 14:117–235. London: Hogarth Press, 1957.
——— (1914–1915), Papers on metapsychology. *Standard Edition,* 14:117–235. London: Hogarth Press, 1957.
——— (1917a), Mourning and melancholia. *Standard Edition,* 14:239–258. London: Hogarth Press, 1957.
——— (1917b), Introductory lectures on psycho-analysis. *Standard Edition,* 16:243–496. London: Hogarth Press, 1963.
——— (1918), From the history of an infantile neurosis. *Standard Edition,* 17:7–122. London: Hogarth Press, 1955.
——— (1920), Beyond the pleasure principle. *Standard Edition,* 18:7–64. London: Hogarth Press, 1955.
——— (1923), The ego and the id. *Standard Edition,* 19:12–66. London: Hogarth Press, 1961.
——— (1926), Inhibitions, symptoms and anxiety. *Standard Edition,* 20:87–174. London: Hogarth Press, 1959.
——— (1937), Analysis terminable and interminable. *Standard Edition,* 23:216–253. London: Hogarth Press, 1964.
Friedman, L. (1980), Kohut: A book review essay. *Psychoanal. Quart.,* 49:393–422.
Fromm, E. (1941), *Escape from Freedom.* New York: Farrar & Rinehart.
——— (1947), *Man for Himself.* New York: Rinehart.
Gedo, J. (1979), *Beyond Interpretation: Toward a Revised Theory for Psychoanalysis.* New York: International Universities Press.
——— (1981), *Advances in Clinical Psychoanalysis.* New York: International Universities Press.
Gill, M. M. (1979), The analysis of transference. *J. Amer. Psychoanal. Assn.,* 27 (Supplement):263–288.
Greenson, R. R. (1967), *The Technique and Practice of Psychoanalysis.* New York: International Universities Press.
Grunberger, B. (1966), Some reflections on the Rat Man. *Internat. J. Psycho-Anal.,* 47:160–168.
Guntrip, H. (1971), *Psychoanalytic Theory, Therapy, and the Self.* New York: Basic Books.
Hanly, C. & Masson, J. (1976), A critical examination of the new narcissism. *Internat. J. Psycho-Anal.,* 57:49–66.

Hartmann, H. (1939), *Ego Psychology and the Problem of Adaptation.* New York: International Universities Press, 1958.

——— (1948), Comments on the psychoanalytic theory of instinctual drives. In: *Essays on Ego Psychology.* New York: International Universities Press, 1964, pp. 69–89.

———, Kris, E. & Loewenstein, R. M. (1949), Notes on the theory of aggression. *The Psychoanalytic Study of the Child,* 3/4:9–36. New York: International Universities Press.

Holt, R. R. (1965), A review of some of Freud's biological assumptions and their influence on his theories. In: *Psychoanalysis and Current Biological Thought,* eds. N. S. Greenfield & W. C. Lewis. Madison: University of Wisconsin Press, pp. 93–124.

Horney, K. (1937), *The Neurotic Personality of Our Time.* New York: Norton.

——— (1946), *Our Inner Conflicts.* New York: Norton.

——— (1950), *Neurosis and Human Growth.* New York: Norton.

Jacobson, E. (1964), *The Self and the Object World.* New York: International Universities Press.

Jaffe, D. S. (1971), Discussion of paper, New developments in object relations theory, by O. F. Kernberg. Annual Meeting of the American Psychoanalytic Association, Washington, D.C. (unpublished).

——— (1975), Book review of *Psychodynamically Based Psychotherapy* by L. J. Saul. *Psychoanal. Quart.,* 44:480–482.

——— (1979), Moderators discussion of papers by J. Klauber and by P. H. Ornstein, on: Formulating interpretations in clinical psychoanalysis. 31st International Psychoanalytical Congress (unpublished).

——— (1984), Book review of *Advances in Clinical Psychoanalysis* by J. Gedo. *Internat. J. Psycho-Anal.,* 65:223–229.

——— (1986a), Book reviews of (1) *Revolt of the Middle Aged Man* (2) *Money and Emotional Conflicts* (3) *The Psychology of Gambling,* by E. Bergler. *Internat. J. Psycho-Anal.,* 67:507–509.

——— (1986b), Empathy, counteridentification, countertransference: A review, with some personal perspectives on the analytic instrument. *Psychoanal. Quart.,* 55:215–243.

Jones, E. (1957), *The Life and Work of Sigmund Freud,* Vol. 3. New York: Basic Books.

Jung, C. G. (1915), *The Theory of Psychoanalysis.* New York: Nervous and Mental Disease Monograph Series, No. 19.

——— (1953), *Two Essays on Analytic Psychology. Collected Works,* 7. New York: Pantheon.

Kanzer, M. (1952), The transference neurosis of the Rat Man. *Psychoanal. Quart.,* 21:181–189.

——— (1979), Developments in psychoanalytic technique. *J. Amer. Psychoanal. Assn.,* 27 (Supplement):327–374.

Kernberg, O. F. (1970), Factors in the psychoanalytic treatment of narcissistic personalities. *J. Amer. Psychoanal. Assn.,* 18:51–85.

——— (1974), Further contributions to the treatment of narcissistic personalities. *Internat. J. Psycho-Anal.,* 55:215–240.

——— (1975), *Borderline Conditions and Pathological Narcissism.* New York: Aronson.

Klein, D. B. (1970), *A History of Scientific Psychology.* New York/London: Basic Books.

Klein, G. S. (1976), *Psychoanalytic Theory.* New York: International Universities Press.

Klein, M. (1948), *Contributions to Psycho-Analysis.* London: Hogarth Press.

Kohut, H. (1966), Forms and transformations of narcissism. *J. Amer. Psychoanal. Assn.,* 14:243–272.

——— (1971), *The Analysis of the Self.* New York: International Universities Press.

——— (1972), Thoughts on narcissism and narcissistic rage. *The Psychoanalytic Study of the Child,* 27:360–400. New York: Quadrangle.

——— (1977), *The Restoration of the Self.* New York: International Universities Press.

——— (1978), *The Search for the Self,* ed. P. H. Ornstein. New York: International Universities Press.

Kris, E. (1951), Ego psychology and interpretation in psychoanalytic therapy. *Psychoanal. Quart.,* 20:15–30.

Lacan, J. (1977), *Ecrits: A Selection.* New York: Norton.

Lampl-de Groot, J. (1976), Personal experience with psychoanalytic technique and theory during the last half century. *The Psychoanalytic Study of the Child,* 31:283–296. New Haven: Yale University Press.

Leites, N. (1977), Transference interpretations *only? Internat. J. Psycho-Anal.,* 58:275–287.

Levine, J. M. (1967), Through the looking glass: An examination of some critiques of Freudian psychoanalysis. *J. Amer. Psychoanal. Assn.,* 15:166–212.

Lichtenberg, J. D., Bornstein, M., & Silver, D., eds. (1984), *Empathy I.* Hillsdale, N.J.: The Analytic Press.

——— (1984), *Empathy II.* Hillsdale, N.J.: The Analytic Press.

Lipton, S. D. (1977), The advantage of Freud's technique as shown in his analysis of the Rat Man. *Internat. J. Psycho-Anal.,* 58:255–273.

Loewald, H. W. (1971), On motivation and instinct theory. *The Psychoanalytic Study of the Child,* 26:91–128. New York: Quadrangle.

——— (1973), Book review of *The Analysis of the Self* by Heinz Kohut. *Psychoanal. Quart.,* 26:493–506.

Loewenstein, R. M. (1958), Remarks on some variations in psychoanalytic technique. *Internat. J. Psycho-Anal.,* 39:202–210.

London, N. J. (1985), An appraisal of self psychology. *Internat. J. Psycho-Anal.,* 16:95–107.

Mahler, M. S. & Furer, M. (1968), *On Human Symbiosis and the Vicissitudes of Individuation.* New York: International Universities Press.

———, Pine, F., & Bergman, A. (1975), *The Psychological Birth of the Human Infant.* New York: International Universities Press.

Malcolm, J. (1983), Annals of scholarship. Trouble in the Archives- II. *New Yorker,* December 12.

Meissner, W. W. (1985), Psychoanalysis: The dilemma of science and humanism. *Psychoanal. Inquiry,* 5:471–498.

Menninger, K. A. & Holzman, P. S. (1973), *Theory of Psychoanalytic Technique.* New York: Basic Books.

Muslin, H. L. (1979), Transference in the Rat Man case: The transference in transition. *J. Amer. Psychoanal. Assn.,* 27:561–578.

Nunberg, H. (1930), The synthetic function of the ego. In: *Practice and Theory of Psychoanalysis.* New York: International Universities Press, 1960, pp. 120–136.

Ornstein, P. H. (1978), Introduction: the evolution of Heinz Kohut's psychoanalytic psychology of the self. In: *The Search for the Self,* ed. P. H. Ornstein. New York: International Universities Press, pp. 1–106.

Panel (1953), The traditional psychoanalytic technique and its variations, E. Zetzel, reporter. *J. Amer. Psychoanal. Assn.,* 11:526–537.

Panel (1954), Psychoanalysis and dynamic psychotherapy: Similarities and differences, L. Rangell, reporter. *J. Amer. Psychoanal. Assn.,* 2:152–166.

Panel (1958), Papers on variations in classical psycho-analytic technique. *Internat. J. Psycho-Anal.,* 39:200–242.

Peterfreund, E. (1971), *Information, Systems, and Psychoanalysis: An Evolutionary Biological Approach to Psychoanalytic Theory* [*Psychological Issues,* Monog. 25/26]. New York: International Universities Press.

Rado, S. (1956), *Psychoanalysis of Behavior: Collected Papers.* New York and London: Grune & Stratton.

Rangell, L. (1979), Contemporary issues in the theory of therapy. *J. Amer. Psychoanal. Assn.,* 27 (Supplement):81–112.

——— (1981), Psychoanalysis and dynamic psychotherapy: Similarities and differences twenty-five years later. *Psychoanal. Quart.,* 50:665–693.

Rank, O. (1923), *The Trauma of Birth.* New York: Harcourt, Brace; and London: Routledge & Kegan Paul, 1929.

Reich, W. (1928), On character analysis. In: Fliess, R., ed., *The Psycho-Analytic Reader.* New York: International Universities Press, 1948, pp. 106–156.

——— (1945), *Character Analysis.* New York: Orgone Institute Press.

Richards, A. D. (1982), The superordinate self in psychoanalytic theory and in the self psychologies. *J. Amer. Psychoanal. Assn.*, 30:939–957.
Rothstein, A. (1980), Toward a critique of the psychology of the self. *Psychoanal. Quart.*, 49:423–455.
Sandler, J., Dare, C., & Holder, A. (1973), *The Patient and the Analyst.* New York: International Universities Press.
Saul, L. J. (1972), *Psychodynamically Based Psychotherapy.* New York: Science House.
Schafer, R. (1976), *A New Language for Psychoanalysis.* New Haven: Yale University Press.
Schwartz, L. (1978), Book review of *The Restoration of the Self* by Heinz Kohut. *Psychoanal. Quart.*, 47:436–443.
Segel, N. P. (1981), Narcissism and adaptation to indignity. *Internat. J. Psycho-Anal.*, 62:465–476.
Slap, J. W. & Levine, F. J. (1978), On hybrid concepts in psychoanalysis. *Psychoanal. Quart.*, 47:499–523.
Stein, M. H. (1979), Book review of *The Restoration of the Self* by Heinz Kohut. *J. Amer. Psychoanal. Assn.*, 27:665–680.
——— (1981), The unobjectionable part of the transference. *J. Amer. Psychoanal. Assn.*, 29:869–892.
Strachey, J. (1934), The nature of the therapeutic action of psychoanalysis. *Internat. J. Psycho-Anal.*, 15:127–159.
Sullivan, H. S. (1947), *Conceptions of Modern Psychiatry.* Washington, D.C.: The William Alanson White Psychiatric Foundation.
——— (1953), *The Interpersonal Theory of Psychiatry*, ed. H. Perry & M. Gravel. New York: Norton.
Treurniet, N. (1983), Psychoanalysis and self psychology: A metapsychological essay with a clinical illustration. *J. Amer. Psychoanal. Assn.*, 31:59–100.
Valenstein, A. F. (1979), The concept of "classical" psychoanalysis. *J. Amer. Psychoanal. Assn.*, 27:113–136.
Waelder, R. (1936), The principle of multiple function: observations on over-determination. *Psychoanal. Quart.*, 5:45–62.
——— (1953), Paper presented to panel on the traditional psychoanalytical technique and its variations, E. Zetzel, reporter. *J. Amer. Psychoanal. Assn.*, 1:526–537.
Wallerstein, R. S. (1953), The bipolar self: discussion of alternative perspectives. *J. Amer. Psychoanal. Assn.*, 29:377–394.
——— (1981), The bipolar self: discussion of alternative perspectives. *J. Amer. Psychoanal. Assn.*, 29:377–394.
Weiner, N. D. (1973), Aposiopesis: a special type of silence. *Bull. Phila. Assn. Psychoanal.*, 23:281–287.
Winnicott, D. W. (1960),The theory of the parent-infant relationship. In: *The Maturational Processes and the Facilitating Environment.* New York: International Universities Press, 1965, pp. 37–55.
Yorke, C. (1972), Some suggestions for a critique of Kleinian psychology. *The Psychoanalytic Study of the Child*, 26:129–155. New York: Quadrangle.
Zetzel, E. R. (1963), The significance of the adaptive hypothesis for psychoanalytic theory and practice. *J. Amer. Psychoanal. Assn.*, 11:652–660.
——— (1966), Additional notes upon a case of obsessional neurosis: Freud 1909. *Internat. J. Psycho-Anal.*, 47:123–129.

May 1986

The Defensive Function of Psychoanalytic Theories

DAVID S. SPIRA, M.D. (Chicago)

This paper grew out of an interest in the role of theory in psychoanalytic practice and the choice of theory that analyst and patient make in the course of an analysis. Patients present with certain theories about their own behavior even though these are not always well formed or conscious. Analysts also have theories with which they organize and reorganize the patient's material. Psychoanalysis has now developed and expanded to the point where there are a number of theories available which offer different perspectives on the patient's dynamics and refer to different developmental constructs.

Freud (1908) was the first to describe the power that theories could hold in shaping the development of the individual, such as the theories of sexuality which children develop and often retain unconsciously into adulthood. Gedo and Goldberg (1973) have described how different models within classical psychoanalytic theory are appropriate to different clinical situations. Roy Schafer (1985a) has recently described in his paper on "Wild Analysis" how psychoanalytic technique is theory dependent and how one theoretical position may lead to techniques considered "wild" by another theoretical position. Mitchell and Greenberg (1983) point to the apparent theoretical incompatibility of theories based on a drive psychology with theories organized around the primacy of object relations. A comparison of psychoanalytic theories raises questions as to which thread of experience a particular theory is addressing, which theory addresses it best for which patient, which holds most therapeutic value for a particular patient, and

This paper received the 1986 Edwin Eisler Prize, Institute for Psychoanalysis, Chicago.

whether there is any relationship between these issues and historical or psychological "truth."

These are timely but broad questions in psychoanalysis today and beyond the scope of this paper, but I begin a consideration of these issues by addressing that aspect that refers to the patient's "choice" of theory as he presents to an analysis and as it develops and changes during the course of the analysis.

In this paper I describe two patients who presented with very powerful, conscious, preconceived notions as to which psychoanalytic theory was required to meet their needs. While these patients presented with quite different theories, both demonstrated during the course of the analysis how their chosen theory served a defensive function.

The psychoanalytic theories these patients chose helped to bind anxiety related to the uncertainty of starting analysis, attempted to avoid the disorganizing pull of a therapeutic regression, attempted to avoid humiliation and narcissistic injury and the emergence and experience of primitive impulses and intense affects. They also seemed particularly well suited as an effort to minimize the dependency longings that later revealed themselves following analysis of the defense transference. (See Freud [1937] on resistance to dependency in men.)

There was another aspect of these defensive structures that was particularly interesting and that made the particular theories chosen uniquely equipped to bind anxiety. These theories in some way "touched" and evoked genuinely felt early life experiences; and the theories paralleled and expressed specific aspects of the patients' preexisting character defense. That is, the psychoanalytic theory "fit" with an already established personal theory. For example, one patient who had long ago developed a character trait of blaming others for his own shortcomings and anxieties was able to use his understanding of Kohut's theory to support this lifelong defense by now blaming his parents for being "unempathic." The patient had in all likelihood been mistreated at many critical times in his life, and in this way the theory touched on and correctly described one aspect of reality.[1]

These psychoanalytic theories were able to assume especially powerful

[1]Roy Schafer (1985b), in a recent article in the *Journal of the American Psychoanalytic Association* on the "Interpretation of Psychic Reality," has pointed out how the psychoanalyst is not in any position to know the historical reality of the patient's past but only the patient's description, a description which will often change with analytic insight. In this paper, when I refer to aspects of "reality" I refer to the patient's description of his own psychic reality as it developed during the course of the analysis and the corrections that the patient was able to make in his own initial narrative.

defensive value by connecting with a part of the personality that valued the understanding which these theories offered.

It is worth noting that the theoretical constructions used by the patients I describe are different from the kind referred to in Glover's paper on "The Therapeutic Effect of Inexact Interpretations" in that the constructions or interpretations are not inexact but rather incomplete. The preconceived theoretical stance is also different from the binding of anxiety that accompanies a paranoid system or a religious conversion in its connection with actual happenings in the patient's past. Of course, like a religious conversion, the theoretical stance gains large support from the particular psychoanalytic group adhering to that theoretical position which often makes persuasive arguments in favor of a particular theory's desirability. This often presents the patient with ready arguments to use in pleading his case to the analyst, and it can pose interesting countertransference dilemmas to an analyst who is by nature involved in theoretical debates and disputes. Savvy patients are well versed in analytic-community debates and often attempt to convert the analysis into just such an event, particularly at moments of renewed resistance.

In the patients referred to in this paper, the analysis of the defense revealed not only its defensive function but also the kernel of "truth" or real experience that helped to give the theory its powerful additional value as a defense. Gill (1982) has described the way in which transference will often attach to a real aspect of the analyst as a hook and stresses that this plausible reality regarding the analyst must be acknowledged in analyzing the distortions which the transference creates. So, too, in these patients the plausibility of these early life experiences on which the theory rests must be explicitly acknowledged by the analyst if their defensive function and incompleteness are to be clearly elucidated.

Lest this defense be confused with intellectualization which binds anxiety through intellectual activities, it is important to note that the defensive use of psychoanalytic theory as described here, in contrast to intellectualization, actually touched on affective experience. It induced affect, often quite powerfully so, and allowed for apparent emotional "insight" and abreaction. But the insight was partial and incomplete and the incompleteness of it was obscured by the psychoanalytic theory's attempt to explain all phenomena and the patient's use of the theory in the same way, to explain *all* of his behavior and development. Because the theory attempts to explain *all* phenomena, as any good or at least complete theory should do, it may function analogously to a paranoid system in that the system is "closed." In some ways it may seem even more powerful than a paranoid system in serving the resistance in that it is based not on a false premise but on a real one, and one that is affectively charged. The more a theory is equipped to explain the more it may be used to explain away in this defensive manner; and the more it allows the expression of affect, the more resistance may be served against even more intense, disturbing affect states. It is important that the analyses referred to in this paper revealed the presence of more disturbing affect states following analysis of the defense transference-theory. Had this not been the case one could very well have argued that the patient's theory was correct all along and the analyst simply contrary. Here again is a potential source for countertransference difficulties. But it is not that the patient is not to be believed but rather that the patient must be convinced he is believed if one is to gain access to deeper affect states and a more complete understanding.

Greenberg and Mitchell (1983) have described the way in which different psychoanalytic theories can be organized around the position they take with regard to object relations. Theories that understand relationships as primary in the development of psychic structure can be contrasted with those that view drives as primary in the development of psychic structure. They argue for the incompatibility of theories based on "drive/structure" models with those based on "relationship/structure" models. Clinically, however, one finds oneself often switching from one theoretical/technical position to another, much like light can be understood as a particle or a wave. In the cases I describe what was significant was not merely a matter of switching from one theoretical perspective to another or the patient's use of theory as a tool to describe and understand his own mental life, but also the patient's need to cling to a theory that pointed to the underlying anxieties.

Given the fact that both patients described are in the mental health field and hence potentially identifiable, I have chosen to omit significant biographical data. My sense is that such data would not give the reader any greater or lesser conviction about the matters discussed.

Description of Analyses

CASE OF MR. K.

Mr. K. came to analysis at age 30 because of feelings of emptiness and depression and an awareness that he was unable to get close to people. He had read the work of Heinz Kohut extensively and had attended many workshops on Self Psychology. He had become interested in Kohut's work because it touched something very deep inside him, and in reading it he felt understood for the first time. It was clear to him as he started analysis that he needed to be understood in Self Psychology terms. Mr. K. held the belief that his parents had been "unempathic" and presented memories to "prove it." His father was described as depressed and unavailable. His mother was forever critical of the patient and his father, and out of touch with the patient's need to be mirrored and appreciated.

During the initial phase of the analysis the patient challenged and scrutinized the analyst, the analyst's comments, and his office. Tentative attempts to understand the patient led to his feeling criticized and angry and to his further examination of why the analyst was saying what he was saying, particularly as it related to the patient's understanding of good psychoanalytic technique "according to Kohut." The patient tried to teach the analyst the kind of appreciation and response that the patient felt he needed and prided himself on a greater understanding of Kohut than the analyst. "You are not being empathic!" was a common complaint during the early years of the analysis and was accompanied by intense and sincere affect.

The dynamics of the transference in which the patient felt that the analyst was depriving and unempathic were accompanied by very "real" memories and powerful affects of sadness, pain, and rage. He tried to support his claims of parental failure, to plead his case. He described long hours of silence during which he and father did not interact. He recalled horrendous stories of his mother's preoccupation with her own concerns and her being out of touch with the needs of a small boy. He described a time when as a child of six he had been physically injured in a fall and mother talked on the telephone making him wait for attention rather than rushing to his aid. Numerous episodes were described during which his parents missed important opportunities to encourage his autonomy and growth. One got the impression in the patient's retelling of these events of their power, of his sadness and despair, of his longing for the analyst to agree that, yes, of course he had been abused and let down.

Of course these affects were reexperienced in the transference as the patient became enraged at the analyst's "lack of empathy" and the patient despaired at being misunderstood and insufficiently appreciated. If, for example, the analyst interpreted the patient's associations as alluding to a fear of unconscious homosexual wishes, the patient would focus on the analyst's lack of appreciation at how difficult it had been for the patient to bring up that material, and the analyst's lack of comment at the patient's ability to associate more freely. The analyst misunderstood just as his parents had misunderstood him.

These patterns ultimately came to be understood as mechanisms of defense and attack that were designed to bring the analyst down, destroy the impact of the analyst's interpretations, and keep the analyst at a distance while preserving the patient's precarious self-esteem. During the course of the analysis it became clear that these accusations also represented defensive maneuvers preventing the emergence of oedipal material, both positive and negative. It also described a piece of psychic reality that was deeply felt and in being deeply felt had affected the patient's development and world view. It contributed to the nature of his defense transference in which he replayed the experience of being let down by all those around him—wife, friends, and business associates. It also became clear, however, that his cries of "lack of empathy" were an attempt at controlling the analyst and the course of the analysis. That control satisfied his wishes to be the one in charge without expressing that desire more directly. He could appeal to theory and Heinz Kohut and admonish the analyst for incorrect technique rather than face his competitive strivings for control and his fear of retaliation and castration.

Interpretations such as these were not met with sadness or despair as the analysis progressed, but with anxiety, and dream material confirmed the presence of the conflicts. The defensive use of Kohut's theory also served as an attempt to avoid further regression that would accompany the deepening of the analysis with more powerful experiences of sexual and aggressive impulses and greater fears of empathic ruptures in the transference itself. Those impulses only became clear when the defensive function had been analyzed. He gained power, prestige, potency, and control by knowing it all before he ever entered the analysis and by attempting to teach the analyst/father the error of his ways.

The patient's psychic reality underwent interesting revisions during the analysis. It became clear that his accusations that father (analyst) was depressed represented a disguised oedipal attack by which he made father impotent. He then felt deprived. He, in fact, remembered strong, positive attributes of the father and understood his resistance to recognizing these attributes lest he feel small and impotent himself and anxious about competing with such a strong and competent figure. For example, he recalled how father taught him to work on cars and to use tools around the house and how, as a child, he was unable to hit a nail straight. Even as he learned and acquired skills he was aware of his lack of skill and power compared to father's powerful use of his tools.

In addition to recalling periods when mother was out of touch with his needs he reconstructed his needs to avoid her and focus on her disappointing him in order to avoid responsibility for his sexual curiosity and excitement. Mother had previously been characterized only as unavailable and inappropriate rather than also exciting.

What was most instructive about this analysis was not only that oedipal pathology emerged with confirmatory associations and reconstructions but also that this patient's use of Kohut's theory derived from its ability to address some very emotional moments in his life. The theory did not simply avoid or reduce anxiety but had itself a powerful emotive effect in stimulating the reexperience of early childhood anxiety and depression. That theory was useful and correct for a part of his emotional life.

It is important to note that the patient's use of Kohut's theory not only protected him against the awareness of disturbing affect states best characterized as derivatives of sexual and aggressive drives, but may also have been an attempt to protect the patient against feared states of fragmentation, emptiness, and depletion more associated with self pathology. I am not making a case here for one theory over another, and I am avoiding debate as to which theory would best describe this patient's difficulty or would best lend itself to the most appropriate technical interventions. What I am making a case for is the way in which this patient's use of theory was especially well suited to protect against an awareness of intense affects even though it appeared to induce, or at least reflect, his affect.

CASE OF MR. F.

Mr. F. desired to become a psychoanalyst. He had read Freud extensively and, for the first time in his life, felt that someone had addressed his problems. He loved the certainty with which he felt Freud made constructions in his case material. He discussed psychoanalytic theory with friends and often involved himself in interpreting their dynamics. He wanted a classical Freudian analyst. It was clear to him from the start that what he needed were interpretations of his unconscious sexual and destructive impulses, and that once these had been made conscious his symptoms of depression and worthlessness would disappear. He described his neurotic pattern of always messing up when he was about to achieve some greatness. For example, if he were working on a par golf game and hitting up to the eighteenth green, he would hit into the water and mess up the whole experience. He was likely to be so enraged and depressed by this that he would break a club and walk off the golf course in despair. Were it not for his symptoms he was convinced he might have been a great athlete, and there was some evidence that that might very well have been the case. Similarly with women, he could win them over and was able to perform sexually but would be seized by a powerful force that led him to confess his "sickness" to them, or to try to physically hold on to them so tightly that he was at the point of hurting them. Here, too, he managed to ruin his opportunity for success.

Phenomenologically, he was aware of intense impulses. Rage and the wish to destroy, desires to possess women and be the envy of other men, were consciously felt daily experiences that lent conviction to his reading of Freud and the descriptions of powerful drives that need to be tamed by making them conscious. This patient was, of course, eminently conscious of strong desires to kill and seduce, and what lay underneath his concerns was a profound conviction that he was sick and "worthless" inside, that he was nothing but a "wimp" which was the lowest form of life, "even worse than being a fag."

The patient was intently focused during the initial phase of the analysis on whether the analyst was making interpretations addressed to the patient's unconscious. He continually berated the analyst for his seeming inability to offer such interpretations. He quoted chapter and verse of Sigmund Freud and prided himself that he knew Freud better than the analyst. He described how Freud would interpret the unconscious impulse and the patient's symptoms would disappear, and why wasn't that happening?

In his attempt to "uncover" the repressed impulses the patient focused relatively little on his relationships with his parents and sibs. In fact, there was evidence of tremendous disturbances in the family relationships from quite early on. Father had been psychotic and would fly into rages and brutally humiliate the patient according to his earliest memories. Every success that the patient attempted as a child resulted in just such humiliation. For example, if the patient at eight years of age went next door to visit the neighbors to be friendly he was berated for "sucking up" to them. If his sibs began to dance to music at home and encouraged the patient to join in, as soon as he began to dance along and relax the sibs would stop and laugh at him, saying that he had been fooled again. The sibs, it appeared, took the lead of the father and harshly criticized the patient for any initiative, enthusiasm, or attempt at growth. Intimacy and desire in his home became a weapon that could and would be used against him.

Mother, on the other hand, was depressed. She might very well have had a postpartum depression—that remained unclear—but she seemed preoccupied with herself. When she took care of the patient and his sibs she appeared to be doing so reluctantly and begrudgingly. Often, as in changing diapers, she showed blatant signs of disgust. When the patient was born mother had less time to devote to his older brother. Brother apparently became enraged and blamed the patient for his very existence, which seemed to the older brother to rob him of what little attention he had. The patient turned to this older brother for comfort and support during times when father was away or cold and cruel, and in the face of mother's preoccupation. The brother, whom the patient continued to look up to, took this as an opportunity to vent his rage and attacked the patient with even more scorn and contempt.

The patient's sense of himself developed in a reciprocal way in feeling that yes, he was worthless, evil, bad, and a fitting object of contempt. If only he could have his pathogenic impulses made conscious, he hoped that he could be rid of the evil within him.

The patient, as the reader may have inferred, did not experience his difficulties as arising from early failures in maternal and paternal care. That is, he experienced his difficulties not as arising from impaired, non-responding, and hostile relationships, but rather as resulting from drives that had produced his symptoms.

The patient's experience of very powerful impulses which he could not explain seemed to confirm Freud's theory and fit quite well with the theory the patient had constructed from quite early on that there was obviously something in him, something biological and inherent, that made him bad and repulsive. He resolutely defended against the suggestion that there might have been some parental failing that led to his symptoms.

As the analysis developed, it turned out that the patient had additional reason for clinging to his theory and his understanding of Freudian theory. To accept the notion of a failure in relationships, and to feel that I now understood this, presented him with a frightening dilemma of increasing intimacy with the analyst and an increasing awareness of longings that had long ago been dismissed.

The fear was that he would reexperience the longings to be cared for and responded to which he had long ago given up any chance of finding. It was the intensity of these longings and the fear that they would lead to greater rejection and humiliation that also led to the appeal which his version of Freudian theory held for him. When interpretations such as these were offered they led to anxiety and discomfort. For example, the patient described how he felt uncomfortable that if he and the analyst were to have a better relationship he would not know how to act. He felt a tension that he could not explain. While he had argued for adherence to Freudian theory all he was aware of feeling was anger.

The appeal of Freudian theory, then, involved both its value in defending against deeper regression and an increase in longing for maternal support, and the fear he would be abandoned and rejected with greater feelings of longing, emptiness, and fragmentation. It also appealed to his experience of intense aggressive and sexual feelings which had always gotten him into trouble. Here lay the kernel of truth that seemed to fit with his preconceived notion that these "drives" could be troublesome, represented his "evil, bad" self, and needed to be "removed" or at least modified through interpretation.

In addition, he hoped for "The Interpretation" which he could "hold in his head" which would work as a counterforce to neutralize the badness of his impulses. The appeal of this idealized "Freudian" interpretation was that it required no relationship. That is, he could rely on the interpretation and not have to rely on the analyst who, as a person in the real world, could only fail him as others had failed him in the past.

Discussion

While the patients described in this paper presented with quite different theories about their psychological states, a number of similarities existed. Both patients took tremendous pride in their knowledge of theory, and both felt that they knew that theory much better than the analyst did. Both patients often referred to specific chapters or phrases by their chosen author to make their case. Both patients had been profoundly affected by their reading. They felt understood by the author, and it was their first experience of feeling so completely understood. They also felt a sense of hope that their problems were being addressed and were hence potentially resolvable. They were thus ardent defenders and proponents of the theory. Neither had read other theoreticians to any significant degree; it was not that they had chosen from many. Both tended to have powerful idealizations not only of the theory but of the men who had created them as well. They hoped to have an experience with Freud and Kohut via the analyst. It was as if the analyst were a vehicle to a union with Freud and Kohut—the ultimate "supervisors." Insofar as there was any deviation from the patient's understanding of theory and technique implied by the theory, the analyst became not only a rival, but also a heretic, a nonbeliever. As might be expected, affects of anger were common early on in the transference, particularly at any imagined "departure" from orthodoxy.

The consideration of an alternative view led not simply to more intense affect states—that is, once the defensive function had been cleared—but also to different affect. The anger and rivalry apparent during the initial phase of the analysis and during the analysis of the defensive function of their use of theory were replaced by anxiety. It was the appearance of this anxiety, objectively and subjectively experienced, that served as an indication to both the patient and the analyst of conflicts which were being defended against. This recognition of anxiety served both patients as a convincing sign that they were frightened of the feelings they would have experienced if they did not cling to their theories. One often sees patients who have some theory concerning their behavior and feelings. When one makes suggestions about alternative views, or points out conflicts the patient might not have been aware of, one is often struck by a sense of consideration or interest, or even pleasure at consideration of another perspective. There was none of this sense of interest or wonder on the part of these patients, but rather a sense of rage that one would tamper with their already-arrived-at perfect system.

The anxieties of both patients included conflicts over dependency. If they needed the analyst to help them through the uncertainty of not knowing during an analytic regression they could not avoid the dependency that they were struggling to minimize.

Another interesting feature of these patients' use of theory was that it seemed to relieve them of responsibility for all that had gone wrong in their lives. Mr. K. felt that Kohut validated his feeling that his parents had failed through a lack of mirroring and his idealized father through a lack of availability, and thus he was not responsible for his neurosis and distress. He was not "depraved," he was "deprived."

Mr. F., on the other hand, felt that Freudian psychoanalysis, with its emphasis on biological drives, relieved him of responsibility in that he suffered from a biological disorder. It was not his fault if powerful drive states led to his symptoms. He was not evil or bad as a person; he was burdened by biological drives.

Hence the appeal of the patients' theories was their value in helping them to feel without responsibility; alternative explanations or a different perspective threatened to make them feel "responsible" for their symptoms.

As stated earlier in the paper, the theory also came between patient and analyst. The patient related to the analyst through the theory, interpreted interpretations through the perspective of that theory, challenged the analyst by referring to the theory, and measured the analyst by his adherence to the theory. In this way the theory served as a buffer in the relationship. It was as if the patients referred to a higher authority: "We have to do it; it's the law."

The choice of theoretical position is a complex one. Often in clinical conferences one will hear persuasive arguments in support of quite different theories, and with seemingly relevant clinical data put forth to support their claims. This paper obviously points to the need to consider, next, the analyst's role in the choice of theory and technique. This is an examination best left for another paper.

It ought to be mentioned that patients do present to treatment with all sorts of theories, and occasionally one will see a patient who, in retrospect, had a relatively good grasp of the dynamics involved. This, of course, often serves the defense of intellectualization insofar as it may take quite some time for the patient to be affected by his intellectual understanding.

REFERENCES

Freud, S. (1908), On the sexual theories of children. *Standard Edition,* 9:205–226. London: Hogarth Press, 1959.

——— (1937), Analysis terminable and interminable. *Standard Edition,* 23:209–254. London: Hogarth Press, 1964.

Gedo, J. & Goldberg, A. (1973), *Models of the Mind: A Psychoanalytic Theory.* Chicago: University of Chicago Press.

Gill, M. (1982), The actual analytic situation in analysis of transference. In: *Analysis of Transference.* Vol. 1: *Theory of Technique.* New York: International Universities Press, pp. 107–120.

Glover, E. (1931), The therapeutic effect of inexact interpretations. In: *The Technique of Psycho-Analysis.* New York: International Universities Press, 1955, pp. 353–366.

Greenberg, J. & Mitchell, S. (1983), *Object Relations in Psychoanalytic Theory.* Cambridge: Harvard University Press.

Schafer, R. (1985a), Wild analysis. *J. Amer. Psychoanal. Assn.,* 33:275–299.

——— (1985b), The interpretation of psychic reality, developmental influences, and unconscious communication. *J. Amer. Psychoanal. Assn.,* 33:537–554.

October 1986

Disavowal: A Review of Applications in Recent Literature

CHARLES M. JAFFE, M.D. (Chicago)

Psychoanalysis has always been fundamentally concerned with the content and process of what is included or excluded from awareness, yet disavowal has been assigned various explanations as psychoanalytic metapsychology and clinical theory have evolved. This paper will examine the variety of meanings assigned to the phenomenon of disavowal as influential critiques and revisions of psychoanalysis in recent years have broadened its emphasis from a specific defense to a more inclusive concept. Rather than attempting an exhaustive review, the intent of this work is to highlight the expanding application of disavowal and to suggest some implications of its current use. At present, disavowal is assigned its broadest meaning as a description of the brain's ordinary process of selectively screening the affective significance of information in the service of overall ordered function. As such, it forms a basis for personality organization and defense. In a narrower application, disavowal refers to a mode of selective attention utilizing preoperational thought in the service of defense. It is suggested that disavowal in its current use serves as a bridge between clinical observations of self-protective processes and the general study of the circumstances and methods in which the integration of affectively laden information is facilitated or foreclosed.

Kohut (1971) focused attention on disavowal when he postulated that it was the operant defense in patients who seemed to have two conscious, but noncommunicating aspects in their mental life. He wondered about the nature of the defense which created a barrier that did not allow the "psyche's right hand (the centrally located reality ego with its low self-esteem, lack of initiative, and its shame propensity and hypochondria) [to] know what the left hand (the grandiose, split-off sector) is doing" (p. 242). In a modification of Freud's concept of "splitting of the ego," Kohut explained this phenomenon on the basis of a "vertical split in the psyche," created by disavowal, and resulting in the persistence of two contradictory currents of mental life. The vertical split is characterized as "the side-by-side existence of cohesive personality attitudes with different goal structures, different pleasure aims, different moral and aesthetic values" (p. 183). Kohut noted the similarity of his concept to Schafer's description of the ego split as "suborganizations of motives, representations, and mental processes. These suborganizations include elements of the id and superego as well as of the ego system" (1968, p. 99).

Although Kohut associates a split in the ego with disavowal, this association is not always present in the literature. A brief review of Freud's uses of splitting may help clarify its relationship to disavowal.

Lichtenberg and Slap (1973) point out that Freud used splitting in relation to the topographic and structural models and as a general term to describe divisions between parts of the mental apparatus.[1] Freud referred to splitting in relation to the "splitting of consciousness" of some thoughts from a dominant mass of ideas (1893), to the "splitting of the ego" which results in the persistence of two contradictory psychical groups in the fetishist (1927, 1940a), and to "two different attitudes . . . one of these . . . belongs to the ego and the contrary one, which is repressed, belongs to the id" (1940a). They divide the applications of the term into four categories: (1) a general organizing principle in psychic development and function, (2) a process connected to the organization of mental contents, (3) a defense, and (4) a process associated with the formation of contradictory psychical groups.

As a principle of mental functioning, synthesis and splitting are considered to be counterparts in the general tendency toward simplification and unity. Nunberg labeled this tendency the synthetic function of the ego. He considered it to be a relatively mature ego function, arising in the oedipal phase. Lichtenberg and Slap criticize this use of splitting because of the confusion between pathological and normal processes. They prefer Hartmann's concept of the ego's organizing function because it contains the same idea of division and integration without the confusion in terminology. Used this way, splitting is not related to the defense of disavowal. However, as will be noted later, in the recent literature disavowal has been expanded

[1]The quotations from Freud that follow are taken from Lichtenberg and Slap (1973).

from a specific defense to a general organizing principle of mental functioning.

Lichtenberg and Slap (1973) note that splitting has also been used to mean "the adaptive pattern in which the affective coloration of infantile experience dictates the separate grouping of memory traces of those experiences . . . [into] . . . good and bad self- and good and bad object representations. . . ." (p. 780). This use originated in Freud's (1915) discussion of a purified pleasure ego which results from the incorporation of pleasurable sensations and the projection of that which is unpleasurable. It is splitting in this sense that is referred to by M. Klein, Mahler, Kernberg, and Fairbairn (although Fairbairn considers the reason for the split to be frustrations in maternal object relations, while the other authors mentioned consider the reason for the split to lie in the necessity of defending against aggressive instinct). Also related are Jacobson's description of the early fusion and separations of self and object images and Glover's concept of ego nuclei. This elaboration of splitting bears little resemblance to disavowal because the defense requires a more mature ego that has coalesced into whole object and self representations.

Once the various affective experiences become integrated into whole self and object representations, splitting refers to a defense as opposed to a failure of integration. It is in this category of a defense that splitting and disavowal are most closely associated. Splitting results from a defensive maneuver of an integrated ego and serves to keep separate two currents of mental life that would arouse anxiety if experienced simultaneously. The separation of psychical groups is accomplished by this process. This meaning of splitting most closely applies to Kohut's vertical split in the psyche which he attributed to the defense of disavowal.

In summary, splitting is a most evocative concept used by Freud in a number of contexts, each of which has received separate emphasis. There are some applications of splitting that may be said to occur on the basis of disavowal, but there appears to be no consistent relationship between the terms. Splitting is referred to as a general organizing principle of mental functioning, as a defense, as the result of a defense, and as a division process that occurs before a defense of disavowal would seem possible. In short, disavowal results in a split, but not all splits are on the basis of disavowal.

At the time Kohut proposed the concept of a vertical split, he was working within the assumptions of ego psychology to account for certain transferencelike phenomena (narcissistic transferences, later to be termed selfobject transferences) that he noted in patients who did not meet the ordinary criteria for analyzability and who did not improve with the usual interpretations. Kohut's formulation was that patients with unmodified, archaic narcissistic energy defended against instinctual danger with repression (horizontal split) or disavowal (vertical split). All patients had a horizontal split, but the most common presentation was those patients who had a vertical split as well. Psychoanalysis was intended to modify and redirect the narcissistic energy in a two-part process. The first part was concerned with undoing the disavowal that separated the reality ego and the unmodified infantile narcissism, and the second part was concerned with undoing the repression that kept the enfeebled self-representation in the reality ego from being imbued with narcissistic energy.

Kohut's dissatisfaction with the limitations of ego psychology and his move to view the development of the self as the supraordinate organizing concept for psychoanalysis is well documented by himself (1984) and by others (Ornstein, 1978). Kohut's (1984) last formulation of psychopathology was that disturbances in development were the result of faulty selfobject relationships early in life. That is, the relationship with caretakers did not proceed by way of optimal frustration in the context of adequate empathic in-tuneness to a healthy self that could sustain itself in adult life, but instead remained reliant on archaic self-selfobject relations for maintenance of self cohesion. It was these repressed or split-off aspects of the self that persisted into adulthood and accounted for symptoms. These remnants continued to search for "appropriately responsive selfobjects from the first years of childhood or from a later period (e.g., the oedipal phase)" (p. 71). Psychoanalysis is the process of establishing empathic intuneness between self and mature selfobjects to supplant the previously split-off archaic narcissistic relationships.

As can be seen, the concept of a vertical split continued to figure prominently in Kohut's theorizing despite his shift away from a drive-psychological explanation for the phenomenon. Kohut did not concern himself specifically with the relationship of the vertical split to disavowal, but his emphasis on psychological development and psychopathology as a consequence of the actual relationships with caretakers did emphasize the importance of defenses against external reality.

In a series of papers, Basch (1974, 1976a, 1976b, 1977, 1979, 1981, 1983a, 1983b, 1983c, 1985) has explored disavowal as a defense against external reality, and has placed disavowal into a general scheme of development based on the integration over time of communicated affects and cognitive maturation. In so doing, he has suggested that disavowal is a developmental achievement as well as a defense. Actually, in his work to place psychoanalysis within communication science, Basch has placed self psychology on a theoretical foundation not supplied by Kohut, a foundation that defines the broader implications of disavowal for development and defense. Basch has made the most thorough exploration of disavowal, so his work requires extended review.

Basch (1983c) traces the development of Freud's theory of disavowal and summarizes as follows:

> Freud described disavowal as a defense available when the need to preserve the reality testing function comes into conflict with the perception of a significant environmental reality that is potentially traumatic. Unable to simply turn away, a compromise is formed that attempts to serve both the pleasure and reality principle. This is accomplished by bringing about an ego split, one arm of which acknowledges the reality, while the other repudiates the meaning of the perception and substitutes a fantasy that protects the individual from the anxiety he would otherwise have to face. Disavowal defends against anxiety-provoking external perceptions and is the counterpart of repression, repression being directed towards similar demands from the inner world of instincts. Disavowal is a ubiquitous process whose presence is not in itself indicative of pathology, general or specific [p. 136].

Basch also cites the concepts of Tulvig and Vygotsky to explain the difference between patients using disavowal and repression. Essentially, Basch says that patients using disavowal have a block that precludes left-hemisphere activity ("verbal or other forms of discursive language") from involving right-hemisphere activity ("totality of experience and its affective significance") and that patients using repression have a block precluding communication in the opposite direction. Either way, there is an interruption in the free exchange ("inner speech") between episodic and semantic memory that ordinarily would allow a continuous feedback and monitoring to occur between the self and experience (pp. 150–151). In other words, repression precludes the verbal representation of an affectively meaningful experience and disavowal precludes the appreciation of the affective significance of reportable events.

Basch takes issue with A. Freud's use of disavowal to indicate a psychotic process in adults and with the many reports confusing denial (a psychotic process involving decathexis of reality) and disavowal. He suggests that denial be used to indicate psychotic or nonpsychotic mechanisms which interfere with sensory signals (as described in Basch, 1974) and disavowal be used to indicate those circumstances where only the expected meaning of the percept is repudiated. Thus, Basch defines disavowal as the "separation of personal meaning from some perceived aspect of external reality judged to be potentially anxiety provoking" (p. 146).[2] This is a more limited definition than Freud's since not all defense against external reality is encompassed by disavowal.

Basch (1979, 1983a, 1983c, 1985) places disavowal within the framework of the development of cognition and affects. As part of the brain's ordering function, inborn affects organize and amplify communication signals between infant and caretaker. Stimulation of affects is the basic motivation for action. Through interaction, experiences are encoded (in the sensorimotor cognitive mode) as affectively toned action patterns. These action patterns form the basis of expectation for later experience. With the capacity for symbol formation (preoperational cognition), a concept of self becomes possible. A concept of self, defined as the symbolic transformation of experience into an overall goal-oriented construct, allows the child to sort stimuli by relevance to the self. Whereas in an earlier stage the child reacted to excessive stimulation with withdrawal, now the child can screen information in a more sophisticated manner that enables more complex interactions to occur. Basch (1983c) suggests that this process of ignoring information that is not relevant to the self (and does not, therefore, initiate action) is nondefensive disavowal: "In the interest of our psychic economy we are continuously making decisions, consciously and unconsciously, as to whether or not, and to what degree, given experiences should mobilize our affective reactions" (p. 147). Disavowal becomes defensive when information is screened out, not because it is irrelevant, but because it represents some danger and creates anxiety. Here it can be seen that Basch uses disavowal as a general principle of mental functioning as well as a specific defense.

Gedo has also made significant revisions of clinical psychoanalytic theory. In this work, disavowal is placed in a developmental context. With Goldberg

[2]Lichtenberg and Slap's (1973) definition of the defense of "splitting of representations" sounds very similar to Basch's definition of disavowal. They state: "The specific function of this defense is to separate two currents of strong feelings that would arouse anxiety if experienced simultaneously towards an object" (p. 781). As Basch (1983c) does disavowal, they consider splitting of representations to be a factor in splitting of the ego as defined by Freud. Furthermore, there is a link between splitting of representations and a vertical split in the psyche based on disavowal, since both Lichtenberg and Slap and Kohut liken their concepts to Schafer's (1968, p. 99) description of "suborganizations of the ego."

However, there are important differences between these concepts. Lichtenberg and Slap state that disavowal involves whole percepts, whereas splitting of representations "separates along affective lines the self and object representations involved in a disturbing percept" (p. 781). This is confusing because Basch, too, talks about separation of affect. In addition, the currents of feeling referred to are said to be derivatives of libidinal and aggressive drives (i.e., internal dangers) whereas Basch's definition refers to external dangers. Lichtenberg and Slap's emphasis, then, is on the division of self and object representations in the service of drive defense, while Basch is concerned with a more general process of ignoring meaning.

(1973), he states: "In later stages of psychic organization, when the loss of self-cohesion no longer threatens actual fragmentation, the differentiated ego may be able to utilize the regressive pathway of splitting of the self in the service of defense. This is the process that was called 'disavowal' by Freud. When the defense is in operation, the nonrecognized or unacknowledged aspects of mental activity do not lie behind a repression barrier; they are separated from the acknowledged parts of the self by a failure of synthesis or integration" (p. 65). Disavowal is the "typical defense" between the time that the self becomes defined as a psychic unit and the internalization of moral standards. The hypothesized explanation for the phenomenon was an abandonment of the synthetic function of the ego. Disavowal is concluded once the synthetic function has matured, making regressive fragmentation of the cohesive self impossible.[3]

In *Beyond Interpretation,* Gedo (1979) revises his epigenetic hierarchy and places self-organization, a hierarchy of personal aims, as the supraordinate organizing principle for psychoanalysis. In his new formulation, disavowal plays an expanded role. In Gedo's view, disavowal maintains self-esteem during that period between the time of the achievement of a cohesive hierarchy of personal aims ("primary identity") and the time when self-esteem is no longer threatened by the absence or failure of empathic caretakers. During this time, the child is aware of his actual dependence on caretakers and his separateness, having achieved a unified self-schema. However, the child continues to expect limitless assistance. The unrealistic aspects of these wishes are disavowed, since the child cannot maintain self-esteem without the illusion of parental perfection. Beneath the reality-oriented recognition of separateness lies a fantasied merger with the omnipotent parent. With this formulation, Gedo applies the concept of disavowal specifically to this disregard for separateness, resulting in a split in the self. Disavowal is considered a necessary operation during that period of time of the internalization of self-esteem, made possible by the immaturity of cognitive functioning (preoperational thought) that allows mutually exclusive personal aims to be pursued concurrently. Cognitive development has replaced the immaturity of the ego's synthetic function as the explanation for disavowal, and the phenomenon is no longer considered regressive at this phase. The transition away from disavowal to repression also occurs because of cognitive maturation, concrete operations requiring logical connections between thoughts.

[3]Interestingly, Gedo adds that with the formation of the superego, it is "no longer sufficient merely to keep dangerous ideas to oneself" (p. 99). The implication is that keeping thoughts private facilitates disavowal. Stern (1985) addresses the relationship of privacy and disavowal and concludes that they result from different processes.

Gedo employs Basch's theory of cognition and affect as the foundation for the development of self-organization, although he disagrees with Basch in certain respects regarding development of self-cohesion and therefore the timing and use of disavowal as a defense. Basch associates disavowal with the development of self, made possible by symbol formation and preoperational thought. Used nondefensively, disavowal allows the newly formed self to screen relevant stimuli. Disavowal, for Basch, is a generic ignoring of stimulation that may be used defensively and that is available from about eighteen months. Gedo presents disavowal in a somewhat narrower sense as a typical defense associated specifically with the maintenance of the illusion of parental perfection. He applies disavowal to a somewhat later phase than Basch, about the middle of the third year of life, citing projection as the typical defense in the earlier stage of self formation. The difference between the two may be in part related to Basch's emphasis on brain function and the discontinuous nature of cognitive development and Gedo's emphasis on the gradual process of the development of stable self-cohesion. It may be noted that where Basch views disavowal as generic and Gedo viewed it as in the service of maintaining specific illusions of parental perfection to safeguard self-esteem, Kohut saw disavowal as maintaining infantile grandiosity, resulting in diminished self-esteem.

G. S. Klein's (1976) exposition of the core clinical propositions of psychoanalytic theory also addresses disavowal in relation to self development. Klein's definition of repression bears close resemblance to definitions of disavowal, and therefore requires inclusion in the present exploration. He states: "The central objective of psychoanalytic clinical explanation is the *reading of intentionality;* behavior, experience, testimony are studied for meaning in this sense, as jointly exemplifying directive 'tensions,' avowed, disavowed, repressed, defended" (p. 26; Klein's emphasis). The core principles of his clinical theory state that psychic structure is the result of resolution of incompatible aims or dispositions, experienced as pleasurable or anxiety-producing by a developing self. Incompatible aims are resolved through active reversal of passively endured experience or through repression, resulting in schemata of interpersonal relationships based on identifications or introjects. New crises occasion the repetition of previous modes of resolution.

Central to Klein's theory is that, in the face of incompatible aims, repression maintains self-schema when experienced dissonance is of traumatic proportions and cannot be made part of the self by reversal of voice (passive into active). Klein views all defenses as variants of repression, and defense mechanisms as means of implementing repressive dissociation. The aim of defense is "to prevent an intolerable understanding of a critical meaning . . . and may focus on intellection, emotion, or motor activity, separately or together" (p. 304).

Klein defines a number of qualities of repression, the core being "an unconsciously active idea which is dissociated from the person's self-experience. It is "the refusal to acknowledge the *meaning* of a tendency . . . [to the self]. Through repression, a meaning or tendency is taken outside these limits: disowned. Repression produces an incapacity to attend to and comprehend the meanings of one's own actions and creates a gap between meanings that are acknowledged by the self and meanings that are 'lived out' without comprehension" (p. 242; Klein's emphasis). Failure to comprehend meaning may include perceptual failure, breaks in awareness of causal sequences, or failure of judgment (p. 243). Indicators of an unconscious fantasy include excessive or inappropriate responses, absence of expected response, or repetition of certain responses (p. 300). "The critical core of the repressive process is the loss of responsiveness to one's own actions and ideas" through a failure to accommodate or respond to feedback (p. 244). Klein also addresses the relationship of repression to memory and consciousness. He notes that remembering an event does not itself undo repression, as it is not memory that is repressed, but its meaning: "To undo a repression means to bring about comprehension of the terms of a previously uncomprehended relationship, the perception of a causal link to which the person had been impervious, and a new level of understanding" (p. 248). In a related argument, Klein stresses that the theory of repression does not require either of Freud's concepts of consciousness as a system or as brought about by energy deployment. Unconsciousness is to be taken not as a state of consciousness but rather as "a gap in understanding, . . . the condition of a cognitive schema in relation to an observer-self" (p. 252). In other words, unconsciousness is synonymous with lack of awareness of meaning, not with lack of consciousness (i.e., absence from memory).

Klein places repression in a developmental context. Intolerable experiences in infancy are managed by a split wherein both the experience and its source are condemned (i.e., massive withdrawal). He follows Balint's idea that a child moves from a stage where location of a painful sensation outside the self serves as a defense, to a stage where increased reality testing necessitates repression. Klein places repression at that stage of cognitive development where the child can experience conflict with self-conception and seems to equate this with Balint's stage wherein the child's cognitive development has become like an adult's.

Stern (1985) addresses disavowal as part of the developmental sequence and expands its use even further. He considers a splitting of experience to occur from the beginning of life as a result of the selective attunement of parents to the child's behavior. He states: "In essence, attunement permits the parents to convey to the infant what is shareable, that is, which subjective experiences are within and which are beyond the pale of mutual consideration and acceptance. Through the selective use of attunement, the parents' intersubjective responsivity acts as a template to shape and create corresponding intrapsychic experiences in the child. It is in this way that the parents' desires, fears, prohibitions, and fantasies contour the psychic experiences of the child" (p. 208). He views this exclusion of intersubjective sharing as the earliest form of what later becomes a part of the "true self"-"false self" split, disavowal, or repression.

Stern uses Basch's definition of disavowal as the separation of felt experience from its language representation (episodic from semantic memory) to explain the existence of two versions of reality that appear with the advent of the sense of verbal self. One version, the false self, consists of those self-experiences that are enhanced because they meet the needs of someone else. The other, the true self, consists of those self-experiences that are closer to the child's naturally occurring experiences. As mentioned, this split occurs from the beginning of life, but with language the false self receives special endorsement. Stern suggests that Winnicott's concept of the true and false self which implies pathology be discarded. He suggests a terminology that includes disavowal in a normative context: "social self" instead of false self, "disavowed self" instead of "true self," and a third category, "private self," which implies certain experiences that are neither disavowed nor part of the social false self, but have nevertheless come to mean something that one does not share. The disavowed self results from the process that prevents, in Stern's words, the "lived-experience . . . true self" from becoming linguistically encoded (i.e., disavowal). Stern leaves to the clinicians the matter of maladaptation in later life as it relates to the different selves, although he does not consider the mere presence of the various selves an indication of future pathology.

In his critical review of Freud's theory of instincts and his discussion of the impersonal and instinctual, Eagle (1984) summarizes the expanded role of disavowal in theories concerned with the integration of aims into overall coordinated functioning. Eagle states:

> . . . the id-ego model, with id as instinctual "seething cauldron" and ego as controlling structure is neither accurate nor useful. What does seem useful . . . is the idea of disowned versus owned aspects of the personality. . . . The dichotomous division of personality into a structure with motivational aims . . . and a structure the function of which is to channel . . . these aims gives way to the conception of persons as attempting to carry out a variety of aims—some in conflict with each other and others

> harmoniously, some infantile and others more mature, and all with varying degrees of conscious awareness and acknowledgement of one's own aims, ranging from full conscious awareness . . . to total lack of awareness and disavowal. The development of selfhood enables one to acknowledge one's thoughts, memories, experiences, feelings, wishes . . . *as one's own.* It also permits one to . . . *disavow* . . . those "engagements" which are inimical to the maintenance of . . . self-esteem. As Fingarette and Schafer note, such disavowal is the essence of the psychoanalytic concept of defense [p. 123; Eagle's emphasis].

Eagle argues that Freud's division of an "it" and an "I" gains meaning by removing the reference to instinct and by emphasizing disavowal versus owning rather than impulse versus control. The crucial aspect of the "it" experience is not presumed instinct but the "not-me" status referred to by Sullivan. What is not experienced as part of one's self cannot be reflected upon and is therefore removed from the influence of experience or judgments. Eagle, like Klein, compares his position with Freud's earliest formulations of the splitting of consciousness. Eagle notes the consistency of Freud's concept with those of Fairbairn, Federn, Fingarette, Sullivan, G. S. Klein, and Schafer: "What all these related ideas have in common is an explicit emphasis on the integration of cognitive-affective complexes into a supraordinate structure as the core of psychic health, and *lack of integration* . . . as the core of psychopathology. In all pathology there is failure . . . to integrate conflicting sets of aims, cognitions, feelings, etc. Furthermore . . . self-cohesiveness is defined in terms of range and adequacy of integration of these cognitive-affective complexes" (p. 125; Eagle's emphasis). This same emphasis is implied in Basch's (1985) definition of narcissistic personality disorder as a disease of excessive disavowal and in Kohut's description of the prevalent personality organization of our time as the "multifragmented (vertically split), and disharmonious" (1984, p. 60) Tragic Man.

Discussion

This paper reviews the phenomenon of disavowal in order to highlight its assigned explanations. Theories of psychic structure that derive from instinct theory refer to disavowal primarily as an ego defense against external reality accomplished through an ego split and resulting in the repudiation of the meaning of a percept. Disavowal may be explained by hypothesizing an immature synthetic function of the ego, although it is not a theoretical abstraction on par with the organizing functions of the ego. By contrast, the critiques and revisions of psychoanalytic metapsychology and clinical theory in recent years, examples of which are represented here, have sought to make explanations for clinical observations more experience near and epistemologically sound. Kohut was, of course, instrumental in shifting the focus from ego psychology to a psychology of the self where the fulfillment of ideals and ambitions in the context of adequate selfobjects serves as the basis for personality organization and pathology (Kohut, 1984). In Kohut's self psychology disavowal refers to the process that maintains split-off archaic self-selfobject relations. In Gedo's revision of clinical psychoanalytic theory personality constitutes a hierarchy of aims, represented prepsychologically and psychologically, which forms a person's self-organization. Gedo (1979) emphasizes disavowal as a typical defense during the years of self consolidation that serves to maintain the child's self-esteem. Among others, G. Klein attempted to disentangle valid clinical observations from indefensible metapsychology. Klein (1976) redefined repression as the refusal to acknowledge meaning to oneself and viewed disavowal, as all defenses, as mechanisms of repression. Stern (1985) implies that disavowal operates in a normative context during the development of a sense of verbal self to create a "disavowed self" that is separate from affective integration. He suggests that disavowed aspects of self, per se, are not indicators of future pathology.

In the theory of communication science, Basch (1973, 1976b) supports the clinical revisions of other authors with a more useful explanatory theory than Freud's metapsychology. He regards the foundation of psychological development to be the brain's function of processing and organizing affectively toned information from biological and environmental sources in a context of cognitive maturation and empathic responsiveness from others. Affectively toned predispositions to action expressed in the framework of cognitive development form the basis for motivation. In this context, disavowal has two meanings. Disavowal classifies the generic inclusion (avowal) or exclusion (dis-avowal) of affectively laden information through selective attention in the ordinary expectable service of coordinated functioning. What is avowed or disavowed influences meanings and motivation throughout life.[4] In a narrower sense, disavowal refers to the specific defense of

[4]At times the explanation for disavowal remains mixed. For example, when disavowal is considered a defense against external reality (Basch, 1983c), it remains part of a theory that maintains instinct gratification as its central assumption. Although Basch says Freud went too far when he made disavowal the counterpart of repression, he modifies the breadth of application of disavowal, not the relationship of disavowal to repression. On the other hand, the view of disavowal as a general means of preserving self-continuity (the nondefensive ordering process of the brain) seems more consistent with a model that views a perception of being "driven" as serving such self-continuity, and avowal and disavowal as organizing principles of mental life.

ignoring the meaning of an anxiety-arousing percept (Basch, 1983c). There is continuity between the explanatory theory of psychological function and the classification of disavowal as a specific pattern of defense.

An implication of the broad definition is that disavowal, when employed to screen out awareness of affectively meaningful information that would prove disruptive to self-organization, is at the root of all defense and is essentially synonymous with repression. A comparison of Basch's (1983c) and G. Klein's (1976) respective definitions of disavowal and repression may serve as an illustration. They may be compared by examining each concept's core assumptions and the relationship of the concept to the origin of the danger, quality of consciousness, and phase of cognitive development.

In the first area of comparison, disavowal and repression share the same core; the separation (dis-avowal, disowning, dissociation) of the meaning of an experience from the self in the service of protecting the person from self-discontinuity and its accompanying painful affective state. Both concepts view precluding feedback as essential to the origin and maintenance of the defense, and both imply origins of the exclusion in the infant's inborn capacity to order and selectively respond to information.

Next, it would appear that the defenses are against different dangers, since Klein states that repression is the refusal to acknowledge the meaning of one's own actions (tendency, wish, impulse) whereas Basch refers to refusal to acknowledge the meaning of an external event. Basch does, in fact, differentiate disavowal and repression by identifying the origin of the danger (external reality versus instinct) as well as by differentiating the method of exclusion from self-awareness (semantic or episodic memory being dissociated). Yet in both views the important parameter of self-consistency remains constant. If the "event" that is blocked from meaning is either one's own actions or actions originating outside the person, then origin of the danger ceases to be a distinguishing factor.

The quality of consciousness is a third area of possible comparison between disavowal and repression. Basch equates disavowal with awareness of the fact of the event and repression with forgetting. In his clinical examples, he notes that disavowal may persist after repression has been lifted. Klein specifically separates repression from the quality of consciousness, making possible the conscious awareness of a repressed idea. In fact, Klein states that consciousness may be enlisted in the service of repression. (Actually, Basch seems to agree with this, when he states that disavowal may serve to maintain repression.) Once repression is defined as a conscious idea, the meaning of which has been disowned, the difference between repression and disavowal disappears.

Mode of cognition is one area of comparison that differentiates disavowal from repression. Klein suggests that repression occurs with the advent of an "increased sense of reality," and equates this with the stage where the child can experience conflict with self-conception and adult-like thought (p. 301). He notes a previous stage where the child simply locates the problem outside himself, but he does not distinguish this from repression. Basch contributes a more considered explanation of the evolution of the defensive processes that occur as cognitive development and stability of self-continuity proceed, when he states that disavowal blocks sensorimotor from preoperational thought at an early phase of self formation where as repression blocks preoperational from concrete cognition when a more stable self has been formed. The difference between repression and disavowal appears to reside in the available mode of cognition at the time of the occurrence of a threatening event.

As disavowal is assigned its narrower meaning as a specific defense, the emphasis on mode of cognition is most pertinent. From a developmental viewpoint, cognitive maturation determines the specific modes available for the selective attention to affectively charged information in the service of preserving overall goal-directed functioning. The earliest form may be withdrawal of any attention. Over subsequent years there may be failure to encode action patterns as language or a variety of symbolic transformations of meaning. Of particular interest has been the separation of symbolically encoded patterns of expectation (i.e., feelings) from their significance when taken together. Such a phenomenon wherein a person may "know" and "not know" simultaneously in the service of avoiding the implications of full awareness is often associated within a developmental context particularly connected to the period of life between the middle of the second and the third years. Discussions of the consolidation of the self have classified disavowal as a typical defense during that time (Gedo, 1979; Gedo and Goldberg, 1953), and the occurrence of disavowal as an important phenomena in the transference has been associated with the reconstruction of preoedipal self pathology (Basch, 1985).

Using the evidence of infants' goal-directed organized behavior from birth and the cognitive psychology of Piaget, Basch (1977) proposes a maturation of defensive processes. The first defense is withdrawal from stimulation ("denial" in Freud's sense of withdrawal of cathexis from reality). Primal repression is the mode of defense at the earliest stages of the capacity for symbol formation (self concept), and it occurs by blocking the sensorimotor action-schemata from symbolic representation. Repression proper is the mode of defense used when concrete operations and a more solid self preclude the child from allowing illogical percepts to consciously exist side-by-side. Between primal repression and repression proper, disavowal operates by ignoring the meaning to the self of a potentially anxiety-provoking percept. In other words, these defenses are all ways of screening information and controlling affect to facilitate the maintenance of the self, made more sophisticated by the development of cognitive capacities.

Basch (1983a) describes some typical presentations by patients that correspond to his conceptualizations of primal repression, disavowal, and repression. He describes patients with primal repression (inability to link words with affect) as those who respond to something in the analytic situation or to the analyst, but who display only an increased tension state, and otherwise "feel nothing." These patients must be treated by helping them to scrutinize their reactions so that they can eventually learn to symbolize their affective states. Patients who use disavowal are portrayed as rather dull and intellectualized, speaking words without much affect. These patients require the analyst's active engagement to create anxiety and mobilize the appropriate affects. Patients in whom repression plays the dominant role come into analysis with a "pressure of affect," and the analyst need only avoid interfering with the unfolding transference.

Basch (1983c) also illustrates a variety of presentations of repression and disavowal. In discussing a neurotic patient, for example, he states that it is not uncommon to find disavowal mobilized in the service of maintaining a repression. He states that in such patients interpretation of the repressed conflict is all that is necessary for the disavowal to be automatically resolved. Elsewhere in the same paper, however, he notes that even after a repression is lifted it may be necessary to work through the disavowed meaning of the memory. Disavowal may also be used as a defense against the development or exploration of a transference. Finally, disavowal may result in a developmental arrest, as in the case of parent loss where the meaning of the loss has not been experienced.

Basch's clinical descriptions of primal repression, repression, and disavowal illuminate questions about how one recognizes and differentiates these phenomena in the clinical situation, where it may be quite difficult to isolate a patient's inability to acknowledge a complex of emotions as a failure to form symbols for one or many experiences, exclusion from awareness of aspects of current or past experience through symbolic transformation, or minimizing the relationship of events or feelings. Is it true that patients who disavow the meaning of an event (or set of experiences, or an aspect of their own behavior) present without a sense of tension or pressure and that anxiety must be induced through confrontation by the analyst as the first step in undoing the disavowal? When a patient is asked and honestly reports no feeling about an event (despite having demonstrated behavior that would lead one to expect otherwise), how is one to know if this is disavowal or if the patient really has no word for the experience? It may be hard for the patient to know if there is a word for the experience, because to know the word is to initiate the process of inner speech, interfering with the disavowal. When the patient is able to describe the experience with associated emotion, has a disavowal been undone or has a new concept emerged where there was none? Following Freud, Basch (1983c) states that all defense is against affect and that the meaning of an event, "the dispositional power of the percept," is determined by the affect mobilized (p. 146). However, what seems to be missing in patients using disavowal is not affect, but its dispositional effect; that is, the power of affect to move the patient to act in an overall self-consistent fashion. It may be that interpretation is directed at helping the patient tolerate the tension state long enough to consider the implications of the connection between two, separated aspects of the patient's life, and not at mobilizing affect.

In a paper on the development of empathic understanding, Basch (1983b) described a progression from affect (described as an autonomic response and by definition unconscious), to feeling (affect plus symbolic representation), to emotion (a mixture of many feelings existing in a particular context at a particular time). Ultimately, it is the emotion aroused by an experience that determines what a person thinks or does, not solely the presence of an affective response. Using this progression, one might extend Basch's thoughts to say that disavowal protects against the full appreciation of the complex relationship of many feelings in context which, if appreciated, would lead to anxiety. That is, primal repression blocks affect from feeling, and disavowal blocks feeling from emotion. Repression also blocks feelings from emotion, but it does so in another way because the more solidly integrated self (and more mature cognitive functioning) will not allow incongruous feelings to exist consciously side by side.

This formulation of disavowal would still fit into the same developmental stage, where symbolic representation has occurred. It would allow for the fact that some patients using disavowal may have "pressure of affect." Such patients do indeed require active confrontation and involvement by the analyst, but not so much to generate affect as to call attention to the fact that the patient is refusing to acknowledge the relatedness of a variety of feelings. Furthermore, it would more closely coincide with Kohut's and Schafer's concepts, which emphasize two aspects of the patient existing side by side with both aspects containing thoughts and associated affective states, and would avoid the equation of disavowal and "isolation of affect" or "flat affect."

Finally, insofar as disavowal is explained broadly as an organizing function of the brain related to the development and maintenance of continuity of function and as a specific means to maintain self-organization in extraordinary circumstances, it serves as a useful bridge between the psychoanalytic theory of development and defenses and the study in other areas of science of the circumstances and consequences of events in which integration of affectively laden information is facilitated or foreclosed. Many of the authors cited in this review illustrate the value of experimental evidence in child development, affect, and cognition for an understanding of disavowal as a phenomenon of development and defense. Psychoanalysts who witness the rich tapestry of integrations and exclusions that form personality and influence adaptation are in a special position to offer refinements to the experimental study of factors influencing development. In this way, mutual contributions are possible that may modify or validate the knowledge in psychoanalysis and developmental psychology.

REFERENCES

Basch, M. F. (1973), Psychoanalysis and theory formation. *This Annual,* 1:39–52. New York: International Universities Press.

——— (1974), Interference with perceptual reality in the service of defense. *This Annual,* 2:87–97. New York: International Universities Press.

——— (1976a), The concept of affect: A re-examination. *J. Amer. Psychoanal. Assn.,* 24:759–777.

——— (1976b), Psychoanalysis and communication science. *This Annual,* 4:385–421. New York: International Universities Press.

——— (1977), Developmental psychology and explanatory theory in psychoanalysis. *This Annual,* 5:229–263. New York: International Universities Press.

——— (1979), Mind, self, and dreamer. In: *Sexual Excitement: Dynamics of Erotic Life,* ed. R. J. Stoller. New York: Pantheon Books, pp. 224–231.

——— (1981), Psychoanalytic interpretation and cognitive transformation. *Internat. J. Psycho-Anal.,* 62:151–175.

——— (1983a), Interpretation: Toward a developmental model. Presented at the Sixth Annual Conference of the Psychology of the Self. Los Angeles, October 8–9.

——— (1983b), Empathic understanding: A review of the concept and some theoretical considerations. *J. Amer. Psychoanal. Assn.,* 31:101–126.

——— (1983c), The perception of reality and the disavowal of meaning. *This Annual,* 11:125–153. New York: International Universities Press.

——— (1985), Psychosis and failure of cognitive development. Discussion of plenary session, Eighth Annual Conference on the Psychology of the Self. New York, October 4.

Eagle, M. (1984), *Recent Developments in Psychoanalysis: A Critical Evaluation.* New York: McGraw-Hill.

Gedo, J. (1979), *Beyond Interpretation.* New York: International Universities Press.

——— & Goldberg, A. (1973), *Models of the Mind.* Chicago: University of Chicago Press.

Klein, G. S. (1976), *Psychoanalytic Theory.* New York: International Universities Press.

Kohut, H. (1971), *The Analysis of the Self.* New York: International Universities Press.

——— (1977), *The Restoration of the Self.* New York: International Universities Press.

——— (1984), *How Does Analysis Cure?* Chicago: University of Chicago Press.

Lichtenberg, D. L., & Slap, J. W. (1973), Notes on the concept of splitting and the mechanism of the splitting of representations. *J. Amer. Psychoanal. Assn.,* 21:772–787.

Ornstein, P. (ed.) (1978), *The Search for the Self,* vol. 1. New York: International Universities Press.
Schafer, R. (1968), *Aspects of Internalization.* New York: International Universities Press.
Stern, D. (1985), *The Interpersonal World of the Infant.* New York: Basic Books.

October 1986

The Emotional Implications of Learning Disabilities: A Theoretical Integration

BENJAMIN GARBER, M.D. (Chicago)

I. Introduction

For years child psychiatrists and psychoanalysts were divided into two camps, those who felt that psychotherapy and/or psychoanalysis could cure all learning problems and those who felt that the presence of organic factors precluded psychological intervention (Giffin, 1968).

The psychoanalytic literature about the learning process and its interferences has been sporadic in recent years as most of the significant studies were published prior to 1970. In the 1950s and 1960s the prevailing impression in the psychoanalytic literature was that most interferences with learning were psychologically based (Pearson, 1952).

Since the last ten to twenty years have brought an increasing appreciation of the heterogeneity of neurologically based learning deficits (Hallahan and Cruickshank, 1973) there has been a corresponding diminution in psychologically oriented research. With the increased emphasis on the neurological determinants of learning disabilities, developmental and educational psychologists have come to the forefront of the important research on learning. While pediatricians and pediatric neurologists have maintained an important role in the diagnosis and treatment of the learning-disabled child, psychiatrists and psychoanalysts have drifted into the background.

It is equally significant that behaviorists, and educators steeped in behavior-modification techniques, have been dominant in the work with learning-disabled children (Hallahan and Cruickshank, 1973).

If that is indeed the wave of the recent past as well as the present, then it is understandable why psychoanalysts, who are preoccupied with the deeper motivations of learning, have had a negligible impact on this field. It is also plausible that the learning experience of the child, which is constantly being assessed and monitored by means of grades and testing scores, would not be congenial to the more personal scrutiny of the psychoanalytically oriented observer. In spite of the secondary position in the area of learning disabilities that these deeper motivations have assumed, there is a rich heritage of psychoanalytic research which is crucial to the understanding of the emotional sequelae of learning interferences.

II. Review of the Psychoanalytic Literature on Learning Disabilities

One of the earliest psychoanalytic studies of reading disabilities was described by Blanchard (1946). She concluded that there was no single situation or personality maladjustment which could be isolated to explain the development of a reading disability. She felt that a complexity of factors came together in a focal point around reading, particularly where the disability had an emotional origin. In this respect the neurotic reading disability conforms to the psychoanalytic concept of neurotic symptoms as being overdetermined.

In a discussion of reading disabilities of a nonneurotic etiology Blanchard called attention to the impression that the attitudes of parents and teachers often exaggerate the problem until it grows into a real disability. The latter point is exceptionally significant because it implies the possibility that reading disabilities in the child can be induced and perpetuated beyond the point at which the child is actually disabled.

Gerald Pearson (1952), in an extensive survey of learning difficulties, noted the marked increase in learning problems which were screened by educators and subsequently referred for psychiatric and/or psychoanalytic evaluation. While Pearson considered a segment of learning difficulties due to organic factors he felt that a diminished capacity to learn was a problem of ego psychology. Consequently, he detailed the various factors that inhibit learning in the ego itself, those which result from the influence of the external world on the ego as well as those influences which may emanate from the superego or the id. While Pearson was exceptionally thorough and complete in touching on the whole range of learning interferences, he dealt with learning problems as an intrapsychic conflict with only a passing reference to external precipitants. Nevertheless, Pearson's work is probably the first attempt by a psychoanalyst to understand the whole range of learning disabilities from a psychoanalytic perspective.

One of the earliest efforts to relate specific psychopathology in the parent with learning difficulties in the child was elaborated by Hellman (1954). Her clinical observations were based on mothers who had difficulties in testing reality and to compensate for this deficit resorted to compulsive lying and deliberate withholding of secrets from their children. The children then proceeded to create an appearance of stupidity by an identification with the mother's symptoms.

Jarvis (1958) proposed that a reading disability is a displaced attempt to solve an oedipal problem that is complicated by a strong scoptophilic instinct and a confusion of father and mother roles. While derivatives of oral and anal impulses are noted in reading it is important to keep in mind how easily the reading situation can be associated with dangerous objects in the oedipal constellation.

DeHirsch (1963), who has made some outstanding contributions to the association between learning disabilities and language deficits, presented one of the earliest studies of learning disabilities in adolescents. DeHirsch described two categories of intelligent adolescents with severe learning difficulties who were quite different from each other.

In group A the academic difficulty was related to ego impairment and a manifestation of a severe character disorder indicating a primary learning disability. In group B scholastic dysfunction was secondary to residual language deficiencies and psychological problems; difficulties in school were the result rather than the cause of the disability.

This paper is significant because it attempts to delineate the heterogeneous nature of learning deficits and it recognizes the presence of learning disabilities in adolescents.

Giovachini (1963) detailed some exceptionally insightful dynamics about the various parent-child interactions that contribute to learning problems in the child. Giovachini indicated,

> If the external world does not supply the gratifying experience that leads to learning at a time when the physical apparatus has acquired the ability to master certain skills, a deficit occurs which is reflected in the structure of the ego and later in character structure [p. 279].

Giovachini (1963) then goes on to delineate the specific interactional matrix which contributes to the child's sense of defectiveness:

> If the child cannot do something, he feels furious and anxious and may express this in temper tantrums, he then expects his mother to come to the rescue. He will not attempt to learn anything that he cannot do since he is used to his mother doing for him whatever he cannot do himself. When he is with her he has the feeling that he can do anything

> without even trying. He cannot assess his own ability or his own strength, and not knowing his own strength or weakness makes it impossible to use that of others. The child who feels all-powerful cannot learn because learning itself is an admission of not knowing, an admission of weakness. He is dependent on his mother in the function that she has taken over for him and this results in a defective ego function of the child. His learning ability, one of his most important ego functions, has been crippled and is defective and disturbed [p. 281].

Although the psychoanalytic literature on the parental response to learning disabilities has been sparse, one of the more thorough papers on this subject was written by Edith Buxbaum (1964). In this study she addresses the parental role in the etiology of learning disorders.

Buxbaum points out that the literature on learning difficulties is almost exclusively concerned with intrapsychic processes and conflicts, while the interpersonal conflicts of childhood are only implicitly considered as contributing to the problem. Yet for some time analysts have been aware of the fact that parents participate in a most important way in the etiology of learning difficulties. Buxbaum then goes on to generalize that the child who suffers a functional deficiency of the kind described by her is often unable to learn in school. His inability to function independently carries over into the area of academic learning. She then concludes that an all-pervasive learning difficulty constitutes a disturbed ego function which is based upon a partially symbiotic relationship between mother and child.

While Buxbaum's (1964) study is more interactional than previous psychoanalytic works, it still does not account for the mother-child interaction in those instances where a learning disability is neurologically based.

One of the first psychoanalysts who attempted to integrate organic deficits and psychopathology in the learning-disabled child was Rappaport (1961, 1966). He also tried to understand learning disabilities by means of ego-psychological principles. Rappaport (1961) focused on the brain-damaged child and emphasized that damage to the neural tissue does not play the major role in either learning failure or behavioral problems. The early insult to the integrity of the central nervous system may bring about deficiencies in the primary ego apparatuses. The child whose basic ego functions such as perception, concept formation, motility, and language are not fully developed at the appropriate time will then experience major difficulties in interacting with his environment in an adaptive manner. Rappaport's contribution emphasized an important shift from a circumscribed organic orientation to a more psychologically focused understanding of brain damage.

In a 1966 article Rappaport notes that the ego functions are adversely affected if the central nervous system is not intact and is not maturing in a normal and even manner. A disturbance in such functions as motility and perception leads to an inadequate development of ego functions. The child's attempts at mastery of various tasks leads to frustration rather than to a sense of accomplishment. Instead of building up self-esteem his activities produce an attitude of self-derision. The child's activities and accomplishments do not stimulate a parental sense of pride; instead they cause the parents to experience anxiety and frustration which may then lead to rejection and overprotection. For the learning-disabled child the feelings within himself and the responses from others mold a concept of an insecure and threatening world. His concept of himself is that of an inept person who does not receive the normal satisfaction of recognition, achievement, or affection.

A study by Dudek and Lester (1968) in which they explored the personality dynamics and cognitive functioning of chronic underachievers by means of the Rorschach Test and the Wechsler Intelligence Scale yielded the following conclusions:

1. The core area of anxiety in these latency-age children centered around the handling of aggressive impulses.
2. The typical defenses in dealing with aggression was a retreat into passivity, compliance, reaction-formation, and a characteristic "good child persona."
3. Underachievers experienced a blocking of oral-aggressive energy.
4. Intellectual functioning was uneven, showing deficits in the areas of attention and concentration.
5. Those abilities which depended more on motivation and acquisition of learning skills tended to be weak (i.e., arithmetic, general information).
6. Chronic underachievers did not do well in psychotherapy.

Dudek and Lester (1968) concluded on the basis of the various publications that there would be considerable evidence for the presence of an underachievement syndrome which is characterized by poor motivation, passive resistance to authority, difficulties with constructive self-assertion, a depreciated self-concept, and a generally depressive attitude toward the world.

One of the earliest studies in the psychoanalytic literature dealing with outcome and prognosis with learning-disabled children was described by Giffin (1968). Using an ego-psychological point of view Giffin concluded the following:

"Insofar as children with learning disabilities have poor perceptual and other organic problems the child by definition has an ego defect. Training, experience and motivation will compensate in part for this defect but probably never entirely overcome this ego deficiency" (p. 78). While this is a rather strong statement about prognosis it nevertheless has a certain validity. Psychotherapists have often described adults who are successful in most areas of their life yet exhibit a circumscribed cognitive deficit. These deficits may range from an inability to balance a checkbook, getting confused and lost in a new locale, or being unable to pronounce or spell common, everyday words.

Some of the more recent psychoanalytic work on learning disabilities includes a study by Berger and Kennedy (1975). They described a number of children who were treated for a type of pseudobackwardness which made them seem retarded. These children were not unusual or different except for the fact that their mothers lacked a sense of pride and pleasure in the child, which was accompanied by a complete lack of admiring approval from the parents. One of the prominent dynamics was that the parents unconsciously needed the particular child to be stupid or ignorant; the child then responded by conforming to the parental need in order to preserve their love. In most of the cases described, the mothers were strikingly ambivalent toward the child and had an intense need to denigrate him or her. Some of the mothers had fantasies about producing a damaged child and subsequently they were fearful about the child's limited intelligence even though there was no objective basis for such anxiety. Consequently, any minor deviation in the child was seized upon as a source of excessive preoccupation and concern.

In some instances the mother assigned a specific role to her child who was perceived as an inadequate and damaged product. The children appeared to be unusually compliant in accepting the role that was assigned to them by their mothers.

Berger and Kennedy (1975) concluded that while the functioning of these children improved substantially with treatment considerable vulnerability in the area of self-confidence and self-esteem remained.

DeHirsch (1975) addressed herself to the pitfalls and problems that may emerge from the indiscriminate labeling of children with language deficits. All the diagnostic labels—underachievement, learning disability, minimal brain injury, arrested ego development—have some essential validity. None of them, however, take into account the complex interactions between the psychological and the physiological aspects of functioning, interactions which are crucially affected by the emotional climate in the child's home.

Abrams (1970) in discussing some common dynamics of the learning-disabled child described how parents, who have been disappointed in their child's achievements, exacerbate the problem because of their great anxiety to alleviate the condition. When the child is not functioning in accordance with the expectations of the parents then he becomes a threat to the parental narcissism rather than the wished for extension of themselves.

In a further elaboration of the above position, Abrams and Kaslow (1976) indicated that parents may, either explicitly or implicitly, desire offspring who possess all the characteristics that they admire in themselves and who will not have the traits that they dislike in themselves. There is usually some disparity between the parent's dream child and their actual child. The child with a learning disability may accentuate such a discrepancy and consequently disrupt the whole familial gestalt.

In these papers by Abrams (1970) and Abrams and Kaslow (1976) there is a striking emphasis on parental narcissism as a major contributing element to the learning-disabled child's psychopathology.

From the early beginnings of psychoanalytic interest in learning problems it has been assumed that a diminished capacity to learn was a problem of ego psychology (Pearson, 1952). Since the early 1950s were considered the period of flowering of ego psychology in psychoanalytic theorizing (Hartmann, 1950, 1952; Hartmann, Kris and Loewenstein, 1949), it is not surprising that the initial considerations of problems in learning would be influenced and shaped by an ego-psychological point of view. It is plausible that the meshing of psychoanalysis and experimental psychology would be strengthened by means of the natural bridge which is afforded by problems in learning. Since various ego functions such as perception, language, concept formation, memory, and motility are the foundations upon which the learning process is built, then a learning deficit would be represented by the impairment of such functions.

While the ego-psychological approach was inherently useful up to a point, it eventually led to a blind alley of theoretical understanding and clinical applicability. The enumeration of multiple ego-functions and the isolation of which ones might be affected by a learning disability did not contribute to a deeper understanding of the clinical problems. Since so many functions are affected by a learning disability a therapeutic approach would have to extend beyond such sterile listings. The therapeutic understanding would need to encompass the totality of the limitations and their impact on the developmental progression of the child. Consequently, a parallel line of psychoanalytic inquiry into learning disabilities addressed itself to the etiology of nonneurologically based problems and explored the impact of the primary caretakers in the etiology of learning deficits. Such an approach allowed for the exploration of the interactional matrix between parent and child which provided a fertile ground for the formation of a learning disability. In other words what was it that motivated the child and the parents to engage in the type of interactions that resulted in a learning inhibition? While such explorations were global in nature and did not possess the seeming precision that is implied by ego psychology, they were more congenial and experientially consonant with a clinical orientation. That is why the studies of Blanchard (1946), Hellman (1954), Giovacchini (1963), Buxbaum (1964), and Berger and Kennedy (1975) possess a psychodynamic orientation that seemed inherently useful in attempting to understand certain youngsters with learning deficits.

Only the recent clinical studies of Abrams (1970, 1980) and Abrams and Kaslow (1976) have begun to consider the impact of the child's learning problems on parental narcissism.

Estelle Shane (1984) picks up on this point in an attempt to understand just what goes wrong between the learning-disabled child and his parents. She notes that a parent who is in good empathic contact with the child can sense when he can achieve for himself and when he needs just the right amount of help. The child thus learns when it is reasonable to expect to accomplish on his own and when it is appropriate, without a sense of shame or humiliation, to ask for and expect help from others. The child is capable of functioning without the mother's physical presence since he is self-confident, reasonably tolerant of himself and his occasional need for help, and able to expect success and to endure failure. He is a child with adequate self-esteem and an adequate capacity to attend to the learning process.

Shane (1984) addresses herself to the dynamics of those children who do not possess innate limitations but have not been either empathically mirrored or optimally disillusioned and who may seek constant gratification for their grandiosity. Such a youngster is so archaically self-centered that he does not recognize or appreciate the competing needs and rights of others in an age-appropriate fashion. He is unable to take another's point of view or exercise minimal empathy for another child. In school he may persist in his grandiose fantasy in which he omnipotently attains his ambitions without acquiring the necessary skills for realistic success.

III. The Impact of the Learning-Disabled Child on Parental Narcissism

In order to gauge the depth of the parental narcissistic injury from a child who is learning disabled it is essential to examine the psychoanalytic literature that has dealt to some extent with learning interferences and the varieties of psychopathology that may be a part of as well as the expression of a learning problem. There is very little in the literature about the psychological reverberations of a neurologically based learning disorder.

What is the impact on the child and the parent once a learning disability is diagnosed? What is the nature of the interactional process between parent and child from the very beginning of life and specifically when the child begins formal education? What transpires between parent and child during the period of indefiniteness when neither teachers, parents, nor psychologists are absolutely certain that the child is educationally impaired?

In order to approach such questions we need to examine some of the psychoanalytic research that has addressed itself to the psychological implications for the parent when there is a suspicion that the child may be damaged and the deficit becomes substantiated. Some parents may suspect within the first few months that something is wrong with the child. Consequently, the parents fluctuate between seeing the child as damaged or intact. While at times the parental suspicions of a deficit are indeed accurate there are other times when the parents project the damaged aspects of themselves onto the child.

The bulk of the psychoanalytic literature about parental reactions to a damaged child has focused on the initial disappointment, followed by rage and then a persistent ambivalence which is transformed into a chronically depressive state.

The psychological preparation for a new child during pregnancy normally involves the wish for a perfect child and the fear of a damaged child. It is very likely that there is always some discrepancy between the mother's wishes and the actual child. To work out and come to terms with this discrepancy becomes one of the major tasks in the establishment of a healthy mother-child relationship. However, when the discrepancy is too great, as in the birth of a defective or damaged child or where the mother's wishes are too unrealistic, a trauma may occur.

The parental image of the expected child is a composite of the representations of the self and of various love objects: mother, husband, father, and siblings. This composite representation includes the image of the expected child which has been conveyed to the mother by her own mother.

Although most learning-disabled children are "normal" in the early years, since by definition a learning disability is not diagnosed until the child enters school, a number of parents may experience the uneasy feeling that the child was not right from the beginning. In many instances, when the child starts nursery school and kindergarten, teachers may comment that the potentially learning-disabled child is different. However, the observations defy specificity and consequently they contribute to parental anxiety and dread.

When parents are informed that their child has a learning disability their initial reaction is one of shock and disbelief, although they will ultimately concede that on some level they sensed that the child was different before he started school. After the shock and disbelief there sets in a feeling of hopelessness, sadness, and loss. Some authors have described this as a mourning process for the perfect child. The most common parental psychological response (Solnit and Stark, 1961) has been an initial grieflike reaction in which the parents mourn the loss of the idealized image of the perfect child.

It may well be that in some instances the parents experienced a sense of relief once the diagnosis was made. The years of tension, suspicion, and not knowing were finally swept aside as the problem was clarified and focused. Since the diagnosis served as an organizer, purposeful remediation can now be pursued. However, this type of relief is short-lived as the parents became anxious about the prognosis and outcome.

Trout (1983) has placed great emphasis on the impression that the parent, who finds out that the child is handicapped, will engage in a chronic mourning process for the perfect child that has been fantasized. This ongoing mourning process, which is manifested by a depressive state, is confusing because the parent is mourning for something or somebody who was never seen but only imagined. Such vagueness and lack of clarity as to just who or what is being mourned contribute to a sense of confusion and embarrassment in the parent.

Olshansky (1962) describes chronic sorrow and grief as a natural reaction and not a neurotic one to the realization that a handicapped child has been born instead of a normal one. Such grief is a part of the experience of the other fantasized perfect child. The loss of the narcissistically invested or perfect child and the simultaneous demand to adapt to the defective child constitute a conflict which has the potential of being overwhelming.

Fajardo (1983) has added another dimension to our understanding of the rage, ambivalence, and chronic depression often experienced by the parents of damaged children. According to the self-psychological perspective the damaged child is a disappointing selfobject for the parents. The author envisions the massive disappointment and ensuing depression or rage in parenting a defective child as a serious interference to the transformation of narcissism which is normally and expectably an outcome of parenthood. Fajardo makes the rather cogent point that the overwhelming disappointments of parenting these children may precipitate self-fragmentation in the parent who must be vulnerable to some degree to such an assault on the self.

The various studies that have been cited tend to agree that the presence of a damaged and defective child can have a profound psychological impact on the parental sense of competence and well-being. Not only is this impact relevant to the parental sense of stability but it can also be destabilizing to the familial equilibrium. The depth of the impact may relate to the severity of the child's damage so that one may not necessarily equate a learning disability with mental retardation or a serious physical illness. Nevertheless, for parents who are exceptionally invested in the child's scholastic performance, a learning disability may become unconsciously equated with a cancerous growth.

IV. Psychodynamic Integration

Since the dynamic forces that permeate human interactions are so complex and subtle, an attempt to reduce a psychopathological configuration to one pivotal interaction is at best a gross oversimplification. The dynamic interchanges between parent and child in their multiple shifts and variable fluctuations encompass such a complex network of interactions that they defy easy patterning. Nevertheless, there may be certain recurrent interactional trends that do stand out from the all-encompassing matrix of parent-child interchange. Such an interaction may not necessarily be the most prevalent one, yet it seems to convey an intense valence as well as a rather unique significance. Such an interaction may elicit a high level of recognition because it tends to explain a variety of behaviors which on the surface do not appear to be related, yet on a deeper level seem to be internally consistent.

Why a particular dynamic formulation would take precedence over other equally appropriate formulations is difficult to answer except by the subjective sense that it seems to fit and to explain the clinical problem more thoroughly. Although clinicians embrace those formulations that are fashionable as well as those that are espoused by respected teachers and fellow clinicians, a particular formulation has to contain nevertheless a certain inherent appeal in its explanatory potential.

The learning problems of children with emotional difficulties have been studied in the past using the more traditional psychoanalytic formulations. Ego-psychological approaches have been used to explain the inherent deficits of the learning-disabled child since the limitation-of-function approach possessed the highest explanatory power. The inability to utilize effectively one's cognitive skills, the inability to compete age appropriately with peers contributed to a lowering of self-esteem. The frustration and subsequent rage with parents for not providing the necessary skills, with teachers for making demands, with peers for being better, and with oneself for not being able "to do it" contributed to a feeling of guilt and a further accentuation of the depressed state. These children then resorted to a passive-aggressive interactional style and/or became overly compliant in an attempt to diffuse the smoldering hostility. Specific learning blocks in and around the symbolic meaning of "knowing" about sexual matters also interfered with learning. The symbolism denoted by various subjects, numbers, and letters added another dynamic dimension to learning problems. As the contributing elements of the learning disability were traced to parents and teachers the interpersonal aspects of the learning problem were then recognized (Buxbaum, 1964; Berger and Kennedy, 1975).

With the more recent studies of Abrams (1980) and Shane (1984) psychoanalytic workers have begun to appreciate the profound impact of narcissistic injuries on the genesis of the learning-disabled child's psychopathology. The parental narcissism that becomes so invested in the child's learning and, by extension, the child's own narcissism as an individual and a student become the interactional matrix from which much of the subsequent psychopathology originates.

While the infant is dependent on parental love, caretaking and nurture, with maturation he enters interactions with other adults in which he depends on emotional responses that are far more complex and intricate. Whenever the child achieves a developmental milestone, masters a new skill, or learns in school, there is a powerful sense of pleasure and pride in the new accomplishment. There is the wish to share the feeling with parents as a means of validation as well as a means of prolonging the good feelings. Kohut (1971) described such an interaction as the gleam in the "mother's eye" or a mirroring of the child's sense of pleasure and excitement.

In his excited and grandiose state the child will idealize the parent who is reflecting and mirroring his every move and accomplishment.

Not only does the child seek the appropriate parental response, but he is also looking for some validation of his accomplishment and the parental pleasure in his growth and progression. To the growing organism such parental joy and pleasure usually signify that he is indeed ready and capable of progressing and moving ahead. So that when the child examines the parent's face for the pleasure and approval that he wishes to share he is also looking for the implicit permission and reassurance to move ahead and to master new skills. If the child should fail or be less than successful, then he will keep trying again and again, for such is the developmental imperative or perhaps the self-propelled nature of the instinct of mastery.

When the child attempts to move forward, checks back at the parent's face, and happens to notice sadness, indifference, anxiety, or concern, he may experience a reaction quite different from the one described previously. He may hesitate and wonder how and why his doing something different is causing his parent's anxiety or distress.

When the child is placed in a position of uncertainty he will invariably look up to the mother to read her face and to get a secondary appraisal. If she smiles the child crosses over the edge of uncertainty but if she looks frightened the child retreats, and may get upset. The mother's affective state determines and modifies the child's affective state (Stern, 1985).

If the parental response is less than enthusiastic, or if it is perfunctory while the parent is distracted or preoccupied with other matters, then the child will sense this and react with disappointment. If the parental response to the child's accomplishments is one of "it's ok" or it is "pretty good" instead of an unqualified "good," then the child will also react with an inner sense that he did not measure up to the parental expectations. Even if the parent uses the right words, as most parents insist that they do, the facial expression may be far more indicative of the true response.

At this time there will emerge the beginnings of the child's sense of disappointment and disillusionment with himself and his own performance. Since he may not know exactly what is not working, he will experience a sense of perplexity about why the previous good feelings are gone or at least do not possess the same pleasurable intensity.

The overly compliant child may choose to fail because he interprets this to be the maternal expectation. Even when the child succeeds he will return and check back (Mahler, 1963) with the mother as to whether she has the confidence or the trust in his moving ahead and doing well the next time. If he is unable to read the mother or to determine her response he will become more anxious and will then develop direct and indirect methods of eliciting her true reactions to his accomplishments.

The recent work of Bryan (1974, 1977), Bryan and Bryan (1981), and Garber (in press) suggest that children with learning disabilities have not only problems reading books but also rather serious problems reading the reactions and responses of others. Because of this inability, which may stem from cognitive limitations, the learning-disabled child is often observed to be self-centered, callous, and insensitive to the feelings of others. It can be concluded that the learning-disabled child is grossly deficient in his empathic skills.

The learning-disabled child will encounter greater difficulties in determining the true parental response because of certain cognitive limitations within himself. The child's primary obstacle may be his inability to sense, to question, and then to assess the true nature of the parental reply.

When the child is unable to determine how the parent sees and feels about him, he resorts to indirect questions, or acts in ways that are inappropriate or bizarre, since he knows that such questions or behaviors will elicit a predictable, reliable, and for him calming response. Adults interpret such behaviors as bids for attention but they are not; they are indirect attempts to determine how the other person sees him and how he or she feels about him and his progress. The learning-disabled child will engage in similarly inappropriate behavior in school in an attempt to test and to make sense out of an unfathomable environment. Such children are usually described as being exceptionally tense and anxious; this tension persists until such a time when the child can elicit and assess a reliable and predictable environmental response. If he cannot, the anxiety will escalate to ever higher levels until adults impose structure from without and a subsequent relief from tension.

Just the way the child becomes disillusioned with his own omnipotence and begins to recognize the limitations in restoring the good feelings from an earlier time, he also begins to experience a disappointment with the parent who is unable to make him feel good and to restore his sense of competence in school. The parent is incapable of compensating for the child's deficits. In the early phases of increasing school problems, behavioral and academic, the child will turn to the mother to restore his equilibrium with the expectation that she will intercede with teachers and make the other children comply with his demands for recognition and appreciation. However, when this is not forthcoming or when it is not long-lasting then the child realizes that in matters pertaining to school the parent has clay feet. The child may experience a similar anticipation of recognition and then deflation and disappointment with each new teacher. It is as if the parent and every teacher were put on a pedestal only to be knocked down and shattered over and over again. It should be noted that each period of idealization of the omnipotent object is accompanied by excitement while each disillusionment is accompanied by an empty, depressed state. The child will experience this as the roller-coaster phenomenon of his own moods which he is unable to modulate effectively.

Because of the learning disability certain cognitive skills as well as their associated ego functions are impaired. The child's ability to perceive, to discriminate, to interpret, and to compare complex affective states and their origins will most likely be limited. Consequently, he may not know, and he may become confused about, what he feels, what he understands, or what he should feel. Since his own perceptual apparatus and synthetic functions are not intact, he will be exceptionally vulnerable to the parental emotional states. Therefore he will internalize the parent's concerns and anxieties and proceed to make them his own. In fact he may not know or understand his own reactions to a new situation until such a time when he can check back the parental reactions and then reflect them as a part of himself. When the parent feels optimistic about the child, following a high mark on an exam, then the child will also feel excited and exuberant; when the parent becomes disappointed with the child for not completing an assignment, then the child will become depressed and see himself as inadequate. It is these fluctuations in parental confidence and trust in the child's progressive hopes and aspirations that probably constitute some of the most crucial interactions that contribute to the child's unstable sense of himself.

At this point it may be useful to digress and examine why the previously elaborated parent-child interaction has been considered so pivotal in the formation of the psychopathology. In attempting to tease out the various strands of psychopathology in such a child it was concluded that the recurrent fluctuations in mood were the most troublesome clinical phenomena. While these children might be described as experiencing a chronic depression, a more accurate assessment of their clinical state would be a combination of self-doubt and self-depreciation interspersed with periods of excitement and grandiosity.

Although the child is not a blank screen and he exerts an influence on the parental feeling state, I am addressing a situation in which a parent experiences fluctuating assessments of the child. I am describing parents who are beset with doubts, anxieties, and instabilities because of each parent's unique history.

If the situation involved these same parents and a child who did not possess the vulnerabilities of the learning-disabled child, then the abovementioned interactions would have minimal impact. All children are exposed to parental mood shifts about their present accomplishments and future aspirations; however, the learning-disabled child, because of his developmental deficits, seems to be uniquely sensitized to such fluctuations. Since the learning-disabled child is unable to distance himself and to disregard the parental insecurities, ultimately he internalizes them and makes them his own. In so doing he incorporates and re-creates the parental feeling states which he then experiences as fluctuations of his own self-esteem.

Since the child is uncomfortable with his fluctuating moods and since there may be an awareness that the stimuli for such come from others, he may often choose to withdraw and engage in solitary activity. Such isolation is not necessarily to avoid people, but it may be in the service of being less dependent and vulnerable to the moods of others.

However, the child is not a static organism for children develop, mature, and quite often they even manage to change.

So the parents in their discouraged state watch intently for signs of progress and/or signs of change; eventually the child feels that his every move is being evaluated, measured, and charted. If the child should exhibit progress then the parent will feel happy, excited, even ecstatic. It may be that this is only a temporary shift; however, it may well be that the child is changing and that the learning deficit is being overcome or perhaps it was never there in the first place. The more primitive-thinking parent may announce that due to some obscure incident the child has undergone a miraculous cure. Since development is not a linear process but rather a to and fro, a back-and-forth fluctuation of progressive and regressive trends, then the child may retreat from a recent achievement. The response of the ever-watchful parent is once again disappointment and hopelessness. Occasionally the child may regress as a means of diminishing the parental and his own excitement which may become too uncomfortable. The child may also regress in compliance with the negative side of the parental ambivalence and as a means of diminishing the parental expectations which become grossly exaggerated.

A common concern about the learning-disabled child is how well he copes with competitive issues. Given an ongoing history of school failure and failure in other areas of his life it would seem self-evident that such a youngster would not deal effectively with competitive strivings. While this is probably a valid overall appraisal, the issues are more complex than at first glance.

When the learning-disabled child is experiencing a period of stability and intactness, when he feels supported and appreciated, then his competitive strivings emerge in an age-appropriate, well-modulated manner. Whether the competitive issues are school related or interpersonal triadic confrontations, such a child is capable of dealing with winning, losing, and the accompanying anger in a relatively appropriate, nonregressive manner.

However, when the child is in a period of disequilibrium, which includes most of the school year, then his competitive feelings are dealt with by a profoundly regressed state. Since the child's self-image is one of being damaged and limited in most spheres, then being confronted with a competitive situation will elicit a position of not knowing and helplessness.

V. Summary

Based on observations of a large number of learning-disabled children I am postulating the following interactional process between such a youngster, his parents, and teachers. Because of certain narcissistic vulnerabilities, the parents of the learning-disabled child become disappointed, disillusioned, and depressed in the course of having to raise such a youngster. Their self-esteem as competent parents will be sufficiently threatened so that they will maintain a stance of confusion and uncertainty in the daily interchanges with the child. Because of the learning disability and their inflated expectations they will relate to and treat the child as an inherently damaged and defective product.

The learning-disabled child, in addition to having difficulties in school, may also have a problem in his ability to determine how other people see him, what they think of him, and how they feel about him. Consequently, he may experience problems in sensing and knowing how he feels about himself. In other words such a youngster is exceptionally vulnerable to the development of an unstable sense of self. He will then become more and more dependent on how others (i.e., parents and teachers) see him and what they think of him and his abilities. In response to such not knowing he will become extremely anxious, and/or depressed. As he internalizes the negative environmental perceptions and expectations he will resort to a variety of regressive behaviors in an attempt to bind the anxiety. If the environment mirrors him positively or feels optimistic then he will become overly excited and grandiose. The net result of such interactions is a labile emotional state.

What I am suggesting, then, is that as a result of such an interactional process between the learning-disabled child, his parents, and teachers, he may ultimately develop a chronically unstable sense of self and narcissistic psychopathology.

REFERENCES

Abrams, J. C. (1970), Parental dynamics—their role in learning disabilities. *Reading Teacher*, 23:751–760.

——— (1980), A psychodynamic understanding of the emotional aspects of learning disability. In: *Advances in Special Education Perspectives on Applications*, ed. B. K. Keogh. Greenwich, Conn.: J.A.J. Press, 2:161–178.

——— & Kaslow, V. (1976), Learning disability and family dynamics: A mutual interaction. *J. Clin. Child Psychol.*, 5:35–40.

Berger, M. & Kennedy, H. (1975), Pseudobackwardness in children: Maternal attitudes as an etiological factor. *The Psychoanalytic Study of the Child*, 30:279–307. New Haven: Yale University Press.

Blanchard, P. (1946), Psychoanalytic contributions to the problem of reading disabilities. *Psychoanalytic Study of the Child*, 11:163–189. New York: International Universities Press.

Bryan, T. H. (1974), Peer popularity in learning disabled children. *J. Learning Disabil.*, 7:621–625.

——— (1977), An observational analysis of classroom behaviors of children with learning disabilities. *J. Learning Disabil.*, 9:26–34.

——— & Bryan, J. H. (1981), Some personal and social experiences of learning disabled children. In: *Advances in Special Education: Socialization Influences on Exceptionalities,* ed. E. K. Keogh. Greenwich, Conn.: J.A.J. Press, 3:261–279.

Buxbaum, E. (1964), The parents' role in the etiology of learning disabilities. *The Psychoanalytic Study of the Child,* 19:421–447. New York: International Universities Press.

DeHirsch, K. (1963), Two categories of learning difficulties in adolescents. *Amer. J. Orthopsychiat.,* 33:87–91.

——— (1975), Language deficits in children with developmental lags. *The Psychoanalytic Study of the Child,* 30:95–125. New Haven: Yale University Press.

Dudek, S. Z. & Lester, E. D. (1968), The good child facade in chronic underachievers. *Amer. J. Orthopsychiat.,* 38:153–160.

Fajardo, B. (1983), Parenting a damaged child: Mourning, regression and disappointment. Unpublished manuscript.

Garber, B. (in press), Deficits in empathy in the learning disabled child. In: *From Motive to Meaning,* ed. K. Field, G. Wool, & B. Cohler.

Giffin, M. (1968), The role of child psychiatry in learning disabilities. In: *Progress in Learning Disabilities.* New York & London: Grune and Stratton, 1:62–82.

Giovacchini, P. (1963), Integrative aspects of object relationships. *Psychoanal. Quart.,* 32:262–285.

Hallahan, D. & Cruickshank, W. (1973), *Psychoeducational Foundations of Learning Disabilities.* Englewood Cliffs, N.J.: Prentice-Hall.

Hartmann, H. (1950), Psychoanalysis and developmental psychology. *The Psychoanalytic Study of the Child,* 5:7–17. New York: International Universities Press.

——— (1952), The mutual influences in the development of the ego and the id. *The Psychoanalytic Study of the Child,* 7:9–20. New York: International Universities Press.

——— Kris, E., & Loewenstein, R. M. (1949), Notes on the theory of aggression. *The Psychoanalytic Study of the Child,* 3/4:7–36. New York: International Universities Press.

Hellman, I. (1954), Some observations on mothers of children with intellectual inhibitions. *The Psychoanalytic Study of the Child,* 9:259–273. New York: International Universities Press.

Jarvis, B. (1958), The visual problem in reading disability. *The Psychoanalytic Study of the Child,* 13:451–470. New York: International Universities Press.

Kohut, H. (1971), *The Analysis of the Self.* New York: International Universities Press.

Mahler, M. (1963), Thoughts about development and individuation. *The Psychoanalytic Study of the Child,* 18:307–324. New York: International Universities Press.

Olshansky, S. (1962), Chronic sorrow: A response to having a mentally defective child. *Social Casework,* 43:190–193.

Pearson, G. (1952), A survey of learning difficulties in children. *The Psychoanalytic Study of the Child,* 7:332–385. New York: International Universities Press.

Rappaport, S. J. (1961), Behavior disorder and ego development in a brain injured child. *The Psychoanalytic Study of the Child,* 16:423–450. New York: International Universities Press.

——— (1966), Personality factors teachers need for relationship structure. In: *The Teacher of Brain-Injured Children: A Discussion of the Bases of Competency,* ed. W. Cruickshank. Syracuse, N.Y.: Syracuse University Press, pp. 231–248.

Shane, E. (1984), Self-psychology: A new conceptualization for the understanding of learning disabled children. In: *Kohut's Legacy: Contributions to Self-Psychology,* ed. P. Stepansky & A. Goldberg. Hillsdale, N.J.: Analytic Press, pp. 191–203.

Solnit, A. W. & Stark, M. (1961), Mourning the birth of a defective child. *The Psychoanalytic Study of the Child,* 25:523–537. New Haven: Yale University Press.

Stern, S. D. (1985), *The Impersonal World of the Infant.* New York: Basic Books.

Trout, M. D. (1983), Birth of a sick or handicapped infant: Impact on the family. Unpublished manuscript.

February 1987

Psychoanalysis and Psychotherapy: Relative Roles Reconsidered

ROBERT S. WALLERSTEIN, M.D. (San Francisco)

My intent in this presentation is to bring together two lines of intellectual interest, one theoretical and one empirical, with which I have been somewhat separately preoccupied over a thirty-year period. The theoretical concern has been with the nature of psychodynamic or psychoanalytic psychotherapy in all of its complex relationships with its psychoanalytic parentage. The empirical concern has been with the careful tracing of the therapeutic courses and outcomes, the treatment careers and the long-term, posttreatment follow-up life careers, of a cohort of 42 patients, 22 in psychoanalysis proper and 20 in other kinds of psychoanalytic psychotherapy, who comprised the patient population in our Psychotherapy Research Project of The Menninger Foundation, started in 1952 and brought to final closure with my completion in 1982 (and publication in 1986) in book form of the overall clinical accounting of these "42 Lives in Treatment."

The Psychotherapy Research Project was established within a context of the then-prevailing theory, the theory of psychoanalytic psychotherapy, as well as the theory of psychoanalysis as a therapy. I do not have the time here to review any of that theoretical context as it was reflected via the range of issues, or rather controversies, both conceptual and technical, comprised in the varying understandings at that time of the relationship among psychoanalysis and its derivative dynamic psychotherapies. If I just

Presented as a plenary address at the Boston Psychoanalytic Society and Institute Symposium on "Psychoanalysis Today: The Integration of Theory and Practice," Boston, October 20, 1983.

mention the names of Gitelson, Alexander, Fromm-Reichmann, Gill, Bibring, Rangell, Leo Stone, Anna Freud, and Edward Glover, you will no doubt at once resonate with the positions that these principal protagonists articulated in the ongoing debates on those issues during the early fifties. On another occasion, at the Rome Congress of the International Psychoanalytic Association in 1969, I undertook to review that history and the then (1969) current status of the major scientific issues in this arena. The point I tried to document in that presentation was that the very same conceptual and technical issues existed in a precisely unaltered form some fifteen years later than the original debates and position taking of the early 1950s, even when viewed in 1969 from the presumably wider standpoint of the newer clinical and theoretical knowledge of that time, and also as then collectively expressed and lived in the now worldwide (not just American) psychoanalytic community that was being canvassed. I need hardly add that today, almost another fifteen years later, with but one or two exceptions about which I cannot take the time here to digress, the same situation obtains, of the principal psychoanalytic protagonists in these discussions still holding conceptual positions that have been essentially unaffected by whatever clinical experience and/or empirical study have meanwhile accrued in our literature.

I can indicate what these continuing central questions and issues have been by stating them in the same schematic form in which I summarized them at the very end of my 1969 Rome presentation.

(1) Is there a scientific psychotherapy apart from psychoanalysis?
(2) What are the similarities and the differences between psychoanalysis and dynamic psychotherapy?
(3) How important are the differences (or the similarities)? Should the differences be blurred or should they be sharpened?
(4) What are the proper boundaries of each therapeutic modality? *or* when does "modified" psychoanalysis or psychoanalysis with parameters become psychotherapy?
(5) How are differential treatment indications determined? Is the patient fitted to the treatment, or the treatment fitted to the patient?
(6) What are the proper dividing lines across the range of psychotherapies conceptualized within the framework of psychoanalytic theory? Is the major dividing line between the expressive-uncovering therapeutic modalities (of which psychoanalysis is one) and the suppressive-supportive therapeutic modalities? Which divisions are meaningful, in theory and in practice?
(7) What is the relation of psychoanalytic to nonpsychoanalytic therapy?

Can a theory of psychoanalytic therapy extend to a psychoanalytic theory of therapy?

(8) Can derivative conflicts, can any conflicts, be substantially resolved by means short of psychoanalysis?

(9) What are our problems as psychoanalysts in doing psychotherapy?

It is within the framework of these issues and these questions that The Psychotherapy Research Project (hereafter called PRP) of The Menninger Foundation was launched in the early fifties, within a major psychiatric institution strongly committed to the psychoanalytically guided treatment of patients in need of long-term and intensive psychotherapy. The patients who came to or were brought to The Menninger Foundation usually did so because it was felt that the severity of their illness (the range of severe character problems, addictions, and perversions, as well as varieties of narcissistic and borderline states, in addition to the more severe forms of the traditional and classical psychoneuroses) required treatment within an overall sanatorium setting with its range of available hospital and day-treatment supporting resources.

Within this context, the intent of The Psychotherapy Research Project was then to follow the treatment careers, and insofar as possible, the subsequent life careers, of a cohort of patients (ultimately 42 in number), half in psychoanalysis, and half in other psychoanalytic psychotherapies—and each in the treatment deemed *clinically* indicated for him/her—from the period of their initial pretreatment, two-week-long comprehensive psychiatric evaluation, over the whole natural span of their treatments, however many years this might take, and then into planned follow-up inquiries, formally for at least several years after their treatment terminations and their (usual) return to their home communities, and with as much of an open-ended follow-up thereafter as circumstance might make possible and as our span of interested observation might last. Actually, the whole cohort of patients entered into their treatment over the span of the mid fifties; their periods of treatment ranged from as short as a half-year in the case of unanticipated treatment disruptions up to a full dozen years; they were all reached—100 percent of the research sample—for formal follow-up information at the designated two-to-three-year mark; and over a third of the patients could be followed for periods ranging from 12 to 24 years beyond their treatment terminations, four of them actually still in ongoing treatment as of this year, and some of the total observation spans up to 30 years until the time of writing of my book, *42 Lives in Treatment,* with its final clinical accounting from this project written over the year 1981–1982.

The aim of this Psychotherapy Research Project was to learn as much as possible about *what* changes actually take place in psychoanalysis and other psychoanalytically based psychotherapies (the outcome question), and *how* those changes come about or are brought about, through the interactions over time of what variables in the patient, in the therapy and the therapist, and in the evolving life situation that together codetermine those changes (the process question). How the project created and carried out a research program geared to try to answer those questions maximally has been described in detail over the now thirty-year span of this research enterprise in some six published books and monographs and close to seventy articles. None of that will (or could) be repeated here. At this point, I want only to iterate that we set up *three* overall treatment groupings—psychoanalysis, expressive psychotherapy, and supportive psychotherapy—in terms of the then-consensus in the psychoanalytic therapy literature on defining characteristics of these (discrete) therapeutic modes, together with differential indications derived from the dynamic formulations of the nature of the patients' lives, developmental history, character structure, and presenting-illness picture.

I should make clear that our psychotherapies in that setting (expressive and supportive alike), though less frequent and less intensive than psychoanalysis—usually two or three times weekly—tended to be equally long in time duration, spanning an equal number of years, and usually several hundred hours. They were also psychoanalytically conceptualized and carried out by psychoanalytically knowledgeable therapists. They were not, and this should be emphasized, the equivalent of what is usually meant by therapy, especially supportive therapy, in institutional outpatient settings. This caveat needs to be kept clearly in mind when considering later the results actually achieved with these approaches as here defined. Within this conceptual frame there were, then, three clear therapeutic modalities with distinctive technical characteristics; they were differentially indicated for different categories of patients, they worked toward differing (kinds of) goals, and they would expectedly lead to different kinds of results, different in scope and depth and different in their promise of stability and duration, because they were based on differing mechanisms of change—albeit with the caveat that in specific cases, some admixture of modality and therefore of consequent course and outcome might be appropriate.

Our project expectations within this framework were twofold: on the one hand, the relatively modest one of giving a firmer empirical evidential base to this received conceptual wisdom and, on the other hand, the more ambitious one of discerning and specifying in more accurate detail both the particular reach and limitation of the therapeutic outcome for each kind of patient appropriately treated within each of the proffered therapeutic approaches. We were also interested in the more empirical elaboration of the psychological change mechanisms operative within both the uncovering (expressive) and the "ego-strengthening" (supportive) therapeutic modes. Given this overall intent, what can we now say about the actual therapeutic processes and outcomes as assessed at this point—some thirty years after the project start—after our fullest possible study of our patient cohort across their treatments and their lives over this time span.

A first major finding was that psychoanalysis was not actually carried out in fully "classical" form with a single one of the 22 of our PRP patients recommended for and ostensibly started in analysis, if by "classical" form we mean that the therapeutic activity within the treatment hours was steadfastly and constantly focused upon the interpretive uncovering of intrapsychic meanings, a constant internally directed scrutiny of the manifest therapeutic content. Certainly, this at least partially reflects the fact that must always be borne in mind, that the patient population at The Menninger Foundation, in psychoanalysis and all, is a sicker population than the usual (psychoanalytic) population treated in the customary outpatient setting. The fact that 10 of the 22 patients in psychoanalysis required hospitalization, either just for some initial period, or initially and with readmissions as indicated, and for varying time periods ranging up to eighteen months, with all of the dimensions of hospital control and care, attests to both the difference from the usual psychoanalytic patient population as well as the substantial modification of the usual understanding of the analytic process as something focused exclusively in the private transference-countertransference interplay between just two people.

But beyond something so gross as concomitant hospitalization, there were all the other kinds of modifications of properly analytic procedure, of episodic or more prolonged sitting up, of termination by what at times became a rather prolonged "weaning process," of extra contacts either by phone or ad hoc additional hours in relation to emergencies that so often arose with so many of these patients—as well as all the other ways in which analysts can feel called upon to intervene to help patients manage their lives or to protect them against the consequences of destructive behaviors. In all, we ended by (somewhat arbitrarily) declaring 10 of our 22 patients designated for psychoanalysis as having had treatments that adhered "well enough" to the model of classical analysis, albeit with some clear departures in every instance, which were however "minimal" within the context of that group of quite sick individuals treated within the traditions and expectations of that setting. (Certainly in other settings, and with more "usual" psychoanalytic patients, even these so-called minimal deviations might well be regarded as much more consequential, enough to get them designated as substantially "modified" psychoanalyses.)

With another six of these psychoanalytic patients, the analyses were *more* significantly "modified," along a variety of parameters, mostly differing from those felt to be more fully proper psychoanalysis along *quantitative* dimensions of alteration, of how often, how intensely, etc., but still adjudged overall to be essentially psychoanalyses, albeit with modifications. And with the other six of this overall twenty-two, there was either a modification of analytic procedures substantial enough so as to be adjudged—by independent research judges—a "conversion" to psychotherapy, *or* an explicit conversion to psychotherapy, clearly presented and acknowledged within the treatment. Clearly, in the experience with these twenty-two patients taken into psychoanalysis, there occurred a marked blurring of the supposedly clear conceptual interface between (proper) psychoanalysis and intensive psychoanalytic psychotherapy.

A second major finding was that a comparable situation existed among the twenty patients in the project recommended for psychoanalytic psychotherapy along the expressive-supportive dimension. Even to begin with, such a distinction started out as a difficult one. There were very few patients recommended initially for a "purely" expressive psychotherapy, and perhaps even fewer recommended for a "purely" supportive psychotherapy. In the great majority of those twenty, plus in those six converted from psychoanalysis to psychotherapy, the issue over the whole therapy was rather one of the varying admixture of supportive and expressive techniques that would properly fit the particular clinical needs of the specific patient. As is made amply clear in the detailed clinical accounting in the book from which these conclusions are drawn, any effort categorically to distinguish the more purely expressive, the truly mixed, and the more purely supportive treatment approaches with these cases, either in treatment planning and prognostication, or in the assessment of therapeutic course and outcome, would not have emerged as a useful or even possible endeavor.

In terms of our project's conceptual starting point, there is considerable surprise to this finding. After all, we began with the seeming fundamental distinction that the expressive (uncovering, interpretive, insight-aiming, etc.) techniques—including here expressive psychotherapy and psychoanalysis together—were those directed toward *analyzing* the defenses (resistances, transferences) as the essential intervening step toward an eventual reintegration (with expressive psychotherapy and psychoanalysis varying of course in the breadth of the effort across the personality structure, and its depth of probe into the developmental history), while by contrast the supportive (ego-maintaining or ego-building) techniques were those presumed polar-opposite approaches directed toward "strengthening" the defenses in order to make the repression of conflict more effective. The underlying assumption in all this was that a very fundamental demarcation line existed between the supportive psychotherapies and the expressive psychotherapies (the latter including psychoanalysis); perhaps even more than that between the expressive end of the range of psychoanalytically oriented psychotherapies and proper psychoanalysis. This is, however, not the way our findings emerged. Rather, as I have already indicated, a real blurring of the interface zone between psychoanalysis and intensive psychoanalytic psychotherapy appeared in our findings. And equally clearly, in looking at the treatment courses of just those PRP patients in analytic psychotherapy (whether the twenty from the start or the additional six who were converted from psychoanalysis proper), this same blurring of the interface, this one between the expressive and the supportive psychotherapeutic modes, also existed from the start in our observed data.

Where, then, do such overall global findings leave us? Just as we decided in our initial PRP conceptualization of patient characteristics to use discrete psychic structures, functions, and attributes, but not overall diagnostic formulations, as a basis for treatment planning and for predicting treatment course and outcome, so we were impressed that individual specification in as detailed a way as possible of the *kinds* of interventions and technical maneuvers that characterized each individual treatment would be far more fruitful in illuminating the relationship among the psychological organization and psychological problems of the patients and the particular treatment courses and outcomes they came to than would any grouping by the widely spaced categories of psychoanalysis, expressive psychotherapy, and supportive psychotherapy, useful as these may be for initial orienting purposes and initial coarse assessments.

There is, of course, a voluminous literature on what makes individual therapies "expressive" and even more on what makes them "analytic." This has to do with all the issues (problematic as they are in ways that I will allude to further on) of interpretation, of insight, of working through, of uncovering (or analyzing) unconscious intrapsychic conflict, etc. What has always been much less clearly specified in both the theoretical literature and in clinical case illustration is what makes therapies "supportive." Actually, our project (PRP) had begun with an array of six different (or at least differently named and conceptualized) operating mechanisms that had been variously said to be differentially characteristic of supportive approaches. It became clear, though, in the actual consideration of the treatment courses of our patients—not only those whose therapy was intendedly largely supportive, but to often a substantial degree as well in those whose therapy was intendedly expressive, and even at times in those explicitly in psychoanalysis—that a major common operative *supportive* mechanism (whether explicitly intended and fostered or not) was the evocation and the firm establishment of a positive, dependent transference attachment (wholly or at least significantly uninterpreted and "unanalyzed"), within which varieties of conflicted transference needs and wishes achieved varying degrees of conscious or unconscious gratification.

This evolved in most clearly visible form in those therapies that went well and were intendedly "supportive" in operation, and seemed in those cases to be as well an essential precondition to the operation of various other supportive mechanisms that were varyingly admixed with it. This is, of course, the basis of the so-called transference cure, the willingness and the *capacity* of the patient to reach therapeutic goals, changes in behaviors, symptoms, and modes of living, as something being done "for the therapist," as the quid pro quo for the transference gratification received within the positive, dependent transference attachment. It is, in effect, a "transference trade"; "I do it—make the agreed-upon and desired changes—for you, the therapist, in order thereby to earn and/or maintain your support, your esteem, your love." That this mechanism operated as clearly and as pervasively as it did in so many of our cases (the putatively supportive and expressive alike) was in itself no great surprise. What was really surprising, however, was how stable and enduring the changes achieved in this way could turn out to be, and in many different ways that are delineated in the individual case descriptions in my book.

Upon this base, then, a further array of supporting maneuvers were built into the various cases studied, designed in each instance to insure individually that the changes achieved on this basis of "transference cure" would indeed become stable, durable, and reasonably secure against adverse environmental vicissitudes. Where the need for the continuing transference gratifications within the established positive, dependent transference attachment could not be otherwise transferred, attenuated, or internalized into new intrapsychic alignments based on a consolidated introjection of the therapeutic relationship and the therapeutic gratifications, this benevolent dependent transference within the therapy could become maintained within the nonending therapy of what we came to call the "therapeutic lifer." This, the risk of the "insoluble transference neurosis" which Alexander and his co-workers saw as a major therapeutic dilemma in so many analyses—especially with severely dependent and masochistic individuals—and which they devoted so much therapeutic effort to counteracting, in order to bring those analyses to a speedier and more effective resolution if possible, became here, rather, the vehicle of continued maintenance of the therapeutically improved psychological functioning. Given the degree of illness and ego deformation in our PRP population, it should be no surprise that in effect five patients in this research population of forty-two became more-or-less such "therapeutic lifers"; it will be more of a surprise that three of those five were among those initially recommended for and started in psychoanalysis.

Those patients with comparable dependent tendencies but with stronger inner psychological resources—a greater capacity to relate helpfully to a consolidated introject of the idealized therapist—were often able to terminate treatments, but through just the kind of pressured tapering and "weaning" process advocated by Alexander in such circumstances. With these instances, where there is successful "weaning" and then continued maintenance of the achieved level of psychological functioning, there is clear evidence of a reasonably consolidated identification with the therapist and the therapist's way of approach toward and mastery of conflict pressures.

Intermediate between those capable of being helped to psychological autonomy via such mechanisms of introjection and identification, and those for whom continued therapeutic contact, possibly lifelong, is necessary to a maintained level of adequate psychological functioning (in a manner quite akin to the continuing maintenance on physical regimens of diabetic patients, cardiac patients, etc.), are those patients with whom the transference attachments and the transference gratifications can be "transferred"—what I have called "transfer of the transference"—within the patient's now improved life situation, a transfer usually, of course, to the spouse. How successful this maneuver in fact turns out to be depends not only on the effectiveness and self-consciousness of the therapeutic work within the ongoing treatment, but also, of course, on the capacity and willingness of the other (the spouse) to carry this transferred transference burden indefinitely. Within our PRP population we observed the full range from an effective and enduring such result, through a total failure because of the ultimate refusal of the spouse to continue to play the assigned transference role. Indeed, the weakness of this kind of resolution of psychotherapy is precisely this question of its dependence on a continuing benign and fully supportive life context, in which some patients are more fortunate than others.

Another, and very specific, change mechanism within the supportive psychotherapeutic mode is that of fostering the displacement (or transfer) of the neurosis into the treatment situation (into the transference) with the alleviation of the external manifestations of the impaired functioning and/or symptoms. The paradigm instance here—but it is not the only kind—is of the conversion of the unduly dependent and submissive individual into more satisfying and assertive life behaviors outside the treatment, on the basis of a (covert) new submissiveness to the therapist, experienced as requiring the altered external behaviors as the price of the continuation of the dependent gratifications within the treatment. That is, the new assertiveness in outer behaviors is on the basis not of having analyzed the roots of the submissiveness so that it is no longer needed as a neurotic compromise formation, but of transferring it into the safer arena of the therapy, and paying the price in return, of chancing the risk of an (obedient) assertiveness in the outer world. What its ultimate success depends upon, of course, is again life circumstance, the reinforcing positive feedback and enhanced self-esteem, when the new behaviors bring not neurotically feared disaster but real reward and gratification.

Quite oppositely to the transference cure and these varieties of maintained or transferred transferences on the behavioral level, though very comparable on the dynamic level, is the mechanism of change by what I have called the "anti-transference cure." These are the cures out of negative transference struggles, the change by defiance and acting out against the therapist, in which the patient changes on the basis of or in the face of perceived contrary expectations by the therapist, usually as an act of triumph over the therapist in the overt or covert transference struggle. By their nature such cures would be far less frequent than the so-called transference cures and would have to be buttressed in some way against their potential instability, whether through the reinforcements from a stabilizing life situation, or from the positive environmental feedback from enhanced life functioning.

A particular concept given much currency by Alexander and French is that of the "corrective emotional experience," invoked by them as the almost all-explanatory construct used to elucidate the mechanisms of the supportive psychotherapeutic approaches, in almost the counterpart role to interpretation leading to insight as the central mechanism in the expressive psychotherapeutic approaches. The concept is, of course, an elastic one and can be used to cover the whole range of supportive therapeutic maneuvers, since by its nature everything that goes on in a psychotherapeutic context is indeed intended in one sense or another to be a corrective emotional experience. I have used the concept in a much more restricted way (and more in accord with a classically psychoanalytic perspective) in relation to treatments that provide a kindly, understanding, reality-oriented figure—the therapist—who in Gill's words is able "to meet the patient's transference behavior with neutrality . . . [and therefore] to give him a corrective emotional experience without the risks attendant on taking a role opposite to that which he expects, as Alexander suggests" (1954, p.

782). The trick here is to be able to do this in a steadily effective way, without falling victim to the transference-countertransference interactions by which the patient has managed to maintain his/her neurotic suffering in the pretreatment life experience.

Actually, only subtly different from such corrective emotional experience is that of the operative mechanism I have called Reality Testing and Reeducation. Here again, reality testing and reeducational activities can be conceived broadly as part of the therapeutic activity in every psychotherapy, from supportive therapy at one end of the spectrum to psychoanalysis at the other end. However, again, I am here using a narrower construction, of educational activities as part of the content focus in a largely supportive treatment, where the therapist plays a direct educational role in the transmission of advice, information, and education according to society's normative behavioral standards and expectations. Again here, at issue is the therapist's capacity to play this role in a way that the patient perceives as nonjudgmental and, if at all coercive, as guided solely by the patient's well-being and best interests. Clearly, the distinction between such activities and the steady provision of a corrective emotional experience cannot be (should not be) a clear one. With both these technical strategies the patient is both supported and educated toward reality-oriented problem solving and reality-corrected emotional responses on the basis of the "borrowed ego strength" that comes from the identification with the therapist in the role of helper and healer. And again, the continued maintenance of changes achieved on this basis in the posttreatment life of the patient is dependent on some appropriate feedback reinforcement from a fulfilling environment admixed with some transfer of the transferences to the significant life other(s).

To shift now in supportive mechanisms under consideration, there is the kind of life-manipulation that was so often involved with the PRP patients—even those in psychoanalysis—and that is in fact so much part of the rationale of the sanatorium treatment setting: the planned disengagement (temporarily or even, at times, permanently) from unfavorable and noxious life situations. This mechanism was indeed a pervasive supporting aspect of so many of the treatments of our patients, supportive *and* expressive, psychotherapeutic *and* psychoanalytic, and indeed became a very central and essential mechanism with some of them. And of course the counterposed position should be kept in mind: that for other patients, it is critical to their best chance for treatment success that their therapy be conducted against the backdrop of an ongoing, maintained interaction *within* their usual life situation. If this cannot be properly maintained, for whatever reason, their chances for an optimal result diminish, at times sharply. Clearly, also in a more usual psychotherapy patient population than that at The Menninger Foundation, treated maximally expressively in the customary totally outpatient practice setting, the tilt is a somewhat different one, with a greater preponderance of the patients needing maximal involvement in and commitment to their usual life situation, and far fewer requiring therapeutically guided disengagements.

And still another and different helping mechanism (hardly curative) is what I have called the Collusive Bargain, quite common perhaps in tacit and in minor ways, though at times quite explicit, and playing a very major treatment role. At issue here is the agreement, however tacitly or explicitly arrived at, to exclude particular areas of personality functioning and/or problems or symptoms from therapeutic scrutiny—leaving more or less consequential islands of maintained psychopathology—in return for the patient's willingness to make agreed-upon and substantial enough changes in (all) other areas of personality functioning and/or problems or symptoms. This is actually dynamically quite akin to the basis of the transference cure, where, after all, the patient is here making changes "for the therapist" in return for a very specific reward within the transference, the shielding from therapeutic probing of a particularly tenacious or rewarding symptom or behavior. The success of such a maneuver obviously depends on the (secondary and primary) value of such a symptom or behavior to the patient—it can be a homosexual life-style—as well as the capacity of the patient to detach the symptom or behavior at issue sufficiently from the other aspects of life functioning, which the patient and the therapist can then commit themselves to trying to change. Since the symptom or behavior "allowed" to the patient in this compromise solution is experienced as at least in some ways rewarding or gratifying, these particular therapeutic outcomes have a built-in stability.

And last in this detailing of specifically supportive therapeutic mechanisms is another kind of transfer of the transference, whether to fortunate life circumstances (and, in our research sample, wealth or other social or cultural advantage could play this role with some of our patients) or to alternative psychological supports selected by the patients often in opposition to their therapists—with our patients we witnessed one turn to Alcoholics Anonymous and another to Christian Science as examples of this. In such various turnings by the patients, whether to external material or alternative psychological supports, for the essential continuing transference dependencies and gratifications, the patients themselves at times "rescued" therapies that otherwise seemed nonprogressive or even failing, and converted them at least to stabilizations if not always to enhancements of levels of psychological functioning.

It is clear from all of this that there are a great variety of different and clearly specifiable ways in which psychotherapies (however expressive and even analytic they can also be) can be supportive of improved psychological functioning, and that ways can indeed be built in to maintain such improvement in stable and enduring fashion over even decades of follow-up (as we have had in our PRP population), far beyond what the conventional wisdom in the psychodynamic psychotherapy enterprise ordinarily allows for. Clearly, these various mechanisms interact in uniquely distinctive configurations in particular therapeutic courses, with varying combinations of meeting transference demands and expectations, of agreed-upon transference trades, of specific substitutions of more adaptive impulse-defense configurations for less adaptive (more symptomatic) ones, of specific agreements and decisions about what to talk about and explore in what directions, and specifically as well what not to talk about, and—equally—of various manipulations in relation to the patient's life situation, various kinds of transfers of the transference, of specific engagements with and disengagements from ongoing life context, and of managing the positive-feedback reinforcements that result in enhanced self-esteem from behaviors and relationships altered in desired directions.

In contrast to this broadly diversified and somewhat untidy array of change mechanisms discerned in our study of the supportive psychotherapeutic approaches has been the central conception in the theory of change in expressive psychotherapy, and of course even more so in psychoanalysis itself, of the dominant role of (properly mutative) interpretations leading to insight into hitherto repressed unconscious conflicts as the basis of "real," structural, change in the personality, and of stable and enduring amelioration of symptoms and alterations of attitudes and behaviors in desired directions. It has always been less clear that every component aspect of this formulation has all along been more or less admittedly problematic, both conceptually and empirically, and that the various controversies surrounding each of these issues have not been, to this point, satisfactorily enough resolved in the crucible of accumulating clinical experience and data-based theorizing.

There is indeed a whole theoretical literature around each of these issues—the nature and the role of the so-called mutative interpretation and the controversy over the special character of the transference interpretation in this regard; the role of insight in relation to change, whether it is a precondition of change, a result of change, or just the ideational representation of the change; the meanings and usages of the concept of psychic structure and of what constitutes true structural change as distinct from "only" adaptive or behavioral change which can presumably occur without insight, on other bases, as in "purely" supportive psychotherapy, or even in the absence of therapy, etc.—but it would be too large a digression to attempt, even cursorily, to review those theoretical controversies here. But certainly, though, the underlying theme through all of that literature, that only such major personality unraveling and reconstruction as psychoanalysis promises is truly able to lead to the kinds of changes—via mutative interpretations, effective insights, and "true" structural alterations in the ego—that are really stable and enduring is one that has been already brought into serious question by our broad finding that treatment changes brought about by way of supportive techniques (and presumably *without* full intrapsychic "conflict resolution" and concomitant achieved insight) have often turned out to be substantially much more stable and enduring over prolonged time spans than we initially anticipated.

To specify now only the highlights of our detailed empirical PRP findings: With a total of 19 or 45 percent of the research population of 42 patients, the achieved changes in their treatments substantially outstripped the working through and the insights developed via the interpretive (psychotherapeutic or psychoanalytic) process. Stated now, this will clearly be no surprise, since I have already described the many ways—the various supportive mechanisms and techniques—through which change and substantial change were reached by many of our patients without a concomitant interpretive-expressive working through of intrapsychic conflict, in fact so often specifically with the avoidance of it. Of these 19, 7 of them were actually among the 22 started in psychoanalysis, while 12 were among the 20 started in psychotherapy. In the case of these 12 of the 20 patients started in psychotherapy who were in the category of change far exceeding the achieved interpretations and insights, with most of them such change represented the appropriate, and mostly successful, kind of mostly supportive-treatment outcome achieved on an expected and appropriately technically implemented basis; with the 7 from among the 22 who started in psychoanalysis, this finding was certainly far less expected.

Alongside these 19 patients where the achieved changes systematically exceeded the acquired working through and insights and were clearly on bases other than the insightful resolution of conflict in response to interpretive uncovering, there were 10 of the 42 patients (almost 25 percent) where the insights achieved via interpretation seemed coordinate with and completely proportional to the changes reached. Expectedly, 9 of these 10 were in psychoanalyses that were maintained as analyses throughout. Not so expectedly, most in this group achieved psychoanalytic outcomes that fell varyingly short of the ambitious goals originally posited for them. For example, 6 of these 10 formed a group with a basically hysterical character structure, with various combinations of depression, anxiety, and phobic symptoms, and with an originally presumed excellent prognosis for thoroughgoing neurotic conflict resolution with psychoanalytic treatment. Though four of these six had very good treatment results (and certainly so by their lights), and two sustained moderate improvements, in all six cases they fell short of a full psychoanalytic result in a very similar way, in the inadequate working through of the preoedipal negative mother transference, and of the patient's unconscious hostile identification with this malevolent, feared, and hateful mother imago. Each in somewhat different ways was able to work around this major area of unresolved conflict, to come to very good therapeutic gains, to draw the analytic work to a close "while she was still ahead," and to maintain to the end an incompletely resolved positive attachment and sustained good feeling toward the analyst. Each successfully avoided the deeper analytic exploration of the earliest ties to the mother, so fraught with painful and hateful affect. Clearly, though these six patients all had therapeutically good outcomes, they also all had psychoanalytically incomplete outcomes, and they each had deficiencies in insightful mastery in precisely the area of analytic incompleteness.

At the other end of this spectrum there were just three cases (only 7 percent of the sample) where the attained insights considerably outstripped the discerned changes. These represented a mixed bag; they included, for example, a long-term psychoanalytic case who ended with a large residue of psychologically undigested intellectual insights and with an essentially unaltered, deeply entrenched, obsessive-compulsive and compliant character structure. And there was still a balance of 10 patients (again, almost 25 percent of the total) where basically there was little meaningful insight and little effective change on any basis—in effect, a clustering of essentially failed cases.

This accounting of the 42 patients does in one large sense add up to data conforming to our expectations; most of the larger group of 19 where the degree of change exceeded the achieved working through and insights and came via other than insight-aiming processes were psychotherapy patients where the kinds of supportive mechanisms I have described operated so substantially, while most of the smaller group of 10 where change and insight tended to be more directly proportional were in analysis, and they were in particular analyses where the supportive modifications were minimal. However, none of this speaks yet to the issue of whether, apart from the degree and proportionality of concomitant achieved insight, the changes arrived at by the two kinds of mechanism, the largely supportive and the largely expressive, differed in the degree to which they represented "true structural changes." This particular issue was specifically addressed in the comparative study of the projective psychological test battery data obtained from our patients at three points in time—before therapy, after therapy, and at the point of follow-up study several years after their treatment terminations. "Structural change" was defined there in terms of adjudged changes in specific intrapsychic configurations, the patterning of defenses, thought organization, affect organization, anxiety tolerance, and ego strength, all variables that can be assessed with special clarity in projective test data.

That data analysis did reveal a clear positive relationship between conflict resolution and structural change—the more conflict resolution, the more structural change. And yet there were significant exceptions since 7 of 16 patients with no evidence of real conflict resolutions nonetheless did show significant structural ego changes. Thus, both points of view—that structural change is associated with resolution of conflict and that it can come about in the absence of conflict resolution—received support from our comparative projective test study. Stated another way, of the 27 of our 42 patients for whom full projective test data were available for comparative assessment across the three points in time, significant conflict resolution was seen in 11, and there was concomitant significant structural change in 10. With the other 16 patients where changes in functioning, behaviors, and symptoms were adjudged to have come about by means other than substantial conflict resolution, structural change in the ego was still discerned in 7 or almost half.

What can we now say overall from this summary of the treatment and follow-up findings from our Psychotherapy Research Project that will throw empirical light on the conceptual issues concerning the relationships between psychoanalysis and the psychoanalytically derived psychotherapies in their similarities and differences, issues that have been specifically debated now in largely unaltered form over more than a three-decade span? I will bring our overall conclusions together as a series of sequential propositions regarding the appropriateness, the efficacy, the reach, and the limitations of psychoanalysis (varyingly "classical" and modified) and of psychoanalytic psychotherapy or psychotherapies (varyingly expressive and supportive)—always of course with the caveat, as this was discerned within this segment of the overall patient population, that my data apply to those (usually sicker) individuals who have been brought to or have sought their intensive analytically guided treatment within a psychoanalytic sanatorium setting.

1. The first proposition has to do with the distinctions so regularly made in the psychodynamic literature between "structural change" (gratuitously

called "real" change), presumably based on the interpretive resolution of unconscious intrapsychic conflicts, and "behavioral change" or change in "manifest behavior patterns" that are (invidiously considered) "just altered techniques of adjustment" and presumably are all that can come out of the other, nonexpressive, noninterpretive, non-insight-aiming change mechanisms, i.e., the varieties of supportive psychotherapeutic techniques and implementations that I have presented in this paper. Intrinsic to this way of dichotomizing between kinds of change has always been the easy assumption that only structural change or real change as brought about through conflict resolution marked by appropriately achieved insight can have some guarantee of inherent stability, durability, and capacity to weather at least ordinary future environmental vicissitudes. It goes without saying that the commonplace value distinction automatically follows: that change brought about by expressive-analytic means is invariably "better," and this is, of course, the basis for the widely believed clinical operating maxim, "Be as expressive as you can be, and as supportive as you have to be." It is clear from the experiences documented from our PRP study that I question strongly the continued usefulness of this effort to link so tightly the *kind* of change achieved (real change, better change) with the intervention modes, expressive or supportive, by which it is brought about. If we accept the observations made from the study of our PRP cases that the changes reached in our more supportive therapies and via intrinsically supportive modes seemed often enough to be just as much structural change, to be just as stable and enduring, just as able to help the patient cope with life's subsequent happenstances, as the changes reached in our most expressive-analytic cases, then we must accept that the one way (the interpretive-uncovering way) does not have such an exclusive corner on inducing true structural change.

2. The second proposition has to do with the conventional proportionality argument, that therapeutic change will be at least proportional to the degree of achieved conflict resolution. Put this way, this proposition is almost unexceptionable, since it is clear that there can be significantly more change than there is true intrapsychic conflict resolution, on all the varying (supportive) bases through which change can be brought about, as well as properly proportionate change where the change is all or "purely" on the basis of conflict resolution with accompanying insight—if such an ideal type ever actually exists in practice—but it would be hard to imagine real conflict resolution (and accompanying insight) without at least proportional concomitant change in behaviors, dispositions, attitudes, symptoms, etc. However, in the closely related arena of the proportionality of therapeutic change to the degree of attained insight (as distinct from conflict resolu-

tion), I have already indicated in passing that we had three instances within our PRP population of achieved "insight" seemingly in excess of induced change. This, of course, is a common enough problem and a frequent enough complaint, both within and about psychoanalytic treatment, and has been the subject of considerable discussion in the psychoanalytic literature. In our own three instances such concepts as undigested intellectual insights or of insights within an ego-weakened or psychotic transference state were invoked. What is meant here, of course, is insights that for varying reasons are not consequent to true conflict resolution and do not reflect it.

3. The third proposition, often linked to the proportionality argument, but in the light of our findings much more debatable and clearly separated from it, has to do with the necessity argument that effective conflict resolution is a necessary condition for at least certain kinds of change. It is certainly clear that an overall finding from our project—and almost an overriding one—has been the repeated demonstration that a substantial range of changes, in symptoms, in character traits, in personality functioning, and in life-style rooted in lifelong and repressed intrapsychic conflicts, have been brought about via the more supportive psychotherapeutic modes and techniques, cutting across the gamut of declared supportive *and* expressive (even analytic) therapies, and that in terms of the usual criteria—stability, durability, and capacity to withstand external or internal disruptive pressures—these changes can be (in many instances) quite indistinguishable from the changes brought about by typically expressive-analytic (interpretive, insight-producing) means.

4. A counterpart to the proposition based on the tendency to overestimate the necessity of the expressive (analytic) treatment mode and of its operation via conflict resolution in order to effect therapeutically desired change has been the other proposition, based on the happy finding that the supportive psychotherapeutic approaches, mechanisms, and techniques so often achieved far more than were expected of them—in fact often enough reached the kinds and degrees of change expected to depend on more expressive and insightful conflict resolutions—and did so in ways that represented indistinguishably "structural" changes, in terms of the usual indicators of that state. In fact, proportionately, each within its own category, the designated psychotherapy cases did as well as the designated psychoanalytic ones. More to the point, the (good) results in the one modality were not overall less stable or less enduring or less proof against subsequent environmental vicissitude than in the other. And more important still, within the psychotherapy group (of 20), the changes predicted, though more often predicated on the more expressive mechanisms and techniques,

in fact were more often actually achieved—often the same changes—on the basis of the more supportive mechanisms and techniques.

And even more, within the psychoanalysis group (of 22), in almost every case there were modifications, parameters, etc., some analytically resolved but mostly not, and all of them in the direction of more supportive modes and aspects, so that even by our liberal PRP criteria, there were only 10 (not quite half) of the psychoanalytic cases who were in overall retrospect viewed as having been in essentially unaltered analyses, 6 who were in substantially modified (in supportive directions) analyses, and 6 who were considered really converted to varyingly supportive-expressive psychotherapies. By the usual stricter criteria of customary outpatient psychoanalytic and psychotherapy practice, just about every single one of our PRP psychoanalytic cases would be considered substantially altered in varyingly supportive directions. Put into overall perspective, more of the patients (psychotherapeutic and psychoanalytic alike) changed on the basis of designedly supportive interventions and mechanisms than had been expected or predicted beforehand, on the basis of either our clinical experience or our theoretical positions.

5. Considering these PRP treatment courses from the point of view of psychoanalysis as a treatment modality, just as more was accomplished than expected, and more stably, and more enduringly with psychotherapy, especially in its more supportive modes, so psychoanalysis, as the quintessentially expressive therapeutic mode, was more limited—at least with these patients—than had been anticipated or predicted. This has been, of course, a function of a variety of factors. In part it has reflected the whole ethos of the psychoanalytic sanatorium and the psychoanalytic treatment opportunities that it is intended to make possible. The dominant theme here has been the concept that the psychoanalytically guided sanatorium, with its possibilities for protection, care, and life management of the (temporarily) behaviorally disorganized and incompetent individual, could make possible the intensive psychoanalytic treatment of patients who could not be helped to resolve their deep-seated personality difficulties satisfactorily enough with any other or lesser treatment approach than psychoanalysis, but who also could not tolerate the rigors of the regressive psychoanalytic treatment process within the usual outpatient private practice setting.

This, of course, is what has led to the concept of psychoanalysis on the basis of so-called heroic indications, which by the nature of the kinds of patients brought to The Menninger Foundation, necessarily comprised such a substantial segment of our PRP psychoanalytic population. In our PRP experience, however, the central tenets of this proposition were found wanting; these particular patients characteristically did very poorly with the psychoanalytic treatment method, however it was modified by parameters, and however buttressed with concomitant hospitalization, and they in fact comprised the great bulk of the failed psychoanalytic treatment cases. On the other hand, there were certainly enough instances of very good outcomes among the very ill and disordered in supportive-expressive psychotherapies that we can feel that the whole broad spectrum of "sicker" patients who are being talked about here can indeed do much better in an appropriately arranged and modulated supportive-expressive psychotherapy, if the ingredients are put together skillfully and imaginatively enough, and if one can ensure truly sufficient concomitant life management. That last stipulation, concerning the need for adequate enough life management, is of course one of the central keys to the success of the treatment recommendations being proposed here, and, by that token, reaffirms a proper role either for the psychoanalytic sanatorium or for some less controlled life regimen made more possible by modern-day, psychoactive-drug management. The big difference is in the departure from the effort at psychoanalysis per se (even modified psychoanalysis) as the treatment of choice for these "sicker" patients in that setting. On this basis, I have spoken of the failing of the so-called heroic indications for *psychoanalysis,* and am instead inviting a repositioning of the pendulum in its swings over time around this issue, more in the direction of "narrowing indications" for (proper) psychoanalysis along the lines marked out by Anna Freud.

6. The predictions made for prospective therapeutic courses and outcomes tended to be for more substantial change and for more permanent change (i.e., more "structural change") where the treatment plan and implementation were to be more expressive-analytic, and where these changes were expected to be more based on thoroughgoing intrapsychic conflict resolution through processes of interpretation, insight, and working through. And pari passu, and again in terms of the conventional psychodynamic wisdom, the more supportive the treatment was intended to be (had to be), the more limited and inherently unstable the anticipated changes were predicted to be. What our research study has revealed in great detail is that all of this was (again, overall) consistently tempered and altered in the actual implementation in the treatment courses. The psychoanalyses, as a whole, as well as the expressive psychotherapies as a whole, were systematically modified in the direction of introducing more supportive components in widely varying ways, and by and large accomplished more limited outcomes than promised (hoped), and, as indicated, with a varying but often substantial amount of that accomplished by noninterpretive, i.e., supportive, means. The psychotherapies, on the other hand, often

accomplished a fair amount more, and in several of the more spectacular cases a great deal more, than initially expected and promised, and again, however the admixture of intervention techniques was originally projected, with much of the change on the basis of more supportive modes than originally specified.

What does all of this labor in our Psychotherapy Research Project add up to? It can be most broadly generalized as follows: (1) The treatment results, with patients selected either as suitable for trials at psychoanalysis, or as appropriate for varying mixes of expressive-supportive psychotherapeutic approaches, tended—with this population sample—to converge, rather than diverge, in outcome. (2) Across the whole spectrum of treatment courses in the 42 patients, ranging from the most analytic-expressive, through the inextricably blended, onto the most single-mindedly supportive, in almost every instance—the psychoanalyses included—the treatment carried more supportive elements than originally intended, and these supportive elements accounted for substantially more of the changes achieved than had been originally anticipated. (3) The nature of supportive therapy, or better the supportive aspects of all psychotherapy, as conceptualized within a psychoanalytic theoretical framework, and as deployed by psychoanalytically knowledgeable therapists, bears far more respectful specification in all its form variants than has usually been accorded it in the psychodynamic literature. And (4) from the study of the kinds of changes reached by this cohort of patients, partly on an uncovering insight-aiming basis, and partly on the basis of the opposed covering-up varieties of supportive techniques, the changes themselves—divorced from how they were brought about—often seemed quite indistinguishable from each other, in terms of being so-called real or structural changes in personality functioning.

In the light of the conceptual and predictive framework within which the Psychotherapy Research Project of The Menninger Foundation was planned and implemented three decades earlier, there is of course considerable real surprise in the overall project findings: that these distinctive therapeutic modalities of psychoanalysis, expressive psychotherapy, supportive psychotherapy, etc., hardly exist in anywhere near ideal or pure form in the real world of actual practice; that real treatments in actual practice are inextricably intermingled blends of more or less expressive-interpretive and more-or-less supportive-stabilizing elements; that almost all treatments (including even presumably pure psychoanalyses) carry many more supportive components than are usually credited to them; that the overall outcomes achieved by those treatments that are more "analytic" as against those that are more "supportive" are less apart than our usual expectations for those differing modalities would portend; and that the kinds of changes achieved in treatments from the two ends of this spectrum are less different in nature and in permanence than again is usually expected, and indeed can often not be easily distinguished. None of this is where, three decades ago, we expected to be today. From another perspective, in terms of the corridor comments made by practitioners in informal interchanges about the conditions and nature of professional practice, which reflect what they regularly find that they do in actual practice as against how technique is conceptualized for formal presentation in professional meetings, our PRP research conclusions are far less surprising.

Which brings me to the conclusion of this paper: What is my view, then, of where this now leaves our field, or rather our concern with both psychoanalysis and psychotherapy? Clearly, just because of the established position of psychoanalysis as the theory of human development and personality organization that informs all of our therapeutic work, whatever its mode, psychoanalysis will retain a very vital position as a specific therapy in the most classical (and unaltered) form in which we can individually fulfill it, first as a research instrument, an unparalleled avenue of access to the dynamic and temporal depths of human mental functioning, and closely linked, as a still unquestioned central aspect of the educational and training process by which individuals become proficient theoretically and clinically so that they will be maximally able to deploy knowledgeably the whole range of psychoanalytically conceptualized therapeutic approaches, from psychoanalysis proper through the whole spectrum of psychoanalytic expressive and supportive therapies, in relation to the patients differentially suited to this range of modalities. For it should be clear from all of the foregoing presentation, that all of these psychotherapeutic approaches, expressive and supportive alike, will be maximally effective with those patients for whom they are differentially suited, only if employed with the utmost of psychoanalytic understanding and skill.

Beyond that, as a specific therapy, the spirit here presented is that of "narrowed indications," of a more circumscribed role for psychoanalysis, with more awareness of its varying degrees of infiltration by nonanalytic, i.e., supportive intervention, techniques, and with more modest expectations in terms of its therapeutic goals, than was the case just a few decades back. The counterpart position is, of course, that of both the "expanded scope" of psychoanalytic psychotherapy, expressive and supportive, and the enhanced therapeutic, heuristic, and also conceptual dignity to be accorded the supportive psychotherapeutic activity, psychoanalytically formulated, with both greater awareness of its presence across the entire psychotherapeutic range, even to the most analytic, and also greater precision in its delineation and the understanding of its mechanisms. Our research project has turned out to be a substantial effort in that direction.

REFERENCES

Gill, M. M. (1954), Psychoanalysis and exploratory psychotherapy. *J. Amer. Psychoanal. Assn.*, 2:771–797.

Wallerstein, R. S. (1969), Introduction to Panel on Psychoanalysis and Psychotherapy. The relationship of psychoanalysis to psychotherapy: Current issues. *Internat. J. Psycho-Anal.*, 50:693–710.

——— (1986), *Forty-two Lives in Treatment. A Study of Psychoanalysis and Psychotherapy.* New York: Guilford Press.

September 1986

III

CLINICAL STUDIES

Apparent Absence of Transference: A Special Instance of Transference Neurosis

BHASKAR SRIPADA, M.D. (Chicago)

This article will review the dynamics of a case during a phase of an apparent absence of transference at the height of the transference neurosis. The discussion will introduce the term *generalization*[1] as a form of general interpretation of the transference which includes transference; extratransference; and current, genetic, psychic, and external-reality possibilities. This article will also describe the transference expectation of countertransference by the patient as well as aspects of the actual countertransference through an analysis of a case by a candidate analyst influenced by the context of the larger psychoanalytic milieu.

Review of Literature

While the centrality of transference in analysis has come to be increasingly accepted, there has been and continues to be debate about the decrease or absence of the transference in a properly conducted analysis. One view is that only a fraction of the potential transference can be engaged in a given analysis, or that transference may even be silent, while another argues that it is always present. Between these views are various positions both for and against these respective arguments.

In "Analysis Terminable and Interminable," Freud (1937) indicates that significant conflicts may not appear in the transference because they are no longer active in the patient's current life, casting doubts about whether the transference neurosis precisely duplicates the content of the preexisting

[1]I am indebted to Dr. Arnold Goldberg for suggesting this term.

infantile neurosis. Glover (1955, pp. 114–115) agrees that the development of a typical transference neurosis in all cases is not only theoretically improbable but contrary to actual experience. However, he notes that the very prolongation of analysis without indications of a transference neurosis may itself be a sign of transference neurosis. Weinshel (1971) comments that in such cases an apparent stalemate in the analytic work rather than the prolongation of the analysis is the crucial but unrecognized indication of the transference neurosis. One interesting transference variation which needs to be distinguished from a true transference neurosis describes a situation where a patient develops a transference to the analysis rather than to the analyst (A. Freud, 1954, p. 66). Fleming (Panel, 1958, p. 564) suggests the term "negative transference neurosis" to describe the dynamic cases which failed to develop a transference neurosis. She attributes the failure to a deep negative transference, accompanied by a fear of reexperiencing early oedipal-rage reactions in the transference based on a male child's actual childhood phallic impotence.

Loewald (1971) indicates that on rare occasions the transference neurosis can be silent despite the accomplishment of significant analytic work. However, Gill (1983, p. 79) disputes this, arguing that if there is no "open emotional involvement with the analyst," any effects obtained must be significantly based on an unresolved transference.

Brenner (1976) also uses a broad definition of transference, noting that it is always present and that some patients, because of the nature of their conflicts, will appear to have no conscious thoughts or feelings of a personal nature about their analyst. But he regards this appearance of indifference and withdrawal of emotions as defensive and, in fact, the manifestation of the transference. Bird (1972), using perhaps the broadest definition of transference, concludes not only that management of transference is the most difficult part of analysis, but also that transference is a universal mental function and the basis of all human relationships. Rangell (1968) cautions against such overarching views, believing that not every affective response to the analyst is transference, but only those displaced by the patient from his unconscious past. Rangell clarifies that the transference can be distinguished and clearly delineated only when the analyst establishes and maintains a proper analytic stance which renders him available and susceptible to transference displacement.

Blum (1983), while asserting that interpretative resolution of the transference neurosis is the central area of analytic work, draws attention to its limitations. He notes that transference is not the entire focus of interpretation or the only effective "mutative" interpretation. He further comments that a "transference only" position is theoretically untenable and may lead to an artificial reduction of associations and interpretations into a transference mold and to an idealized folie à deux. Extreme devotion to analytic transference interpretation could reflect hidden grandiosity in the analyst or in his attitude toward analysis (Lampl-De Groot, 1976).

Even Gill (1983, pp. 123–124), who has advocated the centrality of transference in psychoanalysis, notes that any exclusive preoccupation on the analyst's part may skew the analytic process. A special interest in dreams, for example, may result in a change in the analysand's reporting of dreams. So, too, will an exclusive interest in the transference provoke transference effects which themselves should become the subject of a proper transference analysis. Gill warns against the possibility of an infinite regress, noting that in such cases an interpretation in the transference can have an effect on the transference that is the same as the content of the interpretation. For example, the analyst may interpret that the patient views the analyst's interpretations seductively, and the patient may experience that as a seduction itself. Gill postulates that such situations arise only if the analyst has for some time been engaged in an unrecognized and uninterpreted transference-countertransference interaction. Gill also suggests that in such a circumstance the analyst has not found the appropriate transference interpretation for the particular analytic situation. The analyst must find a plausible transference which the patient cannot dismiss as totally explained by the present analytic situation. While this is clearly true, Gill does not specifically suggest what may be done to reverse this infinite regress once it has occurred, other than to analyze the transference appropriately.

Case Report

The case that follows reports a particular phase of an analysis predominantly in the mother transference in what was an apparent absence of transference during a time considered (retrospectively) the height of the transference neurosis. A summary of relevant aspects of the establishment of the transference neurosis is provided to serve as a background for the case. In this paper, transference neurosis refers to the reactivation of a patient's infantile neurosis in the transference along with the corresponding defenses. The case is presented not with a view to demonstrating correct technique but for the discussion of generalization.

Angela, an Italian Catholic, whose family immigrated to New Jersey when she was seven, is a tall, thin, thirty-four-year-old manager of a cosmetics section in a fashionable suburban shopping center, four years into her analysis. She has been married for one year to a successful real-estate broker. His parents lived nearby in another small town in the vicinity of Milan and were responsible for introducing her and her husband to each other. Her presenting complaints were chronic anxiety, especially with men, and a feeling of being sexually unattractive. She feared rejection and felt extremely jealous toward other women, whom she felt men invariably preferred. (Angela's identity is disguised for the purpose of confidentiality.)

Early in the analysis Angela complained that her boyfriend (later her husband) demanded sex when she was not in the mood. She noted that he made no effort to bring her to an orgasm—that "he gets excited, comes, rolls over and falls asleep," because "he is worse than the stereotype of the Italian selfish man." Because she felt it necessary to make him happy, she frequently—dutifully—consented to sex, or, if they did not have intercourse, she would at least give him a "blow job." She even prided herself on being a good "cocksucker." Later, Angela referred to the analytic couch as "my couch." She wondered whether the couch was primarily for her analysis or for my graduation from the Institute. Soon thereafter, when my watch scraped against the armrest as I shifted in my chair, she thought I was unzipping my fly and fantasized about exciting me by performing oral sex. I interpreted her view of analysis as being not for her but for me, just as she viewed sex with her boyfriend as being for his pleasure. Such feelings were related to the maternal transference. She felt her mother was extremely controlling, frequently deciding what clothes or hairstyle Angela should wear, not only when she was an adolescent growing up in New Jersey, but even now when she visits her parents.

A significant aspect of genetic reconstruction occurred when we explored the circumstances of Angela's childhood bedtime routine. As a child, she frequently asked her mother to help her get to sleep. Her mother, ignoring the needs of her younger brother, would usually oblige by lying down next to her. But occasionally Angela's mother would scream, "What's wrong with you? Leave me alone!" On the nights when Angela was rejected, she was extremely anxious, unable to fall asleep, and would often need to go to the bathroom. She was afraid of waking her mother and irritating her by making some inadvertent noise. Angela therefore would creep quietly to and from the bathroom, a process that could last an hour. This aspect of her childhood neurosis was reactivated in the transference when Angela dreamed that she was an adult in diapers and that I was changing them. She wanted longer sessions and more than one session a day. But she felt that her strong wishes that I be with her or her dream that I change her diapers and be involved with her body might repel me, just as she had disgusted her mother.

The intensity of the transference neurosis caused Angela alternately to express her various wishes and to defend against them. For example, she dreamed that a man raped her and felt I was the rapist in the dream. She felt I was somehow forcing her to be dependent on me. However, she very self-consciously revealed that she was aroused by the rapist in the dream. I interpreted this feeling of being forced upon as a defense to keep from getting aroused by her feelings for me. Angela reported that she did not wish to get too involved, because she feared being like her friend, who spies on her analyst and his family, does not want to leave after sessions, and wishes to call him at nights and on weekends. Angela felt humiliated by the strength of her feelings for me and feared they would become a "burning passion."

Her defense against awareness of her feelings regarding separations, especially vacations, was usually manifested through withdrawal and silences. She was angry that I billed her for vacations that did not synchronize with mine. Further analysis revealed that she was particularly angry because of the fantasy that while she was away I would see another patient, specifically a young, attractive, blond, female patient, during her scheduled appointment times. Consequent symptoms of withdrawal, silence, and jealousy were analyzed and worked through as essentially being related to the transference.

Development of the Phase of Apparent Absence of Transference

What follows is an account of the origin, description, and technical management of Angela's apparent lack of transference after having previously established a workable transference neurosis, aspects of which were described in the previous section.

Angela got married during her third year of analysis, after a few years of a turbulent courtship. Both families had been enthusiastic about the relationship and put pressure on Angela and her boyfriend to marry. The transference during the courtship was intensely felt or intensely defended against. She had a fantasy that I touched her and later had a dream of being in love with two men. One was the Catholic priest that was to perform her wedding ceremony, whom she trusted from her childhood. She felt that her involvement with me was similar to her involvement with her priest and feared that it would diminish her involvement with her fiancé. She felt torn between her involvement with her husband and with me. On her wedding night she had an anxiety attack while she was making love.

After she returned from her honeymoon, she complained of severe anxiety, and she insisted that I give an interpretation of her wedding-night anxiety which she claimed pertained to her relationship not to me but to her husband. She bitterly railed that I was useless because I was interested only in the analytic relationship and the transference. I noted that she did not want me to interpret her anxiety during sex on her honeymoon as being related to her vacation from me. I interpreted her feeling about my uselessness as similar to her feelings toward her father who she had frequently complained was useless. As a child she felt her father had been useless because he could not help her go to sleep. Furthermore during her adolescence he developed Parkinson's disease, which caused him to slow down and which Angela initially attributed to malingering. She agreed that both her father and I were actually ineffectual. From then on she experienced her feelings as related exclusively to her husband and ceased to have any conscious feelings or thoughts directed toward me.

In session 678 Angela announced her plans for a long vacation to Italy a month ahead to visit the village of her birth. She noted her preoccupation with her husband and had little to say in our session. She felt obligated to her husband in many ways, e.g., to have sex with him at his demand; to get pregnant; to have a baby. Yet she had great anxiety about sex, pregnancy, or parenthood. Ideally, she wanted to take a warm bath, eat popcorn, read, and not be bothered by her husband. She soon confirmed the exact dates of her vacation, complained of boredom, and became silent.

I drew Angela's attention to the confirmation of her vacation and interpreted that she was withdrawing from me into her silence, as she had prior to previous vacations. She said the vacation was far from her mind and, besides, her feelings did not relate to me—all her feelings related to her husband. She overslept and was late for her next session, an extremely rare occurrence. She noted that she didn't want to come but that she was on the verge of tears as she left my office after the previous session.

I interpreted her oversleeping and her not wanting to come as a reluctance to analyze her emotions after the previous session and to acknowledge her sadness about her upcoming vacation. She said I was wrong, that she was in fact looking forward to the trip. She said she didn't know what made her sad, but if it were related to leaving me, she was unaware of it. Near the session's end she mentioned that the time had gone by quickly.

The next session, and the last for the week, was on a Friday. Angela felt anxious, remarking that she had also felt anxious the previous Friday. In response to my asking her what she thought about her anxiety on these two consecutive Fridays she replied that on weekends her husband made increased sexual demands, adding that she was willing to "bet" that she knew what I thought about that. She was convinced that I was implying that her Friday anxiety related to not seeing me over the weekends and during vacation. She was further convinced that the expectation that she talk about me was related to the rigidity of the Psychoanalytic Institute, and that I was wrong. I clarified her persistent disagreement with every interpretation I made. She disagreed, saying that we both had an actual disagreement as to whether she had any feelings for me.

On Monday of the following week, Angela remarked about a friend who called her a compulsive people pleaser who never confronted people. Angela was very aggravated with her friend for pushing her to express her anger. She also complained about her mother calling her selfish, on a recent visit, for preferring to go home to watch television rather than to continue shopping with her. Angela also later revealed that her husband mentioned over the weekend, as they drove by a bar, that a few years ago, just when she had begun dating him, he had picked up "a one-night stand" in that bar. She was livid since that had been during a painful period in which she had sorely missed him. While she was alone, pining for him, he had been "screwing" around. She wanted to "cut his balls off" and "murder" him. She could not calm down, often muttering angrily to herself, "you cocksucking mother fucker."

As has been previously demonstrated, Angela presented a curious clinical picture which, on the one hand, revealed a keen, exquisite sensitivity to me and involvement in the analysis, while on the other, an equally adamant refutation at various levels, not only of the importance but also of the very existence of her feelings for me. I was aware, as has been pointed out, that she had various reactions to leaving sessions and was defensively avoiding becoming aware of her previously described reactions to the vacation.

But the usual transference interpretations, some of which have been described, of the resistances to her awareness of them, she had dismissed. I, therefore, did not make a transference interpretation as I felt she was bound to dismiss it as she had in the past. Rather than focus specifically, for example, on the transference implication that she was rejecting my interpretations, feeling sad at the prospect of the vacation, or being angry that I might see another patient during her time, I chose to interpret the common element in her associations that reflected her *general* concern. I interpreted that she felt imposed upon by the expectations of other people. The scope of my general interpretation related to various possibilities including husband, mother, friend, and me for reasons that have been described. Therefore the general interpretation included in its possible scope transference, extratransference, and genetic possibilities. She agreed, expressing a fear of being used by others as was her own mother, who remained a martyr to Angela's father and always tried to please him. Angela cited the example of her, and never her husband, being the one to clean up after their dog. She reiterated that I was essentially correct. It needs to be noted that this was the first time in many months that she agreed to anything I said, indicating some diminution or at least a change in her resistances. Many such generalizing interpretations with transference at the core, but without explicit reference to the transference, were made with similar accepting responses and further elaborations from her.

However, Angela continued to complain about her husband's expectations. But, now, instead of reporting exclusive feelings toward him, she also began to become more aware of her general preoccupation about actual or imagined impositions on her—not only by her husband but by others as well. For example, she talked of her fears that on this camping vacation she might meet new people, have to share toilets, etc. She was afraid of being compromised into joint negotiations regarding anything. She resented conflicts with others and their expectations. Most of all she didn't want to *talk* to others, especially on her vacation. I interpreted this as her expectation that I would want her to discuss her vacation reactions with me.

She said, "Yes, there you go again." She insisted that her position had not changed. She felt, moreover, that I considered her apparent lack of "transference" defensive but that I had probably decided not to prod. But she generally agreed with me, since she didn't feel like paying attention to anybody; she wants to do what she wants, when she wants, how she wants, where she wants, and not worry about others. I pointed out that even though she overtly dismissed her feelings for me, she remained concerned about her perceptions of my thoughts and feelings, whether I thought she was defensive or had decided not prod her. This clarified her transference expectation of countertransference from me toward her.

After this session Angela had difficulty falling asleep. She was irritated by her husband watching television in bed. At her request, he turned it off and she fell asleep, only to be awakened by the blaring television. She was very angry at her husband who had tricked her into going to sleep so that he could again turn on the television. I said perhaps she also felt tricked by my interpretation that she expected me to expect her to talk about the vacation. She laughed and agreed that I was like her husband. This is an example of the gradual relinquishing of the generalizing interpretation and the beginning of a reintroduction of transference interpretations in such a manner that they can be analyzed within the transference.

Soon thereafter Angela reported a dream: "I was trying to make a milkshake at my home in New Jersey. Suddenly I was making milkshakes for others in a girls' boarding school in a place far away from New Jersey—maybe back in Milan. Some girls deliberately kept putting feces in the milkshake, while other girls were helping me."

Angela felt the dream was weird; she didn't understand it at all. She commented that the feces were not hers; it was "other people's shit." I compared the change of location in the dream to the change of her location during her upcoming vacation. She laughed, agreed, and said that if my remark specifically regarded her vacation from treatment it was still a "shitty" interpretation. She noted that if I "generalized" it to be her fear of expectations from others, it would be helpful. She spontaneously elaborated on the similarities and dissimilarities between me and her husband, acknowledging that her feelings for her husband might be a shield against her feelings for me. She felt free to agree or disagree with me and was now not worried that I might "put my shit" on her as she feared with her mother and husband. She said she trusted me and hoped that her pattern of rejecting my interpretations did not displease me terribly. Now she was concerned that I might view her as argumentative.

After Angela returned from her European vacation, she reported that as soon as her previous session had ended, just prior to her vacation, she had cried and became aware of how much she would miss me. She was surprised by the sadness and also by the strength of the feeling. She was glad that I knew more about her in this instance than she did about herself, for that meant that indeed I could help her even though she was reluctant to admit it. She was also glad that I did not go along with her evasion of her feelings pertaining to me generally, or to the vacation specifically. Understanding her feelings toward me was the only path out of her neurosis. Only she and I could work it out. With this important turn came the reestablishment of the analyzable transference neurosis, which had been consciously absent from the analysis for the period described. Gradually, I was able to work through her concern that I might view her as argumentative as well as the surprised awareness of her feelings of sadness within the transference. Prior to her next vacation, she was able to explore her feelings regarding the upcoming analytic break, and to allow time for working through the transference implication without resorting to generalizing as a mode of interpretation. Her progress is reflected by the analysis of a dream reported in the 812th session and herein recounted.

Angela had a baby; it was a baby bird or an insect. Her mother held this creature and killed it. She was shocked but also relieved that she did not have to deal with the baby. The day residue for the dream was a Public Broadcasting Service nature movie about eagles that she had watched with her husband. The topic of birth control and abortion had also been in the news, triggering memories of childhood sexual prohibitions and memories of her parish priest's admonitions. Angela noted that the baby bird was delicate and fragile. She also noted that she had neglected to report the dream the day after it occurred. I interpreted this delay as a way to distance herself from her own neediness in the relationship with me and as being similar to the neediness of the child/bird/insect in her dream. She realizes that she wishes that I would kill the needy bird (like her mother), so that I would not analyze her neediness. This insight allowed her to understand her sense of relief when she felt I could not tolerate her. It meant that she would not analyze her neediness.

Angela felt her mother didn't want to hear her problems, that by Angela's waking her up she would consider herself the inadequate mother of a fearful child. She felt her mother preferred her younger brother. She wondered if I, too, felt inadequate when she displayed no feelings for me—when she would not let me be an analyst and help her with her anxiety. This led to the analysis of her conflicting hostile feelings toward me in the transference and toward her mother during childhood. Angela now reconstructed the events of her childhood and their relevance to the present.

By age seven, Angela had begun a secret life, hiding her anxiety and her true feelings and withdrawing emotionally from her mother. She found it was easier to share her life with the parish priest who had taken a liking to her. A specific aspect of her infantile and childhood neurosis was reactivated in the transference neurosis during the phase of the apparent absence of transference when she was indifferent to me.

Many different and equally or more plausible formulations or technical ways of handling the transference may be entertained. As has already been stated, this case, however, is to be viewed not as presenting correct or good technique, but as a springboard to exploring the implications of a generalizing transference.

Discussion of Generalizing Interpretation

Generalizing from one's experience is natural, and its use in psychoanalysis is not new, but its implications have not been explicitly spelled out. Generalization, as stated earlier, denotes the interpretation of latent extratransference or genetic reference to the transference in a general manner that essentially encompasses the transference, extratransference, and current, genetic, psychic, and external-reality possibilities. A generalizing interpretation is to be distinguished from transference interpretation and extratransference interpretation and clarification.

Freud (1926) noted that transference was a universal phenomenon that dominates each person's relations to his human environment, that transference is not created by analysis, it is merely uncovered by analysis. He notes that an analysis without transference is an impossibility and implies that extratransference is not necessarily nontransference; the former does not deal with the transference to the analyst. Occasionally, transference and extratransference are seen as separate or mutually exclusive and sometimes, as antagonistic. Indeed, from a purely transference perspective, extratransference objects may even be referred to as "objectionable others" (Anthony, 1980). However, the general tendency in psychoanalysis has been to attempt to distinguish clearly the extremely complex border between transference and extratransference. For example, Blum (1983) notes that extratransference interpretation may include transference to objects other than the analyst as well as the real relationship to the analyst.

Schafer (1985), in his discussion of psychic reality, suggests that representations of other people may be communications that bear on the unconsciously conflicted self, a displaced reference to the analyst, a form of remembering the infantile past, or a projected reference, e.g., a dream. Moreover he specifies that when the estimate of the analysand's cognitive ability is high and when the factuality of the representations meets the criteria of a narrative good fit, or when there is sufficient correspondence or consistency, the analyst may take a stand on the factuality of the representation of others. The generalizing interpretation from this perspective would be to include as many categories mentioned, including the representation of the other, in its scope. But generalization would obviate the need for specific comment about the factuality of the representation of others, even if it met the criteria mentioned above. The concept of generalization implies the similarities in the different manifestations of analytic material, which are psychically connected and derived from the same unconscious of a given patient. Therefore, generalization offers a descriptively broader framework that brings together and unites transference with extratransference, the past with present, and inner with outer reality.

Generalization differs from clarification as understood by Greenson (1967, p. 38), who stated that "clarification refers to those activities that aim at placing all psychic phenomenon being analyzed in sharp focus." Generalization aims at broadening the focus and thus is the opposite of clarification unless sharpening the focus could also broaden it. Gill (1982, p. 117) notes that analytic work involves various steps: the first is clarification of extratransference material in order to get a clue to the allusion of the transference; the second is to bring this transference into awareness; and the third is its resolution. From this perspective, generalization differs from clarification because it deals simultaneously rather than sequentially with transference-extratransference.

The risks of abusing generalization are obvious. Just as exclusive attention toward or away from the transference may serve the patient's resistance, so, too, exclusive use or avoidance of a generalization may indeed serve the purpose of resistance. The same principles that guide the proper use of transference also apply to the generalizing interpretation. Generalization is, therefore, not suggestion or a disguised transference manipulation. Rather, it is geared ultimately for insight; it is not intended to be a judgment on the patient's life or objects. Therefore, the analyst needs to be aware of both the benefits and risks of generalization, since it can unwittingly serve to mask countertransference, weaken the transference, and impede analysis.

Transference Expectation of Countertransference from the Analyst

Angela expected that I wanted her to talk only about me and also complained about my need for transference associations and the rigidity of the Institute in always demanding a strict interpretation of transference. While part of her expectation was indeed true and will be discussed later, her own rigidity was externalized onto her expectation of both the Institute and myself. She bemoaned the fact that I was a candidate and said that she believed that after graduation analysts became more relaxed and less concerned with demanding transference. Even if a patient's transference expectation of an analyst's broadly defined countertransference is accurate, the elaboration of its genetic and transferential antecedents continues to be the task of analysis.

This view is supported by Gill (1983, pp. 59–60), who clarified that the proper analysis of transference includes the attitudes the patient believes the analyst has toward the patient. Often the patient may not voice the attitudes and feelings he or she ascribes to the analyst, since the patient may assume that the analyst will either not like or be uncomfortable about those feelings. It is for this reason that the analyst must be especially alert to the attitudes the patient believes the analyst has, and not only to the attitudes the patient shows toward the analyst.

The analysis of a clinic patient is further complicated by the candidate's need to demonstrate his own conceptual and technical mastery of transference. This realistic factor is therefore fertile ground for the patient's resistances and the analyst's countertransference. Windholz (1970) gave the example of patients who developed a split transference to the analyst and to the fantasized supervisor, a split related to the patient's experience with an important parental surrogate in childhood. Windholz describes how a patient developed a brother transference to her student analyst, excluding him in her fantasy from her relationship to the "supervisor-mother." Another patient believed her student analyst needed her as insurance against his possible failure with another patient, in accord with her belief that her mother conceived her as insurance against the possible loss of her other children. Windholz points out that the supervisory constellation may be used to maintain a "replica" of a significant constellation which was real in the patient's childhood. Oremland and Windholz (1971) describe the transference expectation of countertransference of a patient who came to analysis with the assumption that the analyst wanted her to fall in love with him. She was silently contemptuous as she secretly laughed at his audacity.

Discussion of Countertransference

An integral part of the candidate analyst's learning expectation is the ability to demonstrate the proper elaboration, understanding, working through, and resolution of the transference neurosis. These conscious and unconscious needs are realistic, narcissistic, or object related. The candidate may allow this realistic need to mask a countertransference, or indeed, use it to act out. A thorough exploration of my countertransference toward Angela is beyond the scope of this paper, but it was partly influenced by my candidacy. In Angela's analysis during the apparent absence-of-transference phase, I experienced a countertransference—an expectation of transference, as Angela alleged. It seemed that the transference neurosis was displaced onto her husband, and I partly acted out by having a countertransference expectation of transference that facilitated this development. Such an assumption by an analyst of a specific role assigned him by a patient and based on the patient's transference has been described as countertransference role responsiveness (Sandler, 1976). Furthermore, I briefly had a feeling of discovery when I began to conceptualize the use of generalization and feel a sense of mastery, which again played into her defense that analysis was for my pleasure.

Racker (1968) discusses the example of a candidate who reacted for a time with slight annoyance whenever his analysands were much occupied with their childhood. The candidate had the idea that only transference could further the treatment. In reality, Racker notes that the analyst also had a wish that the analysands concern themselves with him. The candidate was, with the help of supervision, able to recognize quickly his countertransference, revive his interest in the analysand's childhood situations, and continue appropriate analysis.

Rosenfeld (1972) warns against countertransference-based transference interpretations. He notes that some analysts, at times under the influence of countertransference, automatically reference all the patient's productions to the transference, e.g., with parrotlike repetition of the patient's words. When undetected, Rosenfeld argues that such "absurd," "stereotyped" responses may masquerade as "an interpretation of the here-and-now transference situation."

The Analytic Milieu

Aspects of the analytic milieu, comprised of the Clinic-Institute, may lend themselves to transference projections, even if accurately surmised by the clinic patient. But it is equally true that the analytic milieu is a real presence and defines the stage on which the candidate's learning occurs. Limentani (1974) discusses the complex matrix responsible for difficulties in the psychoanalytic training situation. He comments on the constant interaction between the analyst and the training Institute, the student and the Institute, the student and other students, as well as the analyst and his colleagues. He draws attention to possible group countertransference in analytic settings that may be very difficult to understand, and sometimes of psychotic proportions. Kernberg (1986) describes the varieties of possible organizational structures of psychoanalytic institutes, and draws attention to such institutional dynamics as an atmosphere of indoctrination, or an uncritical reading of Freud, and their deleterious effects on psychoanalytic education. However, notwithstanding these risks, supervision offers a candidate a live environment, the opportunity to work through and learn and understand the influence of the larger analytic milieu on both the clinic patient and himself.

As Arlow (1963) notes, the most effective influence on the development of the candidate analyst in the supervisory situation is dependent on his ability to form an identification with the supervisor and thereby change or correct the distortions of the image of the professional ego ideal. Dewald (1971) states that, even assuming optimal functioning of the candidate analyst, there will be considerable variation in, and possible disagreement about, whatever conceptualizations and specific interventions he makes in the analytic process. The teaching/learning process of psychoanalysis needs to allow for individuality of style, technique, and understanding of both the candidate and supervisor. While this is occurring there are bound to be periods and areas of uneven progress by the candidate and periods that predispose to countertransference problems, however transitory. Cooper and Witenberg (1983) note that the supervisor must "stimulate" the student's curiosity about his own responses as he listens to patients, and enlarge the student's capacity to use himself as a sounding board. Such stimulation, if and when it is uneven, may be the locus of countertransference or other learning problems. Oremland and Windholz (1971) refer, for example, to a feeling of conviction in the supervisory sessions stemming from a joint discovery. However, after returning to the patient, the treating analyst again felt alone. Oremland and Windholz term this a misplaced site of conviction. They indicate that the supervisor may be reluctant to discuss the patient's reactions to the analyst's student status for fear of humiliating the student, and the student and patient may be reluctant for other reasons. In such situations Mayer (1972) notes that all three of them, as well as the entire organization of the Institute as well, may wish to view the supervised analysis as a "real" analysis and, consequently, deemphasize those elements that make the analysis by a candidate different from "real" analysis.

However, when the transference nature of such splits is recognized and there is an open attitude to exploring such complications, working through is possible. This awareness, of course, goes a long way toward enhancing not only the analysis itself but the learning and teaching of psychoanalysis.

Summary

An analysis in which there was an apparent absence of transference was analyzed as a specific form of transference neurosis, and was managed through the use of a "generalizing interpretation." The latter term has been defined and demonstrated as an intervention with a wider scope than that encompassed by concepts of transference interpretation, extratransference interpretation, clarification, or genetic reconstruction. The parameters for using a "generalizing interpretation," the limitations of its use, and its potential benefits and risks have been outlined. The potential influence of the training needs of the candidate and the analytic milieu of the analytic Institute on an analysis performed by a candidate have been briefly explored.

REFERENCES

Anthony, E. J. (1980), The family and the psychoanalytic process in children. *The Psychoanalytic Study of the Child,* 35:3–34. New Haven: Yale University Press.

Arlow, J. A. (1963), The supervisory situation. *J. Amer. Psychoanal. Assn.*, 11:582–583.
Bird, B. (1972), Notes on transference: Universal phenomenon and hardest part of analysis. *J. Amer. Psychoanal.*, 20:267–301.
Blum, H. P. (1971), On the conception and development of the transference neurosis. *J. Amer. Psychoanal. Assn.*, 19:41–53.
——— (1983), The position and value of extratransference interpretation. *J. Amer. Psychoanal. Assn.*, 31:587–617.
Brenner, C. (1976), *Psychoanalytic Technique and Psychic Conflict.* New York: International Universities Press.
Cooper, A. & Witenberg, E. G. (1983), Stimulation of curiosity in the supervisory process of psychoanalysis. *Contemp. Psychoanal.*, 19:164.
Dewald, P. A. (1971), The clinical conference in the psychoanalytic process. *This Annual,* 1:270–277. New York: International Universities Press.
Freud, A. (1954), The widening scope of indications for psychoanalysis. *J. Amer. Psychoanal. Assn.*, 2:607–620.
Freud, S. (1926), An autobiographical study. *Standard Edition,* 20:3–76. London: Hogarth Press, 1959.
——— (1937), Analysis terminable and interminable. *Standard Edition,* 23:216–253. London: Hogarth Press, 1964.
Gill, M. M. (1982), *Analysis of Transference.* Vol. 1: *Theory and Technique.* New York: International Universities Press.
Glover, E. (1955), *The Technique of Psychoanalysis.* New York: International Universities Press.
Greenson, R. R. (1967), *The Technique and Practice of Psychoanalysis,* vol. 1. New York: International Universities Press.
Kernberg, O. T. (1986), Institutional problems of psychoanalytic education. *J. Amer. Psychoanal. Assn.*, 34:799.
Lampl-De Groot, J. (1976), Personal experience with psychoanalytic technique and theory during the last half-century. *The Psychoanalytic Study of the Child,* 31:283–296. New Haven: Yale University Press.
Limentani, A. (1974), The training analyst and the difficulties in the training analytic situation. *Internat. J. Psycho-Anal.*, 55:71–77.
Loewald, H. W. (1971), The transference neurosis: Comments on the concept and the phenomenon. *J. Amer. Psychoanal. Assn.*, 19:54.
Mayer, D. L. (1972), Comments on a blind spot in clinical research: A special form of transference in the psychoanalytic clinic. *Psychoanal. Quart.*, 41:384–401.
Oremland, J. D. & Windholz, E. (1971), Some specific transference, countertransference, and supervisory problems in the analysis of a narcissistic personality. *Internat. J. Psycho-Anal.*, 52:267–272.
Panel (1958), Technical problems of transference, D. Leach, reporter. *J. Amer. Psychoanal. Assn.*, 6:560–566.
Racker, H. (1968), *Transference and Countertransference.* London: Hogarth Press.
Rangell, L. (1968), The psychoanalytic process. *Internat. J. Psycho-Anal.*, 49:19–26.
Rosenfeld, H. (1972), Critical appreciation of James Strachey's paper on "The nature of the therapeutic action of psychoanalysis." *Internat. J. Psycho-Anal.*, 53:455–462.
Sandler, J. (1976), Countertransference and role responsiveness. *Internat. Rev. Psycho-Anal.*, 3:43–47.
Schafer, R. (1985). The interpretation of psychic reality: Developmental influence and unconscious communication. *J. Amer. Psychoanal. Assn.*, 33:537–554.
Weinshel, E. M. (1971), The transference neurosis: A survey of the literature. *J. Amer. Psychoanal. Assn.*, 19:67–88.
Windholz, E. (1970), The theory of supervision in psychoanalytic education. *Internat. J. Psycho-Anal.*, 51:393–406.

October 1986

Intelligence and Analyzability

PHILIP RUBOVITS-SEITZ (Washington, D.C.)

During the third year of his analysis a 36-year-old man who had not dated prior to his treatment became seriously involved with an attractive, intelligent, and successful businesswoman. After they had "gone steady" for six months and lived together for a month, subtle indications of ambivalence toward Marilyn began to appear, against resistance, in John's free associations, fantasies, and dreams. The resistance was a response to fears that finding fault with her might spoil their chances of staying together.

The source and nature of the ambivalence surfaced rather suddenly in the following manner. John started an appointment by saying that he had been grumpy toward co-workers recently but they had not really done anything to justify his irritability. He wondered whether the anger might be coming from some other source. He blocked for about half a minute, then said that he hadn't been sleeping well lately. He went on a bit sheepishly to say that he had been drinking more during the past couple of weeks. He recalled that in the past he drank more when he felt "lonely, unhappy, and misunderstood." He then blocked for about a minute. Asked what he was thinking he said: "I thought about a woman who was having trouble working the intercom at your outer door when I arrived today. She didn't seem to realize that it has a temperature switch—she was pressing it with her glove on. I tried to explain to her that she had to take her glove off

The author gratefully acknowledges the collaboration of John and Marilyn in the preparation of this report and dedicates this work to them.

The author is indebted also to Randi Rubovits-Seitz, M.D., and to George H. Pollock, M.D., Ph.D., for helpful suggestions concerning preparation of this report, and to Barbara P. Jones, Ph.D., for neuropsychologic and personality testing.

This essay was awarded the Annual Research Prize, Washington Psychoanalytic Society, May 1985.

so the warmth of her skin would activate the switch; but she didn't seem to understand what I was trying to tell her." He then blocked again.

I commented that the incident might contain clues about what had been bothering him recently. He responded immediately that he had thought of something while telling the incident. When he mentioned "warmth of the skin" he recalled that he and Marilyn had not been sleeping as closely to each other as they did previously. "She doesn't come over close to me," he added with a tone of hurt and sadness. Her tendency to withdraw and remain distant seemed to increase after they started living together. He had tried as tactfully as possible to tell her that he needed more closeness and contact but she didn't seem to understand him. She had replied that they were close enough for her. Having said all this he recalled the intercom incident and recognized spontaneously how his conflict with Marilyn was reflected in it: i.e., his trying to explain the need for close, warm contact in order to promote communication and relationship but feeling that neither Marilyn nor the woman at the door understood him.

John's ability to construct and comprehend symbolic structures such as the intercom incident gives an impression of both psychologic-mindedness and of relatively high general intelligence. His actual full-scale I.Q., however, was only 107! He had required a great deal of special tutoring throughout school and had barely completed high school. His intellectual limitations had cost him a number of jobs because he consistently overreached himself occupationally. John's cognitive problems were most evident in his frequent misuse of words. He attempted to overcompensate for his lack of higher education by using words that he did not really understand or know how to pronounce. Some examples follow:

"She is so *'POSSESSIOUS'* [possessive] that she called to see if I was there."

"I feel guilty that I have gone behind their *'BACKWARDS'* [backs]."

"She bought a *'REMLANT'* [remnant] of carpet."

"I took it as a personal *'FRONT'* [affront]."

"She was *'AMADENT'* [adamant] about our leaving together."

"He made it sound *'INMORAL'* [immoral]."

"My parents look on me now as a *'WHORE-MONGREL'* [monger]."

"You probably thought I was *'INDATED'* [inundated] with work that made me late."

"To me the word 'kike' does not have a good *'CONDENSATION'* [connotation]."

"I didn't used to believe in *'MAHOGANOUS'* [monogamous] relationships."

"I can't stand it if a woman whines. My mother *'WHOUNED'* [whined]!"

"I've been very busy, going *'HITHER AND NON'* [yon]."

"I wanted her to drop to her *'FEET'* [knees] when she saw me!"

"She *'WRAPS HER FINGER AROUND ME'* [wraps me around her finger]."

"We saw the movie, *'IRVING COWBOY'* [Urban Cowboy]."

"The dehumidifier has a *'VERITABLE'* [variable] fan."

"The apartment has floor to *'GLASS'* [ceiling] windows."

"They're *'OOZING'* [easing] me out."

"In the old days the woman gave the man a *'DIARY'* [dowry]."

"I was like an *'OYSTER'* [ostrich] with its head in the sand."

"Religion must be quite a cross to bear. Hah! that's a *'PUN ON WORDS'* [play on words]."

"My mother zeroes in on sick people—a real *'SCARLET O'HARA'* [Florence Nightingale]."

"If you're on a *'STATUE'* [pedestal] you can get knocked off!"

"She was Jewish and since I'm not I thought I might be *'IN GROTTO'* [*persona non grata*] with her."

John's malapropisms appeared to contain motivated slips of speech occasionally but by far the majority were cognitive errors. He simply did not understand or know how to pronounce many of the words he used. He regularly misused the word "condensation," for example, in place of "connotation." He was sensitive about his mistakes being corrected so I did not call attention to them. Usually I knew what he meant from the context in which such a word or phrase appeared. If I did not understand him I would ask what he meant without referring to the specific word that had confused me.

About a year after his treatment began an occasion for psychologic and psychometric testing presented itself in a natural way. He had been fired from another job and felt at a loss about what sort of work to try next. I asked if he had ever taken vocational aptitude tests to determine the kinds of work for which he was best suited. He seized the idea eagerly and undertook extensive testing at a vocational counseling service. As a result of those tests additional studies of his hearing and speech were carried out and neuropsychological tests were administered. The results of the various tests will be presented later.

The present report focuses upon the relations of cognitive functions, psychologic-mindedness, and analyzability. A summary of John's therapeutic process will be presented to illustrate (a) that he was analyzable in spite of his intellectual limitations, speech disorder, and other cognitive deficits; and (b) that his analyzability appeared to result from relatively intact psychologic-mindedness, the latter representing a complex, largely cognitive set of ego functions which are at least partially independent of general intelligence (Gardner, 1983). Reviews of the literature on cognitive functions, psychologic-mindedness, and analyzability are presented and the relations of cognitive processes to psychologic-mindedness and analyzability are discussed.

Case Report

John was the younger of two sons in a well-to-do southern family that prided itself on illustrious Civil War ancestors. The elder son, Bob, had been the "fair-haired boy" of the family since birth. He was intellectually gifted and became very successful in his career. John remembered him fondly as, "the nicest person in the family." Bob had been an unusually good brother to John—patient, kind, and helpful.

Unlike his brother, John was both sickly and a slow learner. He was born with several congenital defects which included fibrous cortical defects of both femurs, bilateral talipes varus, and pilonidal fistula in addition to brain damage. The club feet were corrected during infancy but the pilonidal fistula was not repaired until John was seven years old. One of his clearest memories from early childhood was of holding his mother's hand and going from doctor to doctor for treatment of his various ailments. Throughout his childhood—in fact, his life!—he had been perceived and treated by his mother and brother as fragile and in need of protection. His father on the other hand was critical of weakness in John, tried to shame him into more macho behavior, and accused his mother of making a "sissy" of him.

John's father had been a high-level executive in industry. His inheritance made it possible for him to retire at a fairly young age but alcoholism may have contributed to the early "retirement." Both parents drank excessively during John's early childhood. His mother sometimes joked that she had breast-fed John with milk that contained some of the gin she had been drinking. On at least one occasion, according to his mother, baby John had become intoxicated. Both parents stopped drinking sometime during John's early childhood. He recalled feeling proud of them that they no longer drank. When he was nine years old he heard his mother tell a neighbor that his father had "fallen off the wagon." John felt very saddened by that and disappointed in his father. His father's carousing with golfing buddies became the source of endless quarrels between his parents, his mother repeatedly threatening to leave. From the age of nine therefore John lived in dread of the family breaking up. He attached himself even more closely to his mother and brother in an attempt to relieve the insecurity.

John was distinctly a "momma's boy." He preferred staying at home and helping her with cleaning and cooking rather than going out and playing with other boys. His mother seemed to enjoy his companionship and sometimes joked to people that John was the daughter she had wanted. When John developed a "crush" on a vivacious and attractive young neighbor woman his mother expressed intense dislike of the woman, objected to her wearing lipstick, and succeeded in stamping out John's interest in her. As he grew into adolescence his mother actively discouraged him from dating; she found fault with every girl toward whom he showed interest, her usual disparagement being that the girl was "not of our class."

John also became something of a nurse to his mother because she was sick frequently, spent a great deal of time in bed, and complained openly about her symptoms. It seems likely that much of her illness was hypochondria. His father on the other hand was robust, hale, and hearty and expected his sons to be the same. At some point during John's childhood, however, his father seemed to have given up on trying to make a man out of his younger son. From then on John felt that his father largely ignored him. When contact with each other was unavoidable his father was often irritable toward and critical of John.

John was a very slow learner who had difficulty with most of his courses in school. He began having "crushes" on other boys during high school which he only half admitted to himself, rationalizing that he merely admired and wanted to be like them. At the age of fifteen he attempted suicide by taking an overdose of his mother's sleeping medicine. He must have taken a potentially lethal dose because he was unconscious for several days and had been placed on the hospital's critical list. Ostensibly, the suicide attempt was precipitated by his getting caught for cutting a certain class in school repeatedly. He said at the time that he could not face his father's wrath and felt the only way out was to kill himself. In the course of his therapeutic process, however, we discovered that the actual precipitant which had been repressed was homosexual panic activated by attraction to a handsome boy in the class he cut. He felt his father's direst prediction about him had come true—that he was a disgrace to the family and that the only honorable thing he could do was to kill himself. In this dynamic context cutting the class represented a desperate and ironic effort to identify with his father by turning away from homosexual stimulation.

From the time of his suicide attempt until his treatment with me he had been in therapy almost continuously with a series of psychiatrists. Presumably because of his intellectual limitations the therapies had been more supportive than exploratory. When I first saw him and heard the history of his life, I too assumed that his treatment would have to be considerably less than analytic. It was only after he had been in treatment with me for about six months that I began to sense more potential in him for a depth-psychologic approach. His somewhat awkward, unsophisticated, adolescent manner in addition to his difficulties with language and pronunciation made it fairly easy to underestimate him. In due time however his sensitivity, psychologic-mindedness, and capacity for symbolic conceptualization and insight became apparent. After six months of psychotherapy, therefore, I explained analysis to him and asked if he would like to try it. He said that he would so his appointments were increased to four a week and he began lying down to free associate.

To demonstrate the patient's analyzability his therapeutic process will be presented both longitudinally and cross-sectionally: i.e., after summarizing the ongoing analytic process in terms of principal conflicts, defenses, and phases of the transference neurosis, an example of a "good analytic hour" (Kris, 1956, pp. 255–260) will be reviewed in greater detail:

> The good hour is actually an observable *cross section of the optimal process at a particular moment.* It is a "marker" of the presence of an optimal process. The presence (or absence) of good hours enables us to make an ongoing evaluation of the state of the process. These hours serve as a gauge or indicator to "measure" the [evolving] development of the process (Peterfreund, 1983, pp. 67–68).

Summary of the Therapeutic Process

PREANALYTIC PSYCHOTHERAPY

When he started treatment with me, John felt lonely and isolated. His parents had moved from the family home in the south to the northwest in order to live near their older son and his family. John felt abandoned and responded by moving to a new city in the north where he knew no one. Despite severe loneliness, however, he did nothing to seek companionship.

When he had been away from his parents in the past John had relieved loneliness by making occasional friendships with couples—usually older couples who were like parents to him. Asked why he had never dated his answer was vague but alluded to intense shyness and awkwardness with women. Since his treatment at that time was psychotherapeutic and because I did not anticipate that it might become analytic I encouraged him gently to try dating. He was extremely reluctant to do so. I increased the encouragement gradually, pointing out that dating might benefit his treatment: i.e., underlying conflicts about women would be activated giving us a better chance to understand them. I made a note at the time that despite his protests John seemed to appreciate the implication that he might be capable of something from which he had always felt disqualified.

His initial attempts at dating were acutely uncomfortable for him. With support and encouragement from me, however—as well as patience and compassion on the part of the women he dated—he persevered. Eventually he felt somewhat less shy about approaching and going out with women. One day I mentioned that from what he had told me about his dates the women seemed to like him. Rather than making him feel better about dating my comment aroused considerable anxiety, the reason for which soon appeared. A long-standing fantasy emerged—a paranoid idea inculcated originally by his mother—that women would pretend interest in him because of interest in his money. In the course of the therapeutic work on this fantasy and attitude we found that he believed women would be interested only in his money and not in him as a person. He recognized eventually that the fantasy of "women's greed for money" was more applicable to his mother and to himself, both being obsessed with money.

Thus far John's relations with women had been platonic. He insisted that sexual relations would be morally wrong (his mother was puritanical about premarital sex); but also sex posed the threat of entrapment. He had been warned repeatedly by his mother that women would try to ensnare him by becoming pregnant which would force him into marriage. I raised questions about whether such notions were realistic, in the process of which he revealed his naiveté about sex generally and contraception in particular. I recommended a simple book on sex for him to read and offered to answer any questions that might occur to him in connection with the reading. He read, asked questions, and gradually learned the basic facts about sex.

Eventually with the understanding, assistance, and initiative of a woman whom he had dated frequently he learned how to get into bed with her and to make love. Not surprisingly, he ejaculated prematurely at first. Defensively, this symptom appeared to be a way of keeping his distance from a potentially entrapping woman. Contiguous associations about premature ejaculation and suicide suggested that at a deeper level guilt about hostility toward the woman contributed to the premature ejaculation. To my surprise carefully worded interpretations of both the defensive and deeper symbolic meanings of the sexual symptom appeared to strike a responsive chord in John. He seemed to understand symbolic representation of that kind more easily than he did simpler, concrete ideas, words, and meanings. His understanding of the depth-psychologic interpretations was attested also by an acceleration of the therapeutic process. For the first time he began to express hostile feelings toward his mother, in the course of which the thought occurred to him that *she* was the entrapping woman in his life. Soon after these developments in his therapy he became fully potent with his sexual partner.

It was at this point, approximately half-a-year after his treatment with me had begun, that I considered the possibility of psychoanalysis for John. I explained psychoanalysis to him and indicated how it would be different from his previous treatments. Although I could not be certain that he really understood what I had said he agreed to try analytic treatment. From then on he came four times a week instead of two and lay down to free associate.

PSYCHOANALYTIC PROCESS: DEVELOPMENT OF THE TRANSFERENCE NEUROSIS

John had little difficulty in adjusting to the changes in his treatment. Lying down, not seeing me, and my talking much less than before all occasioned reactions and comments from him but actual disturbance about the changes was minimal. He seemed at home with free association—if anything more relaxed and spontaneous than when he had sat up and talked conversationally.

Within a month after starting analytic treatment feelings of exultation about his first successful sexual experiences reactivated childhood fantasies and associated conflicts about getting rid of his father and taking over his mother:

> *Dream:* An old Civil War pistol in the family that my father is very proud of and shows off to people. I got rid of it somehow. My mother and I were there by ourselves.
> *Associations:* He and mother sometimes went on trips together without his father. They shared the same motel room, even the same bed at times. "Confesses" with embarrassment that recently he had sexual feelings about a man and his penis.
> *Interpretation:* The homosexual feelings attempted to cover up competitive feelings toward his father. He responded: "That *scares* me—*both* ideas are scary to me!"

During the next several weeks the competitive conflict toward his father was transferred to me and acted out in the form of delaying payment of his bill. He associated money with his father because his father was wealthy. Many times over the years John had attempted to get out of paying his father money that he owed him, and occasionally he had gotten away with it. Money is power to his father and he guards it very closely.

> *Dream:* I was Secretary of State "Lance" (Vance) and was ordering Mary (his girlfriend at that time) what to do about the closed Iranian embassy.

Associations: "Lance" was a slip—he meant "Vance." "Lance" made him think of Burt Lance, the crooked banker who had been budget director. Patient has been dishonest in trying to gyp his father about loans. Lately he has done that with analyst's fee. He was a big shot in the dream and could dominate Mary—the way his father dominates his mother. Adds anxiously that he saw analyst's wife recently and thought she was attractive.
Interpretation: Perhaps he wants to take more than money from analyst. He responded with anxiety, then became deferential in subsequent associations.

The foregoing developments led to a moderately prolonged (four-month) phase of defensive homosexual transference to me which barely concealed his underlying envy and competitiveness.

Dream: I was afraid to ask your age for fear of it seeming I was sexually interested in you.
Associations: He is puzzled about my age. Analyst's wife seems to be about patient's age. He has always liked older men.
Interpretation: Could the compliment conceal a put-down? He responded with anxiety, then a protest of admiration for analyst.

During this phase of the analytic process he recalled numerous occasions since his adolescence when he became intensely involved with other boys and men—what he called having "crushes" on them. He had not engaged in overt homosexual relations, however. Conflict about homosexual interests was warded off with rationalizations and compensatory macho attitudes. The homosexual father-transference gave way eventually to a further defensive displacement of the homosexuality to older-brother figures:

Transitory obsession: He became obsessed with men approximately his own age or a little older who had red hair.
Associations: His older brother, Bob, has red hair. John idolized Bob, followed him around, and tried to emulate him.
Interpretation: Homosexual feelings toward his father were too frightening so he shifted them to his brother. He agreed with the interpretation, adding that Bob welcomed his affection whereas his father gruffly rejected it.

During the previous phase of obsessive-erotic interest in red-headed men the father-transference to me continued but was no longer erotized. He was cooperative and respectful—a positive but platonic father-transference. The highly erotized, obsessive transferences to red-haired brother-figures persisted for approximately another four months with gradually increasing conflict—i.e., fear that his homosexual preoccupation might be discovered. When that conflict became too intense a further defensive regression occurred to a dependent and at times demanding attitude toward brother-figures:

> *Behavior pattern:* He mentioned several instances of trying to extract favors from brother-figures, asking them to do things for him, go out of their way for him.
> *Interpretation:* Getting them to do things for him seemed to be a substitute for getting sexual pleasure from them.
> *Associations:* He never would have dared to be sexual with his brother, who was a "straight arrow." But Bob was always very good to him and often did go out of his way to help John.

Recapitulating the first year of his analytic treatment, the principal transference trends were: (1) First an early and somewhat abortive reactivation of oedipal conflict in which phallic-competitive feelings were transferred to the analyst, and phallic-incestuous and domineering feelings were transferred to a girlfriend and to the analyst's wife. (2) A defensive homosexual transference to the analyst during which libidinal interest in women was withdrawn and attached to father-figures. (3) Conflict (mainly anxiety) about the homosexual father-transference led to a defensive splitting of tender and erotic feelings toward men, the tender love feelings remaining transferred to me (as father-figure), and the erotic feelings displaced to brother-figures. (4) Conflict about exposure of his erotic feelings to brother-figures led to still further defensive regression during which dependent and demanding feelings replaced the erotic transference to brother-figures.

WORKING THROUGH OF COMPETITIVE FATHER AND BROTHER TRANSFERENCES

Since the purpose of reviewing the therapeutic process in this case is to demonstrate that the patient was analyzable in spite of only average intelligence and other cognitive limitations, the remainder of the case report will focus upon the working over/working through of a representative sector of the patient's pathology rather than presenting an extended review of the total analytic process. The competitive father and brother complexes—i.e., phallic-oedipal conflicts alternating with defensive patterns of self-defeat, homosexuality, and dependence upon men—were among the most prevalent dynamic trends in John's analysis. Transference reliving of these conflicts and defenses recurred at intervals throughout the analytic process, each time with further elaborations of childhood fantasies and memories. This working-through process will be illustrated with clinical material from serial phases of the ongoing analytic process.

Early in the second year of his analysis John was awarded a prize for bringing in the most new business at his company. He responded to the success initially with surprise and satisfaction followed soon by reactivation of oedipal fantasies and conflict (cf., the same dynamic sequence following his first successful sexual experiences six months previously).

> *Paired dreams:* A woman at work wanted to kiss me but I was afraid the boss would see us so I told her not to kiss me when he was around. In another dream I was angry at the Pope for backing Iran.
> *Associations:* He recalled his father telling his mother that she was making a sissy of John by petting and pampering him and keeping him around the house so much. During his teens he once kissed his mother very passionately which startled her. Afterwards he was afraid she might tell his father. Associations to the Pope backing Iran brought out anger at his father for not rescuing him from mother by whom he was "held hostage."
> *Interpretation:* In the first dream he blamed mother for the kiss. In the second dream he blamed mother for holding onto him and father for not rescuing him. He blames them to avoid feeling blame himself. He responded sheepishly that he had to admit that the kiss was his own idea; and he probably could have gotten away from his mother if he had really wanted to. But the truth is that he liked being with her.

During the next several months an important defense mechanism against phallic-oedipal conflicts became evident, viz.: a need to fail—the pattern that Freud (1916, pp. 316–331) called, "wrecked by success." Soon after receiving the award for new business, for example, he very nearly got himself fired for failure to attend required meetings. Another manifestation of the same self-defeating pattern could now be recognized in his history of job-hopping—never staying with a job long enough to compete for advancement. We found also that the masochistic mechanism was coupled with a passive-dependent gratification, i.e.: having been a sick child he could obtain considerable attention from his family by appearing unable to compete. A year later in the analytic process still another motivation for this pattern appeared: by being sick as a child he could sometimes have his mother to himself.

In the middle of his second year of analysis, while anticipating a visit from his father to discuss family business, he reported the following pair of dreams:

> *Dreams:* In the first dream I was eating semen. I awakened sexually

excited. Later that night I dreamed about an aquarium that had a shark in it.
Associations: He didn't know why but he associated the first dream with his father coming to visit, sleeping in the same room with him. The second dream reminded him that as a child he had been angry at his father for not letting him have an aquarium.
Interpretation: The sharklike feelings beneath the surface would eat more than his father's semen! Those feelings would "go for the jugular"—and the penis! He shuddered at the idea. Subsequent associations were about how much money his father had and how ashamed he felt about occasional "greedy" fantasies of getting it all.

By the end of his second year of analysis the guilt and fear about competing with his father and brother had been reduced sufficiently that he was able to go into business for himself. It was only a matter of time, however, before anxiety developed about the career advancement and also about further success in his love life. He had begun "going steady" for the first time with a well-educated and attractive woman toward whom he felt both compatible and in love. As anxiety mounted in response to his competitive successes, defensive homosexual fantasies toward brother-figures reappeared. Conflict then developed about the homosexual feelings, whereupon the erotic obsession about brother-figures changed to dependent wishes for a brother's help in getting the new business started. Pride conflict about needing help stimulated a dream in which he was the helper rather than the one receiving help.

The foregoing sequence of conflicts and defenses was followed by reemergence of sibling rivalry, transferred this time to the analyst. The same series of defenses, as well as conflicts about the self-defeating, erotic, and dependent defense-transferences, soon asserted themselves. The homosexual transference was acted out symbolically one day by his coming into my office without being called and without knocking. Soon afterward he reported an undisguised homosexual dream:

Dream: I was getting my hair cut and the barber got interested in me sexually. He licked my face. I lay down and the barber got on top of me. My penis went into his rectum and ass-fucked him.
Associations: He blocked about the possibility that the barber—"the man working on his head"—was the analyst. That made him too anxious. He preferred to think it was a colleague from his new business whom he had seen the night before. His associations shifted to the incident of coming into my office uninvited. Sometimes he feels lonely and eager to see me. His friend and colleague the night before didn't seem very interested in him. That bothered him a lot.
Interpretation: It must bother him that I don't show more response to his

feelings about me. He agreed, wishing I were as eager to see him as he is to see me.

After six months of going steady with his girlfriend, Mary, he asked her to move in with him. She declined, telling him candidly that she hoped to find someone with more education. In addition to his disappointment he responded with a dream of going to college in another state, then returning and being desired by Mary. In the context of these events, during which his envy and competitiveness toward "educated men" like his father and brother had been intensified, he reported a moderately disguised dream, the associations to which were rich in oedipal content:

Dream: A death had occurred—I don't know whose. I felt panicky, as though I had lost my parents and was all alone. Then I was at my parents' home. There was a bees' nest shaped like a man's face, an older man. I think of my father. I did something to the hive, maybe tried to remove it, when out came the bees after me! All three fireplaces in the house had fires going in them. People were looking for a church where there was to be a service. I wasn't going to go. People outside the church were smoking dope. I didn't like the smell and said so.
Associations: Sometimes he misses his mother, like recently when he has felt lonely. He and his mother spent so much time together. He liked especially the trips they took together, staying in motels, sometimes even in the same bed. He would cuddle up close to her. Sometimes she walked around nude. He remembers mainly her breasts because they stood out from her body so far. One night when she was asleep he thinks he felt her tit. He was afraid she would wake up and give him hell for it. The beehive looked like father but the angry, buzzing bees remind him of mother. He practiced kissing on mother, would give her passion kisses. She got flustered one time when he kissed her a long time. He was afraid she would tell father and both of them would punish him. He wonders if his father was jealous of him.
Interpretation #1: Your removing the hive suggests that you were jealous of him! John expressed surprise, didn't recall ever feeling that. Associations turned to smoking pot—something forbidden—sex. Not liking the odor of pot reminds him of not liking the odor of women's "genikals." He does not recall seeing his mother's "public" hair (pronounced "pew-blick").
Interpretation #2: Your sexual interest in her must have felt so forbidden that you wouldn't let yourself notice or think about her genitals. You even tried to make her genitals seem undesirable by thinking of them as just hairy and smelling bad. He responded quickly that he didn't think he ever had "intercourse feelings" about his mother! Suddenly he remembered that one of the women outside the church with him in the dream was a nursemaid from his childhood. He then recalled with a

shudder that the nursemaid's husband had had his testicles removed because of cancer.

What followed in subsequent weeks was a return of the homosexual defense-transference, accompanied by increasingly undisguised anal-penetration dreams from which he awakened in panic. At that point in the therapeutic process the masochistic, self-defeating defense had combined with anal-erotic, homosexual fantasies producing a masochistic homosexual defense. When the erotic masochistic homosexual feelings gave way to the further-regressive, dependent homosexual transference, he reported a dream in which he was a young daughter in the analyst's family—the first time that wishes to be a girl had appeared so clearly.

Rather than reviewing every instance in which phallic-oedipal competitive feelings were reactivated in the therapeutic process and followed by dynamic sequences of masochistic, homosexual, and dependent defenses, only a few additional highlights illustrating these transferences will be mentioned. Childhood competitiveness with his father for possession of his mother was transferred to the issue of money on several occasions. He acted out this transference in his relationship to me by withholding payment of the fee, and in relation to his father by trying to gain control of some family funds. As his competitive father-transferences to me became increasingly hostile he blamed me for allowing him to become so involved with Mary—in part a projective defense against oedipal guilt. Insights occurred regarding: (a) using sickliness in childhood as a way of having mother to himself (the dependent defense vicariously gratified his incestuous wishes); and (b) use of a splitting mechanism to cope with ambivalent feelings toward his father and brother—i.e., directing the hostile feelings toward his father and the loving feelings toward his brother.

Frankly oedipal transferences to me and to my wife revealed themselves in dreams such as the following:

Dream: You and your wife and I were in the dream. At the end of a session you said we had to stop because you and your wife were going to a party. I went on talking to your wife. You were building a fire. There were three fireplaces. You burned up a small, ornate dollhouse, small enough to hold in your hand. I wanted to help. You didn't pay any attention to me so I went on talking to your wife—like having a session with her.

Associations: There were three fireplaces in his childhood home. His father often built fires and tended them but would not allow John to help him. He recalled his father stirring up the fire with his long poker. Mother would sometimes squeal nervously as the sparks flew. John recognized the sexual symbolism of these memories and concluded that the dollhouse might refer to a child—perhaps the girl child that he knew his mother had always wanted, that he was afraid his parents might have, and that he had tried to prevent by (a) being like a daughter to his mother and (b) stirring up conflict between his parents.

Interpretation: I agreed with the patient's own conclusions about the dream.

At this point in the third year of his analysis John met and became deeply involved with Marilyn who eventually lived with him for a year before they became engaged and then married. As his involvement with Marilyn deepened some erotic mother-transference developed toward her—e.g., dreams of a voluptuous woman showing him her body, associated with many more memories of seeing his mother nude, sleeping with her, etc.—but significantly not followed by self-defeating, homosexual, or dependent defenses. When he told his parents that he and Marilyn planned to live together his mother became furious and withdrew from him for several months. For several more months, after she had resumed contact with John, his mother refused to mention Marilyn or discuss John's relationship with her. John stood his ground courageously during this difficult period—shaken, though not in his resolve, and without moral support from either his father or his brother. His father sided with John's mother, although it is doubtful that he felt strongly about it one way or the other, and his brother told John that he should have kept the matter a secret. Eventually John's family became somewhat more accepting of his relationship with Marilyn and of his independent attitude toward them.

Early in the fourth year of analysis the working through of competitive conflicts toward his father and brother had proceeded far enough that John could recover obsessive childhood fantasies of being the "richest man in the world"—the owner of many large companies (including a detective agency!)—so successful in making money that his advice was sought by financiers, governments, and royalty throughout the world. (His father had been, and his brother became, very involved in the world of finance.) The purpose of the fantasied detective agency was to uncover financial wrongdoing on the part of rivals, as a result of which they would be put out of business. He had not admitted to himself until now, of course, that the unnamed rivals in the fantasy were his father and brother.

Following a series of dreams in which he defeated his father and brother in competitive situations involving automobiles, his associations included memories of childhood fantasies in which his father and brother were killed in accidents or died from serious illnesses. At some point in his teens that fantasy had been elaborated to include the taking over of responsibility for his brother's "widow": i.e., he would marry his sister-in-law as part of the responsibility for her. In the process, he reasoned, his sexual shyness with girls would be resolved because he felt comfortable with his brother's wife and her sexual experience would make it possible for her to teach him what to do.

As the time for termination of his analysis approached, John's principal conflict was about giving up his dependent status.

> *Dream:* My brother and I went down in a basement. It was like a wine cellar. Marilyn was there. We were going to clean up the place, straighten up the crates and bottles of wine. As I turned over one of the crates a bunch of ants crawled out and started biting my brother. They didn't attack me or Marilyn.
>
> *Associations:* (Note his improved self-interpretive capacity.) In some previous dreams basements were his unconscious. Analyst's office is down a flight of stairs. Cleaning up the basement seems like analysis. The ants biting brother is probably some childish feelings in himself toward brother, or analyst, or both. "Putting the bite" on them; angry about not being baby brother any more. Still wants that support. I asked: "What about the wine?" He said he likes wine, buys it occasionally. Then he beat around the bush, appearing to avoid the subject of wine. I brought him back to the wine again. He hesitated a moment, then said: "Wine gets better as it gets older, doesn't it?" I replied: "As it matures?" He laughed suddenly, adding sheepishly that for someone who couldn't take compliments he seemed to be paying himself one in the dream! I asked: "What do you think is improving in you?" "My mind!," he answered firmly. "I may not be any smarter but I feel a lot more sure of myself!"

FOLLOW UP

John's analysis was terminated four years ago. Approximately six months later he returned for a brief series of follow-up appointments, precipitated by further rejections from his parents and brother. Since that time he has not needed or sought additional treatment. He is happily married, and continues to prosper in his own business. John and Marilyn had their first child two years ago. The child is physically and mentally healthy, and is developing normally.

EXAMPLE OF A "GOOD ANALYTIC HOUR"

To illustrate further that despite his intellectual limitations John was able to benefit from psychoanalytic treatment, a more detailed, "cross-sectional" view of his therapeutic process will be presented in the form of a "good analytic hour" (Kris, 1956, pp. 255–260). Kris (1956) described such sessions in the following way:

> . . . "the good analytic hour" . . . [occurs] with patients well advanced in analytic therapy. . . . It may come gradually into its own, say after the first ten or fifteen minutes, when some recent experience has been recounted, which may or may not refer to yesterday's session. Then a dream may come, and associations, and all begins to make sense. In particularly fortunate instances a memory from the near or distant past—may present itself with varying degrees of affective charge . . . when the analyst interprets, sometimes all he needs to say can be put into a question. The patient may well do the summing up by himself, and himself arrive at conclusions. Such hours . . . seem as if prepared in advance (p. 255).

In a recent discussion of "good hours," Peterfreund (1983) evaluated their significance in this way:

> The good hour is one wherein patient, therapist as well as competent observers would agree that something important happened, something "true," "real," or meaningful, both cognitively and affectively. Often, these are dramatic hours, but they need not be. Good hours are especially important because so many of our sessions are murky, uncertain, confused, and it is often difficult to know what has happened. The good hour is akin to a successful experiment which has given clear-cut, valid, unambiguous results. . . . [pp. 67–68].

The appointment to be reported occurred during the third year of John's analysis, at a time when he was anticipating a visit from his father to discuss family business. During the past year John had convinced his father to let him handle the investment of some family funds; his father retained control of the money, however. In a competitive effort to prove that he could achieve greater returns from investments than his father, John had made some speculative investments which had turned out badly. Knowing that his handling of the funds would be reviewed during the coming visit, John anticipated his father's arrival with dread. The following is a summary of an appointment which occurred during that period.

John started the appointment by asking: Did you know that the bridge near your place is called "suicide bridge"? (cf. Seitz, 1955; Lipton, 1958; Arlow, 1969a, p. 14; and Spence, 1982, pp. 54, 93, regarding the dynamic significance of initial associations). He had heard the bridge called that recently. A number of people have jumped to their deaths from that bridge! Recently he has had a return of his old height phobia which started in his early or middle teens and then went away for a while when he was in the hospital (age 17). The phobia returned after he left the hospital and went to visit an older woman he had met in the hospital. She had an apartment in a high-rise building with "floor to glass" (!) windows. His mother was very opposed to his visiting the woman. When he got there and saw how far down it was to the ground the height phobia returned. He hasn't had it recently; but today, coming over the bridge near the analyst's office, he noticed it again.

He wonders why he has the height phobia. He used to like to climb trees when he was around ten years old. He knew a boy at the hospital who later hanged himself in a tree. [How did you feel about that?] I guess I felt that he succeeded, dammit! [You wish you had?] Sometimes. That way I wouldn't have to face problems all the time. [What problem just now?] Uh—I guess facing my father about the money I lost in the market. I haven't told him about it but it'll come up during his visit.

[This is beginning to sound like what happened just before your suicide attempt.] Hunh?! . . . Oh! . . . Yeah! . . . I was afraid to face my father about cutting that class at school! I was afraid he'd be furious—which I am now, too. That reminds me of a bunch of dreams I had last night.

Dream #1: I was trying to hide from someone I was afraid of. I became a statue in a fountain. Turtles kept nipping at my pants legs.
Dream #2: David Stockman who is in charge of the budget office attempted suicide by swallowing a bunch of pins.
Dream #3: I was living with an older woman whose husband was dead. I think it was the older woman in the hospital.
Dream #4: A statue was covered with ice. I was chipping the ice away. The ice was falling off in big chunks.

He began associating to the dreams spontaneously:

Associations to dream #1: There was a fountain at the mental hospital with a statue in the middle of it. I wasn't just pretending to be a statue—I *was* a statue! Turtles live a long time and have a thick shell, both like my father! That dream sounds like trying to hide from my father but he catches me anyway.
Interpretation #1: [A statue sometimes represents a dead person. You tried to escape from guilt and fear of your father by death. Have you been thinking about doing that again because of guilt and fear about the investments?] Yes, he blurted out. It has crossed my mind! But I wouldn't actually do it now—at least I don't think I would. . . . Uh—
Associations to dream #2: . . . on the other hand, that second dream about David Stockman swallowing pins could be me! My mother says I look like him—but she *prefers* Ronald Reagan!
Interpretation #2: [She prefers the "old man," eh? What about the pins?]

Pins remind him of a man's sperm. They look like sperm cells. He recalls an earlier dream of swallowing semen which occurred when his father was visiting and slept in the same room with him. But how could swallowing his father's sperm be a suicide attempt?
Interpretation #3: [It may mean killing off your manhood to keep from competing with your father.] Competing with him about investments? About mother? I wonder whether the investments, my father's money, is like mother to me. I tried everything to get control of the money, then tried to outdo my father with it.
Interpretation #4: [You also "took liberties" with it!] He laughed suddenly and nervously. Yeah, I did, didn't I? I took some liberties with Mother, too, that I was afraid for Father to know about!
Associations to dream #3: That reminds me of the next dream about living with the older woman whose husband had died. I happen to know that she tried to make a substitute husband of her son. Maybe she would have tried that with me, too!
Interpretation #5: [Maybe that's why the height phobia returned. You probably felt you were getting in over your head with her, which you must have felt at times with your mother, too.] "For sure! Like the time I kissed her so long and she got flustered. I was scared to death she'd tell Father and they'd both punish me for it." [What about the last dream?]
Associations to dream #4: Chipping the ice off the statue seems like what I do in treatment. I chip away at the thick coatings that cover up my feelings and find out what's underneath. Lately I seem to be chipping away pretty fast and deep. In that dream what lies under the ice is someone dead—me. Hmm! I'm getting the feeling that my old suicidal thoughts must have been stronger and lasted longer than I realized!
Interpretation #6: [Right!—and why do you think that is?] He was thoughtful for a while, then said: "Guilt! Guilt about wanting to get rid of my Dad; guilt about wanting to get his money; guilt about wanting to outdo him with Mother; guilt about wanting Mother all to myself; guilt about wanting sex from her. So guilty I should be given the death sentence! (End of session.)

Although I may have been more active interpretively than is usual for "good hours," nevertheless the session flowed associatively and dynamically, from beginning to end, with such clarity and spontaneity that the patient as well as I seemed to experience a sense of inevitability about its momentum and its meaning. Correspondingly, our collaboration in the therapeutic dialogue (cf. Leavy, 1980) was unusually effective and satisfying. For all of these reasons I believe the session represents a "good analytic hour." Such sessions were not rare in John's analysis but occurred several times a year during the latter half of the therapeutic process.

Discussion

The case report demonstrates that despite the patient's intellectual limitations, speech disorder, and other cognitive deficits an analytic process occurred. This finding raises a number of questions: (1) Which cognitive-intellectual functions were deficient in this patient and which were not? (2) What made it possible for him to use a complex cognitive-emotional process like psychoanalysis in spite of his intellectual and other limitations? (3) Do the findings in this case help to answer the question of what kind and degree of intelligence are needed for psychoanalysis? (4) How do the present findings and conclusions compare with those of other investigators regarding intelligence, psychologic-mindedness, and analyzability?

Starting with the question of which cognitive-intellectual functions were deficient and which were not, summaries of the various tests that John underwent, and also the results of psychological tests from age 17, will be reviewed.

SUMMARIES OF SPEECH, LANGUAGE, HEARING, PERSONALITY, AND NEUROPSYCHOLOGIC TESTS

> *Speech, language and audiologic evaluations:* His speech errors appear to result from faulty learning of the pronunciation of specific, infrequently occurring words and of the composition of certain idiomatic expressions. The source of such faulty learning in this patient is uncertain. Hearing is normal in the left ear and normal to low-normal in the right ear. Some conductive pathology was found in the right ear . . . probably from prior middle-ear problems and/or surgical procedures in the right ear. Additional tests of central auditory function revealed no abnormalities.

The patient's essentially normal hearing ruled out the possibility that his difficulty in pronouncing certain words and garbling idiomatic expressions may have resulted from inability to hear such words clearly in the first place. The speech and language tests were unable to specify the basis of his speech problems; but the personality and neuropsychologic assessments were much more specific about the etiology of these problems.

> *Psychologic and neuropsychologic tests administered:* Wechsler Adult Intelligence Scale—Revised; Rorschach; Thematic Apperception Test; Draw-a-Person; Wechsler Memory Scale; Canter Bender Interference Procedure; Wide Range Achievement Test; Gray Oral Reading Test; Wisconsin Card Sorting Test; Boston Naming Test; Brown-Peterson Short-term Memory Test; Neuropsychological Screening Examination.
>
> *Personality assessment:* Psychological testing was suggestive of a narcissistic

personality with hysterical features. Preoccupation with himself and his own needs appears to be based upon an underlying fault in his self-esteem. A sense of intellectual inferiority is the most pervasive theme (e.g., percepts of gorillas, baboons) which, however, is overdetermined, having roots both in his actual neuropsychological problems and in castration anxiety. His emotionality and narcissistic involvement with himself may be important factors in making analytic therapy possible in this otherwise relatively unreflective individual. Perhaps as a result of treatment, he appears to be developing more capacity for delay, reflection, and sublimation.

Neuropsychological testing: His general intellectual functioning is in the average range, with a Full Scale I.Q. of 107 (Verbal 107, Performance 106). Despite real difficulties in language functioning, he has acquired an adequate fund of factual information and an average vocabulary—which may have resulted from a rich early cultural environment and intact learning and retention skills. Common sense reasoning is generally intact, and mathematical reasoning average. However, he has difficulty with some aspects of higher-level verbal concept formation, verbal abstraction abilities being below average on both the Similarities and Proverb Interpretation subtests of the WAIS-R. Among nonverbal abilities tested by the WAIS-R, he did poorly on Digit Symbol—a common finding in patients with reading disability. Memory functioning appears to be generally intact, with the exception of a borderline score on a verbal short-term memory test. Language function tests reveal a mild developmental language disorder, the most important symptoms of which include dyslexia, impaired spelling, and paraphasic errors in spontaneous speech. These findings correspond with Denkla's (1979) category of "dysphonemic-sequencing difficulties"—i.e., in spite of normal vocabulary, verbal I.Q., and articulation he exhibits phonemic paraphasias and inability to decipher or spell words on the basis of phonetic skills. Except for occasional paraphasic errors (e.g., *public* for *pubic*), *spontaneous speech* was normal and *auditory comprehension* was intact. However, *reading* at the single-word recognition level was at grade level 7.1; performance on the Gray Oral Reading Test was at grade level 5.3, with frequent word substitutions and mispronunciations; and *spelling* was at grade level 6.0, with many flagrant errors showing failure of phonetic analysis (e.g., *nessaity* for *necessity, afemate* for *effeminate*). *Verbal fluency* was also low (25th–29th percentile).

In *summary,* the patient has average intelligence and a mild developmental language disorder with dyslexia, impaired spelling, and paraphasic errors (both phonemic and semantic) in spontaneous speech. These weaknesses are probably part of an underlying deficiency in left-hemisphere-mediated skills, for he also shows a borderline score on a verbal short-term memory test and impairments in verbal fluency and verbal concept formation. Also consistent with left-hemisphere dysfunction is a mild deficiency in visuospatial and constructional functioning, in which the *gestalt* is preserved but details are sparse or in error. Whether this array of problems is genetic or due to some early brain injury cannot be determined on the basis of these tests.

Psychologic test results at age 17 (Rorschach; Sentence completion; Thematic Apperception; Wechsler Adult Intelligence Scale; Bender Gestalt Test; Figure Drawings): In his *general behavior,* he stammered and made facial grimaces whenever talking about subjects that made him anxious. He expressed considerable lack of faith in his own abilities as compared with the accomplishments of his father and brother. He made rather strange mistakes in speaking and writing: e.g., he wrote his name incorrectly, fusing the first half of his first name with the last part of his last name.

Personality evaluation revealed him to be a rather isolated person who does his best to keep away from actively engaging in meaningful relationships. Yet he is very concerned about the adequacy of how he is conducting his life, and feels the need for understanding, strong authority, and guidance from others. He also shows fear of the adults around him. He is caught in a bind of wanting to have a strong authority with whom to identify and upon whom to lean, but fearing that to do so would mean losing his own individuality. He has relied upon inhibitory defenses for the most part, but at the present time poorly channeled impulses may be breaking through.

Intellectual functioning is in the Average range with a Full Scale I.Q. of 102 (Verbal 102; Performance 100). Certain areas were within the bright normal range: viz., general information, *ability to form verbal concepts* [*note contrast to recent psychological report*], and sensitivity to common details in the environment. Certain qualitative signs suggest poor judgment: e.g., when asked who Longfellow was he attempted to state Longfellow's full name, which was given as "John Greenleaf Longfellow." When constructing a design with the geometric blocks, instead of maintaining the 3 × 3 stimulus pattern, he changed it to a 4 × 2, discarding one block which he claimed was extra.

In *summary,* he is of average intellectual abilities but functions academically well below this level. His intellectual level would probably be only bright normal at best, however, so he cannot really attain the academic achievements of others in his family.

Both the recent test results and those from age 17 indicate that John's general intelligence was only average—considerably lower than that of other members of his family. In addition his left-hemisphere-mediated impairments included a language disorder (phonemic and semantic paraphasias) with severely impaired spelling, defective verbal short-term memory, and deficiencies in visuospatial and constructional functioning.

Significantly however, psychological tests from age 17, unlike the more recent tests, showed his verbal concept formation to be in the bright-normal range—i.e., higher than his general intelligence score. The latter finding corresponds with the observation during John's analysis of at least average if not better than average ability to produce, understand, and at times to interpret metaphoric and symbolic meanings. Despite his cognitive-intellectual limitations, therefore, his capacity for symbolic conceptualization remained relatively intact and presumably contributed significantly to his psychologic-mindedness and his analyzability. More will be said about this issue following a review of the literature on (1) analyzability, (2) psychologic-mindedness, and (3) the relationship of cognitive functions to psychologic-mindedness and analyzability.

Review of the Literature on Analyzability

The literature on analyzability has been reviewed previously by Waldhorn (1960), Tyson and Sandler (1971), Bachrach and Leaff (1978), and Erle and Goldberg (1979). Tyson and Sandler (1971) introduced the distinction between "indications" and "suitability" for psychoanalysis. Bachrach and Leaff (1978, pp. 892–893) called attention to the difficulty in defining what is meant by and the criteria for analyzability. Some of the many criteria used by various authors have included: resolution of unconscious conflict; degree of "accessibility"; extent of intrapsychic and life change; psychodynamic changes and insight regarding the patient's original problem; circumstances of termination; symptomatic improvement; ability to recognize and tolerate triangular conflict; clinical judgment of the treating analyst; clinical judgment of a supervisor; and independent rating scales.

Bachrach and Leaff (1978, p. 896) concluded that analyzability has multiple meanings and should be viewed as a relative rather than an absolute concept. The analytic process, for example, sometimes makes a seemingly unanalyzable person analyzable (Appelbaum, 1973). In addition patient qualities vary in importance during different phases of the analytic process, and a particular patient's analyzability can change with different analysts.

Erle and Goldberg's (1979) review focused upon problems in developing effective methods of assessing analyzability. They call attention to the "increasing complexity and . . . confusion" (p. 49) and "lack of consensus in approach" (p. 53) regarding assessment of analyzability. Waldhorn (1960, p. 478) had noted the same problem twenty years previously. Increasingly complex, multifactorial attempts to identify reliable criteria of analyzability are illustrated by the elaborate metapsychological/assessment profile developed by Greenspan and Cullander (1973) which allows comparison of the patient initially and at various points in the therapeutic process, as well as comparisons with other patients. Erle and Goldberg (1979, p. 59) concluded that the studies by Greenspan and Cullander (1973), Schlessinger and Robbins (1974), and Graff and Luborsky (1977) did not adequately specify definitions of attributes or evidence of reliability. Knapp et al. (1960) reported, however, that when impressionistic judgments were replaced with clearly stated criteria, evaluation patterns were not significantly altered.

Psychological tests were used for assessment of analyzability by the Menninger Psychotherapy Research Project (Kernberg et al., 1972) and by Kantrowitz, Singer, and Knapp (1975). The latter authors reviewed previous such studies noting possible advantages of tests including standardization, ease of comparison, and assessment of total ego functioning. Theoretically, the assessment of cognitive-intellectual factors in analyzability should be enhanced considerably by psychological testing. Evaluation of test results is complex and difficult however, particularly with respect to criteria such as motivation and affect. Appelbaum (1977) reported that in the Menninger Psychotherapy Research Project outcome predictions based upon test data *interpreted by psychoanalysts* were significantly superior to those based upon interview. The potential value of such an approach has been discussed in detail by Bachrach (1977, 1980).

The number of patient characteristics believed by different investigators to influence analyzability is startling: 390 separate references to such factors in the reports reviewed by Bachrach and Leaff (1978, pp. 884–885). They consolidated these patient characteristics into eight categories containing a total of 42 "main trends" or principal sets of factors influencing analyzability—still a disconcertingly large number. The eight major categories were: (1) Adequacy of personality functioning; (2) object relations; (3) motivation; (4) affect organization; (5) character qualities; (6) superego factors; (7) demographic factors; and (8) external factors.

Cognitive-intellectual functions were not grouped in a separate or even a single category by Bachrach and Leaff (1978) but were divided between two categories, "Adequacy of Personality Functioning" and "Character Qualities". The number of cognitive-intellectual factors included in their review and classification is small compared with the large number of noncognitive patient characteristics, suggesting perhaps that cognitive-intellectual factors are a relatively minor issue in analyzability. Bachrach and Leaff (1978) expressed caution however about drawing such a conclusion:

> A person whose analytic practice is limited to intellectually gifted analysands—such as in a university practice—may regard intelligence as hav-

> ing little prognostic value because there is little variation among his patients . . . [whereas] a person with a more varied practice may find it has considerable prognostic value because of its variability [p. 900].

Intelligence, also referred to in the literature as "learning capacity" and "educability," is one of the specific cognitive-intellectual factors believed by some writers to affect analyzability. Waldhorn (1960), Karush (in Panel, 1960, pp. 147–149), and Namnun (1968) consider high intelligence to be a positive factor in analyzability. Tyson and Sandler (1971) on the other hand do not view low intelligence as a significant factor in this regard. All that is required they believe is sufficient intelligence to form a working alliance and to gain insight. Most writers on the subject seem to feel, however, that *psychoanalytic* insights require more than average intelligence.

In the related category of education, Hamburg et al. (1967) reported that more educated patients did better in analysis; and Weber et al. (1974) concluded that intelligent patients with higher educational achievements did better. Knapp et al. (1960) on the other hand did not find education to be a significant factor in his series of 100 cases, although difficulties in thinking and memory were negatively correlated with analyzability.

Other cognitive-intellectual factors reported to have negative effects upon analyzability include: "Basic ego defects" (Zetzel, 1968); "poor judgement" (Lower et al., 1972); "gross speech defects" and "delayed verbalization in childhood" (Waldhorn, 1960); minor speech defects were not considered significant factors in analyzability (Panel, 1960).

Psychologic-mindedness, a complex, largely cognitive set of characteristics, is believed to correlate very positively with analyzability. Thirteen of fourteen studies including Waldhorn (1960), Aarons (1962), and Diatkine (1968) rated it a highly important factor. Namnum (1968) referred to psychologic-mindedness as "essential" and Kuiper (1968) viewed it as the "most essential quality" in analyzability. In addition several subcategories of psychologic-mindedness have been proposed as important determinants of analyzability: "Ability to observe oneself introspectively" (Karush, in Panel, 1960); "self-reflectiveness" (Tyson and Sandler, 1971); "capacity to split the observing from the experiencing ego" (Diatkine, 1968); "viewing self objectively" (Huxster et al., 1975; Stone, 1954); and "capacity for insight" (Levin, 1960, 1962; Knapp et al., 1960; Lower et al., 1972). Still other elements that may contribute to psychologic-mindedness will be discussed below.

Comparison of the Present Case with Previously Reported Correlations between Intelligence and Analyzability

To summarize the reported correlations between intelligence and analyzability: Despite some disagreements many investigators agree that

1. High general intelligence may facilitate and low intelligence may preclude psychoanalytic treatment.
2. Better-educated people who often have higher intelligence are more likely to be analyzable than less well-educated persons.
3. Among the various components of cognitive functioning that facilitate analyzability, psychologic-mindedness is considered particularly important.
4. Certain specific cognitive deficits have negative effects upon analyzability: basic ego defects; poor judgment; disorders of thinking and memory; major speech defects; and delayed onset of verbalization in childhood.

How does the present case compare with these previously reported correlations between intelligence and analyzability?

1. The present case does not fit the pattern reported by a majority of investigators, viz.: that analyzability is correlated with high general intelligence. The present case corresponds with the minority opinion that *only enough intelligence is needed to form a working alliance and to gain insight* (Tyson and Sandler, 1971). John had only average intelligence but was able to establish a good therapeutic alliance and was quite capable of acquiring insight. Some remarks by Heinz Hartmann (1939) about intelligence are appropriate in this connection: "The failure to recognize the limited role of intelligence in the total personality has occasionally led to a description of the totally rational man . . . as the ideal, the paragon of health. . . . Experience shows that the healthy and the analyzed man are quite unlike this 'ideal' . . ." (p. 69).
2. The present case deviates from the widely reported correlation between educational attainment and analyzability. John barely completed high school, requiring extensive tutoring and special classes to graduate. He fits the less frequently reported observation that *amount of education does not correlate significantly with analyzability* (Knapp et al., 1960).
3. The present case strongly supports the almost universal finding that *analyzable patients are psychologic-minded*—about which more later.
4. Finally, the present case partially resembles but in part does not fit certain patterns of cognitive deficit that have been reported to interfere with analyzability. With respect to "basic ego defects" (Zetzel, 1968) John suffered from deficiencies in certain left-hemisphere-mediated skills. In addition he was born with several physical deformities. Although his judgment did not appear to be affected he suffered from a short-term-memory deficiency. He had fairly severe language

difficulties but his speech defect was mild rather than "gross" (Waldhorn, 1960); and onset of speech had been delayed in childhood. On the basis of cited reports in the literature these multiple cognitive deficiencies would have been expected to make John unanalyzable; but he turned out to be well-suited for analysis despite several specific cognitive deficits.

Review of the Literature on Psychologic-Mindedness

Among the numerous criteria of analyzability that have been reported in the literature the highest consensus among investigators specifies psychologic-mindedness as "important," "highly important," or "the most essential" quality. The patient described in the present report fits that consensus. Despite only average intelligence and several specific cognitive deficits based upon left-hemisphere-mediated impairments he was distinctly psychologic-minded and analyzable. As Appelbaum (1973) has emphasized however:

> . . . psychological-mindedness . . . has remained . . . undelineated and unsurveyed . . . even the assertion that there is such an ability [raises] ambiguous issues. Is [it] one ability or a congeries of related abilities? . . . a capacity or an actuality? . . . constitutional or acquired, autonomous or a function of conflict, culturally or nosologically influenced? How is it different from . . . insight or introspection [p. 35]?

Most writers on the subject view psychologic-mindedness as a mixture of cognitive and affective elements, the combination of the two being considered particularly important. Loewenstein (1967), for example, suggested the term "psychological grasp" in place of "psychologic-mindedness" to emphasize the distinction between genuine psychologic-mindedness with its mixture of cognitive and affective elements in contrast to "intellectualized psychologizing" which serves purposes of defense.

Appelbaum (1973) defined psychologic-mindedness as ". . . a person's ability to see relationships among thoughts, feelings and actions with the goal of learning the meanings and causes of his experiences and behavior" (p. 36; emphasis omitted). This definition focuses upon the psychologic-mindedness needed in patients for psychoanalytic treatment: "The *direction* of a person's psychological thinking for purposes of treatment must be toward himself, in contrast to those who think psychologically only about other people or works of art" (p. 37). Self-observation, introspectiveness, self-awareness, and self-appraisal may be the more important aspects of psychologic-mindedness for purposes of psychoanalytic treatment, but a patient's empathy and intuitiveness toward others is by no means unimportant in therapeutic work. For example, the analyst's interpretations sometimes refer to possible motivations which the patient may have overlooked in other persons. If the patient were not psychologic-minded concerning other people as well as himself he might be unable to grasp the analyst's meaning. Although he did not include this aspect of psychologic-mindedness in his definition Appelbaum (1973) is well aware of its importance:

> To satisfy [the] requirement for psychological-mindedness a person would have to have an interest in people as complex and motivated, to be intrigued by human nature . . . [to] wonder what makes people tick. . . . Human beings are, for them, . . . life histories, caught at a point in time, many selves as well as one self . . . [p. 36].

The object-oriented as well as introspective aspect of psychologic-mindedness has been recognized by a number of writers. Kris (1956), Loewenstein (1967), and Moore and Fine (1967) emphasized that humanistic self-regard *and* object-commitment contribute to genuine psychologic-mindedness. Schafer (1970, p. 292) proposed that the capacity to recognize tragedy and irony also should be subsumed under psychologic-mindedness.

Psychologic-mindedness, therefore, is a complexly overdetermined quality, the definition of which must include cognition, affect, object-relatedness, introspection, empathy, intuition, reality sense, objectivity, curiosity, tragic-sense, irony, humor, and more—especially subtle combinations of these factors plus the ability to bring such understanding to bear upon one's own behavior or that of others when needed: i.e., the so-called availability aspect of psychologic-mindedness.

The relatively new theory of "multiple intelligences" is also relevant to the subject of psychologic-mindedness. Gardner (1983) has described seven separate aspects of intelligence which he believes may be relatively autonomous in their development. Among the sources of evidence cited for these separate entities is the observation that localized brain lesions may impair one but not necessarily others of the several intelligences, a finding that may be relevant to the present case. The seven specific intelligences are: linguistic, musical, logical-mathematical, spatial, bodily-kinesthetic, and the "personal intelligences" or intra- and interpersonal intelligence. The latter form of intelligence corresponds with what clinicians call psychologic-mindedness. Gardner's findings support the conceptualization of psychologic-mindedness as a separate and specific kind of intelligence, about which more later (pp. 207–208).

Research on "split brain" patients by Roger W. Sperry and by Michael

Gazzaniga (1970) also seems relevant to variations in psychologic-mindedness. The right hemisphere is more concerned with emotional and interpersonal functioning; lesions in the right hemisphere can impair recognition of emotion in others. Since my patient John's brain damage was confined to the left hemisphere, compensatory activity by the right hemisphere may have contributed to his better-than-average emotional and interpersonal understanding, i.e., to his psychologic-mindedness. Grigg (1977) has suggested that the differing cognitive styles of therapists—some more logical, others more intuitive—may be based in part upon variations in left-right cerebral specialization.

RELATIONSHIP OF COGNITIVE FUNCTIONS TO PSYCHOLOGIC-MINDEDNESS

Turning to specifically cognitive aspects of psychologic-mindedness, cognition was considered central to the definition of psychologic-mindedness in the Menninger Psychotherapy Research Project (Wallerstein and Robbins, 1956). Appelbaum (1973) also viewed cognition as basic to psychological thinking:

> . . . its at least minimal presence is a necessity no matter how well-endowed a person might be in the other components of psychological-mindedness. Thus mental defectives, excessively literal obsessionals and many organically damaged people . . . tend to be unpsychologically-minded [p. 36].

Although psychologic-mindedness is sometimes considered similar to or the same as insight, Appelbaum (1977, p. 37) distinguishes between psychologic-mindedness as a process and insight as a product of that process. Employing such a distinction, what are the principal cognitive structures and functions that contribute to the process of psychologic-mindedness? Some of the following mental activities are mainly cognitive while others are only partially so:

1. Ideational capacity (thinking)—varies in terms of quantity, speed, variety, complexity, and richness of content.
2. Verbal ability—highly correlated with ideational capacity since thoughts and fantasies are usually expressed through language and speech.
3. Capacity to think both abstractly and concretely as the situation requires. Although most insights proceed from the concrete to the abstract the process of psychologic-mindedness would be overly intellectualized if based entirely upon abstract thinking. Concrete thinking is needed to make the experience affectful. More will be

said about the role of abstract thinking and symbolic conceptualization later in the discussion (pp. 202ff.).

4. Capacity for integration—". . . lies at the heart of psychological thinking" (Appelbaum, 1973, p. 39). The collecting together of related ideas, memories, fantasies, and feelings allows their similarities to be recognized and a new, coalesced configuration (insight) to be formed.
5. Synthesis. If a new configuration produced by integration brings together disparate parts of the personality a capacity for synthesis also exists (Kris, 1956).
6. Self-observation and appraisal—also referred to as introspectiveness and self-awareness.
7. Ability to ". . . view the self and to observe its own functions with some measure of objectivity" (Kris, 1956, pp. 449–450). Namnum (1968, p. 271) referred to this trait as ". . . the capacity to take distance from one's emotional experience. . . ." Sterba's (1934) earlier concept of a "therapeutic split" into experiencing and observing parts of the ego was similar but described the phenomenon as a "fate" rather than an autonomous capacity of the ego.
8. Ability to shift back and forth between fantasy and reality, between past memories and present perceptions of reality (Stone, 1967).
9. Ability to tolerate and communicate the irrational (Erikson, 1964). Cf. also the related capacities of "regression in the service of the ego" (Kris, 1956); "affect tolerance" and "tolerance of frustration and delay" (Appelbaum, 1973, p. 40).
10. Empathy and intuition—". . . the talent that some people have, and others lack, to 'see,' 'know,' 'feel' covert and inexplicit psychological events" (Appelbaum, 1973, p. 36).

These various cognitive and partially-cognitive aspects of psychologic-mindedness are usually conceptualized as ego functions. Loewenstein (1967) emphasized however that psychologic-mindedness is not only an ego function but is also subject to influences from all of the psychic institutions, especially the mature, conflict-free portion of the superego.

Cognition and Psychologic-Mindedness in the Present Case

Appelbaum (1973, p. 36) concluded that mentally defective and many organically damaged patients lack the cognitive capacities for psychologic-mindedness and therefore presumably are not analyzable. The patient described in this report was not mentally defective but had only average intelligence, which was considerably lower than that of other members of his family. He suffered also from a number of left-hemisphere-mediated cognitive impairments. How did this array of neuropsychologic deficits affect the patient's psychologic-mindedness?

So far as ideation was concerned John's thoughts and fantasies during free association seemed at least average in amount and speed, although perhaps somewhat less complex and rich in content than those of intellectually more gifted patients. His thoughts tended to be simpler, less varied, and somewhat more repetitive than average but not to an extent that would be classified as "poverty of thought," "simple-minded," or "unimaginative." On that basis his ideational ability would have to be considered within the normal range.

> [Some psychoanalysts assume] incorrectly that the [patient] needs to have some literary or rhetorical command over language. . . . Not at all, as Montaigne wrote; everyone, including *"vostre chambrière,"* speaks in tropes. Uneducated language uses just as colorful figures [of speech] as educated, but they are likely to be fewer, more repetitious, and less personal [Leavy, 1980, p. 73].

Aside from his mild language and speech disorder which affected mainly his use of certain unusual words and idiomatic expressions John's verbal ability also appeared to be about average. The results of his speech tests were reported as essentially normal in this respect. In free association he expressed himself clearly and naturally with a minimum of affectation, intellectualization, circumstantiality, or severe constriction such as blocking.

John's capacity for both concrete and abstract thinking and his ability to use one or the other as the situation required appeared to be at least average or possibly somewhat better than average during free association. An example is the vignette about the woman who had trouble with the intercom. Not only did John usually grasp the meaning of symbolism interpreted by the analyst but also he possessed considerable ability to interpret metaphoric and symbolic meanings himself, without help from me. His method of self-interpretation was not that of "wild analysis" or "symbol interpretation" but was similar to the disciplined-yet-imaginative approach that analysts themselves use: i.e., he produced, collected, and reviewed his associations, especially to a puzzling fragment of material, searching for similarities, contrasts, repetitions, and contiguities on the basis of which inductive inferences were drawn or sometimes inductive "leaps" were made in the form of "hunches." Although the ability to interpret his own clinical material improved in the course of analysis it became evident early in his treatment, soon after the analytic process was under way. Self-interpretive skill had not characterized the initial psychotherapeutic phase of his treatment; and his previous treatments had not involved such interpretations by his therapists or himself. The sudden emergence of his self-interpretive capacity in the psychoanalytic situation gave the impression of a previously latent talent.

Turning to the cognitive capacities of integration and synthesis, the effectiveness of John's self-interpretive ability suggests that the idiopathic brain damage had not impaired his integrative and synthetic functions.

The cognitive capacities for self-observation and appraisal—i.e., viewing the self and observing its functions with some measure of objectivity; taking distance from emotional experiences; and the "therapeutic split" between experiencing and observing aspects of the ego—appeared to be unimpaired.

The cognitive capacity to shift back and forth between fantasy and reality, between past memories and present perceptions of reality, to tolerate and communicate the irrational, to regress in the service of the ego, control temporary and partial regression, tolerate affect, frustration, and delay—all were essentially intact.

Intuition and empathy, although initially blocked by conflict in relation to women, revealed no basic impairment as a result of John's brain damage and associated cognitive deficits.

Summing up the evaluation of cognition and psychologic-mindedness in John's case: the idiopathic brain damage which had produced impairments in a variety of cognitive structures and functions appeared to have left John's psychologic-mindedness, including its principal cognitive components, essentially unscathed. The emergence within the analytic situation of a previously latent capacity for generating and understanding symbolic psychologic contents concerning intra- and interpersonal human experiences—a highly specific form of abstract thinking which appears to be a necessary condition of psychologic-mindedness and analyzability—is of particular interest. The recent psychological tests did not detect this ability in John but, in fact, gave an impression of some difficulty with test items requiring abstraction. By contrast the psychological tests at age 17 reported his verbal concept-formation to be in the bright-normal range, higher than his general intelligence. More will be said about John's "depth-psychologic competence" in the following section.

Cognitive Functions, Psychologic-Mindedness, and Analyzability

Evidence has been presented that analyzability does not depend upon general intelligence; rather, the cognitive requirements of analyzability are related to that special kind of intelligence called psychologic-mindedness. This conclusion concurs with a consensus of reports in the literature indicating the unparalleled importance of psychologic-mindedness in analyzability.

The principal cognitive components of psychologic-mindedness (and hence analyzability) appear to include: an unusual kind and degree of interest in, curiosity about, alertness to, ability to recognize, and capacity to transform analogically, abstractively, symbolically, and metaphorically certain specific types of phenomena—viz., intrapsychic and interpersonal events concerning feelings, attitudes, motives, and relationships in oneself and others. A question arises whether the specificity of psychologic-mindedness is based primarily upon its content—i.e., the "personal" mental activities and interpersonal relationships of people, including oneself—or whether it results from a distinct set of transformational mechanisms which differ from the cognitive processes that govern other forms of thinking. The latter possibility has been postulated by Wolff (1972, 1978, pp. 260–261) who reasoned in the following way. Gouin-Décarie (1966) had observed that severe environmental disturbances can alter the sequence of affective but not of cognitive development, and that social-affective and cognitive-intellectual development do not appear to follow the same sequence of development. Somewhat similarly, a discrepancy between "intellectual logic" and "social logic" was observed by Serban (1978, p. 230) who investigated the role of cognitive defects in the development of mental illness. Wolff (1978, pp. 260–261) interpreted the findings of those investigators to mean that qualitatively different transformational mechanisms may govern cognitive-intellectual and social-affective development respectively:

> . . . . a formal system of [interpersonal] logic . . . would probably have qualitatively different formal characteristics than the psychological structures that make operational logic possible. Social logic, unlike operational logic, always remains under the control of at least two independent centers of causality [i.e., two persons]; it always operates in a concrete context, and therefore never achieves the same degree of "reversibility" which Piaget associates with operational logic [p. 261].

Although the possibility of separate kinds of transformational processes underlying cognitive-intellectual and social-affective thinking cannot be ruled out categorically, the concept seems superfluous to the present writer. The distinction between psychologic-mindedness and other kinds of cognition appears to be primarily *what* one thinks about, knows about, and is interested in rather than *how* one thinks. The cognitive processes involved in affect-laden perceptions and thoughts about oneself and other people seem capable of explanation by the same transformational processes that govern thinking generally: (a) perception of similarities among phenomena; (b) abstraction of analogies; (c) construction and deconstruction (comprehension) of symbolic structures; (d) construction and deconstruction of communicable metaphoric expressions (verbal and nonverbal). The relations of these cognitive processes to psychologic-mindedness and analyzability will now be discussed in greater detail.

Hunt (1982) observed that logic is not the normal mode of human thought. In logic every statement is true or false whereas in real life many statements are neither. We reason most of the time by noting similarities between things, making best guesses, and reaching conclusions on the basis of likelihood rather than logical certainty. Most reasoning relies on the intuitive recognition of similarities. We reason analogically about anything new in our experience by drawing a parallel to something old. Hirsch (1967) put it this way:

> No one would ever invent or understand a new type of meaning unless he were capable of perceiving analogies and making novel subsumptions under previously known types. . . . To make an analogy is not merely to equate two known types . . . but to create a new one. . . . This can happen in two ways: two old types can be amalgamated, . . . or an existing type can be extended [p. 105].

Although it is generally held that thought begins where perception leaves off, Arnheim (1969) believes that the cognitive operations called thinking are essential ingredients of perception itself. He includes among the cognitive operations of perception: active exploration, selection, grasping of essentials, simplification, abstraction, analysis and synthesis, completion, correction, comparison, problem-solving, as well as combining, separating, and putting in context. Arnheim concludes, therefore, that there is no basic difference between what happens when a person looks at the world directly and when he sits with his eyes closed and thinks (p. 13). Arnheim illustrated his thesis with the following observations from psychoanalysis:

> According to Freud, the human mind groups, at the level at which dreams are made, sticks, umbrellas, knives, steeples, watering cans, serpents, fishes, nailfiles, hammers, zeppelins, and the number three. Another group of dream items comprises pits, hollows, caves, bottles, boxes, chests, pockets, ships, gates, and mouths. This grouping is made because of a vital concern with the organs of reproduction. More specifically, the grouping is not based on just any attribute objects happen to have in common with the genitals but on those crucial to the sexual interest, namely, pointedness and the capacity to rise and pour *versus* concavity,

> receptivity, etc. . . . [In] order for the grouping to occur, an abstraction had to take place beforehand. The crucial attributes . . . had to be distilled from the particular shape and functioning of the sexual organs. Without this prior abstraction there could be no selection of the objects serving as dream images [p. 159].

Whether the perception of similarities includes the actual extraction of analogies is a moot question and does not really matter for purposes of the present discussion. It seems clear that the perceptual process of recognizing similarities and the cognitive process of abstracting analogies are closely integrated. The general literature on the abstractive function has been reviewed by Pikas (1965) who believes that abstractions are produced not in perception but "in and by memory" (p. 128). Concerning *how* abstraction operates, Langer (1948) proposed that it is based upon "the power of . . . regarding everything about a sense-datum as irrelevant except a certain *form* that it embodies" . . . (p. 58). Much the same kind of operation is implied by Kendler's (1961, p. 447) definition of abstraction (or its equivalent, "concept formation") as a "common response to dissimilar stimuli." Arnheim (1969) described a special kind of abstraction that seems to operate somewhat differently and may be particularly relevant to psychologic-mindedness, analyzability, and interpretive competence: viz., ". . . the ability to wrest a *hidden* feature or *disguised* relation from an *adverse* context" . . . (p. 70; emphasis added). Due to the factors of resistance, defense, and disguise the most relevant meanings in the therapeutic process are "hidden" and the context is often "adverse" (obscure). Arnheim's special type of abstractive operation may be applicable, therefore, to clinical interpretation in the therapeutic situation.

Since abstraction occurs in all forms of thinking except the most primitive (during the sensorimotor phase of the first two years) we may ask whether there are particular varieties or developmental stages of abstraction which are prerequisites to psychologic-mindedness and analyzability. The investigations of Piaget (Piaget and Inhelder, 1966) and Vygotsky (1934), ably reviewed by Basch (1981), provide considerable information along these lines. The stage of cognitive development that Piaget called "preoperative" (ages 2 to 6) marks the beginning of both abstraction and symbolic representation—". . . the first truly human phase of development" (Piaget and Inhelder, 1966, p. 158). From that point on objects exist for the child, making evocative recall possible. One abstraction can then represent another and meaning can be attributed to signals. In contrast to other animals which do not seem to develop this ability the human child's capacity for abstraction is virtually limitless.

Impressive as these early developments are, the cognitive achievements of the preoperative period by themselves could not produce psychologic-mindedness and analyzability; the "objects" that can be represented abstractively at this stage are still based largely on subjective experiences rather than being discreet and more-or-less objective objects. Vygotsky called this the period of "syncretic thought."

During the stage of "concrete operations" (ages 6 to 12) abstractive manipulation of symbols becomes possible, the abstraction being of sensory-perceptual qualities (Piaget and Inhelder, 1966). Vygotsky called the ability to classify in terms of perceptual bonds, "complex thinking." So far as psychologic-mindedness and analyzability are concerned, the principal limitation of this developmental stage is that abstractive transformation is confined to these sensory-perceptual qualities. Psychologic-mindedness and analyzability require the capacity for abstractive manipulation of conceptual as well as perceptual relations.

The stage that Piaget called "propositional operations," during which conceptual relations can be manipulated abstractively, appears in adolescence. Vygotsky called this "conceptual thinking." "Thinking then no longer depends on empirical facts but can deal with that which is [inexplicit and] only possible" (Basch, 1981, p. 162). Since the psychoanalytic process depends so extensively upon the ability to "interpret the inexplicit" and to "understand the merely possible," it follows that the abstractive competence required for psychologic-mindedness and analyzability must include "conceptual thinking" (Vygotsky) which begins during the adolescent stage of "propositional operations" (Piaget).

This brief review of Piaget's and Vygotsky's concepts suggests that psychologic-mindedness and analyzability depend upon mechanisms of cognitive transformation from the developmental stages of both "concrete operations" (ages 6 to 12) and "propositional operations" (adolescence). The verbal language of the psychoanalytic process is actually better suited to "complex" than to "conceptual" thinking. The discursive aspect of speech forces thought into atomized sequences which are anticonceptual. An important aspect of the analyst's job is to "prepare the ground for *conceptual* transformation [*by the patient*] of what is discursively communicated" (Basch, 1981, p. 172; emphasis added).

> . . . not until ["concrete operational"] insights become transformed into conceptual thought can their [full] significance and meaning . . . be known to the patient. . . . [The] conceptualization that brings not just more information but new meaning to what is known [is the transformation we call *insight*]. . . . the mutative interpretation is the one [that helps] the patient to perform this task [pp. 167–172].

On the basis of the foregoing developmental considerations I conclude that despite multiple cognitive deficits my patient John's cognitive capacity for transforming "concrete operational" thoughts into conceptual insights was essentially unimpaired, contributing to his being both psychologic-minded and analyzable. The mere functional intactness of these cognitive processes would not account for his psychologic-mindedness and analyzability, however. According to the present thesis those traits would depend also upon the development of a lively interest in, curiosity about, alertness to, and ability to recognize intrapsychic and interpersonal events concerning feelings, attitudes, motives, and relationships in people, including himself. No one in John's childhood family possessed such traits; the family norm and tradition was to eschew psychologic perceptiveness and candor. How, then, did John develop his psychologic-mindedness? Assuming that this trait is not simply an innate talent, I suspect that the environmental model for it was his relationship with a therapist during adolescence. Although his treatment at that time was not psychoanalytic it was dynamically oriented and therefore may have provided a model of psychologic-mindedness with which John could identify. The preanalytic absence of *overt* psychologic-mindedness may have resulted from John's characteristic conformity to family expectations. The appearance of surprisingly proficient psychologic-mindedness in his treatment with me therefore may have represented the emergence of a previously latent adolescent identification with a previous therapist.

Before leaving the subject of abstraction a recent and possibly relevant concept from cognitive science will be mentioned: viz., the concept of "modularized psychological systems":

> What seems to be characteristic of such modular systems is that they are concerned with highly specific problem structures. For example, there seems to be one such system involved in speech perception . . . there seems to be another one that is involved in rather low level analyses of visual forms. . . . There may be another one involved in face recognition; [another] in voice recognition. What is characteristic of all these mechanisms is that they do very highly specialized jobs (in a way that thought at large does not) [Fodor, 1983, p. 95].

According to this concept the brain may be partly modularized for special purposes and partly diffuse and functionally equipotential. The language of thought in the specialized areas may be different from that in the general association areas. The representational capacities of the modular systems appear to be highly specialized, too—finely tuned for the specific jobs they do—hence the individual systems may have separate, private languages (pp. 97–98). The question arises in this connection whether psychologic-mindedness might represent such a modularized cognitive system. (Cf. also Gardner's [1983] concept of "multiple intelligences," p. 44.)

Whether psychologic-mindedness is a modularized system or not, the assessment of analyzability is probably facilitated by our proceeding operationally as if it were. We are not really interested, after all, in whether a potential patient's abstractive capacity makes it possible for him or her to perform complex mathematical calculations—which is another specialized use of abstraction employing a different kind of symbols (numbers)—or even whether he/she is adept at abstraction generally. To be able to use the psychoanalytic process effectively the prospective patient needs to have an abstractive competence that is well-developed primarily and specifically in relation to people, including him- or herself: i.e., he/she needs to be analogically perceptive about inner feelings, fantasies, motivations, conflicts, sensitivities, defensiveness, relationships, capacities, limitations, etc. The psychoanalytic patient needs to have formed extensive representations of him- or herself and others in a wide variety of human contexts, the sum of which contributes to the development of a specialized perceptive-analogic-abstractive competence concerning people, their motives, and relationships. It is this more "modular" and specialized rather than general abstractive capacity that must be assessed clinically in the determination of psychologic-mindedness and analyzability. Although psychologic tests attempt to measure general abstractive capacities, the more specialized abstractive competence involved in psychologic-mindedness probably cannot be assessed satisfactorily in that way. John's *verbal* concept formation and abstractive abilities, for example, were reported as below normal on the basis of the more recent psychologic tests; but his abstractive capacity for emotionally significant intrapsychic and interpersonal events, which could be observed readily and repeatedly in the therapeutic situation, indicated better-than-average ability in this specialized, "modular system" of abstractive functioning.

With regard to the cognitive function of symbol formation, Langer (1948) stated that:

> The symbol-making function is one of man's primary activities, like eating, looking or moving about. It is [a] fundamental process of his mind [that] goes on all the time . . . following its own law it is actively translating experience into symbols, in fulfillment of a basic need to do so [pp. 32–33].

Langer (1948) considered psychoanalysis and symbolic logic to be the two fields "which have . . . developed beyond all prediction, by the discovery of the all-importance of symbol using" . . . (p. 17). Edelson (1972) observed that Freud's dream studies established psychoanalysis as a science of symbolic functioning that studies symbolic systems: "Psychoanalysis inherently aspires . . . to a general theory of symbolic functioning" (p. 206). Blum (1978) proposed a broad psychoanalytic framework from which to view symbolic processes and symbol-formation: a spectrum of symbolic representations extending from primary-process derivatives to the most abstract symbolizations.

The relatively recent field of cognitive science has become increasingly interested in the symbolic function. Recognizing the need for some sort of internal representation of reality (Miller, 1983, p. 15) cognitive scientists now theorize that "Man . . . represents the world symbolically . . . [which] gives us a way to represent things at levels quite different from the concrete, perceptual level" (p. 28). Mental representations themselves are symbols, and mental activities such as thinking and fantasy are carried out by means of symbolic representations.

> The . . . mind is . . . essentially a symbol processing device. . . . [Thought] in general is a matter of deploying these symbols in some disciplined way. . . . [Furthermore, in] contemporary cognitive science . . . mental processes have gone underground . . . cognitive scientists now assume that the most interesting thought processes are unconscious [Fodor, 1983, pp. 85–86].

Fodor called attention to a far-reaching parallel between mental activities such as desires and beliefs on the one hand and certain properties of symbols on the other: ". . . mental states and symbols are the only things in the universe—at least the only things we know of—which have semantic properties. . . . [In constructing] a theory of mind . . . that parallelism [should not be considered] simply an accident" (p. 85).

The specific kinds of symbolic representations that are of greatest significance to the clinician in assessing psychologic-mindedness and analyzability are those symbolic structures that concern the patient's observations and evaluations of mental activities and relationships in him- or herself and others. An important but sometimes overlooked aspect of evaluating the symbolizing function is that the capacity for both *constructing* and *comprehending* symbolic representatives must be assessed. Is the patient able to *produce* interpretable symbolic structures and can she or he *understand* symbolic meanings? The former is a constructive and the latter a "deconstructive" process (cf. Palombo, 1978, 1984). The intercom incident in John's analysis illustrates both aspects of psychologically minded symbolic competence: i.e. (a) his ability to transform a highly specific intrapsychic and interpersonal conflict involving his girlfriend into an analogous interpersonal event entailing a contact and communication problem between himself and another woman; and (b) subsequently the ability to "deconstruct" the abstractively analogized and symbolically substituted event in order to understand its unconscious meaning.

I turn now to the cognitive function of *metaphoric expression* and its relationship to psychologic-mindedness and analyzability. The goal of the therapeutic process is to learn as much as possible about what transpires in the repressed enclave of the patient's unconscious, the mental activities of which operate according to the primary processes. The latter processes are characterized by displacements and substitutions of emphasis, condensations of meanings, and by symbolizations. Since it is primarily meanings that we interpret we are particularly interested in derivatives of the repressed unconscious that have a symbolic form—but not simply the everyday discursive type of symbolism that lends itself to linear expression in words. We are even more interested in what Langer (1948) calls "presentational" symbolism which is not readily expressed verbally but occurs in art, music, ritual, dreams, fantasies, and in *metaphorical forms of expression.* This type of symbolic representation manifests itself in phenomena such as images, attitudes, moods, and dispositions; it operates metaphorically, and the significance of its symbolic content is felt or sensed rather than clearly identified. Bringing together the concepts of analogy, abstraction, presentational symbolism, and metaphor Langer (1948) observed that:

> Where a precise word is lacking to designate the novelty which the speaker would point out, he resorts to the powers of . . . analogy, and uses a word denoting something else that is a presentational symbol for the thing he means. . . . Metaphor is our most striking evidence of abstractive seeing [and thinking]. . . . Every new experience or new idea about things evokes first of all some metaphorical expression [pp. 111–116].

Sharpe (1940) was one of the first psychoanalysts to recognize the significance of metaphor in the therapeutic process. Shengold (1981) considers metaphor important in therapeutic work because it originates in "that period of wonder" during the second year of life when the child is establishing both a sense of self and a recognition of the external world by forming mental representations which both equate and differentiate the inner and outer worlds. Metaphor therefore expresses and evokes analogic similarities and differences between the inner and outer worlds. Arlow (1969a, b) also noted the "ubiquitous foreground character" of metaphor, associations to which regularly lead to unconscious fantasies typical for the patient. Arlow (1979) agreed with Langer (1948) that metaphor is a fundamental component of human thought, a basic mechanism for integrating experience and organizing reality. Perception and memory, for example, are integrated analogically in terms of similarities and differences by means of metaphor. Leavy (1973) and Isay (1977) have called attention to the inherent ambiguity of speech; but ambiguity makes metaphor possible and metaphor provides an infinite number of potential meanings for the expression of overdetermination (Lacan, 1970; Leavy, 1973).

Metaphor is a form of figurative speech—language which says one thing but means another. Hawkes (1972, p. 59) considers metaphor the most fundamental form of figurative speech. The mechanism of metaphor is transfer of meaning from one object to another. Metaphor gives language flexibility, expressibility, and the ability to expand. "It is the [mechanism] whereby language, even with a small vocabulary, [can] embrace a multimillion things" (Langer, 1948, p. 116).

Arlow (1979) considers psychoanalysis itself to be ". . . essentially a metaphorical enterprise. The patient addresses the analyst metaphorically; the analyst listens and understands in a corresponding manner" (pp. 373–374). Transference, too, according to Arlow (1979) is related to metaphor; in fact they mean the same thing, the carrying over of meaning from one set of objects to another. "Transference in the analytic situation is a particularly intense, lived-out metaphor of the patient's neurosis" (p. 382).

> Sometimes large segments of an analysis center about the understanding of one or two leading metaphors. . . . The different variations of the basic metaphor take on special and clearer meaning as they become related to each other . . . in time, contiguity, and context. Metaphoric expressions may be said to relate to each other as the syntax of unconscious fantasy [pp. 379–380].

Voth (1970) found that metaphorical expressions appear when the transference relationship is most intense. Although the metaphoric expression is concrete and specific its meaning is abstract and general; the meaning therefore must be grasped cognitively rather than empathically. Shengold (1981) suggested that the therapeutic process can be conceptualized as an investigation of the patient's characteristic metaphors: ". . . what and how they connect; how they are coordinated; what prevents or arrests the connective flow; . . . [evoking] the patient's awareness [of] and responsibility for his metaphors, and especially for the passions attached to, or contained in, them" (p. 302). Shengold also proposed that metaphor and insight are related by virtue of both "making connections." The word "insight" itself is a metaphor, meaning originally "seeing with the eyes of the mind." Both metaphor and insight function by connecting and integrating experiences.

To illustrate that psychologic-mindedness and analyzability depend upon the cognitive capacity to produce and understand metaphors, I turn once again to the intercom incident in John's analysis. At the time of creating the metaphor John's mind was in a state of readiness to perceive phenomena that somehow resembled his inner frustration, hurt, and anger about Marilyn's withdrawal. When the intercom incident occurred, perceptual and projective processes seized upon the event instantaneously; and cognitive processes promptly abstracted several analogies or common denominators between the intercom incident and his problem with Marilyn. Starting with some of the simpler similarities between the two experiences: (1) Both situations involved a disturbance in interpersonal relationships; (2) the participants in both cases involved a man and a woman; (3) the nature of the disturbance between the man and the woman involved an insufficiency of close, warm physical contact and a breakdown of communication; (4) in both instances the women contributed to the problem by failure to understand that close, warm physical contact was needed from them to facilitate communication; (5) in both cases the man reacted with unresponsive silence to the women's lack of understanding about what was needed from them. John used the intercom incident therefore to construct a metaphor of his problem with Marilyn, later deconstructing it to grasp its meaning.

One final observation will be mentioned to complete this discussion. The developmental paradigm that I have used for the cognitive functions involved in psychologic-mindedness is based upon the investigations and concepts of Piaget and Inhelder (1966) and Vygotsky (1934). From the standpoint of that paradigm psychologic-mindedness as we know it in certain adults should not occur in the unprecocious preadolescent child. Consonant with that prediction I have been unable to find any reports in the literature of child psychoanalysis that deal directly with psychologic-mindedness. A report by Ritvo (1978) emphasizes the cognitive-developmental limitations of the child in that regard:

> With the child a crucial question, quite apart from resistance and defense, is the degree to which the child's development makes it possible for him to have the self-awareness, objectivity, and intellectual comprehension [for] full partnership in the [therapeutic] process (p. 298). . . . The inability of the child to [observe himself and maintain conflicting beliefs] may not be a resistance as much as it may be an inability of the child to comprehend and carry out the steps of abstraction, conceptualization, and generalization which are [needed for those purposes]. In the initial phase the adult analysand, too, has to be educated to this feature of the analytic process, but he has the fully matured capacity for abstract think-

> ing and generalization to bring to the task. The analytic process may stimulate precocious development of this capacity in the child, but the usual situation is one of limitation in this regard [pp. 301–302]. . . . The immaturity of the child's capacity for conceptualization, generalization, and abstraction limits his capacity for the self-observation and comprehension of meanings which are an important part of ego becoming where id was [p. 304].

Along similar lines Neubauer (in Panel, 1980, p. 731) quoted Anna Freud to the effect that "The child lacks introspection and consequently has diminished insight into [his or her illness]." Neubauer added, however, that because of the child's curiosity, need to arrive at causative connections, and "closeness to drive influence" the child does "theorize" about his or her experience, which might be considered a "forerunner of true insight" and perhaps also of psychologic-mindedness.

Summary

The case of an analyzable patient with multiple left-hemisphere-mediated cognitive deficits including a speech disorder and a full-scale I.Q. of only 107 suggests that analyzability does not depend upon general intelligence. The cognitive requirements of analyzability appear to be associated with that special kind of intelligence called psychologic-mindedness which is at least partially independent of general intelligence.

The principal cognitive components of psychologic-mindedness include an unusual kind and degree of interest in, curiosity about, alertness to, ability to recognize, and capacity to transform analogically, abstractively, symbolically, and metaphorically certain specific types of phenomena, viz.: intrapsychic and interpersonal events concerning feelings, attitudes, motives, and relationships in oneself and other people. The cognitive transformations of these particular types of intrapsychic and interpersonal events are presumably the same as for thinking generally, i.e.: perception of similarities among phenomena; abstraction of analogies; construction and comprehension (deconstruction) of symbolic representations; and construction and comprehension (deconstruction) of communicable metaphoric expressions (verbal and nonverbal).

Reviews of the literature on analyzability, cognitive functions, and psychologic-mindedness are presented, and the relations of cognitive transformations to psychologic-mindedness and analyzability are discussed. The focus of the present investigation upon cognitive functions and psychologic-mindedness does not imply that these are the only important factors determining analyzability.

REFERENCES

Aarons, Z. A. (1962), Indications for analysis and problems of analyzability. *Psychoanal. Quart.*, 31:514–531.

Appelbaum, S. A. (1973), Psychological-mindedness: Word, concept, and essence. *Internat. J. Psycho-Anal.*, 54:35–46.

——— (1977), *Psychotherapy: The Anatomy of Change.* New York: Plenum.

Arlow, J. A. (1969a), Unconscious fantasy and disturbances of conscious experience. *Psychoanal. Quart.*, 38:1–27.

——— (1969b), Fantasy, memory, and reality testing. *Psychoanal. Quart.*, 38:28–51.

——— (1979), Metaphor and the psychoanalytic situation. *Psychoanal. Quart.*, 48:363–385.

Arnheim, R. (1969), *Visual Thinking.* Berkeley: University of California Press.

Bachrach, H. M. (1977), Psychoanalysis and diagnostic testing: With special reference to the assessment of analyzability. *J. Phila. Assn. Psychoanal.*, 4:147–161.

——— (1980), Analyzability: A clinical-research perspective. *Psychoanal. & Contemp. Thought*, 32:85–116.

——— & Leaff, L. A. (1978), "Analyzability": A systematic review of the clinical and quantitative literature. *J. Amer. Psychoanal. Assn.*, 26:881–920.

Basch, M. F. (1981), Psychoanalytic interpretation and cognitive transformation. *Internat. J. Psycho-Anal.*, 62:151–175.

Blum, H. P. (1978), Symbolic processes and symbol formation. *Internat. J. Psycho-Anal.*, 59:455–471.

Denkla, M. B. (1979), Childhood learning disabilities. In: *Clinical Neuropsychology*, ed. K. M. Heilman & E. Valenstein. New York: Oxford University Press, pp. 535–573.

Diatkine, R. (1968), Indications and contraindications for psychoanalytic treatment. *Internat. J. Psycho-Anal.*, 49:266–270.

Edelson, M. (1972), Language and dreams. *The Psychoanalytic Study of the Child*, 27:203–282. New York: International Universities Press.

Erikson, E. H. (1964), *Insight and Responsibility.* New York: Norton.

Erle, J. B. & Goldberg, D. A. (1979), Problems in the assessment of analyzability. *Psychoanal. Quart.*, 48:48–84.

Fodor, J. (1983), Imagery and the language of thought. In: *States of Mind*, ed. J. Miller. New York: Pantheon, pp. 82–98.

Freud, S. (1916), Some character-types met with in psycho-analytic work: II. Those wrecked by success. *Standard Edition*, 14:316–331. London: Hogarth Press, 1957.

Gardner, H. (1983), *Frames of Mind: The Theory of Multiple Intelligences.* New York: Basic Books.

Gazzaniga, M. (1970), *The Bisected Brain.* New York: Appleton-Century-Crofts.

Gouin-Décarie, T. (1966), *Intelligence and Affectivity in Early Childhood.* New York: International Universities Press.

Graff, H. & Luborsky, L. (1977), Long-term trends in transference and resistance: A report on a quantitative-analytic method applied to four psychoanalyses. *J. Amer. Psychoanal. Assn.*, 25:471–490.

Greenspan, S. I. & Cullander, C. C. H. (1973), A systematic metapsychological assessment of the personality—its application to the problem of analyzability. *J. Amer. Psychoanal. Assn.*, 21:303–327.

Grigg, K. A. (1977), Implications of left-right cerebral specialization for psychoanalytic data collection and evaluation. *Internat. Rev. Psycho-Anal.*, 4:440–457.

Hamburg, D., Bibring, G., Fisher, C., Stanton, A., Wallerstein, R., Weinstock, H., & Haggard, E. (1967), Report of Ad Hoc Committee on central fact-gathering data of the American Psychoanalytic Assn. *J. Amer. Psychoanal. Assn.*, 15:841–861.

Hartmann, H. (1939), *Ego Psychology and the Problem of Adaptation.* New York: International Universities Press, 1958.

Hawkes, T. (1972), *Metaphor.* London: Methuen.

Hirsch, E. D., Jr. (1967), *Validity in Interpretation.* New Haven: Yale University Press.

Hunt, M. (1982), *The Universe Within: A New Science Explores the Mind.* New York: Simon and Schuster.
Huxster, H., Lower, R., & Escoll, P. (1975), Some pitfalls in the assessment of analyzability in a psychoanalytic clinic. *J. Amer. Psychoanal. Assn.,* 23:90–106.
Isay, R. A. (1977), Ambiguity in speech. *J. Amer. Psychoanal. Assn.,* 25:427–452.
Kantrowitz, J. L., Singer, J. G., & Knapp, P. H. (1975), Methodology for a prospective study of suitability for psychoanalysis: The role of psychological tests. *Psychoanal. Quart.,* 33:371–391.
Kendler, T. S. (1961), Concept formation. *Ann. Rev. Psychol.,* 12:447–472.
Kernberg, O. F., Burstein, E. D., Coyne, L., Appelbaum, A., Horwitz, L., & Voth, H. (1972), Psychotherapy and psychoanalysis: Final report of the Menninger Foundation's Psychotherapy Research Project. *Bull. Menninger Clin.,* 36:1–275.
Knapp, P. H., Levin, S., McCarter, R. H., Wermer, H., & Zetzel, E. (1960), Suitability for psychoanalysis: A review of 100 supervised analytic cases. *Psychoanal. Quart.,* 29:459–477.
Kris, E. (1951), Aesthetic ambiguity. In: *Psychoanalytic Explorations in Art.* New York: International Universities Press, pp. 243–264.
——— (1956), On some vicissitudes of insight in psychoanalysis. *Internat. J. Psycho-Anal.,* 37:445–455. Also in: *Selected Papers of Ernst Kris.* New Haven: Yale University Press, 1975, pp. 255–263.
Kuiper, P. (1968), Indications and contraindications for psychoanalytic treatment. *Internat. J. Psycho-Anal.,* 49:261–264.
Lacan, J. (1970), The insistence of the letter in the unconscious. In: *Structuralism,* ed. J. Ehrmann. Garden City, N.Y.: Doubleday, pp. 103–136.
Langer, S. K. (1948), *Philosophy in a New Key.* New York: Mentor.
Leavy, S. A. (1973), Psychoanalytic interpretation. *The Psychoanalytic Study of the Child,* 28:305–330. New Haven: Yale University Press.
——— (1980), *The Psychoanalytic Dialogue.* New Haven: Yale University Press.
Levin, S. (1960), Problems in the evaluation of patients for psychoanalysis. *Bull. Phila. Assn. Psychoanal.,* 10:86–95.
——— (1962), Indications for psychoanalysis and problems of analyzability. *Psychoanal. Quart.,* 31:528–531.
Lipton, S. D. (1958), A note on the connection between preliminary communications and subsequently reported dreams. *J. Amer. Psychoanal. Assn.,* 6:237–241.
Loewenstein, R. (1967), Comments in Kris Study Group Monograph II: *Indications for Psychoanalysis,* E. D. Joseph, ed., H. F. Waldhorn, reporter. New York: International Universities Press, pp. 44–45.
Lower, R., Escoll, P., & Huxster, H. (1972), Bases for judgments of analyzability. *J. Amer. Psychoanal. Assn.,* 20:610–621.
Miller, J. (1983), *States of Mind.* New York: Pantheon.
Moore, B. E. & Fine, B. D. (1967), *A Glossary of Psychoanalytic Terms and Concepts.* New York: American Psychoanalytic Association.
Namnum, A. (1968), The problem of analyzability and the autonomous ego. *Internat. J. Psycho-Anal.,* 49:271–275.
Palombo, S. R. (1978), *Dreaming and Memory: A New Information Processing Model.* New York: Basic Books.
——— (1984), Deconstructing the manifest dream. *J. Amer. Psychoanal. Assn.,* 32:405–420.
Panel (1960), Analyzability and the factors in ego-integrative strength, S. Guttman, reporter. *J. Amer. Psychoanal. Assn.,* 8:141–151.
Panel (1980), Insight in child and adult psychoanalysis, E. Chaitman, reporter. *Psychoanal. Quart.,* 49:729–733.
Peterfreund, E. (1983), *The Process of Psychoanalytic Therapy: Models and Strategies.* Hillsdale, N.J.: Analytic Press.
Piaget, J. & Inhelder, B. (1966), *The Psychology of the Child.* New York: Basic Books, 1969.
Pikas, A. (1965), *Abstraction and Concept Formation.* Cambridge: Harvard University Press.

Ritvo, S. (1978), The psychoanalytic process in childhood. *The Psychoanalytic Study of the Child,* 33:295–306. New Haven: Yale University Press.
Schafer, R. (1970), The psychoanalytic vision of reality. *Internat. J. Psycho-Anal.,* 51:279–297.
Schlessinger, N. & Robbins, F. P. (1974), Assessment and follow up in psychoanalysis. *J. Amer. Psychoanal. Assn.,* 22:418–444.
Seitz, P. (1955), Relation of initial associations to focal conflict in analytic interviews. Presented to the Chicago Psychoanalytic Society, February 22.
Serban, G. (ed.) (1978), *Cognitive Defects in the Development of Mental Illness.* New York: Brunner/Mazel.
Sharpe, E. F. (1940), Psycho-physical problems revealed in language: An examination of metaphor. *Internat. J. Psycho-Anal.,* 21:201–213.
Shengold, L. (1981), Insight as metaphor. *The Psychoanalytic Study of the Child,* 36:289–306. New Haven: Yale University Press.
Spence, D. P. (1982), *Narrative Truth and Historical Truth: Meaning and Interpretation in Psychoanalysis.* New York: Norton.
Sterba, R. F. (1934), The fate of the ego in analytic therapy. *Internat. J. Psychoanal.,* 15:117–126.
Stone, L. (1954), The widening scope of indications for psychoanalysis. *J. Amer. Psychoanal. Assn.,* 2:567–594.
——— (1967), Comments in Kris Study Group Monograph II: *Indications for Psychoanalysis,* E. D. Joseph, ed., H. F. Waldhorn, reporter. New York: International Universities Press, pp. 41–43.
Tyson, R. & Sandler, J. (1971), Problems in the selection of patients for psychoanalysis: Comments on the application of the concepts "indications," "suitability," and "analyzability." *Brit. J. Med. Psychol.,* 44:211–228.
Voth, H. M. (1970), The analysis of metaphor. *J. Amer. Psychoanal. Assn.,*18:599–621.
Vygotsky, L. S. (1934), *Thought and Language.* Cambridge: MIT Press, 1962.
Waldhorn, H. F. (1960), Assessment of analyzability: Technical and theoretical observations. *Psychoanal. Quart.,* 29:478–506.
Wallerstein, R. S. & Robbins, L. (1956), The Psychotherapy Research Project of the Menninger Foundation. *Bull. Menninger Clin.,* 20:221–278.
Weber, J., Bradlow, P., Moss, L., & Elinson, J. (1974), Predictions of outcome in psychoanalysis and analytic psychotherapy. *Psychiat. Quart.,* 40:1–33.
Wolff, P. H. (1972), Operational thought and social adaptation. In: *Play and Development,* ed. M. Piers. New York: Norton, pp. 28–42.
——— (1978), Critical remarks on essays by Lawrence Kohlberg, George Serban, Aaron T. Beck, & John Rush. In: *Cognitive Defects in the Development of Mental Illness.* New York: Brunner/Mazel, pp. 258–265.
Zetzel, E. (1968), The so-called good hysteric. In: *The Capacity for Emotional Growth.* New York: International Universities Press, 1970, pp. 229–245.

July 1986

A Parameter

JULES GLENN, M.D. (Great Neck, N.Y.)

After four years of psychoanalysis, Mrs. V., now 31, who had sought treatment because she took Valium nightly in order to prevent panic dreams, decided that she was ready to stop the medication. However, as she might well be addicted to the hypnotic after fourteen years of regular use, she appealed for my help to avoid adverse physical withdrawal reactions. She wanted *me* to establish a regimen because when an internist had attempted to help her gradually withdraw a year previously, he had failed: she had maneuvered him into providing other drugs rather than stopping the Valium. In effect she requested that I institute a parameter. For a number of reasons I did.

Eissler (1953) has stated that in the model technique the analyst's interventions consist only of interpretations. The introduction of any other intervention, which he called a *parameter*, should occur only when the ego structure of the patient requires it to allow the analysis to progress. Further, according to him, the meaning and effects of the parameter should undergo analytic scrutiny so as to abolish its effects. Adverse results of a parameter include the transference intrusion of the intervention. In addition, the parameter should never exceed the least necessary degree of deviation.

Loewenstein (1957) has challenged Eissler's approach. He observed that there need not be any ego modification in order to employ an intervention other than interpretation. Indeed, what Eissler designates as parameters and Loewenstein prefers calling interventions are not unusual. They are employed in every analysis. One does so at the start of every analysis when

Much of the clinical material in this article was presented and discussed at a meeting of Group 1 of the Center for Advanced Psychoanalytic Studies, of which Dr. Samuel Lipton was a member. However, he was ill and did not attend that particular meeting.

one informs the patient about the use of the couch and free association, for instance. Further, there are a variety of preparations for interpretation, including pointing out patterns of thought, behavior, and mechanism, clarifications and confrontations that are necessary for the analysis to proceed. It is often difficult to differentiate preparatory comments from interpretations, Loewenstein observed.

I believe that most analysts subscribe to Loewenstein's views and agree with his statement that the fewer noninterpretive interventions the better. Neither he nor Eissler opposes the use of parameters. They both assert that they should be used when appropriately and rationally dictated. They both agree that there are times when the analyst employs rather unusual methods that are neither interpretations nor preparations for interpretations in order to overcome resistance when interpretation fails to suffice. Such was the case with Mrs. V.

Case Material

Before I discuss the parameter itself, I will describe the analysis briefly. I will sketch the background setting in which the intervention occurred.

Mrs. V.'s analysis was characterized by her talking freely for periods and then withholding her thoughts. She also withheld payment of her bill to me and accumulated debts to other people. The retention was a derivative of obstipation following a tonsillectomy when she was three years old. Mrs. V. had imagined the operation was punishment for sex play with a male baby sitter. She believed she had been castrated for oedipal wishes, and retained her bowel movements to undo the loss and prevent further loss. The withholding also appeared to be based on earlier toilet-training battles with her mother who was rather demanding and intrusive.

A new meaning of the periods of silence then appeared. She had to be quiet when her parents returned home in order to keep them from overhearing her sexual behavior with the babysitter at three. Her fear of being apprehended continued. It became so great that when she had another operation, an appendectomy, shortly after her first sexual relations at seventeen years of age, she developed nightmares for which she took the Valium. The drug combated the anxiety chemically but also served as an oral defensive gratification and provided justification for a fantasy that she would replace that which she had lost. She could hide envy of men and their genitals by ingesting the Valium.

Narcissistic determinants of the silences then emerged. Mrs. V. feared she and I would realize that she was imperfect if she uttered illogical thoughts during free association. She therefore remained silent. Extreme rage occurred when she felt that my interpretations were critical and demonstrated her failure to be an omnipotent and omniscient person. First her penis envy appeared to be the central reason for her feeling so deficient. Then a symbioticlike relationship with her husband, based on a similar attachment to her mother, revealed itself. Her husband would insist they were a team capable of playing beautiful music when she played the violin at his direction. Although she resented this view, she joined with her husband in actualizing the fantasy.

At this point in the analysis Mrs. V. determined that she no longer needed the Valium. She and I had accomplished a great deal of analytic work together, the outline of which I have presented. Mrs. V. felt she understood why she had required it, and she requested that I help her stop taking it by helping her establish a withdrawal regimen. I did not immediately accede to her request. First, through her associations and my interpretations we added to her insight. She could see that the ingestion of the Valium her husband supplied represented the union of mother and infant. Without the sense of fusion it engendered she would become furious and anxious. She arranged for her husband to stop supplying the medication, but had quite a few tablets in her possession.

For reasons I will describe in the discussion section, at the time I agreed to the following arrangement which Mrs. V. and I decided upon. She threw out most of the Valium and gave me the rest. I would give her a few pills at a time daily or every few days on a prearranged schedule, thus enabling her to withdraw completely in a period of less than a week. She would receive less Valium each day.

This plan worked out rather well. In even less than the time we had arranged, Mrs. V. was no longer taking medication. The panic dreams did not occur. Feeling extremely confident, she started to talk about ending the treatment. She felt in control of things. Indeed, we noted, she had controlled the withdrawal by stopping the Valium in a shorter period than planned. Her need for control was related to her lack of control before and during surgery in her childhood and adolescence.

To a great degree the meaning of the parameter, my keeping and doling out the Valium to the patient, was analyzed, as Eissler recommended. Mrs. V. told me a joke in which Martians have sex relations and produce children, not through intercourse, but through finger contact. She associated this joke to our hands having made contact when I gave her the pills. She recognized her intense affection for me, her sexual desires, but wanted to push them out of her mind. She also wanted to avoid recognizing her desire for me to take care of her as a mother looks after an infant. In a rather symbolic stream of associations she talked of diminishing the dosage from three tablets a night to two tablets. I had first given her three pills, which she associated with the male genitals. I had, she imagined, given her my penis and testicles. Then, when I handed her two tablets, she felt as if I were a mother offering her my two breasts.

When she stopped the medication she felt extremely independent and wanted to continue to feel that way. She was able to end the analysis, she said. She experienced a similar feeling of confidence with her husband and mother. Now her sexual relations with her husband were excellent and they didn't argue as they had previously.

For the first time Mrs. V. recalled a frightening event that occurred when she was about three years of age. Her parents went away for a vacation for several days, leaving her in the care of an adolescent girl. One night this girl held a big party at the house; many teenage boys and girls attended. When the patient went to bed early, the guests played a dreadful prank. They put sheets over their heads and hid in different parts of the patient's room. When she entered the room to go to bed, they suddenly revealed themselves, terrifying the little girl. She cried uninterruptedly for hours. Finally neighbors heard the commotion and intervened. They dismissed the baby sitter and informed the patient's parents, who returned the next day.

Mrs. V. immediately saw the connection between the event and her panic dreams. She remembered that as she awoke from a repetitive frightening dream she would feel her body, including her arms and legs, but especially her head, was becoming very large. She became dizzy and felt pins and needles all over her body. She saw flashing lights and spots in a domelike pattern, and heard buzzing sounds. This phenomenon, similar to what Isakower (1938) had described, had been analyzed earlier in the treatment as a memory of an oral feeding experience which appeared defensively to ward off forbidden oedipal wishes, and as a repetition of sensations that occurred during her anesthesia at three and again in adolescence. Now she connected the hypnopompic phenomenon with her terror at seeing the children with sheets over them. They were ghostlike figures. She recalled that she had nightmares following this traumatic event and agreed with my reconstruction that the dreams repeated the trauma in an attempt at mastery. The adult panic dreams were a new version of these, following separation from her parents when she left for college and underwent surgery. Mrs. V. had a vague feeling that the original traumatic event was somehow connected with sexual activity on the part of the patient or the teenagers, but could reach no firm conclusions.

After this piece of analysis, Mrs. V. felt excellent and wanted more than ever to terminate the analysis. We discussed resistance aspects of this desire. She did not want to go further into the traumatic experiences that were so upsetting. She wanted to control things, her fears, the upset that might occur if *I* stopped the treatment rather than she. I suggested that she wanted to avoid her affectionate relationship with me by ending the analysis, but she was skeptical. She agreed that she wished to be independent and correct about everything. Mrs. V. became rather argumentative at this time, but argumentativeness alternated with friendliness.

The interpretation of the resistances to continuing did not result in any diminution of the desire to stop. She suggested a termination date two months hence, and I agreed to it. She then had a dream:

I am in a crowded elevator which I am taking to the twentieth floor. I get off the elevator and go through a gate into an office.

The office in the dream reminded Mrs. V. that her brother had just passed the bar examination and was opening an office. She had selected a painting to give to her brother, a painting of the scales of justice, which in turn reminded her of male genitals. She recalled seeing her father's genitals including his testicles when she was a young girl. The painting also had a gavel, like one her father, a judge, possesses. Its color is the same as the wall of my consultation room. Indeed the appearance of the twentieth floor reminded her of my address and the gate in the dream a chandelier in my office. She thought of giving me a gift—a painting. To the people in the elevator she associated a party. She hopes to see me at a party after the analysis ends, perhaps at a Bar Mitzvah. In fact she met an analyst I know who looks like me, and she even danced with him. As she associated to the dream, Mrs. V. protested that her associations were not valid, even though she believed in their appropriateness. Her tone was argumentative.

I suggested that perhaps she enjoyed doing what lawyers do—argue in a tortured way. Mrs. V. recognized her pleasure in arguing with me and recalled that her father and brother love to dispute. Feeling accused by me, she added, was like a lawyer or judge accusing her. Feeling judged by me was like her father, a judge, judging her. She suggested that her argumentative relationship with me could be a way of hiding her love for me and before that, for her brother and father. It was also an expression of that love, we both agreed. She recalled feeling guilty and accused of sexual thoughts in childhood. She connected this with the episode when her parents were away and the teenagers partied. She disagreed with my suggestion that something sexual occurred at that time.

Mrs. V. got to see that her argumentation, her desire to see me at a party, her wish to give me a picture stemmed from increased love for me due to plans to terminate the analysis. She could not see that she was angry about ending. She took her son to a psychiatrist with the expectation that he would treat him. Through her contact with this man she could vicariously continue contact with me.

With the analysis of her desire to maintain her attachment to me as a father figure, the treatment ended. She was pleased that there was no return of symptoms and confident that that state of affairs would continue. She was delighted that she was getting along with her husband and that her sublimatory activity continued. She was notably forceful and assertive. Indeed, as she predicted, the therapeutic effects of the analytic work did continue after termination. When I saw Mrs. V. five years after the analysis regarding problems of one of her children I learned that she had remarried and was an independent, assertive person able to deal with difficult life situations. Her creative sublimations continued and her symptoms did not reappear.

Discussion

The conditions that justify a parameter include the occurrence of a stalemate in the analysis or the likelihood that it would enter an impassable cul de sac. Certainly Mrs. V.'s analysis at the time of the parameter had not reached the former state. The patient had been analyzing certain preoedipal defenses; things seemed to be going very well. In my judgment, however, the analysis was in grave danger of coming to a standstill if I did not take some action. Mrs. V. felt ready to put a halt to her use of Valium, but she needed medical help to do so. There was a realistic aspect to her request. Withdrawal from Valium can produce severe symptoms, including convulsions. True, she could gradually decrease the amount she took, but a physician's guidance would entail a sounder judgment, a greater safety. I felt I had to respond with some action or find myself confronted with Mrs. V.'s unanalyzable reaction to not pursuing a reasonable and protective medical path. Some readers may think the emotions that I predicted would indeed allow a deepening of the analysis and a sounder result, but I do not think so. I thought that the patient might stubbornly continue to take the Valium, and that this continued acting out would be destructive to the analytic work.

It is generally agreed that acting out beyond relatively minor and analyzable limits is destructive to the analytic process. As Freud (1914) has noted, acting out is a form of remembering that substitutes for more conventional recall. Rather than remember the patient repeats in distorted form past events in action and hides the repetition of childhood experiences in the transference. With intense action, the analysis of the transference and tracing its roots back to childhood become seriously compromised.

Acting out played a major role in Mrs. V.'s analysis. I have mentioned the fact that she had earlier in the treatment withheld words and money from me. Eventually, that was analyzed. Here I want to emphasize that Mrs. V.'s action included the nightly ingestion of Valium, a behavior instilled with drive satisfaction and defensive impact. In order to achieve optimal analytic work, the acting out had to come to a halt. If that were accomplished one would expect a forward surge.

Paradoxically, the means of diminishing acting out involved a cooperative action between patient and doctor, usually an ominous occurrence. Nevertheless, it seemed to me that, balancing one action (the ingestion of drugs) against another (helping the patient stop the medication), we would achieve the greater good if the drug abuse halted.

The question arose as to what action I should take, and thus encourage the patient to take, what would be the minimal effective parameter. I strongly suspected that if I once more referred Mrs. V. to another physician to help her withdraw, we might well have found that she again remained on the drug. The reader will recall that exactly that had occurred the previous year.

Another possibility was that I would advise her as to how she should gradually diminish the use of the Valium. I decided that getting her off Valium was of such great import that I would go further and dole out the medicine, a course she thought would be best. In that way I would be able to control the dose and alter it if medical necessity required. I believed I could probably analyze the complications this parameter would bring about. At any rate, the benefits of ending serious acting out were so great as to justify the risk.

The gamble paid off. Mrs. V. stopped taking Valium. We were then able to analyze many of the essential unconscious meanings of the parameter to the patient. The interpretive work soared and the analysis terminated successfully.

The significance of the parameter was ultimately related to the unconscious meaning of the taking of the Valium. The ingestion of the drug gratified the patient libidinally. It represented sexual intercourse with oedipal male objects including, in the transference, the analyst. It also signified preoedipal attachments to the mother, especially oral and symbiotic aspects, which could serve defensive as well as gratificatory purposes. The analyst who helped the patient stop taking the drug was to her the protective, seductive father and the feeding, caring mother. Antagonism to the therapist was rather muted and well defended against, possibly because the mutual interaction of patient and doctor hid her aggressive drives. This defect of the analysis may have resulted from the encouragement of acting out, but the reader should also recognize that intense rage did appear in the transference earlier in the analysis and could be interpreted effectively. The defect was but a relative deficiency. Drive derivatives and defenses were analyzed earlier in the treatment as well as after the implementation of the parameter.

Although one may suspect the patient's decision to terminate the analysis soon after she stopped the Valium was merely defensive, that is not so. Mrs. V.'s confidence and sense of autonomy were the result of a developmental advance, an overcoming of a regression. Defensive aspects were not ignored but they did not comprise the entire picture.

The upsurge of positive oedipal transferences and the recall of oedipal memories resulted from the patient's achieving a firm oedipal position. Ceasing to act out removed a defensive layer that enabled the patient to remember more and progress further. She recalled the traumatic incident at three when her baby sitter arranged for a wild party and the teenagers present terrified the patient. That event fortified fears of oedipal wishes and pushed the patient into a regressive seeking for protection, even into symbioticlike states. Her need for control, which had interfered with adaptation earlier, could be further analyzed so that she became able to utilize it more adaptively.

The patient was able to recognize attachments to her father and brother, and the defenses involved, as her fear of oedipal wishes decreased after the memory was recovered. She was able to feel greater affection for her husband, and achieve greater autonomy and greater ability to sublimate.

My justification of the parameter is not the same as the justification Eissler suggested. He said that when the patient suffers an ego modification which limits purely interpretive work, a parameter should be employed. In my justification I suggested that the parameter would decrease acting out and hence further analysis. One of the examples Eissler offers is the case of the phobic patient who can prevent intense anxiety in the analysis by avoiding phobic situations. In such a case the analyst suggests that the patient enter the feared arena. A claustrophobic patient may be told to enter enclosed spaces, or an agoraphobic may be encouraged to walk in the streets. Eissler does not state the exact nature of the ego modification here. In the case of the Wolf Man (Freud, 1918), where a major parameter consisted of setting a termination date while the patient had serious symptoms, the ego defect was clear (Blum, 1974). The Wolf Man was a borderline patient with a seriously defective sense of self, a feeling of deficiency that required close and continued contact with the analyst for repair. As part of this picture he utilized primitive defenses as projection and identification to extremes. Reality testing was shaky. Indeed the Wolf Man's ego defects were so severe that the parameter was only temporarily effective. Although it did propel the patient to more intense analytic exploration, the good results of the analysis were only temporary. The Wolf Man returned to treatment with psychotic symptoms which were then alleviated. But the patient's defective self-representation was such that he required the support, help, and appreciation of the psychoanalytic community to adapt. He rather grandiosely viewed himself as Freud's famous patient.

Mrs. V.'s ego modification was much milder than the Wolf Man's, but it was in some ways similar to his. She, too, felt incomplete and tended to experience symbioticlike states, but for her the defensive regressive element was prominent, whereas the Wolf Man's narcissism bore the mark of serious developmental arrest.

Further Comments on Parameters

Despite the fact that the concept of the parameter is frequently employed in colloquial clinical discussions it is a controversial one. In the written literature, even though there is general agreement that interpretation is the main instrument of psychoanalysis, there is little discussion of other interventions on the part of the analyst that are necessary for the analytic work but require special caution or particular means of dissipating their adverse influence. Menninger and Holzman (1973) describe parameters in a matter-of-fact way. Neither Greenson (1967), who points out many interventions other than interpretations, nor Brenner (1976) uses the term. Loewenstein (1957) prefers the broader concept of an "intervention." Stone (1961) decries the rigid conduct of analysis, and indeed has influenced technique in advocating greater flexibility. The concept of the parameter, he feels, is an extreme example of a "rigidly outlined conception of the [psychoanalytic] situation [which] is, for an increasing number of analysts, as important as our fundamental metapsychological concepts" (p. 18). Child analysts, noting that a purely verbal interpretive technique is inappropriate for their patients, differentiate parameters and modifications (Maenchen, 1970; Glenn, 1978).

Although the concept of the parameter rarely appears in the literature, it has indeed caught the imagination of analysts. If it is not used frequently in the literature, it is nevertheless often used in clinical discussion. Frequently, the term carries a pejorative connotation and the analyst who employs a parameter finds he has to defend himself. This is unfortunate as such interventions are often necessary and wise. If the analyst feels guilty about its usage he will find himself too restrained in the performance of good work (Stone, 1961).

The dictionary definitions of parameter are a far cry from the psychoanalytic definition. Webster (1956) cites an obsolete astronomical meaning ("an element of an orbit") as well as extant crystallographic and mathematical definitions and a more recent usage: "An independent variable through functions of which may be expressed other variables, as the coordinates of a locus" (p. 1773). Two dictionaries add recent colloquial usage of the term. A Supplement to the *Oxford English Dictionary* (1982) describes extended uses: "any distinguishing or defining characteristic or feature . . . ; an element or aspect *of* anything; *loosely*, a boundary or limit" (p. 263). The *American Heritage Dictionary* (1982) states: "The scientific term has been adapted to general usage. It is sometimes used in the sense of 'a constant, a given, or a precondition' and sometimes in the sense of 'a limit or boundary' (perhaps influenced by *perimeter*) . . . None of these examples are acceptable to the majority of the Usage Panel" (p. 901). The etymology of the term is relevant. The Greek Pará means beside, near, beyond, against. The prefix Para in English means past, aside, beyond, i.e., perverted, amiss, wrong, irregular, disordered, abnormal. Meter means measure (Hinsey and Campbell [1970], Partridge [1959], Webster [1956]). The etymology justifies the pejorative connotation some attach to the parameter. According to its derivation it is not merely an alternate intervention different from the usual; it may be considered incorrect and out of order.

The *Chicago Psychoanalytic Literature Index,* (1920–1984) lists a wide variety of articles under parameter, suggesting that the compilers define it as the varieties, i.e., the range and limits, of psychoanalytic psychotherapeutic techniques (and even theory). They include books and articles on psychosis, borderline conditions, geriatrics, the use of medication in psychotherapy, dream interpretation, giving advice to parents of children in treatment, to mention but a few. Glenn Miller (personal communication) has informed me that the compilers had no definition in mind and simply list articles in which the term appears frequently regardless of the author's meaning.

The indexes of the *Journal of the American Psychoanalytic Association,* the *Psychoanalytic Quarterly,* the *International Journal of Psycho-Analysis* and *The Psychoanalytic Study of the Child* since Eissler introduced the term do not include "parameter," even when articles on the subject appear in the journals. Probably this lapse indicates both the paucity of articles on parameters and a skepticism as to its importance.

Grinstein's (1956-1975) index refers to but a few articles. One, by Calogeras (1967), employs Eissler's definition, and gives an example of the use of silence as a parameter to deal with a patient's silence. Lipton's (1967) paper, delivered at the Chicago Psychoanalytic Society, has not been published but an abstract has been printed. Here Lipton is critical of the concept of the parameter, but in another of Lipton's papers (1977) he emphasizes that a pejorative connotation of the term *parameter* cannot be found in Eissler's paper. Grinstein does not refer to Olinick's (1954) article on questioning which also follows Eissler's usage but does not provide clinical details.

In this article I have provided clinical details from an analysis. I have used the term *parameter* to refer to an intervention of the analyst that is neither an interpretation nor a preparation for the analytic work (such as statements at the start of the treatment of the methods employed), or a preparation for interpretation (such as a description of patterns or a confrontation) carried out in order to further the analytic work or to avert a stalemate when interpretation does not suffice. As Eissler (1953) has stated, a quantitative as well as a qualitative factor must be considered; I emphasize that the deviation from the usual interpretive technique must be sufficiently great to warrant calling it a parameter.

I believe this way of viewing the matter is in the spirit of Eissler's article. He clearly states that he does not include as a parameter telling a patient to free associate when the analysis starts. He implies that questioning a patient falls outside that province also. Indeed, his article does not display the rigidity some have ascribed to it and others have used it to justify. Rather he recognizes the need for flexibility. He states, for instance, that "It is doubtful if any person was ever analyzed without being asked questions by the analyst in the course of psycho-analytic treatment . . . [T]he question is a basic and therefore indispensable tool of analysis and one essentially different from interpretation" (p. 109). Flexibility also appears when Eissler asserts that although analyses of some patients are seriously compromised by an analyst's deviation, the majority of patients are quite flexible: "Whatever may, in them, be wakened in terms of transference formation by trivial wish fulfillments can easily be analyzed and does not become a stumbling block to further treatment" (p. 112).

I suggest, then, that my modification of Eissler's ideal and abstract definition is appropriate in that it derives from sound analytic theory and practice and allows the use of parameters without rigidity. In clinical discussions, despite Eissler's flexibility, the concept of the parameter is frequently invoked to advocate a narrow and restrictive technique.

In addition to those mentioned above, certain misconceptions may interfere with the analyst's flexibility:

1. Although analysis of the effects of a parameter and its meaning to

the patient is certainly warranted, one should not adhere to the illusion that one can always do so and completely eliminate its effects. In this regard Eissler points out that Freud's setting the Wolf Man's termination date was not analyzed and its effects could not be eliminated. This certainly was not ideal and did compromise the analysis. However, I suggest that without the parameter, the results would have been more deficient.

2. Stubbornly insisting that one must analyze the effects of a parameter may interfere with the work. Some deviations from a purely interpretive technique are so minor that one need not necessarily point them out to the patient or pursue their significance relentlessly. It would be ludicrous to analyze the effects of every question that the analyst asks, even when they are used as parameters, but it would be wise to understand the analyst's frequent or excessive use of that technique, whether the inquiries are parameters, preparations for interpretations, interpretations, or errors.

3. What appears on the surface to be a noninterpretive intervention may in fact not be a parameter. Interpretations may be made in the form of jokes, stories, or questions (Eissler, 1958).

A parameter should be differentiated from a number of other interventions mentioned in the literature. A parameter, which furthers analytic work, should be differentiated from deviations which are errors and either do not further it or impede the process.

It would be well to distinguish between the parameter and what Sterba (1944) has called the formative activity of the analyst. He suggests that *following* his interpretative activity, which is basic to analysis, the analyst must often use his personal influence to steer the patient to adaptive patterns of thought, feeling, and behavior. The patient on his own may not be able to integrate his insights in such a way as to overcome his neurotic patterns. Recognizing that colleagues may disapprove of this approach, he bolsters his argument by quoting Freud (1915–1917, 1926) who said that analysis involves suggestions and reeducation. Sterba gives no examples of "formative activity," and I believe such maneuvers are not generally required. Certainly such activity did not appear in Mrs. V.'s analysis. The parameter instituted was not the final step in the analysis. It removed an impediment to further analysis. When that was accomplished, the process continued and the patient was able to achieve a new synthesis on a more advanced level of functioning. An essential difference between the two technical procedures is that the parameter is intended to overcome a roadblock so that interpretations may once more be effective, while formative activity occurs *after* the interpretative work and is not intended to lead to more analysis. Although my helping Mrs. V. withdraw from Valium involved the use of my personal influence to overcome a symptom, the primary function of my activity was to further interpretive work and achieve insight through the eventual ending of particular acting out.

Parameters should also be distinguished from what Lipton (1977) has designated as interventions "outside of technique" and "not technical." When Freud sent the Rat Man a postcard or fed him, Lipton maintains, he did not intend to influence the analytic work and did not do so adversely. Nevertheless, he observes, the repercussions of Freud's activity were not excluded from the analysis. (Possibly, however, they were insufficiently interpreted.)

One may consider Freud's use of a number of techniques early in analysis and throughout analyses as attempts at bolstering the therapeutic alliance. In addition to sending the Rat Man a postcard and feeding him, Freud complimented him, as he did the Wolf Man, for his capacity for understanding. He also praised Kardiner (1977) for his producing a perfect first analytic session and showed H. D., the famous Imagist poetess, his collection of antiquities during her analysis in 1933-1934 and offered to lend her any book she wished to borrow (Doolittle, 1956). These activities were neither formative activities nor parameters. Generally such activity on the part of the analyst compromises the treatment. The patient receives gratifications the effects of which are very difficult to analyze. The patient may work harder for the analyst who approves of him, but in doing so he also hides conflictual aspects of his personality through a defensive compromise. What seems to be the "unobjectionable part of the transference" may not be analyzed, to the patient's detriment (Stein, 1981).

REFERENCES

American Heritage Dictionary (1982). Boston: Houghton Mifflin.

Blum, H. P. (1974), The borderline childhood of the Wolf Man. *J. Amer. Psychoanal. Assn.*, 22:721-742.

Brenner, C. (1976), *Psychoanalytic Technique and Psychic Conflict.* New York: International Universities Press.

Calogeras, R. C. (1967), Silence as a technical parameter in psycho-analysis. *Internat. J. Psycho-Anal.*, 48:536-558.

Chicago Psychoanalytic Literature Index (1920-1984), Chicago: Institute for Psychoanalysis.

Doolittle, H. (1956), *Tribute to Freud.* New York: Pantheon Books.

Eissler, K. R. (1953), The effect of the structure of the ego on psychoanalytic technique. *J. Amer. Psychoanal. Assn.*, 1:104-143.

——— (1958), Remarks on some variations in psychoanalytic technique. *Internat. J. Psycho-Anal.*, 39:222-229.

Freud, S. (1914), Remembering, repeating, and working through. *Standard Edition*, 12:145-156. London: Hogarth Press, 1958.

——— (1915-1917), Introductory lectures on psycho-analysis. *Standard Edition*, 15 & 16. London: Hogarth Press, 1963.

——— (1918), From the history of an infantile neurosis. *Standard Edition*, 17:7-122. London: Hogarth Press, 1955.

——— (1926), The question of lay analysis. *Standard Edition*, 20:183-258. London: Hogarth Press, 1953.

Glenn, J. (ed.) (1978), *Child Analysis and Therapy*. New York: Aronson.

Greenson, R. R. (1967), *The Technique and Practice of Psychoanalysis*. New York: International Universities Press.

Grinstein, A. (1956-1975), *The Index of Psychoanalytic Writings*, vols. 1-14. New York: International Universities Press.

Hinsey, L. E. & Campbell, R. J. (1970), *Psychiatric Dictionary*, 4th ed.

Isakower, O. (1938), A contribution to the psychopathology of falling asleep. *Internat. J. Psycho-Anal.*, 19:331-335.

Kardiner, A. (1977), *My Analysis with Freud*. New York: Norton.

Lipton, S. D. (1967), Observations on rapid manifestations of drives and defenses. Read at Chicago Psychoanalytic Society, May 23. Summarized in *Bull. Phila. Assn. Psychoanal.*, 17:176-177.

——— (1977), The advantages of Freud's technique as shown in his analysis of the Rat Man. *Internat. J. Psycho-Anal.*, 58:255-273.

Loewenstein, R. (1957), Variations in classical technique: Concluding remarks. In: *Practice and Precept in Psychoanalytic Technique: Selected Papers of R. M. Loewenstein*. New Haven: Yale University Press, 1982, pp. 164-169.

Maenchen, A. (1970), On the technique of child analysis in relation to stages of development. *The Psychoanalytic Study of the Child*, 25:175-208. New York: International Universities Press.

Menninger, K. A. & Holzman, P. S. (1973), *Theory of Psychoanalytic Technique*. 2d ed. New York: Basic Books.

Olinick, S. L. (1954), Some considerations of the use of questioning as a psychoanalytic technique. *J. Amer. Psychoanal. Assn.*, 2:57-60.

Oxford English Dictionary. Supplement (1982), vol. 3. Oxford: Clarendon Press.

Partridge, E. (1959), *Origins*. 2d ed. New York: Macmillan.

Stein, M. H. (1981), The unobjectionable part of the transference. *Psychoanal. Quart.*, 29:869-892.

Sterba, R. (1944), The formative activity of the analyst. *Internat. J. Psycho-Anal.*, 25:146-150.

Stone, L. (1961), *The Psychoanalytic Situation*. New York: International Universities Press.

Webster's New International Dictionary (1956), 2d ed. Unabridged.

August 1986

A Reexamination of Phobias as the Fear of the Unknown

GEORGE MORAITIS, M.D. (Chicago)

During the last several years, anxiety states, phobias, and panic disorders have received a good deal of attention in general psychiatry. Recent studies and reports published in a number of psychiatric journals and other publications have shifted the emphasis in the understanding and treatment of these disorders from the psychological to the biological and the behavioral approaches. New medication and treatment modalities have been introduced, and patients have been advised by their physicians and by the news media of the limitations of the psychoanalytic treatment of phobias and the need to turn elsewhere for the solution to their problems.

Psychoanalysis has, for the most part, kept silent in this regard. Since Freud's early publications on phobias and anxiety hysteria, and the contributions of the early pioneers of psychoanalysis, little has appeared in psychoanalytic literature during the last twenty-five years that specifically addresses the psychoanalytic conceptualization of phobias and the associated panic states and deals with the specifics of the management and treatment of these conditions. It would be ironic if during this period of the widening scope of the clinical applications of psychoanalytic treatment we as psychoanalysts relinquished to the nonanalytically oriented therapist the clinical field upon which psychoanalysis was originated. Instead, I think the time has come to take advantage of the discoveries in the biological field in order to make a renewed effort to reconceptualize phobias by distinguishing between what we really know about them, what we think we know, and, more importantly, what we do not know about them.

Phobias are known as states of unreasonable and irrational anxiety not warranted by the reality posed by a given situation which, in combination with the associated avoidances and obsessive-compulsive symptoms, drastically affect the patient's sense of well-being, self-esteem, and level of functioning. Originally, Freud explained phobias as the outcome of the projection and displacement of unacceptable and repressed wishes and irrational fears of punishment. Phobias were conceptualized as a compromise symptom against a more diffuse and crippling anxiety state. A patient identifies a more encapsulated area of danger in order to limit the anxiety to specific and, it is hoped, manageable proportions. In the process, the patient presumably denies the inner source of the sense of danger by externalizing it onto a given object or situation.

Freud's (1909) formulations about phobias placed the symptom within the boundaries of hysterical neurosis upon which the whole foundation of psychoanalytic theory was established. Phobics were identified as the hysterics who are unable to repress their unacceptable wishes and fears, and instead displace them onto other objects and situations. The phobic symptom, like the dream, has been approached as another royal road to the unconscious, the analysis of which could well lead to the uncovering of the pathological neurotic fantasy and to the resolution of the neurosis.

In the actual clinical situation, this proved to be a very hard road to travel. Attempts to utilize the psychoanalytic conceptual model in the treatment of phobias have been consistently frustrated. Freud (1919) identified this difficulty early in the development of psychoanalysis when he wrote: "One can hardly ever master a phobia if one waits till the patient lets the analysis influence him to give it up. He will never in that case bring for the analysis the material indispensable for a convincing solution of phobia" (p. 165). He urged analysts to recommend to their patients to "struggle with their anxiety" in order to try to achieve "a considerable moderation of the phobia" that would produce the necessary memories and associations that would lead to the successful analysis of the symptoms. One of Freud's explanations for the tenacity with which phobic patients are attached to their symptoms pertained to the intensity of the impulse. He assumed that the analyst's recommendation to his patient to struggle with his anxiety would reinforce the ego's capacity to deal with the strong instinctual impulse.

In the panel discussion on phobias and their vicissitudes (Panel, 1959) at the American Psychoanalytic Association, the change in thinking among many analysts about the nature of the unconscious fantasy in phobias was clearly evident. The participants in the panel described phobias primarily in association to pregenital pathology and in individuals whose character structure was oral or anal. Several investigators, such as Ralph Greenson,

Leo Rangell, Brodsky, and others, felt in a sense confronted with a choice either to revise the explanatory theory of hysteria or dissociate the phobias from hysteria. It is important to point out that at that time most of these thinkers were primarily trying to identify the content of the phobic patient's fears and the nature of the fantasy associated with them. The concept of structural defect was only beginning to emerge as attention was drawn to the phobic patient's internal representations and structure.

In 1959, Greenson, in his paper "Phobia, Anxiety, and Depression," explained panic states as the reaction to the loss of both the external object and the internal representation of an object. Brodsky (1959) referred to the extinguishing and disintegration of the self-image in association to phobias, identifying them as the fear of annihilation. More recently, Heinz Kohut (1984) elucidated the concept of agoraphobia as a structural and functional deficiency of the patient's self, related to insufficient selfobject milieu. Kohut's formulations pertain to both parents' empathic failures—the father unempathically overstimulates the little girl while the mother fails to provide the necessary mirroring and soothing that will help her daughter cope with the situation.

In reviewing the psychoanalytic literature on phobias I can distinguish two basic directions in conceptualizing them. One aims to uncover the unconscious fantasy operating behind the symptom no matter what the nature of this fantasy may be—oedipal or preoedipal. The other direction approaches phobias as a manifestation of a more general and basic pathology. Accordingly, the symptom does not become the main focus of the analyst's attention. Instead, the analyst aims to help the patient better regulate the tension produced by the phobic symptoms, so that he can address the fundamental structural deficit upon which all pathology presumably rests.

The analyst who operates within the first premise is likely to come across to his patient as a sleuth, who aims to uncover the unconscious pathological fantasy by systematically gathering small pieces and details and piecing them together until the unconscious part of the scenario becomes evident. The eagerness and determination that this attitude involves will probably resonate with the patient's sense of urgency for relief and comfort and thus win the patient's cooperation and positive response for a while. Often, however, this does not last very long. The analyst's notion that what the patient fears represents only a compromise for a much more dreaded thought and impulse will inevitably be perceived by the patient, who may respond with apprehension and even panic to the notion that a dreadful unconscious wish must be uncovered before achieving symptom relief. The patient's reservations and objections will probably be interpreted as resistances, whether this is justified or not.

The analyst who operates with the basic premise of structural defects is bound to be more prepared to cope with the tenacity of the phobic patient's symptoms. He will be more patient, open-ended, and empathic with the patient's sense of helplessness. The analyst's efforts to reduce tension, however, may come across as an inability on his part to appreciate the urgency of the situation. Furthermore, the notion of an all-encompassing structural defect may well be perceived as lack of appreciation of the strength of the patient's overall psychological organization as manifested in many other areas.

In my experience, both of these two approaches provide considerable relief to the patient but not the "convincing solution" of the phobias Freud referred to in his 1919 paper. By and large, the phobic patient who is motivated and capable of remaining in analysis for a long time will probably experience a gradual lessening of the intensity of the fears regardless of how the pathology has been conceptualized by his analyst. With time and patience phobias may fade away, but they seldom, if ever, disappear. By and large the phobic orientation remains and, given certain circumstances, the fear can strike again and often when least expected.

Obviously, there are many kinds of phobic patients. The patients I refer to in this paper are the ones who can abide by the procedure and structure of the psychoanalytic situation, and whose manifest psychopathology is primarily organized around the phobic symptomatology. In my experience, these phobic patients have had little difficulty in acknowledging their tendency to misinterpret, to exaggerate and distort in their reality testing. They are aware of their impairment in the perceptual process and the troubling split between what they perceive on a logical, cognitive level, and what, on a deeper level, they feel and experience. In a way, such patients behave like people with learning disabilities. Facts and persuasion have little effect on their beliefs and fears, and they act as if they have a hidden source of knowledge, on the basis of which they have constructed a highly idiosyncratic and often ridiculous image of external reality, which they systematically reinforce through an elaborate system of avoidances and obsessive-compulsive behavior. Often the phobic patient's strong sense of conviction about the nature of the dreaded external reality parallels the analyst's sense of knowing the content of his patients' unconscious. Under such circumstances, the presumption of knowledge implicit in the attitudes of both analyst and patient obstructs the awareness of their mutual ignorance and erects obstacles to a more honest and effective therapeutic interaction.

I believe that for some patients a different and more promising approach to the understanding of their phobias could be devised with the systematic exploration of this clinical phenomenon: the phobias could be seen as the fear of the unknown rather than as the fear of a wish or danger presumably known on a conscious or unconscious level. Instead of assuming that all phobic patients dread the rediscovery of the repressed and displaced we may, in selected cases, proceed with the hypothesis that it is the new and the unknown that are feared. For these patients, avoidances do not represent the outcomes of fears, rather, the fears are in the service of avoiding the new and unfamiliar. By avoiding the novel and the unknown they try to maintain a rigid, familiar, and rather limited perception of the self and the universe within which the self is experienced. The obsessive-compulsive symptomatology commonly observed in phobic patients represents a restitutional effort, no matter how awkward and logically unattainable, to bring the input of novelty under the rubric of more archaic perceptual patterns and configurations. The patient's effort to avoid the unfamiliar and maintain a perceptual world designed to his or her own specifications can best be addressed if the analyst himself comes to terms with his own exaggerated need to confirm in his patient's history and symptoms the validity of his own perception of the patient, in accordance with preexisting theoretical schemata. To facilitate the patient's capacity to deal with the encounter with the strange and novel, the analyst must cope with his own sense of strangeness that the phobic patient arouses in him. To accomplish this he must appreciate the ambiguity of the clinical situation and avoid unwarranted presumptions of knowledge.

In the clinical presentation that will follow I will attempt to illustrate some of these issues and differentiate between the encounter with the truly unfamiliar and novel and the concepts of repression and disavowal, in which the perceptual input is familiar on a conscious or unconscious level but set aside in one form or another. The therapeutic advantages and disadvantages of the new conceptualizations will be discussed as they pertain to the handling of the patient's transference and the analyst's countertransference response.

Mrs. K.'s analysis began five years ago when she was thirty-five years old. She is a married woman, mother of three children, whose phobias began approximately three to four years before the beginning of the analysis, and were precipitated by a cervical biopsy. Despite the fact that the results of the biopsy were negative and the patient was properly reassured, she developed intense fears of cancer. As a result of these fears she instituted an elaborate system of avoidances of people and situations designed to prevent her being contaminated with "cancerous materials." The subsequent development of obsessive-compulsive symptomatology gradually made this patient virtually a prisoner in her own house.

In the beginning, the patient attempted to hide her symptoms as most phobics usually do. Yet, as the intensity of her symptoms increased, inevitably she revealed her fears to her family with considerable embarrassment. At the height of her illness, the patient's efforts to avoid contamination precipitated some strange and bizarre behavior. She would not use the entrances and part of the house, she would engage in compulsive washing of clothes or discarding of clothes that were presumably contaminated, and she would avoid certain important people in her environment and stay away from all doctors. Under the circumstances, seeking psychiatric help was out of the question until, paradoxically, her condition improved slightly three years later, following the death of her father. It took her, however, another two years before she finally entered analysis.

Mrs. K. is a good-looking woman who conveys a sense of intensity and high energy. She was born and raised in this country, but her parents came to the United States as refugees from Europe in the early twenties, having been the victims of political persecution. Her father achieved some prominence as a political figure in the United States, but her mother remained uninvolved in his activities. Mrs. K. has an older brother, very successful professionally, and three, much younger, married sisters. The patient was a very creative student who achieved several distinctions in high school and college. She was raised in a strict Christian environment in which her parents' code of behavior and set of values were presented in no uncertain terms. Although the patient reported some mild fears in childhood, there is no history of phobias prior to the onset of her present illness. The patient's father conveyed a good deal of pride and interest in his daughter, but both parents seemed to favor the older brother, toward whom she also felt very attached. Mrs. K.'s mother consistently identified the patient as "lucky." That conveyed to the patient a sense of envy and competition. Mrs. K.'s mother was indeed very "unlucky." Due to the dramatic circumstances in the country of her origin, she was forcibly separated from the patient's grandmother and placed in an orphanage at the age of six. The patient's mother and grandmother were reunited in the United States several years later, while the maternal grandfather died in the meantime.

The patient describes herself in childhood and young adulthood as an energetic, outwardly directed individual, eager to experience something new, and capable of distinguishing herself in whatever she was doing. As an adolescent and young adult she had experienced some sexual inhibitions which she had partially overcome after her marriage. They reappeared, however, when she became phobic. Despite her neurosis, Mrs. K. is a very effective and caring mother, who encourages her children to do the things she is phobic about. She has helped her husband very substantially in his professional development. At the time the phobias appeared, her husband had achieved some important successes in business, and the family had become very secure financially. It was at the same time, however, that both her father and her husband underwent major operations. Her father died some years later from another illness.

It was easy to identify the fear of death in the patient's phobic preoccupations. I linked the illness and death of her father to her fears about cancer, a fact that led me to believe that Mrs. K. was in a state of pathological mourning reaction. This assumption was further reinforced by information she provided about her parents who apparently both suffered from fear of doctors, superstitions, and strong belief in their longevity and, implicitly, immortality. The patient, who quickly sensed from my questions the line of my thinking, had no difficulty with this formulation. The presence of an idealizing and somewhat eroticized transference provided some further indication of the patient's effort to replace the lost object and lessen the frightening identification with her deceased father.

As the process unfolded, however, I was impressed with the fact of how well things were progressing in the analytic situation and how little difference this seemed to make as far as the phobic symptomatology was concerned. I brought this to the attention of the patient, and this produced a somewhat explosive response. She felt she had displeased me. She became frightened and apologetic. She made a deliberate effort to overcome her fears and engage in some activities she had difficulty with, but despite some minor successes, by and large the fears remained. I thought the time was ripe to address the issue of her desire to please, an issue that helped us focus primarily on her relationship with her mother. She recalled with pain some agonizing efforts to please her mother and her consistent failure to do so. She took care of her younger sisters as if she were their mother, did many chores at home, was a straight-A student in school. Yet her mother remained unimpressed and continued to perceive her as "lucky," privileged.

My familiarity with the patient's cultural background placed me in a position where I could not only empathize with her but could also appreciate what traumatic experiences of her mother's probably contributed to her failure to empathize with her daughter's psychological needs. During that period of time my patient became increasingly more curious about my background, asking me to provide her with information about historical events which she assumed I was familiar with, and which her mother had directly experienced. She had never asked her mother such questions or, if she had, she had never felt she received satisfactory answers. In analyzing her curiosity, once more I had the feeling of a very meaningful and intense analytic process in the clinical situation, but the same question remained: how did this really affect the phobias, the symptoms that originally brought her into analysis? It was quite evident that the patient's episodes of panic were gradually diminished; she was less anxious in the clinical situation, and thus capable of performing her daily activities at home. Although her fears were greatly reduced, the avoidance of places, situations, and people who could activate these fears remained very strong. The patient became better able to master the anxiety, should anxiety erupt, but both of us were keenly aware of the potential for a new outbreak of fear, and of the fact that her basic phobic orientation to life had remained the same. At that time I considered of particular importance the fact that these outbreaks of fear, whether intense or mild, did not seem to be linked in any apparent way to the analytic process in general and to the transference in particular. Consistently, the patient's phobic responses would be mobilized when confronted with a situation in which she had to take some action in a direction she was unfamiliar with. It did not seem that such incidents represented the acting out of a conflict mobilized in the clinical situation.

After the third year of analysis, the patient acknowledged that her self-awareness and her self-esteem had increased, and she had reached a better understanding of her past. She was still very frightened of the future, but capable of preventing her fears from turning into panic. Her life, however, remained very restricted by a series of avoidances which, like an iron curtain, interfered with the fulfillment of her ambitions and ideals. The patient could not pursue a professional career, enter into new social or civic activities, or cultivate relationships outside her immediate and extended family. Perhaps many phobic patients are prepared to settle for such results, which does not necessarily mean that they will terminate analysis. More likely, phobic patients will attempt to mold the analytic process within the boundaries of their small world by collaborating with the analyst in the clinical situation, as long as no demands are placed upon them to alter their phobic orientation to life and the constrictions that such an orientation entails. Under such circumstances, the phobic patient would readily acknowledge the validity of the analyst's interpretations by providing corroborative evidence, but would stubbornly resist any attempt to take action as a result of the understanding reached.

Through appropriate interpretations, Mrs. K. realized the danger of bringing the analysis to a standstill by her inactions, and was not prepared to settle for such a result. Instead, we embarked on another attempt to approach her phobias from a different vantage point. I thought it necessary to avoid redundant interpretations of the patient's phobias as displacements originated in archaic wishes and fears. From this experience, and from experiences with other phobic patients, I assumed that the displacements evident in certain phobias are epiphenomena of behaviors which have deeper roots.

It is important to clarify that I did not direct my attention to the early developmental determinants of my patient's behavior because I assumed that she was incapable of dealing with imagery and symbolism, and of developing an object-related interaction with me. On the contrary, I assumed that the oedipal and narcissistic issues were clear and evident both in the transference and in the patient's history as presented, and that our analytic work was effective insofar as these issues were concerned. The erotic attachment to her father, the issues of envy and competition with her mother and brother, as well as her archaic needs for a holding environment, were properly recognized and addressed. None of these issues, however, generated the intensity of the affects of the phobic reaction, the abrupt outburst of which would overshadow everything else. It seemed that these episodes had, to an extent at least, an independent existence.

It is hard to overestimate the frustrating effect such outbursts have upon the patient and the analyst, and the ease with which they can facilitate a sense of therapeutic pessimism, a sense of resignation to an interminable process of containing the symptom within manageable proportions. Some analysts may elect to identify such behaviors as being purely biological in nature, and delegate their treatment and management to the pharmacological approach. Although in some cases this may indeed be the treatment of choice, the analyst should not abandon the search for the understanding of the phobic symptom and attempt to incorporate this understanding into the whole spectrum of the patient's personality and structure. Simply to dismiss it as biological is an easy and unacceptable way out that presumes an unwarranted dichotomy between the biological and psychological factors in human behavior.

In pursuing a broader psychological understanding of phobias, I found the comparative studies between cognitive development and psychoanalytic theories (Basch, 1977; Lichtenberg, 1983; Stern, 1985) quite relevant. Piaget's concept of the sensorimotor schemata as action patterns that constitute the fundamental elements of thought has been further elaborated by Basch (1977) who postulates that the establishment of these schemata during the first year of life forms the basis for the organization of all future thought and self-awareness. More recently, Stern (1985) has postulated the existence in the infant of a sense of self long before the development of self-awareness and language. In other words, we can presume that the infant is capable of organizing perceptions and creating models of the universe and of the self within it that later on will drastically affect the nature of self-awareness and the awareness of the nonself. It is very unlikely that such early models can be brought into conscious awareness during psychoanalytic therapy. Nevertheless their existence can be presumed indirectly from their restrictive effect upon the patient's behavior and experiences.

In my analytic work with Mrs. K. I have been impressed by the restrictive nature of the universe upon which her perceptions rest, and the dread with which she approached any possibility of expanding the boundaries of it. The invisible "iron curtain" I referred to, which defines her idiosyncratic world, seems to serve two basic functions. On the one hand, it skews the impact of information so as to confirm the validity of earlier perceptual schemata in a way that is excessive and compulsory. On the other hand, it impedes the necessary action needed for the expansion and revision of the boundaries involved.

I hypothesize that the archaic model upon which Mrs. K.'s perceptions were organized was designed systematically to discourage curiosity and search and avoid states of doubt and bewilderment. Accordingly, trial-and-error experiences were limited, while circular, repetitive patterns of behavior were reinforced. Such an organization may be particularly effective when it operates within the boundaries of a limited universe within which very little is presumed not known and unfamiliar on a conscious or unconscious level. The phobic symptoms appear when at some point, under the influence of certain experiences, a large input of discrepant stimuli demand processing and ordering for which the individual can use neither repression nor disavowal.

I define such perceptual input as novelty in the sense that the discrepant stimuli has on some level been registered but there is insufficient correlating registration or symbolic meaning on a conscious or unconscious level in the individual's self experience or self organization, with which the new input could be accommodated. The phobic patient's distress resembles the infant's stranger anxiety because the generated emotional response results from the individual's inability to use repression or disavowal. For an individual who cannot tolerate a state of doubt and ambiguity, withdrawal becomes the only defense available.

The psychological organization of some phobic patients can be compared to a totalitarian state which, in order to maintain the consistency of its rigid organization, must avoid threatening strangers and the informational input which contact with strangers generates. If avoidance is impossible, a state of emergency will be created, a state of panic that will block the input of any further stimulus by the powerful affects mobilized. Panic represents the brutal force that will obliterate all perceptions and give priority only to one—the phobia—which thus becomes the instrument through which an obsolete model of the world and of the self will be maintained.

The metaphor I used is designed to illustrate both the intensity with which the phobic patient experiences his or her condition as externally imposed, as well as the possibility that the patient's perception of danger is not necessarily illusionary in nature. The danger may not be reminiscences repressed or displaced, but alien perceptual input that threatens the phobic individual's psychological organization due to its limited capacity to cope with ambiguity and ignorance.

Mrs. K. experienced her phobic symptoms as a programmed response to repeat thoughts and actions despite her strong sense of conviction that she "ought to know better." Repetitions in life and in the analytic situation are of course always observed and associated with transferences. There is, however, a substantial difference in the versatility and variability with which these repetitions appear and are experienced. Hypothetically, we can place on one end of the spectrum repetitions with greater versatility and variability. Such repetitions may be difficult to recognize, for both analyst and analysand, without the use of symbolism and imagination, because the repetitive elements involved are intertwined with several novel elements each time they appear. At the other end of the spectrum we can place repetitions with little versatility and variability which are probably close to what Freud referred to as repetition compulsion. Phobic responses constitute the compulsive repetition of affective states and avoidances that does not allow for any novel element to enter into it. They can better be compared to repetition compulsions than to transference reactions. The phobic patient's persistent perception of the symptom in concrete and external terms frustrates the analyst's effort to influence it through a systematic search of its meaning. When this occurs, both patient and analyst assume the presence of a master who dominates the patient's life experiences, which neither can control. Under such circumstances, biological explanations are tempting, and the use of medication may become a necessary step in alleviating the soaring anxiety and panic states. When this occurs, it would be erroneous to assume that the analyst should relinquish to biology the search for the "master" responsible for the patient's condition. Instead, medication provides a much-needed symptomatic relief that makes the continuation of the analytic work possible.

Early in the analysis I informed Mrs. K. of her option to be medicated for her condition by offering to refer her to a colleague experienced in biological psychiatry. She elected not to pursue this, partly because she was phobic about medication and partly because she had already been involved in the analytic process and intrigued by our efforts to understand by whom and how she had been "programmed."

In reviewing Mrs. K.'s history, it is relatively easy to identify the masters who systematically programmed her early experiences. Being the daughter of two frightened and severely traumatized refugees, she was raised in an atmosphere of suspicion, superstition, and relative isolation. Her physical activities were systematically restricted to protect her from unrecognized dangers. The patient was only conditionally allowed to play with other children and bring them home. She could understand with difficulty the daily exchanges of her parents, who were speaking another language in her presence and did not bother to teach her the language they spoke. A set of unnegotiable and unexplained prohibitions had been imposed upon her from early childhood. Paradoxically, the patient did not resent these prohibitions and did not object to them. It gradually became evident that she did not perceive her parents' attitudes and prohibitions as the reflection of their own narcissistic need to intimidate and control. Instead, she perceived their behavior as the outgrowth of their true conviction of the actual nature of the reality they lived in, and their sense of parental responsibility to protect and guide. Under the circumstances, it would have been impossible for her to doubt and question her parents' perceptions, which by all indications were based on their actual experiences. With ingenuity and hard work she managed for a long time to avoid a direct confrontation between the small world upon which her perceptions were organized and the larger world she was operating in. She went through the developmental period of adolescence and young adulthood with little discomfort. But gradually she became increasingly more phobic in her middle thirties, several years after her marriage and the birth of her children. At the time the phobic symptoms appeared she had distanced herself from the family of origin. The professional success of her husband, the increasing affluence of the family, and involvement in a larger social and family milieu had created for her a world both different and apart from the one she was raised in.

The appearance of a phobic symptom can be described as a developmental crisis, which builds up gradually, often below the level of the patient's awareness, until at some point a rather trivial event precipitates a major emotional outburst. I doubt that the precipitant of a phobic reaction is, in itself, so important. Only the overall evaluation of the patient's personality and pathology will give the strategic information needed to understand the depth of the crisis involved. I hypothesize that, in the case of Mrs. K., the phobic symptoms emerged as a result of a large input of novel and discrepant stimuli, accumulated over a period of time, for which she could use neither repression nor disavowal. More specifically, such a sense of novelty was precipitated by an increasing awareness of the finiteness of life as associated with the illness and death of her father, the illness of her husband, the approaching end of her reproductive period, and her awareness of an aging process. It can be assumed that the mentally and physically disintegrating image of her father, in combination with her own physical and environmental changes, created for her a frightening image of novelty. (At some point, when her father's condition deteriorated, he would mistake the patient for somebody else. She had become a stranger to him and he appeared a stranger to her as well.)

The capacity to come to terms with the deepening awareness of the finiteness of life constitutes a developmental passage. An individual's ability to cope with such awareness depends on the tools available, starting with the earliest experiences in life. There was probably little in the survivor mentality of her family and cultural background that provided Mrs. K. with the necessary tools to deal with the inevitable and irreversible.

In Mrs. K.'s family and personal history there had been many opportunities to learn how to avoid and defend against threatening situations. Her parents were survivors of a catastrophe who managed to reverse passive and helpless situations into the activity of escape and reconstruction in a new country. They retained their survivor type of mentality through their lives and taught it well to the patient from the beginning of her life. It is not surprising, therefore, that she has always been an outwardly directed, stimulus-hungry individual, who tested the boundaries of the small and restrictive world of her early childhood. Her difficulties arose when she encountered the novel (to her) notion that not all dangers are avoidable or reversible. Her delayed awareness of the finiteness of life aroused in her a sense of novelty that she could not effectively deal with, with the schemata familiar to her. We can assume from the intensity of the patient's reaction that the novel and discrepant stimulus was registered. Once this occurred, the stimulus could not be erased or ignored, or processed through the means available to her. Its presence created a disruption in the patient's personality organization which she attempted to restore through the utilization of an obsessive-compulsive symptomatology, the predominant mechanism of which was that of undoing. Such symptomatology is restitutional in nature, and its aim is to undo the registration of the novel stimulus by reinforcing old beliefs and convictions, even beyond the boundaries of what the patient herself considered logical and reasonable.

An individual's capacity to come to terms with the inescapable biological realities of his or her existence requires the utilization of inward-directed, thoughtful reflection. Such reflection may take the form of an open inquiry involving doubting and questioning, or it may be more structured in the form of philosophical, psychological, and theological beliefs and convictions. In the absence of an individual's ability to alter external reality through some form of outwardly directed activity, the change of its internal image produces the needed sense of control and mastery. This function is the reverse of what George Klein (1976) referred to as the principle of self-initiated, active reversal of passive experiences, and could be referred to as the self-initiated, passive reversal of active experiences. Both of these functions operate on the basis of the same principle, but in opposing directions. Together they constitute an essential duality in the service of the regulating and processing of novel and discrepant stimuli.

Individuals traumatized by prolonged exposure to painful and rigid external realities which have rendered them helpless and ineffective are skilled in reversing a passive experience into an active one and are quite eager to do so, but quite reluctant to proceed in the reverse order. Thoughtful reflections and the open inquiry associated with them represent to them something intolerable, something to be dreaded and avoided. Such attitudes have been described as counterphobic responses designed to conceal the underlying fear or wish. It is important to keep in mind that Mrs. K. had not experienced such traumata directly. These were her parents' experiences which she borrowed from. More specifically, her difficulty lies in her inability to tolerate not knowing and the uncertainty and ambiguity associated with it.

The awareness of biological changes, occurred and impending, does not exactly represent a well-defined reality an individual must come to terms with. Growth, aging, and death arouse a sense of uncertainty and bewilderment in response to which all reassurances and explanations are limited at best. To deal with such awareness the individual must tolerate a state of doubt, ambiguity, and disbelief, and accept with relative comfort the awareness of ignorance. Even for those who possess a wide range of factual information and a well-developed capacity for conceptualization, the known and knowable world is bound to be a limited one. As the individual matures, he or she becomes increasingly more aware of this basic fact. How well he or she will respond to such an awareness depends on some of the very early experiences in life.

Freud often postulated that the unconscious perceives no time limits or contradictions, and there is no room in it for a correlative of death as a concept (1923). He found little meaning and justification for the notion, "every fear is ultimately the fear of death," and assumed that the fear of death is something that occurs between the ego and superego (1923). In a later paper he postulated "that the fear of death should be regarded as analogous to the fear of castration and that the situation to which the ego is reacting is one of being abandoned by the protecting superego—the powers of destiny—so that it has no longer any safeguards against all the dangers that surround it" (1926, p. 130).

The fear of abandonment was easy to identify in my patient's history and associations. So was her fear of death. Both were conscious, and references to them could hardly be construed as interpretations. They were simply statements of the obvious. I have little difficulty accepting the proposition that ultimately every fear is the fear of death, as well as Freud's proposition that all fears of death involve the individual's sense of abandonment by his protective agency. Such broad generalizations, however, have limited explanatory power and clinical use. The crucial question to address is in what sense Mrs. K. felt abandoned. What made her feel unprotected and vulnerable? Freud drew the analogy between castration anxiety and the fear of abandonment. Contemporary investigators, as already stated, tend to focus on preoedipal pathology and structural defects associated with loss of boundaries, the need for selfobjects, and fusion states.

In my work with Mrs. K., I saw some relevance to all of these conceptualizations, but considered particularly important the issue of pathological mourning. I assumed that the loss of Mrs. K.'s father, and her awareness of an aging process, represented to her not simply the loss of an object she had to replace, but also the collapse of a perceptual system upon which the self-nonself organization depends. Pollock (1978) has described the "liberation process" that the successful completion of the mourning process precipitates, which involves the freedom to follow new creative paths. To achieve such liberation Mrs. K. had to overthrow the totalitarian state that dominated her experiences and achieve a degree of personality reorganization that can be described as reprogramming. At the time the phobias appeared she was faced with the dilemma of either retreating into a private world of her own specification or reorganizing her whole perceptual system in order to accommodate the novel and discrepant input. Once her resolve not to retreat into a private world was consolidated, the analytic work focused on facilitating her capacity to deal with the novel and unfamiliar, and thus liberate herself from a tyranny that was hardly known to her up to the time the symptoms appeared.

More specifically, my clinical approach was expanded to provide my patient with the opportunity to develop the awareness and tools necessary to broaden the boundaries of her restricted world by increasing her capacity to deal with ambiguity, doubt, and ignorance. I proceeded with the notion that the better these qualities are developed, the broader will be the boundaries of the undifferentiated totality, of the universe upon which the self experiences have been based. It is primarily the awareness of what we do not know and of the limitations of our knowledge that extends these boundaries and enables an individual to transform rigid and obsolete perceptual schemata into more flexible and adaptable structures. Although only few of us can reach the level of Socrates' awareness, as expressed in his famous, "I know one thing, that I know nothing"—the closer we come to it, the better we can deal with discrepant stimuli for which no immediate assimilation is possible. To be consistent with the therapeutic aims as I conceptualized them I had, to begin with, to be aware of the relative value of my own knowledge of the patient's pathology and make no effort to conceal such awareness from my patient.

Gedo (1979) has indicated that "psychoanalytic therapy should be able to produce a maximal variety of meaningful reformulations of the analysand's experiences . . . preferably, analysands should arrive at as many of these insights as possible through their own integrative efforts for . . . no outside observer . . . is really competent to judge the relative importance of the various determinants" (p. 262).

Put in different words, Gedo advocates that the analyst must tolerate a reasonable level of doubt and ambiguity of his own perceptions of the patient's experiences, to which I would like to add that, for some analyses, it may be particularly therapeutic to help the patient recognize the analyst's limitations, as well as the particular way in which he deals with them. In the analysis of Mrs. K. I thought it essential to share with her my perceptions and misperceptions, my sense of conviction and my sense of bewilderment. I operate with the notion that she can benefit more from her awareness of how I deal with my sense of ignorance than from the accuracy of some of my interpretations.

From the beginning of the analysis, Mrs. K. conveyed to me a "transference readiness" in the sense that she quickly identified in me certain real or imagined similarities with her caretakers, which she reenacted in the clinical situation. I approached such reenactments as a defensive effort to maintain an obsolete perception of herself and the world around her, by simply replacing a lost object with another that she assumed was similar, and thus maintaining a sense of continuity at the expense of a better appreciation of the differences involved. Mrs. K. achieved a higher level of self-awareness when she realized how different from her parents I am. When this occurred, she experienced a form of "stranger anxiety" which was vividly reflected in her dreams and associations.

Mrs. K. had originally perceived my introspective and reflective posture as a form of endorsement of her own active participation. She was comfortable with my silence and with brief, nonconfronting responses to her long and elaborate communications. Self-confrontations were abundant, but it was hard for her to assume the position of a listener when I addressed an issue in a manner substantially different from the way she had thought of it. Consistently, I had the impression that she wanted to prevent the input of any new ideas and observations that would disrupt the repetitive cycles of her thoughts and perceptions. When, despite her resistances, I provided her with some feedback to catalyze the process, she would respond with anxiety that often would make her unable temporarily to comprehend what I had said. The basic aim of my interpretations has been to facilitate a continuous input of novel stimuli by offering observations, open-ended questions, and brief commentaries that would raise the patient's curiosity about the issues at hand and introduce an approach to them from another vantage point, thus systematically avoiding premature closure. I have systematically avoided conveying to her that I know the answers even when I suspect I do. I operate with the principle in mind that self-awareness increases as one progresses from an assumption of knowing the answer to the search of the proper question.

Characteristically, during this stage of her analysis Mrs. K. became considerably more "phobic" in the analytic situation, with reverberations outside of it. Her fears took the form of worrying about my health and mortality, as well as about the extent of my knowledge and wisdom.

The patient's pathology and the analytic process as I described it can easily be conceptualized along the familiar lines of narcissistic pathology. We can assume that her illness was the result of a narcissistic mortification generated by a traumatic challenge to her infantile grandiosity and to her primitive idealizations. To restore the cohesiveness of the self she developed an idealizing and mirroring transference. Accordingly, my therapeutic approach consisted of tension-regulation techniques and a gradual disillusionment, aiming to resolve the transference and restore the narcissistic balance. According to this formulation, her phobic symptomatology can be conceptualized as episodes of fragmentation in association with a possible biological predisposition.

My basic objection to such a conceptualization pertains to the use of the terms grandiosity and idealization. Such terms refer to an exaggerated perception of one's own worth and abilities or to those of somebody else. It implies a distortion in the perception of reality which presumably is relatively clear to everybody else. I do not believe that such clarity exists. Value judgments are always subjective in nature. To appreciate their meaning, the observer must place them within the context of the subject's psychological and cognitive world. For example, we often assume that children idealize their parents when they believe that father or mother "knows best." Their perception may not be as exaggerated as it appears when one takes into account the limited universe they operate in, within the boundaries of which the parent indeed seems to know best. Many adults operate within very narrow boundaries as well—geographically, perceptually, and experientially. Within their small world they may experience themselves as very powerful and omnipotent, or attribute to somebody else near them, comparable powers. Their perceptions may not be as distorted as presumed if one takes into account the narrowness of their vision.

I believe Mrs. K.'s "grandiosity" and "idealization" of her parents and of the analyst were the outgrowth of a very constricted perceptual world that could not accommodate discrepant stimuli generated by internal and external input. When novel input could no longer be avoided, its registration precipitated in her a powerful response that aimed to reinforce old and familiar themes, in an effort to assimilate the new input as if it were old. These transference reenactments were defensive in nature. I identified the basic problem as the absence of the necessary schemata that would enable her to tolerate a delay in assimilating novel input. Due to the absence of such schemata, she resorted to mobilizing old, unresolved oedipal issues and some more archaic phenomena best described as repetition compulsions or archaic transferences. In a therapeutic sense, tracing the origins of these reenactments and compulsive repetitions does not necessarily address the basic pathology involved, which pertains to what has not been learned and developed.

What I referred to can be described as a deficit, but I am reluctant to use this term because of its pejorative meaning, which implies a primitive psychological organization. Experience has taught me that an individual's limitation in accommodating novel input is by no means limited to those with primitive character structure. To introduce new ways of looking at their experiences and facilitate the construction of a new sense of reality may be difficult not only for the psychologically limited and uneducated, but also for some of the psychologically better-organized and well-educated individuals.

The boundaries of the perceptual universe in which an individual lives in are only partially affected by the extent of factual knowledge, the wealth of personal experiences, the geographic boundaries, and a cohesive psychological organization. No matter how far an individual extends his awareness of the known and knowable world, his boundaries of the universe will remain limited unless he also maintains a level of awareness of what is not known or knowable. The more closed the perceptual system within which an individual operates, the more difficulty this individual will have in accommodating the novel and the unfamiliar, and the more vulnerable he will be to phobic avoidances. Maintaining an open perceptual system is not necessarily the product of formal education and of a well-developed psychological organization. It is a quality of perception and experience that enjoys a certain autonomy and has its roots in some of the earliest experiences in life. To doubt and to question, to wonder and to inquire are qualities of thinking and experiencing substantially different from both dreaming and fantasizing, as well as from logic and reasoning. I believe psychoanalytic therapy can facilitate the study and the development of this quality if the analyst himself operates within an open system.

It is not the purpose of this paper to present a more systematic discussion of the concept of novelty in psychoanalytic theory and clinical situations. In this paper I presented fragments of the analysis of a phobic patient in an effort to illustrate a new approach to conceptualizing and analyzing phobias for selected cases, which has some more general clinical and theoretical implications.

REFERENCES

Basch, M. F. (1977), Developmental psychology and explanatory theory in psychoanalysis. *This Annual*, 5:229-263. New York: International Universities Press.

——— (1983), The perception of reality and the disavowal of meaning. *This Annual*, 11:125-154. New York: International Universities Press.

Brodsky, B. (1959), The self-representation and the fear of dying. *J. Amer. Psychoanal. Assn.*, 7:95-108.

Freud, S. (1909), Analysis of a phobia in a five year old boy. *Standard Edition*, 10:3-152. London: Hogarth Press, 1955.

——— (1919), Lines of advance in psychoanalytic therapy. *Standard Edition*, 17:157-168. London: Hogarth Press, 1955.

——— (1923), The ego and the id. *Standard Edition*, 19:3-68. London: Hogarth Press, 1961.

——— (1926), Inhibitions, symptoms and anxiety. *Standard Edition*, 20:77-178. London: Hogarth Press, 1959.

Gedo, J. (1979), *Beyond Interpretation*. New York: International Universities Press.

Greenson, R. (1959), Phobia, anxiety and depression. *J. Amer. Psychoanal. Assn.*, 7:663-674.

Klein, G. (1976), *Psychoanalytic Theory: An Exploration of Essentials*. New York: International Universities Press.

Kohut, H. (1984), *How Does Analysis Cure?* Chicago: University of Chicago Press.

Lichtenberg, J. (1983), *Psychoanalysis and Infant Research*. Hillsdale, N.J.: Analytic Press.

Panel (1959), Phobias and their vicissitudes, reported by L. Farber. *J. Amer. Psychoanal. Assn.*, 7:182-192.

Pollock, G. H. (1978), Process and affect, mourning and grief. *Internat. J. Psycho-Anal.*, 59:255-277.

Stern, D. (1985), *The Interpersonal World of the Infant*. New York: Basic Books.

July 1987

Countertransference: Its Role in Facilitating the Use of the Object

KENNETH M. NEWMAN, M.D. (Chicago)
with discussions by
CHARLES KLIGERMAN, M.D. (Chicago)
and
DAVID M. TERMAN, M.D. (Chicago)

I. Introduction

The tragedy of character is that it so often works to interfere with what the subject needs most—a usable object. This is most poignant with people who have suffered significant early traumata and therefore have reorganized their psychic structures with highly protective mechanisms. Frequently, the pathological character repetitively works to achieve the conviction of the unusability of the current objects through evoking complementary responses from the companion object to the restitutive structure. Even when the response produced is a positive one, sought out by the patient, the way this transaction was evolved as well as the history and motives for eliciting this response will render the object and the experience invalid, i.e., not truly usable. Whether intentionally induced or not, whenever the external object enacts the complementary role to the patient's character, once more the patient gains conviction that distance must be maintained. Thus, the new object in the patient's mind becomes identified with and contaminated by the original object, and is thereby disqualified for use as a new object. When the patient's character presentation is more obviously imbricated with frustrated expressions of rage, acute sensitivity to slights, and massive defensive reactions, the analyst will experience, typically, negative attitudes, painful affects, and demeaned self states.

Whether motivated by intentionality or now simply a manifestation of an addictively driven sector of the psyche (false self, vertical split), the patient who seeks and gains apparently positive responses by selectively accommodating to the needs of others is inducing responses which serve, ultimately, only to duplicate the failures and misunderstandings of the earlier objects.

We come to know about the patient's internal objects through our countertransference experiences. I contend that many patients develop a sense of experience-near conviction of their inner world *only after* the stimulating effect of the analyst's countertransference enactments and failures. The power to induce in us such countertransference enactments gains impetus from two directions. We are most likely to be attracted and delighted by those patients who have a talent for divining our needs, enhancing our self-esteem. Correspondingly, we are susceptible to injury most often when the patient somehow withholds his attachment needs and subtly induces in us the feeling that our efforts are as meaningless, incompetent, and helpless as were the efforts of his earlier selfobjects. Because of the power of the wind to chill or of the sun to warm, many of our patients have a capacity to induce us to dress up in the complementary clothes suggested by the climatic conditions they create. Our job, in turn, is to make use of this to create an atmosphere in which they feel less rigidly doomed to failure by their inner experience and hence freer to relive their old traumas in a more hopeful way under safer skies. Thus, how *well* we eventually come to manage our profound countertransference reactions and even failures will determine the milieu out of which can emerge a mutative experience, or out of which can emerge the hoped-for new object that the patient is able to use creatively. However, when we become caught up unknowingly in a complementary identification (Racker, 1968) with the internal archaic object of the patient we frequently remain unaware of the affects activated in ourselves. The result is a stalemate in the analysis, duplicating the situation which originally froze the patient in this maladaptive defensive stance.

Recognizing that it is often very difficult to reach a point with our patients where they can use us, we must learn how to provide the setting necessary to facilitate this. Usability encompasses not only the capacity to use the object to provide emotional strengthening, structural growth, modification, and reorganization, but even more crucial, our "usability" requires that the patient find us sufficiently trustworthy in order to dare to relive early transferences (and their inevitable frustrations) under these more secure conditions.

Often the shift to usability can evolve spontaneously as we help our patients recognize and identify the nature of the internal environment, their specific relationship to earlier objects and their introjects, and the meaning of resultant defensive-adaptive psychic organizations. Much of the time our empathic grasp of this and the communication of our insight will be sufficient to facilitate the process and begin the mobilization of deeper transferences. But with other patients a protective characterology has been erected in such a way as to create a poor compromise, comprising a continued need for objects, and yet a chronic need to mute, control, or prevent awareness of that same need.

These patients require exquisitely tuned environmental responses, yet so often the new character organization they have forged out of the earlier traumata sets up "resistances" and protections which can, in turn, operate in an analysis to induce profound reactions (affect states or symptomatic behavior) in the analyst. These latter can be expressions of "failure" paralleling those of the parents and thus serving to freeze the analytic process.

These patients, as infants, missed a satisfying and sufficiently understanding object and therefore needed to wall off and bury painful affect states, forming tenacious defenses to protect their vulnerable core. Fortunately, however, these states can be communicated in the form of intersubjective transactions whereby the unconscious of the patient can profoundly influence feelings in the analyst. As often occurs, the analyst is induced into repeating the introject or selfobject counterpart to these nuclear traumata, and becomes identified with the original failed, rejecting, or unavailable object, or the object relationship that developed as a compromise out of this failure. Whichever negative identification predominates, the end result of this countertransference enactment is the patients' feeling of the need for defense. The major focus of this paper is to underscore how this event can serve to maintain the analyst as *unusable*: the rigid and near-addictive need of the patient to reenact these situations acts in the negative as a potent obstacle to the progression and increasing depth of the analysis.

However, the *way in* and the apparent resistance created also offer a marvelous opportunity to find the *way out*. Through the process of actually identifying with the dramatis personnae of the patient's early history, the authentic feelings and psychic reality of the patient's nuclear life can be brought to the surface. As the analyst emerges from the eye of the stormy feelings to a decentered position, he can begin to help the patient by putting words and understanding gleaned through direct reliving with the heretofore unarticulated affects. From this point of maximum urgency the current disruption can be lived in a less toxic way, in effect providing a new function. I believe that it is through a series of such transactions that the lifelong attachment of these patients to the archaic introject, both as motive for and source of defensive organization, can be modified. As long as the patient continues to view all objects unconsciously as derived from the original defensive and unusable object, and finds this repeatedly confirmed by the collusive responses of the complementary object, it is a static and nonproductive relationship. However, it is clung to because it maintains cohesiveness and quiets the noise of the underlying depression.

The implication for treatment is that it is necessary to create a breach in the vicious cycle so that the analytic object can be differentiated from the archaic original. To this end I believe we must accept the idea that the affective availability of the analyst and his ultimate capacity to embrace and make sense out of the complex feelings engendered in an intense two-party system may be crucial to effecting mutative changes. We may also have to accept the fact that often we inevitably fail our patients, but that through these failures, if we can manage the associated disturbances in ourselves, we may provide a new object. This new object may serve in a variety of ways (to be highlighted here), not the least of which involves supplying a missing or inadequately internalized holding or container function. The traditional belief that it is chiefly the patient's distortions which cause the intense transference distortions and which need to be corrected by the objective reality of the analyst, then, requires some modification. For, if the unconscious of the patient, the power of regressed and often inexpressed need states, and the impact of complex defenses, influences our unconscious in a universal (and not just idiosyncratic) way, then what is stirred up in us and, in turn, affects our patients must be given a significant position in understanding current disruptions in them. The therapeutic benefit emerges out of the resultant work that eventually can be done as the patient, in the context of a shared experience, gains a new appreciation for the source and meaning of his earlier and heretofore unarticulated feelings and desires.

That we can learn such facts from the transference material and our countertransference reenactments is no startling revelation. But this phenomenon has, in my opinion, the unique capacity for being *the* most important starting point for fundamentally eroding the old set of projections, for rejecting the attachment to the old introject (especially the addiction to the false self), and for establishing the possibility of a mutative experience.

II. An Operational Construct of the Patient's Inner World

It is my operational view that the patient's internal atmosphere arises in the context of early-developmental failures from which the pathological character solutions have been forged. My emphasis will be on the nature of the internalized object relations and their chronic influence on the organization, cohesion, and tone of the self, as well as their motivating role for the walling off of early affect states and continuing libidinal needs. Rather than striving for precise metapsychological consistency, I shall focus on deriving a working set of concepts for clinical application. Although the model will show the influence of Kohut and Winnicott, I hope to provide a unique integration and synthesis which add dimensions not apparent or sufficiently emphasized in their individual theories.

Cumulative traumata in the mother-child (self-selfobject) dyad interfere drastically in what otherwise would allow, through mirroring, good-enough adaptation to needs of the infant, resulting in the establishment of a positively toned self connected to a reliable self-enhancing introject (or selfobject). In its stead we have a self prone to melancholia or depression or, in self-model terms, a self vulnerable to depletion or fragmentation anxiety. Kohut's work stressed the subjective experience of the child in terms of the threats to continuity, vitality, and the danger of overwhelming tension states. To this I would add a more concrete picture of the inner state, i.e., a self endangered by enforced contact with an insufficiently reliable mirroring object, whether due to that object's indifference, pathological narcissism, or excessive needs of its own. In my experience, this more concretized picture of the selfobject failure explains the specificity of the child-patient's attempt to conceal from himself the awareness of this failure, and also the need to control the original needs for the longed-for (good) object.

Similarly, Winnicott (1960) and his followers have spoken of the failure in maternal adaptation and the resultant characterological developments (especially the pathological false self): The child's primary anxiety is the result of impingements on the child's efforts to experience and actualize in a lively and responsive atmosphere his true self. Instead of the child focusing on affective self-realization and the self-enhancing and self-strengthening benefits of optimal maternal adaptation to his gestures, his energies are distracted into a preoccupation with accommodating to the mother. What are left understated in this formulation are the complex reverberations such a failure evokes. The emergent self preconsciously experiences the loss in primary terms of neither being valued nor given time enough to find himself or his object in a "transitional space." Abandonment, loneliness, and a secondary reactive rage are the hallmarks of this state. These affective states and the nature of the specific internal object result in a hostile and frightening internal world. In object-relations terms, the end result of these early failures is not simply a potential patient fearful of awakening primary need, and dreading impingement anxiety, but also a world viewed as consisting of a self in contact with an introject which is excessively narcissistic, critical, or unavailable in the face of deeper libidinal needs. Contributing significantly to the fear of revival of direct contact with this internalized object is a second crucial failure, equally as important as the primary presenting failure.

I believe that the latter failure is underemphasized in the self model. Any major interferences with the positive sense of self traumatically distort the developmental pathway to a true nuclear self. But the same parental environment that failed to meet primary needs for mirroring and optimal maternal adaptation reacts to the child's protest, i.e., affective reactions of hurt, loneliness, and rage, in a most unfortunate way. In the face of the child's negative, withdrawn, or depressive reactions, such parents are unable to provide a soothing, calming, holding atmosphere which confirms for the child that such affects are bearable and that the object will not be lost in the face of these states. Instead, exactly the opposite too frequently results. The self is experienced as locked into a relationship with objects that will withdraw in the face of one's ordinary—but misperceived—affect states. Thus, the inner atmosphere, concretized as self and object (introject or selfobject) is doubly viewed as dangerous, not only in terms of a failure in the face of primary needs, but also in its inability to contain the psychic consequences of the primary failure.

Thus the term "fragmentation anxiety" would include this expanded concept. The source of this "anxiety" is much more than feared breakup of the self-selfobject unit. The break with the selfobject activates primary affect states, such as painful loss and rage, which, because of the defect in the earlier selfobject's container function means that there is no organizational structure available to hold these affects. The patient's anxiety is not just a consequence of the danger that the remobilized needs emanating from a true self will once more be injured by impingements. Rather, it is the fundamental threat of revival of affects associated with the *original memory of having been abandoned (emotionally) in the face of basic needs, together with the memory of the primary object's (defensive) vulnerability in the face of the feelings the child had in response to the frustration of those basic needs*.

Thus, a crucial understanding, whatever model one uses for patients with chronically melancholic, enfeebled, or fragile selves, is that these patients do remain fixated at a level of intense primary need states. But tragically these needs are mostly walled off, or only find muted, distorted, or compromise outlets in the character to be developed. Awareness of the complex expression of these libidinal needs and their corresponding attachments to an object (or selfobject) are repressed, because the reawakening of these needs will bring patients to an awareness of their core attachment also to an intrusive, critical, excessively narcissistic, unavailable object. And they fear the affects which are connected to these basic attachments because, as in childhood, the new object might remain unavailable to them in the face of inevitable disappointment.

III. The Development and Motivational Side of the Pathological Character

The character structure forged out of these early developmental failures serves at least three main objectives. It is designed to ward off recognition of the pain coming from the internal atmosphere; it provides, in its more positive and adaptive motives, the illusion of connectedness to objects; and yet it controls the depth of attachment to a new object in order to keep in repression the core regressive needs and the accompanying intense affect states. The object emerging from this characterological organization is, then, part of a complex compromise—for some patients the major emphasis is on the adaptation to the needs of others and the addiction to gaining the illusion of the object's responsiveness. For others, the stress will be more on controlling the object through a complex of protective mechanisms which attempt to maintain the object at a distance. In all cases, this restitutional (defense transference) object is at depth a "relatedness," not a usefulness (using Winnicott's [1971] term). The intent is to control the external object to prevent recognition of its direct connection with the original and feared object. But the nature of this defensive object relationship is so obviously shaped from and has so clearly emerged out of the original traumata that the shadow of the *original* object naturally must fall on it. Thus, when the analyst in the treatment situation senses, and then becomes, this relationship, he is in effect echoing an aspect of the failed original.

When there has been a failure in the early dyad, self-selfobject, or symbiotic relationship, the child, rather than going on with a developmental process which includes progressive turns toward reality and modification of needs for omnipotent or subjective control over the environment, becomes instead fixed on more archaic modes, which include the fantasied subjective control of the object. As Winnicott (1958) has stated, fantasy is not a defense against external reality but a defense against a painful inner reality. No matter how compliant or accommodating the child may become, the attunement to what brings forth responsiveness, praise, a smile, attention, etc., renders for the child the illusion of control. The final organization and honing of this style is the false self. Kohut's (1971) vertical split works in a fairly similar way—the child, after perceiving the inability to gain responses to himself as the unique center of initiative, and in the face of painful affects associated with disillusionment, loss, or fragmentation, will shift to performing or identifying with activities and interests which are selectively responded to by the needs of the parental selfobjects. A similar dynamic is true for Mahler's (1971) concepts of the symbiotic character which emerges out of the failure in the late separation-individuation phase, more specifically due to the inability of the mother to manage the loss of the child as symbiotic object.

In all of these models, the object relationship is the product of a reorganization formed after the original needs were thwarted, and after powerful affective disturbances and tension states were so poorly managed that the psyche could not go on with its normal program of development. Character, as a complex attempt to master a number of issues, influences how the child will relate to the object and attempt to gain responses which provide an illusion of self-cohesion and, at the same time, serve to quiet the noise associated with the earlier disappointments. However, as soon as the object indeed does enact the complementary role to the restitutive or defensive character, he or she is automatically suspect and in danger of becoming invalidated as a useful object. For example, if a man has learned, in childhood, after a series of disappointments in the early relationship with his mother, how to adapt to her moods and becomes invaluable to her in this function, he can then transfer this talent onto later relationships. However, the moment a new girlfriend begins to be charmed and "warmed" by his specific capacity to know her mood, etc., he already feels a sense of despair. Yet this man sadly will be addicted to repeating this experience because it seems temporarily to quiet the lifelong feelings of abandonment and deadness which would come in the recognition of the initial unavailability of the mother he needed. His success in inducing a complementary response only unconsciously confirms the persistent idea that the current woman needed, like his mother, to have him shift *his* central need to that of meeting *hers*. The despair he begins to feel is due to the mobilization of this defended and feared recognition.

Another form of defense depicts more open use of withdrawal, disavowal, or frank depreciation. This is not only evidence of the disturbed earlier relationship but also reflects more manifestly the shift to shaping a character which strives for self-maintenance by employing more distancing defenses (schizoid, paranoid) to reinforce the walling off of needed but feared libidinal strivings. Much as there is more open evidence of the negative transference, there is also a heavy component of defense involved here.

Once again, the object is invoked at one level to conform to a subjectively held view, in this case the overly self-centered, indifferent, or excessively vulnerable parent. Naturally when, as a result of the intensity of complementary affects stirred up in us by these specific narcissistic offenses and defenses of our patients, we reenact an aspect of the earlier relationship, we at least temporarily confirm our untrustworthiness. But it is here that the mutual work can begin. No matter how persistently the patient maintains this "bad-object" defense (Green, 1975), our managing of our own complicity and injury in order to see the human side of our patient and to remember the injured child in need of an accepting object may offer the best opportunity to erode the frozen interior of our patient attached to an archaic introject.

The character, as it acts as an addictive bond invoking responses which may stabilize temporarily and ward off melancholia or fragmentation anxiety, actually interferes with attachment to nourishing new objects unless and until something can occur to facilitate a mutative experience. For many patients, this may only happen as a result of the analyst finding his way to the patient's true interior self through the recognition and then resolution of his/her countertransference.

Essentially, two major kinds of patients will be described here. In one group the central defensive pattern can be categorized as a form of false self or vertical split where the emphasis is on denying the affects associated with disappointments in the early dyad. Ultimately, the countertransferences elicited recapitulate aspects of primary failures in optimal-mirroring and/or early-idealizing functions.

The other group, by contrast, more openly clings to the experiences with the "bad object," and defensive and aggressive components of this activate the countertransference. This latter more closely repeats a secondary failure, i.e., the inability of the parents to "hold" the child in the face of his affects and defenses—reactions that emerge from and were generated by the primary failure.

IV. Clinical Material

The first patients described here *comprise* that larger group who erected a character organization designed in some way to adapt to the needs of their original objects. This character is a restitution emerging out of failure and trauma, a massive compromise motivated by the need (1) to control the depressing and devitalizing experience centered in their core relationship between the self and the internalized object, and (2) to bring the current object under subjective control, hence guaranteeing a form of responsiveness which the psyche can use to maintain variously self-cohesion and/or the illusion of connectedness to the external object.

In essence the child and now patient has learned through highly attuned ego perceptions how to mold himself to, perform for, make himself indispensable to an object, hence forming a "special" bond. This form of relating has been viewed conceptually as a false self (Winnicott, 1960), a vertical split (Kohut, 1971), a symbiotic attachment (Mahler, 1971), achieved in particular by a gifted child (Miller, 1979), or the illusion of symbiotic compliance (Khan, 1975). The character presentation can take many forms—some crude, some extremely subtle—but all developed in collusion with an early relationship and motivated by the multidetermined needs to quiet the pain of disillusionment.

No matter how masochistic, compliant, or conforming the patient is, the external object is experienced as part of the patient's inner world of projections, and hence is quietly but persistently felt to be under subjective control. The control "guarantees" that as a result of the patient's knowing how to be for the other, special responses will be forthcoming. But when they are, the external object confirms the patient's underlying projection that he needs to be this way to insure the minimal relationship of the narcissistic, depressed, or conditionally responsive object.

But this character formation has been so altered and deformed by the various compromises and defenses developed within the earliest relationship, that the all-important capacity to use us as new objects (introjects, selfobjects) is anywhere from mildly to greatly impaired. In addition, the way these patients so often induce others to respond to them unconsciously confirms for them the need to maintain distance. In analysis, one can see the shadow of the original—i.e., we will be able to see in the transferences to us admixtures which speak on one level to the feared core experience which they are attempting to quiet, and on the other to the way they have learned to be in order to keep themselves from being fully aware of the nature of this disillusionment.

The first clinical illustration concerns a patient-analyst experience described to me by a candidate with a patient she had been treating for several months prior to her being assigned to supervision. Not only had she anticipated using this case for supervision but she had been hoping to present the patient at a large regional conference. The male patient, it was clear, saw himself as a man who had been able to charm and delight women, but felt a chronic sense of dissatisfaction and vulnerability to depression. The initial six months of treatment seemed to go very well, with lively material and rich associations. The analyst felt quite candidly delighted until gradually she noted that in rereading the hours, instead of feeling a deepening of understanding she felt a boredom and a sense that the associations were repetitive.

In the prologue to her overall case presentation, the analyst stated a belief that one of the premier ways to augment the analytic alliance and the conditions for a deepening transference would emerge from a shared understanding of the nature of the patient's relationship with internal objects. Thus, it was a departure from the analyst's cognitive insight when, following her awareness that the patient's presentation was in fact a performance staged for the analyst, she then began to withdraw from a more lively involvement with the patient, and began to interpret along the lines of the patient's latent hostility and envy. The patient, in turn, indeed became progressively more depressed and confused, which might have confirmed that such interpretations were finding their mark. Yet the analysis as a whole seemed to be bogging down if not reaching a stalemate.

I believe that the analyst reacted to the feeling of being the colluder with a set of projections that the patient possessed about his own behavior in order to guarantee a lively response from someone. I contend that the analyst's initial (but not fatal) failure here occurred when she became delighted with the patient's restitutional or defense transference; she duplicated the complementary role of the patient's experiences with his responsive mother, adapting to her needs. This transference relationship (or "narcissistic solution") had the shadows of both components of the original, hinting at what failed in the mother-child experience, as well as to how the patient learned to re-form a bond (false self, vertical split, secondary breakdown product, etc.) in order to cover over the pain of that failure.

In essence, once the analyst goes beyond cognitive understanding of what happened to the patient and is drawn into an affectively charged reaction, the moment for a mutative experience is now possible. The patient could be viewed as communicating the following: "I relate to you in this way so that we both can create the illusion of your goodness, responsiveness, liveliness, and I can at least temporarily feel that I am valued, central, mirrored, and in balance. Moreover, I can quiet the noise (of depression, hopelessness, emptiness, or fragmentation emanating from a vulnerable, melancholic, and enfeebled self) that is chronically around me. I, too, recognize a deeper awareness of the kind of self and early-object atmosphere in which I live. But the very fact that I have to enact with you this form of engagement, already renders you, the analyst, as suspect of needing me to be this way, and hence reminds me and once more mobilizes feelings in me resonating with the earlier loss. Since, however, you see and can eventually grasp (for my benefit) and even more urgently reenact with me the defense transference, you may actually provide for me in a more immediate and sense-near way a picture that captures the original disturbance. I treat or react to you now and more importantly in ways I have perfected with others, and now induce you to react. You can help me to really gain access to (1) what I had to do to keep from feeling overwhelmed as a child; (2) what I feel I need to do in order to keep from feeling caught up in the intensity of the unbearable affects concretized by the atmosphere of an insufficiently true self in touch with a narcissistic, indifferent, critical internal object; and (3) what I feel I must do in order to control deeper needs. I would then hope that, having felt that, instead of attacking my defenses, you might have said 'Ah, I now see how hard you have had to work in order to feel you have someone's interest, keep them feeling alive, or whatever. Although I, too, confirmed for you that this was important to me, i.e., to feel excited by your material, etc., I can really begin to sense the driven quality in you to keep me as you felt you had to keep someone earlier involved and interested.' "

Having entered into the patient's inner world of objects and accepting responsibility for repeating an aspect of the failed primary relationship, the analyst now can function as a potential new selfobject. A dialogue is established which opens up contact with the needed good object and in time will permit the process of engaging the disturbing affects (depression and rage) connected with the bad object set in the context of a deepened transference.

A second clinical illustration regards a patient of mine, a young woman in the mental-health field, who had been quietly in services all her life. Over an extended period of time we gained insight into how through precocious ego developments she made herself both indispensable to her mother and also valued by her mother because, unlike her younger siblings, she was able to look after herself. We were progressing with increased understanding of her current life and the way in which she often deprived herself of support because she feared giving up her restitutive character, feeling that she would be exposed to an unavailable and overburdened mother. However, there was something slightly stilted and controlled in her relationship with me that seemed to hinder a deeper regression and a more open expression of earlier need states, until an interesting moment in the analysis. I was leaving for vacation and, as had been a familiar pattern, the patient began to feel more closed up during our last week. We both knew that separations were quite difficult, but the affects and specific feelings of abandonment and increased tension states were more often excluded from the treatment hours, or generally muted. In the second to the last hour the patient was relatively silent, and I began almost unwittingly a reverie which included concern for several other patients and the intensity of their feelings about this separation. I did, though, after several minutes, take time out from my "work with the real patients" to inquire of my "colleague" on the couch what was going on. She replied that she was actually thinking about some patients of her own who were in need of special help. What a beautiful piece of acting out on my part! I had, at an important level, forgotten my here-and-now patient and become worried about the truly needy "others," and she, true to her own character neurosis, was enacting her style of drowning out her own affective distress through identifying with the helper. Both of us were forgetting the forgotten girl in the room.

My recognition of it had an impact on me—i.e., with the contrast between how well I thought I knew about this part of her and yet how I could at some level play the complementary role to her restitutive style, whereby she quietly and on some unconscious level experienced me as needing not to be burdened by her affective needs. Only when I was finally aware of this transference to me and my enacting an identification with the object to which she had turned following a traumatic disappointment in the earlier (core) dyadic relationship, could we together sense the intense and rigid affects the archaic atmosphere erected. A deeper regression began to take place at this point with a genuine shift, whereby I was experienced as a potentially new object vis-à-vis her symbiotic needs and the capacity to handle the objects associated with their inevitable disappointments.

Unconsciously, the patient is always seeking a kind of relationship which will not preempt his own subjective experiences and will, at some level, register his disappointment when this is absent. If the analyst then consciously or unconsciously is induced to impose expectations of his own (through a variety of subtle or not-so-subtle ways we have of communicating our priorities), then a resistance, negative transference, or malignant regression will be mobilized. This parallels Winnicott's concept of the mother impinging her own needs on her infant, and the whole set of unfortunate psychic events which result.

I believe that when we as analysts take responsibility for our part in what may be considered at times a malignant regression (as compared with a therapeutic regression), we facilitate the deepening of the analytic process by acknowledging that there is something environmental (whether due to something idiosyncratic in us or to our complementary response which reproduced an early dyadic failure) that has communicated to the patient that his own needs are burdensome or excessive. This creates a context for resultant feelings of rage and despair. The reexamining of our current role in reactivating aspects of the earlier conditions gives the patient a chance to achieve compassion for the child-in-himself rather than blaming himself for the continuation of his intense needs and powerful affects. The analyst's role here is to emerge from a temporary enactment to a position of offering an understanding and grasp of what went wrong in the past and, from his own firsthand experience, "know" for the patient how the patient had to experience himself and his objects.

There is an inherent tendency on our part to assign responsibility to the patients for our failing to see the intensity of need or pain in them. We soften the blaming quality when we speak to the efficient functioning of their self-maintaining character structure. However, I believe we can go further in supplying a missing function for the patient, that of being an advocate for his needs and supporting the legitimacy of his affect states.

After enacting an identification with the earlier objects whereby we implicitly or explicitly expect more self-sufficient or precocious behavior, it is now possible to reexamine with the patient how this affected the fate of his needs and affects and culminated in a certain pathological identification and negative posture toward them. All of this resonates with the patient's past. For example, with my woman patient, it is true that she had become adept at conveying self-sufficiency. However, in the treatment situation, I acknowledged that if we were to accept and welcome the early child part of her in the room, then of course it would not be her job to know and articulate her pain before being able to expect a suitable response. In this way we supply a missing diatrophic function, giving validity to the patient's need for centrality, legitimizing desire, and shifting the responsibility from the child through reexamining the context of affective upheavals.

There is a further range of difficulties which even more dramatically underscores countertransference issues. With the above patients we are essentially "enjoying" the apparent benefits of the false self or vertical split. The patients attempt to maintain a bond with us by accommodating to our needs through a host of adaptations to the analyst or analytic process. However, there are many patients who not only are addicted to performing, adapting, etc., but whose capacity to differentiate, modify, and shift their view of the external object is also severely hindered by the degree of the original trauma and by the nature of their anxiety. Not only do these patients regard us in the early stages as needing to be treated conditionally, as they felt they had to do with the earlier objects, but once this form of transference is brought into focus the patient seems to present as well as to adhere to an image of us which (we hope) is an exaggerated caricature. At times we may indeed find ourselves conforming to some of the subjective images being attributed to us, but the patient rigidly and automatically takes the part for the whole, and anxiety, depression, and anger can begin to accompany our response, even without our awareness.

What we are responding to, "silently," is at one level the patients' way of protecting themselves from deeper experiences of abandonment fears, emptiness, etc., by maintaining an illusion of control. Thus, a subjective set of obligatory projections maintains us as the "bad object." The bond to this bad object was organized in childhood—parallel to the false self and vertical split, but more malignant and rigid in its form. A vicious cycle developed in childhood: the parent may have recognized the hostility and the distrust involved in the bond, and may have felt injured by it. By clinging to the distrusted parent, but at a distance, the patient (child) never really felt nourished or repaired, and the parent (out of narcissistic-injury motives) might have felt critical, enraged, withdrawn, and/or accusatory of the patient. At times a parent may respond more to feeling unuseful, while at other times it is the underlying rage that cannot be tolerated or absorbed.

Those patients who, in spite of our apparent grasp of their inner atmosphere, resist a shift to viewing us as more usable—thus insisting on maintaining an image of us as conditionally accepting, unresponsive to regressive needs, and unavailable in times of emergency affect states—eventually can cause significant reactions in us. With these often-more-subtle forms of the patients' defensive systems, our reactions to the implied image of us as untrustworthy may evolve slowly. Frequently, the perception that we are being held at a distance is disclaimed by the patient who simply experiences the nonawareness of us as a natural phenomenon. However, it is presently not my intent to delve into the controversy between how much is hostile or defensive in these character presentations versus how much is part of a primary narcissistic disorder. My main concern is the effect the whole presentation has on our analytic instrument.

Kohut has spoken of the kinds of problems we can have when the patient's relationship to us reveals a paucity of traditional (object-instinctual) transference material, but his emphasis has been on helping us see that self-selfobject transferences take specific and often quite primitive forms. He refers to a narcissistic defense against exposure of deeper narcissistic presentations, with the motive for the resistance being the overriding need to maintain self organization. Winnicott (1963) alludes to long periods when the patient is in a state of passive noncommunication, not unlike Modell's (1976) cocoon stage where the emphasis is more on the patient's waiting and preparing for a new and more hopeful relationship and less on defense. Gaddini (1982) writes of patients who need the analyst to preserve the illusion of their nondependence for a prolonged period, since the premature exposure to their dependence on the analyst and the concomitant recognition of vulnerable separateness can lead to disintegration anxiety.

However, while we can be fortified with such sophisticated theoretical insights, a danger exists that we, like the parents, will react to a chronic sense of being "held off," treated as unessential. This threat to our maintaining a positively toned relationship toward our patients is increased when an active defensiveness is imbricated in the character. It has been particularly noticeable in my practice if a patient is not only attached to and organized around the traumatized object of infancy, but also now utilizes this percept of the negative object fairly rigidly, transferring a view of me as narcissistic, demanding, conditionally accepting, etc., as a way of maintaining control over the mobilizing of deeper affects (see the discussion of *Autumn Sonata* in my article "Use of the Object" [Newman, 1984]). For example, a patient has consistently told me that she only wishes that I could be of real significance and use to her, but as it is I am just a person she comes to four times a week who listens fairly well. Between sessions, and during breaks, regrettably I have little meaning. Due to this she has cautioned me repeatedly not to make the mistake of assuming transference as a motive for current disturbances, increase of symptoms, etc. However, what is thrust forward whenever there is a feeling of increased closeness or assurance of my reliability is the emergence of images of me which refer to my need for her transference, my self-centeredness, etc. What we are gradually learning is that what she "worries" about at a more superficial level is an organization used to defend against what is feared at depth, i.e., the fear that her authentic needs, if really exposed, would be met by a self-centered, excessively critical, perfectionist mother.

In the clinical situation, with this patient and with several others previously, I have, consequent to a prolonged exposure to this level and form of relationship, been out of phase at particular treatment junctures. In spite of their manifest disclaimers, spontaneous gestures and the beginning of expression of deeper needs have been proffered, although often in muted, stilted, or even garbled form—I believe because I have not fully embraced the feeling of injury involved in not feeling really important. In my reactive anger I have missed the opportunity to sense positively the patient's potential shifts. While I feel this duplicates early issues and vicious cycles which get activated in childhood between child and parent, my own contribution to this has to be attended to; namely, I have a tendency toward narcissistic vulnerability and thus, at some level, can too readily agree to feeling nonsignificant.

In the treatment, what occurs at times is that the patient will seem to be increasingly defensive and I will, in some way, see this as once more an attempt to control her deeper transference needs. However, this, we are learning, is not always true, and the pulling back is motivated by my being insufficiently responsive to needs that are in ascendancy. In my opinion, it is a countertransference reaction which has interfered with my analytic instrument. In effect, it has rendered me unavailable to be *used* at the delicate moment when the patient's highly vulnerable deeper yearnings would or could emerge.

With another patient early in treatment her overall attitude toward me was a muted but consistent feeling that I was of little help, was too inexperienced. During her last session before my summer vacation she asked me to find an extra weekly session for her in the fall. In spite of my fancying myself an expert on movie trivia and other memorabilia, I happened to forget this request.

Moving along the diagnostic continuum we come to those patients who more openly, actively, and consistently make it clear from the beginning that we are nonuseful, nonmeaningful and, moreover, that we seem to be repeating the same failures as their earlier objects. We are seen as needing the patient's compliance, self-centered, and conditionally accepting. There is often criticism of other shortcomings, regarding either our inability to understand and empathize, our shallow quickness to relate themes to ourselves, or our underlying vulnerability. There seems to be little time when the patient does not feel annoyed, in need of withdrawal, or impatient with our uselessness. Even if it appears to our well-intended therapeutic selves that we seem to be "getting it right" or providing a nonintrusive and empathic background, our patients seem to find aspects of our responsiveness which imply our self-deception and overall insensitivity. Often, following "good" sessions in which we have felt that the analytic bond is strengthening and the conditions may be set for a safer and deeper regression, we are aggrieved to find that our patient is in a state of withdrawal, despair, or has reacted negatively to some issue we perceived as relatively insignificant. Because we are viewed as untrustworthy and excessively narcissistic, we often attempt to "understand" with our patients the intensity and origin of these distortions. This often leads to an increased negative experience as the patient feels that we need to place the blame on him and, because of our vulnerability, reject his criticism. At this point two major questions arise: Has the patient's core self been so damaged that the need for an exquisitely sensitive and perfectly attuned object (selfobject) is so vital that our limitations are constantly threatening the cohesion of the patient's self? Or, we may wonder (especially when we feel ourselves out of balance) whether there is a self-protective quality to the patient's experience. That is, is a set of projections and distortions expressed through a negatively held and often vituperatively voiced view of us rigidly held onto because it serves as a defense against mobilizing deeper transference needs?

Now, obviously, a steady diet of being made to feel useless or meaningless at best, and under a fairly steady barrage of criticism for faulty empathy, incomplete understanding, and so on, provides a marvelous opportunity for activating a countertransference experience, or at least sampling countertransference attitudes and affects. There is a developmental issue which parallels, I believe, the clinical condition which is being dramatized in these tense moments.

As described earlier, failures in the environmental response to the infant's needs are inevitable and lead, in turn, to disruptions in the well-being of the self. Powerful affects are activated, and the relationship to the object (selfobject) can be temporarily altered. In effect the child's disruptive experience may be expressed through aggressive and angry outbursts, painful manifestations of loss, and evident altered views of the important objects which may include highly distorted experiences (the selfobjects may become fragmented or hostile drive derivatives may be displaced onto them). In addition, the child may attempt to retreat temporarily from the objects. This disruptive state, with its intense affects, distorted accusations, and defenses can be a serious challenge for the parent. This is particularly true if, for example, the mother has a vulnerability to loss which is activated by the feeling that her child is accusing her of being a bad mother, or by the child's temporary withdrawal. The injury-prone parent may also unconsciously sense the child's distorted and altered experience of the parent and either attempt to deny the significance of the child's tension states or withdraw. Another major source of failure occurs when the parent's own character pathology is organized around denial of infantile needs and affects, and this then may interfere with appropriate and true identification with the child's distress. The child, left alone with tension states due to parental failure at this pivotal point, may begin to both wall off his primary needs and affect states and shift into a more chronic and potentially pathological character solution, including permanent disillusionment and deformation of the capacity for usable relationships with the needed object.

When these patients subject us persistently and unremittingly to open and frank criticism for our insufficient sensitivity, evidence of our self-centeredness, and/or vulnerability, there is often little doubt that the patient feels that he or she must keep us at a distance. For a number of other patients, more subtle implications of our untrustworthiness are usually combined with reminders of our meaningfulness. Over a period of time, admixtures of our intentions and interventions are constantly "distorted" or reinterpreted to fit the patient's ever-changing subjective experience of an untrustworthy object. Together with the sense that we are rarely ever "truly useful" to the patient, it is this obligatory role positioning by the patient which has the power to activate in us a series of affects which represent, on one level, negative identifications with the earliest objects and, on another, with aspects of the patient as a child.

I believe that the nature and content of much of the patient's manifest reactions to us have important transference meanings, i.e., certainly speak to the underlying rage and disappointment in the parental capacity to listen, to be empathic to needs, and to accept responsibility for the child's feelings of distress. Yet I feel that the crucial issue for consideration is our being asked to relive with the patient a point in time *after* the earlier traumata had occurred—when the child had shifted to a position of chronic defensiveness as well as to an altered experience in relationship to his selfobjects. Just as the parent now is challenged to "hold" her child in the face of distortions and caricatures (mother as witch, for example) and be available to absorb the underlying rage with appropriate doses of empathy and controls, so now is the analyst called upon to "hold" the patient through this period. Further, an ever-more-difficult issue for both parent and therapist is the reaction to the distance and apparent nonattachment of the child-patient. Since we are seeing the child (now adult) after he has attempted to reorganize himself around self-protective, self-maintaining mechanisms (which may include viewing the analyst in a "bad-object" manner, reinforced by near-paranoid and schizoid mechanisms), we are able to be in a position similar to that of the earliest parental objects which *followed* significant developmental disturbances. I feel that we may inevitably fail, at least for a time and regrettably more than once, to provide what I believe these patients require in the long run. But again it may only be through the experience of enacting these failures that patient and analyst can begin to have a mutual understanding based on concretely shared experience—a genuine dialogue can be established which may facilitate the patient's raised hope of a possible new experience.

In my clinical experience, countertransference failures, in spite of my best intentions, have clustered around the following issues: I often find myself attempting to "help my patient" with underlying views of me which reverberate with the archaic objects, i.e., I will make transference interpretations which I hope will sufficiently differentiate me from the intensity of the negative experiences associated with the earlier objects—in order that they can in turn permit deeper libidinal experiences to develop so that the usability can be facilitated. While this can be very helpful with some patients, my persistence with this approach with others has often led them to be more despairing and critical of my need to "defend myself." However well I rationalize this approach as an attempt to help us differentiate so that patients can start to use me to deepen their transference, I am confronted with more protest, retreat, and accusations of self-deception. In addition, however well I think I understand the subtle-to-manifest expressions of disavowal of my meaning, at some point I may react in a way that suggests my feeling deprived or injured.

The needs that these particular patients are conveying to us have been referred to somewhat differently by Winnicott, Kohut, and Modell. Kohut has spoken of the patients' needs to preserve their own integrity and implies that we are called upon to maintain for them the possibility of a selfobject in order for them to start to grow again. What he underscores, though, is that the defective self will need to ward off or maintain its own cohesiveness for a prolonged period of time, and we must recognize and forbear. This forbearance may include acceptance not only of the patients' view of the world but *even* of their right and need to distort it. Winnicott speaks to the patients who begin in a stage of active noncommunication and may only gradually move to a position that may appear as resistance but is actually like a "moment of hesitation." This position is like a transitional space gradually filled by the patient with expressions of needs and desires which belong to id experiences and which are not preemptively encouraged by external impingements—a point from which the patient, given time, may start to use the analyst.

Frequently, in these more "difficult" analyses, I feel that in spite of my getting things right the patient seems either to retreat or to attack me or the analysis. If a patient announces a scheduling difficulty, and I offer to rearrange something for him, I may be surprised to hear in the next session that I seem to need to have him come for the hour, or he suggests that I have found the time to maintain my "nice-guy" view of myself. At these points I begin (out of ultimate motives of my own) to think of the concept of negative therapeutic reaction, or begin to suggest that the patient needs to defend against closeness, etc. Once more this may lead to an outburst of despair, vituperation, or retreat.

From the patient's perspective of his own earlier experiences, we learn repeatedly that there is often something in our responses which activates a danger signal. It is also true that the patient may need to see us in this negative light, perhaps to disrupt the bond in the face of anxiety over potential deepening experiences (such as closeness). But for these particular patients, the interpretation of the concept of negative therapeutic reaction is itself, I believe, some evidence of our countertransference. If due to this we somehow convey our disagreement with their continued nonuse of us, or imply their error in failing to see our goodness, we may indeed find the patient protesting that we are attempting to induce a guilt reaction. We also may feel concern for the therapeutic alliance and rationalize our unconscious feelings of injury with the idea that our patient is possibly unanalyzable.

A case vignette follows which I hope illustrates a number of issues just outlined: the unacknowledged countertransference and its effect on stalemating the treatment; the identification with and attempt to reject a hostile maternal introject; and the manifestation of these occurrences not only in mutual affective storms but in the assigning of the major responsibility to the patient's negative therapeutic reaction.

A young woman patient of mine for several years has chronically expressed disappointment in my "helpfulness," most dramatically conveyed whenever she really "needs" me because of a current stress. A number of such scenes have been replayed during phone calls, where the patient will plaintively communicate, "Why can't you help more?" or "Why is it that as soon as I hear your voice I know this won't be helpful?" At times in the office sessions she will be quite upset about a particular situation, and on one level she will turn to me for aid while on another I feel that I am being almost automatically invalidated as any potential source of help. Earlier in the treatment these office transactions would often heat up, resulting at times in my feeling greatly annoyed and my unfortunate patient at first enraged and finally in despair.

However, it is not these acute reactions that I want to focus on, but the quieter, yet equally insidious phone transactions which for so long have proved anathema to both of us. From my point of view, I often felt that I was providing availability and concern, while the patient, although not hostile, would despair that I was going to be useless. Sometimes I was contrasted with near strangers who for some reason could offer something more helpful; indeed at other times allusions were made to my being a professional or like her "do-the-right-thing mother." It seemed to me that no matter what sort of help or how much time I offered, it never made a difference, and the dominant impression I had was that I was at some level identified with the bad mother.

Needless to say, there has been no dearth of interpretations offered by me to supplement my attempts to be a real and new object. Among my insights, the most frequent related to a negative therapeutic reaction, an anxiety on the patient's part to allow me to be useful and hence activate her feared but longed-for deeper yearnings. My major explanation for her not feeling helped was based on her organizing herself and me around the negative mother. At times I became aware of other disquieting personal reactions, anywhere from pique to rage, or simply a feeling of resignation which amounted emotionally to my withdrawal from her.

What I gradually realized was that what I felt—no matter what the explanation—was that I hated being identified with her almost brutally insensitive mother, and that this feeling was reinforced by my own self needs to be a helpful, caring mother, a more special person. At times, then, my reaction to this feeling of injury led me in effect to become her "bad" mother by shifting the blame for our stalemate onto her in subtle (and sometimes not so subtle) ways. (Thus, even the interpretation concerning her "need" to distance or disavow my meaning was experienced by her as "her fault.") What we have come to learn over time is that the moment she turned to me as a real (not a fantasy) object, she got in touch with disillusionment. I then became the embodiment of the unloving and unyielding mother, who not only was unempathic but who also denied the reality of her daughter's affects. The recognition that I could not be helpful, because of the intense fixation of an all-powerful object who instantly provided soothing, introduced us both to the overwhelming pain and melancholy in this woman and the deep and heretofore unspoken-of disillusionment with and rage at the mother.

Although there are a number of additional interesting insights into this complex patient, most significantly I became aware that an important part of me needed to be helpful and, in many ways, that meant, like her mother, not fully admitting her present pain. As long as I could not completely accept the almost inevitable reality that, of course, I could not be useful and was not immediately taking away her painful tension states, I was demonstrating the same vulnerability as the mother had. Then, when the patient would begin despairingly to protest and I would in some way convey that it was her need to see me this way, absolute depression and feelings of failure would set in. A need of mine to be helpful made me more susceptible to feeling identified with the mother who needed to reject her daughter's unconscious accusations that she was unavailable emotionally. My inability to accept my patient's sense of despair fully was in part caused by my being unable to separate myself from the mother of the past who was subtly being accused in the present. It just so happened that the current disappointment was being deployed onto me and, in my effort to reject it as identification with the cold and empathic mother, I was in fact denying her psychological reality and, in essence, duplicating too closely her mother's response. As I more readily accepted my nonhelpfulness and spoke to the contrast between her subjective idealizing of my usefulness in the absence of contact and the disillusioning limitations of my reality, she felt less alone with the emerging depressive feelings.

In this case I believe the acceptance of the role of nonhelpful mother permitted more of the expression of the real disappointments. The opening up of the issue of needing the illusion to keep from feeling genuine affects was often interfered with by my unconscious resistance to accepting that I could not be helpful, but not because the patient needed me to be the bad mother. The emphasis on this form of negative therapeutic reaction helped disguise for me my part in the stalemate, and certainly interfered with my being able to reopen a dialogue between the patient and a container-function selfobject. Now, as time has gone on, the patient can acknowledge that at times she gets anxious about the deepening transference, worries about my commitment, and then reorganizes around me as a conditionally available object, i.e., starts to retreat to a negative but more controllable object. But this aspect of her resistance was not the whole or possibly even the central *cause* of her chronically finding me nonuseful.[1]

When we react with feelings of helplessness and injury we are unconsciously identifying with the parental objects at a developmental point following disturbances in the core dyadic relationship. Following our own negative experiences, what is wanted of us is a period in which we regain a perspective and remember the injured child in our patient. I believe the patient needs us to live through and absorb the injuries, the rages, and even to accept, without undue vulnerability, their defensive position.

As a general concept, a holding environment is what the patient needs us to be. And this includes for some more than ordinary doses of acceptance—the acceptance of not being (apparently) usable. We are asked to try and see our failures through our patient's eyes and bear what certainly may feel like considerable distortions arising from these often intense encounters. Much depends on how well we are able to take responsibility and even acknowledge how our own injured self-esteem influences our negative attitudes toward the patient. Even though we do identify temporarily with the earliest of the patient's objects, especially as we become critical of our patient's demands on us, or his or her resistance to the relationship with us, it is our capacity to reestablish a dialogue with the patient that offers the creative moment for experiencing a new object. Here the patient may gradually see in us an ability to emerge out of the intense countertransference reactions for the purpose of understanding how earlier traumas were experienced. Our willingness to look at our own vulnerability and not

[1] To reiterate: What caused her to feel hopeless came from two major sources—(1) the contrast between me (or others) as simply real and hence less than the fantasied needed object, and (2) my identification with the mother who could not at depth accept her injured, depressed child, and who could not therefore help her validate her feelings.

shift all of the blame onto the patient may actually be the crucial mutative experience.

One of the most difficult issues arises when the patient seems to take an issue that represents an area of our insensitivity, and then universalizes it. Everything else seems to feed into this, and it is as if we are being viewed in a totally encompassing, subjective way. I call this the part being taken for the whole, and I think it is invariably one of the most devastating kinds of experiences because one feels helpless to alter someone's globally negative view of oneself. It is certainly a source of injury to our wishful view of ourselves as helpful, caring, etc. The source of this attack should be seen as being evidence of the nature of the earlier trauma suffered by the patient and now reversed partly as a way of discharging rage and partly maintained to keep the object at a safe distance.

We are unconsciously being asked to relive with the patient as the object who represents both a past threat but holds a future promise. They are asking us to survive their provocative defenses, their grievances and derivatives of their need states. But this is all being staged at a certain surface level—with the hope that we can help master and embrace both the patient's and our own powerful affects. If we can negotiate the "defense transference" and emerge with our patients out of the intensity of the countertransference enactments, then we may go on to deeper, more regressive transferences, but more ultimately profitable analyses. The initial stages of such analyses are like difficult tryouts. However, if we can handle testy and critical reactions, then we may prove safe enough for our patient to restage the core of his transference needs and affects.

V. Summary

The central work of psychoanalytic action can only take place when the analyst is experienced as a usable object. For many patients restitutional adaptations and character defenses often operate to evoke in the analyst responses that potentially render him or her nonuseful. While these countertransference "failures" can lead to a stalemate, they also provide a vital opportunity to effect crucial mutative changes. Through a series of countertransference enactments the analyst samples intensively complementary identifications with the faulty objects of the patient's childhood. The gradual capacity to manage and embrace the countertransference, rather than remain frozen in it facilitates an authentic recognition of the patient's inner world and in effect supplies a missing function. The analyst now can reconstruct from firsthand experience aspects of the failed original dyad and then through these communications, which revive previously unspoken affects, reestablish a new developmental dialogue. This is a vital part of the "holding" environment which offers both a scaffolding for new experiences and the vehicle for eroding the pernicious attachment to the archaic introject.

Two major groups of patients are presented. The first includes those whose character structure reveals pathological accommodations restitutional to early environmental failures. The analyst's initial countertransference enactment corresponds to a complementary identification with the parental failure at the point at which the child is subtly induced to repress and compromise his own needs and affects as the price of maintaining his attachment.

The second and apparently more difficult group evoke negative responses in the analyst which parallel a specific developmental interference. The analyst is unconsciously asked to "hold" the patient at a point corresponding to the child who, in the face of acute disappointments and rising tension states, has retreated to a negatively charged and protective character organization. The mastering of the countertransference reaction raises the patient's hope and trust and allows a deepening transference with all the attendant affects to unfold.

REFERENCES

Gaddini, E. (1982), Acting out in the psychoanalytic process. *Internat. J. Psycho-Anal.*, 63:57-64.

Green, A. (1975), The analyst, symbolization and absence in the analytic setting. *Internat. J. Psycho-Anal.*, 56:1-24.

Khan, M. (1975), Introduction to *Through Pediatrics to Psychoanalysis*, by D. W. Winnicott. New York: Basic Books.

Kohut, H. (1971), *The Analysis of the Self*. New York: International Universities Press.

——— (1984), *How Does Analysis Cure?* New York: International Universities Press.

Mahler, M. S. (1971), A study of the separation-individuation process and its possible application to borderline phenomena in the psychoanalytic situation. *The Psychoanalytic Study of the Child*, 26:403-424. New York: International Universities Press.

Miller, A. (1979), The drama of the gifted child and the psychoanalyst's narcissistic disturbance. *Internat. J. Psycho-Anal.*, 63:47-58.

Modell, A. (1976), The "holding environment" and the therapeutic action of psychoanalysis. *J. Amer. Psychoanal. Assn.*, 24:285-307.

Newman, K. M. (1984), The capacity to use the object. In: *Psychoanalysis: The Vital Issues*, ed. G. H. Pollock & J. E. Gedo, 2:149-175.

Racker, H. (1968), *Transference and Countertransference*. New York: International Universities Press.

Winnicott, D. W. (1958), *Through Pediatrics to Psychoanalysis*, with introd. by M. Khan (1975). New York: Basic Books, pp. xi-xlviii.

——— (1960), Ego distortion in terms of true and false self. In: *The Maturational Process and the Facilitating Environment*. London: Hogarth Press, pp. 140-152.

——— (1963), Communicating and not communicating—leading to a study of certain opposites. In: *The Maturational Process and the Facilitating Environment*. London: Hogarth Press, pp. 179-192.
——— (1971), The use of an object and relating through identification. In: *Play and Reality*. London: Tavistock Publications, pp. 109-111.

May 1986

Discussion

DR. KLIGERMAN:
Dr. Newman offers an essay full of rich and provocative clinical ideas that bear directly on some of the most basic issues in psychoanalytic therapy. He advances some novel ideas and raises a host of fruitful and intriguing questions, which are in themselves hallmarks of a valuable paper. As I perceive his thesis, it runs roughly as follows: In many persons an unfortunate selfobject derailment with the original caretakers leads to a traumatic walling off of the primary needs, claims, and aspirations, and to the secondary development of an adaptive defensive style, in which the child learns to live with a faulty object in a way that maintains some cohesiveness and fends off disintegration anxiety or hopeless despair, but fails to address the deeper needs and the existing damage of the self. In later life, the child/patient maintains this style in the form of a false self which, however, presents itself as manifest character. He both adapts and defends. In his personal relations, he finds objects who behave in a complementary fashion to this outer layer, or evokes unconscious complementary responses in people who ordinarily might have behaved differently. When such patients enter analysis, the analyst can easily fall into an unconscious complementary countertransference posture, which, if not corrected, leads to a stalemate or negative therapeutic reaction. This state of affairs is then all too frequently attributed to the patient's unanalyzability. On the other hand, when the complementary countertransference is understood and the therapeutic relationship is felicitously handled, instead of a pathological regression resulting, the false self or split-off part is gradually modified, and the patient enters into a fruitful therapeutic regression toward the primary archaic selfobject transference.

So far, the sequence does not seem entirely unfamiliar to us. One might say it represents the pregenital counterpart of the traditional concept of defense transference in structured neuroses, in which the therapeutic regression leads to the nuclear conflict of an oedipal nature. In this case it leads to the primary pathogenic situation of earlier selfobject failures.

But at this point Dr. Newman introduces his most original and challenging idea, namely, that enmeshment in a complementary situation to the patient's pathology, in which the analyst in a sense repeats the original object's reactions not to the original failure but to the type of defensive shell which the patient has built around himself, is not simply an accident which must be surmounted, but a sine qua non which has to be experienced and then understood in order to foster an optimal mutative result. This position strikes me as the end of the line of a long historical development of our attitudes toward countertransference, and I would like to digress for a moment to review this history.

Traditionally, our theory of therapy has always depended on the nonparticipation of the analyst in the transference of the patient. While few have adhered to the mirror model that was originally proposed, there has been more or less general espousal of the idea that the analyst should maintain an objective, nonjudgmental, observing stance, so that the transference projections of the patient could be readily recognized and made clear to the patient through interpretation. Insofar as the analyst had affective or unconscious reactions of a countertransference kind, they were to be analyzed by the analyst and eliminated or seen as signals which inform him about the status of the unconscious in the patient. If the analyst's attitudes or reactions went beyond this then they became a more serious form of countertransference, which had to be cleared up by the analyst in order for the analysis to get back on the track. If this development reached major proportions, then it became critical for the analyst to work through the countertransference, understand it within himself, often discuss it with the patient, in order, again, to clear the air. Sometimes the analyst's candor and honesty could have a favorable effect on the therapeutic alliance and on the patient's regard for the analyst, and both could have learned something from the episode. The general progression of the thinking about countertransference was from something bad, something to be avoided, to be expunged through further self-analysis or actual analysis of the analyst, to a more tolerant view of one's frailties and lending oneself to the patient's transference, and making a virtue out of a necessity by doing analytic work on it, trying to turn it to good account.

Newman now takes this one step further. In the treatment of some patients this is a necessary step to be undergone if the patient is going to be analyzed—in Newman's language, if the patient is to learn to use the analyst as a new object or the analyst is to make himself usable. The early drama must be repeated in the analysis with affective participation by *both* parties of the noxious relationship, in order for the patient to come to grips with the psychic reality of what had happened in the past. In other words, the expectant attitude of the analyst, or the interpretation of defenses against transference, or the interpretation of those transference derivatives which do manifest themselves, are not sufficient in these cases. There must be an actual reenactment of the pathogenic object relationship that pertained in the first place, or rather in the second place, since it deals mainly, as Newman emphasizes, with the defensive structure that emerges after the original trauma. Only in this way can an experience reminiscent of that early trauma become vivid enough to be convincing to the patient, and bring home to him what he has done to render the object unusable, or, more accurately, what he *had to do* in order to make the object both usable and unusable.

This seems rather a tour de force, like injecting noxious substances in order to evoke healthy immune responses. I might say, too, that this technical approach is strongly reminiscent of that advocated by François Roustang in Paris who, in his book, *Psychoanalysis Never Lets Go*, advances the idea in treating patients of this sort that the analyst must allow himself to be caught in what he calls "the game of the other." Naturally, this has to be a dangerous game and raises many thoughts. Perhaps the first thought which arises concerns the danger of retraumatization, that the patient will have yet another damaging experience and be quite justified in his bitter reproaches to the analyst if he still maintains any dialogue at all. So, at this point, a decisive amount depends on the empathy, skill, and honesty of the analyst who, as Newman sagaciously points out, is only too prone to feel bruised and narcissistically wounded himself and, in subtle or not-so-subtle ways, tends to blame the patient. For example, one senses this attitude in the first case cited where the analyst felt "had" by the patient who tried to delight her. Newman's own clinical examples show admirably the high degree of empathy and honesty that is required to resolve the impasse in a constructive way. In some patients, the risk of retraumatization may be the only way to effect any positive change, and it may be inevitable anyway, because few of us are immune from countertransference entanglement with such patients.

The idea of the vivid reenactment might seem to be a temptation to play-act a kind of psychodrama in order to bring about a corrective emotional experience. Such an effort is hardly necessary: the major issue is not to flee when one is caught, but to try to work the problem through with the patient to a new level. There is a certain aspect of corrective emotional experience to this situation, but, in a sense, it is just the reverse of Alexander's suggestion that the therapist deliberately play the opposite role of the pathogenic parent. Interestingly enough, I remember an example given by Alexander which was really more corrobatory of Newman's reasoning.

Alexander described the case of a young man who attributed his troubles to a mean, tyrannical, ungiving father. In the analysis, Alexander determined to be as kind, warm, and permissive as he could for this young man, who was terribly obnoxious and would come in unkempt, unshaven, sloppy, often with filth on his shoes. Alexander bore all this with equanimity but to no avail, until one day, when the patient acted out in a particularly provocative way, Alexander lost his temper and roared, "what's the matter with you anyway?" or words to that effect. Whereupon the patient jumped up and said, "You see, you see, you are just like my father!"—an episode so ludicrous that even the patient had to realize it, and this led the way to a marked character change and a different evaluation of the father. So in this simplistic, encapsulated episode, there was an outburst of negative countertransference that made the patient genuinely aware of his counterproductive, negativistic style. This was a lucky hit, but in general Alexander's method failed to fulfill its promise. Alexander thought he could divine the bad internal object in advance. Newman's cardinal point is that only through actually experiencing the countertransference interaction in a developing situation can the analyst diagnose within himself the pathogenic parent. In fact that takes *lots of time*—time to develop the relevant complementary countertransference and time to work through the impasse.

I recall a patient of mine, a young woman who seemed to be a classical hysteric but, after two years of an apparent classical analysis, suddenly went into a severe regression that lasted many months, if not years, in which she wailed piteously and berated me constantly for not helping her. She would furiously beat her head and face with her fists, as she had indeed banged her head on the floor as a child left alone for long periods—but this interpretation did not help very much. I will not detail all the interventions I made that only increased her despair (and mine too). Inwardly, I considered interrupting the treatment, but finally I decided just to wait it out as a witness. In a sense, I had through sheer exhaustion gone beyond the anguish and narcissistic resentment of feeling helpless and useless. One day she came in very quietly and, after a long silence, said in a small, timid voice, "I'm glad you didn't give up on me." And from then on the work progressed rapidly in a favorable direction. I never quite understood the timing, but there must have been some internal change in me of a greater acceptance that permitted the holding that Newman describes so well.

In the course of his paper, Dr. Newman acknowledges the influence of previous writers, mainly Winnicott and Kohut, whose work he would like to integrate and expand. It is certainly a worthwhile project and, to a great extent, he has succeeded, but at times the concepts do not lend themselves to equation. For example, I don't think that Kohut's concept of vertical split is entirely comparable to Winnicott's false self, although there are certain similarities. Also, I don't believe that two other aspects were quite as neglected by Kohut as Newman implies. One is the issue of understimulation, of faulty mirroring, and lack of response on the part of the selfobject. It was not only "overwhelming tension states" and lack of soothing mechanisms that Kohut was dealing with, but also understimulated, empty personalities, who suffer from lack of attention and input. And, in fact, Kohut saw this as a prevailing pathology of our current era. Second of all, Kohut indeed dealt with developments after the primary trauma and felt that the transference usually represented some later traumatic episode with regression. However, Newman may be right that there was not as much emphasis on later defense and resistance as on the development of primary selfobject transferences. In much of Kohut's writing, for purposes of schematic exposition, there is often the impression that the selfobject transferences develop rather easily and spontaneously with a minimum of interference from the analyst, but he always emphasized that often a great deal of work had to be done by the analyst in the effort to evoke the deeper, primary selfobject transference. Part of this relative neglect of defense in his system may have been due to the fact that he was viewing defense from the structural point of view as an element of the drive-defense model, differentiating this from the selfobject model. I don't think there is any relevant difference between Newman's approach and the self model in these areas.

There may be somewhat more of a difference in the attitude toward compensatory mechanisms. One gets the impression in Newman's approach that on the way to the Big Apple, the defenses are to be eschewed or abandoned as obstructive aspects of the false self, whereas in the self-psychological approach adaptive aspects of the defenses can undergo a meaningful development of their own, which is sustaining to the self and a valuable acquisition. For example, the ingratiatingness can be imbricated with the self as a higher form of charm. Also, it goes without saying that sometimes the compensatory mechanisms should not only not be questioned but also preserved and strengthened when one suspects an underlying emptiness or fragmentation. However, this core state is often very difficult to assess, and one man's borderline might be another man's archaic but analyzable patient. Such people have, in the past, been approached by educative and ego-supportive measures, but it could be that Newman's courageous method might advance us a little farther in the treatment of these patients and also inform us favorably in our analytic work with the better-integrated population.

It has been a pleasure to discuss this most interesting and sensitive paper.

DR. TERMAN:

I am pleased to have the opportunity to discuss Dr. Newman's paper—however, there is a problem. There is so much here with which I agree that I am afraid that I will bore all my readers and contribute very little by saying, "Yes, yes, yes." So I shall stress our differences, some problems with the terms, and a slightly different theoretical perspective, rather than our agreement, even though the latter is far greater than the former.

Dr. Newman describes two, now familiar, clinical syndromes met with in our analytic work. One is the compliant, pleasing patient who seems to do well or "makes use" of us—prospers with our efforts, or lack of effort—and seems to confirm our capacities as analysts. Such an appearance is only a snare and a delusion, we will sadly discover, when it becomes apparent that the patient is enacting an old role of divining the parents' deepest or most comforting wishes and complying with them at the sacrifice of his or her own needs and wishes with the attendant rage, disillusionment, and loneliness that such transactions evoke. The clinical task is to discover this and make both aware of it. The greatest difficulty for the analyst in such a situation is having to dislodge himself and his patient from a position of comfort to one of greater tension and uncertainty.

The other syndrome is far more difficult for both analyst and patient to negotiate. In this, the central source of the analyst's self-esteem is under unremitting assault. Rather than aid, benefit, or enlighten the patient, the analyst has hurt, disappointed, or failed him; and the patient bitterly reproaches the analyst repeatedly with these failures. Interpretation which focuses on the patient's distortions only adds fuel to the fire, and nothing short of accepting the blame will do. Dr. Newman offers us, ultimately, the advice of having to accept such patients as they view us, and to accept, "without undue vulnerability, their defensive position." He goes on to say that "our willingness to look at our own vulnerability and not shift all of the blame on the patient may actually be the most mutative experience." The working through can only be achieved by the analyst's willingness to fail, as it were, acknowledge the failure, and finally understand what it means to the patient and himself.

This is a difficult task indeed. I shall confine my discussion to the technical and theoretical problems raised in dealing with this latter group of patients. I should say at the outset that my own clinical experience corresponds with that of Dr. Newman. And my own approach to these situations also corresponds with his. However, I am not so sure I would use the term "countertransference" to describe the analyst's response to the patient's experience. For countertransference means the stimulation of the analyst's unconscious, repressed conflicts and wishes and the archaic narcissistic needs which make the patients vehicles for their expression. There are real self-esteem issues here for the analyst—as well as for the patient. It is not neurotic to take pride in one's work, to want to perform one's function well, and to enjoy seeing the patient benefit from the relationship and our understandings. To react with distress when that does not occur is natural. To become frustrated is also natural. And when our persistent attempts to become effective are consistently frustrated, to become helpless, enraged, or despairing is also only human. That we must deal with these affects in ourselves and try to keep an eye on our patient and discern what is happening is also true. That is what we are paid for—that is our professional task. But the existence of such affects and responses within us cannot be properly called countertransference.

They may certainly become so. Considering this a negative therapeutic reaction may well be a way of blaming the patient—retaining the integrity of our professional and personal and childhood selves. But likewise, seeing this as countertransference may be equally unfair to ourselves—the outgrowth of a compliance with a sadistic or intransigent, archaic force in which we are deformed and demeaned.

That we repeat the childhood of our patients with our responses, I emphatically agree—and that the recognition of our participation is the vehicle by which treatment moves I also agree. But maybe we can find another term for the in-depth, nonneurotic-negative responses we experience. Would "counterreaction" be better?

We certainly need to "regain a perspective and remember the injured child in our patient," but the difficulty under these circumstances is immense. We may be aided in keeping our balance and perspective by a theoretical framework into which we can put these experiences.

Dr. Newman provides us with one on two levels. He suggests an etiological transaction and a dynamic structural construct. The first—the hypothesis about etiological experience—involves the following two-step process: the child's nuclear self or central needs are thwarted, *and* the child's *reaction* to the primary failures and incompletion—the rage, hurt, and/or loneliness—are then reacted to by the parents in such a way that the child feels hurt yet again. What Dr. Newman calls the "container function" of the parents—the soothing or modulating of the affect engendered by the primary failure—fails at the level of dealing with the affects aroused by the first injury. It is this *second* failure which is reenacted in the transference.

This is an interesting and worthy hypothesis, I think, and my own clinical experience corroborates the frequent encounter of yet another vulnerability once the uselessness of, or disillusionment with, the analyst is, initially, for moments worked through. Some years ago (1975), I reported on just such a case in which what seemed to be at stake was the revival of an excruciatingly traumatic experience of mirroring. The patient was a woman who would become especially enraged and find most fault with me at the approach of a wish to display herself as an adorable girl. It seemed that this was particularly threatening because of her experience with her father. He was a powerful, cold, domineering captain of industry who deemed normal fatherly affection fatuous. The confluence of her need for response with the particularly pointed, self-righteous rejection of it was what, he felt, stimulated her need to self-righteously find me in the wrong.

Yet, in thinking about her case and others which show the characteristic transference Dr. Newman describes, we may ask why it is so important that we somehow acknowledge blame, fault, responsibility for injury. This *quality* of the experience is quite distinctive. I found it instantly recognizable, and I suspect most of us would corroborate it. The two-step process does not quite account for that particular quality, I think. Nor does it account for the central importance—the mutative experience—of taking the blame. In several patients I have seen, including the patient I have just referred to, one prominent characteristic of the dominant parent was his or her *inability* to take the blame, and his or her obliviousness to the pain and/or injury inflicted on the child. In the case of the woman who was most emphatic about Newman's nonhelpfulness, the mother's denial of her daughter's affects may arise from just that kind of psychology. It is the experience of the implacableness of the parent that contributes to the absolute helplessness and rage of the child. The apparent assurance and self-righteousness of the parent with the consequent obliviousness, dismissal, or denial of the child's pain in the face of his or her actions deny any possibility of healing the injury and allowing the parent to perform the requisite functions—in Dr. Newman's term—of allowing the child to find the parent "usable."

Hence, it seems to be that though antecedent injury may frequently have occurred, it is not always at the center of these experiences. That is, the experience of the implacable inability to be responsible has an importance in its own right which needs to be understood and worked through.

I have found that this goes on over long periods of time and that significant changes evolve from its transformation. These changes certainly involve the emergence of greater vulnerabilities, but also include important shifts in how these patients see themselves and others. Quite significantly, there is a shift in the patient's capacity to hold himself responsible and accountable, to see the effects of his own actions and feelings on others, and, hence, to find relationships less puzzling and frustrating.

The corollary of my hesitation in accepting the two-step model of etiological transactions is my concern with the dynamic structural concept Dr. Newman proposes. (I think he is not quite comfortable with it, either, and he is also looking for a way out.) I am referring to the concept of the "bad-object defense." He states that the character is formed so that it uses an introject both to keep others at a distance and to avoid the experiences of need and vulnerability—the "walling off of needed but feared libidinal strivings." It is a "restitutive structure." Rigid, archaic, repetitive, compulsive, driven—yes, but restitutive? Defensive? Maybe—maybe not. "Defensive" gets in the way, clinically, as Dr. Newman points out. It is his having to overcome his—our—temptation, perception that the patient is distorting, misperceiving which is one crucial element in the analyst's part of the therapeutic process.

Why are these perceptions so real to the patient—so real that they are changed not with the interpretation of their distortion or defense, but only in understanding the reality—for them—the correctness of their perception? Is the perception formed only to protect? Or is it formed because it *is*—or *was*—i.e., the reality? It is a protest: "I should not be blamed—you must take the blame for what you do." And in that sense, it is an emotionally accurate rendition of the situation the child sees himself in. The notion of "defense" further implies choice and, to some degree, control. But the emotional reality is the converse, i.e., helplessness and lack of choice. Appreciating the "injured child" involves understanding these qualities of his experience, too.

I am suggesting that the nature of the structure that has formed has less a created, willed character than a quality reflecting the affective givens of the experience-fixed, frozen, and determining of the nature of the "reality" of relationship forevermore. That this fixture does prevent deeper engagement, use of others for appropriate functions, and even real love of others, I have no doubt, but the need to maintain it and repeat it has less to do with defense than with the primary nature of psychological substrate. It is a kind of *Weltanschauung* which is dominant and organizing. It is partly because it exists that other vulnerabilities are so traumatic; for by themselves, longings for tender responsiveness or the feelings of need or safety are not, in and of themselves, difficult. In fact, as they can be engaged more, they are really quite easy and fulfilling. The most difficult task is the slow and repetitive engagement and change in the conviction of uselessness and/or the disappointment of the parent or analyst.

You might object that this is really a nit-picking difference. After all, aren't we saying the same thing? This is a very subtle shift in perspective hardly worth the time it takes to articulate. Yet, it does bear on how we understand our patients clinically and on our notions of the development of psychological organization. In terms of our clinical approach I think my shift encompasses Dr. Newman's clinical experience somewhat more closely. Interpretations of defense or willful construction of this reality are met with rage (or self-blame) with intensification of the negative experience of the analyst. Acceptance of the reality of one's failure for the patient while still maintaining the availability and the capacity to modulate and understand the intense affects stimulated is, as Dr. Newman so rightly and clearly points out, the mutative experience. That is what changes the structure. It exists in its own right, as it were, not just as a protection against other vulnerabilities.

With respect to the second question—the development of psychological organization—I cannot enter into a prolonged dissertation. But though it is true that we construct our realities and that symbolization powerfully affects and determines the structure, the unity of self and object—the functional system that is implied in the term "selfobject"—behooves us to rethink some of our notions of development. That is, the givenness of experience makes a powerful contribution to the nature of the patterning which remains.

Again I want to thank Dr. Newman for his thoughtful and stimulating consideration of these problems. These are difficult and complex issues for all of us, and I think we can all appreciate the help he has given us in wrestling with them.

IV

APPLIED PSYCHOANALYSIS

Pregnant with Joy and Sorrow: Creativity, Androgyny, and Manic-Depression

VICTORIA SHAHLY, M.A. (Ann Arbor, Mich.)

> Every creative person is a duality or a synthesis of contradictory aptitudes.
>
> —C. G. Jung

Two discrete literatures address a bipolarity of sorts in highly creative persons. The first largely anecdotal and theoretical literature proposes that sexual "bipolarity" (Heilbrun, 1964) is prevalent among artists. Scholars frequently refer to a "certain bisexuality" (Hitschmann, 1956), "a shifting, at times, confused sense of maleness and femaleness . . . , a kind of *primal biunity*" (Oremland, 1985, p. 414) among the artistically gifted. The second literature documents somewhat more empirically the disproportionate rate of manic-depression among artists, especially poets. A striking, but previously unreported, observation is the apparent overlap between artists cited as manic-depressive and those described as androgynous.

The present paper reviews both literatures and attempts a more synthetic reading of affective illness and gender disturbance among eminent artists. Unfortunately, neither literature is sufficiently substantial or systematic to permit conclusive statements. Further, not a single paper has been located which addresses the curious coexistence of bipolar affective illness and "bisexuality." Lacking more methodologically rigorous documentation, this paper relies heavily on artists' self-reports, and psychoanalytic case studies

The preparation of this paper was supported by National Institutes of Health National Research Service Award MH17496 from the National Institute of Mental Health. The author wishes to thank Drs. Janet Adelman, Philip Cowan, Ravenna Helson, Sheldon Korchin, Georgine Marrott, Gerald Mendelsohn, and Abby Wolfson for helpful comments.

and theory. The survey is intended as a preliminary inquiry into what may comprise only a subtype of the creative personality.

Method

Before beginning, a word must be said regarding method. In the course of an analysis of feminine identification in the poet Rilke (Shahly, in press), I informally reviewed the psychoanalytic literature on pregnancy envy in men. That literature referenced other writers with apparent gender disturbances and pointed to a bisexual trend among artists. While reading these artists' works and biographies, I noticed an unusual prevalence of affective bipolarity as well. Moreover, their manic phases seemed to coincide with more acutely experienced contrasexual identifications and depressive phases with a return to more "gender-appropriate" experience. As Rilke also demonstrated gender-related cyclothymic tendencies, I became interested in the association between the two traits. Four writers—Nietzsche, Cocteau, Custance, and Wolfe—will be discussed in detail.

I next conducted a systematic search for clinical case studies of men with pregnancy envy, assisted by the Medline computerized database, to determine whether they, too, might have artistic and/or cyclothymic propensities. To my astonishment, all of the adult cases wherein occupation was identified involved professional artists or unusually creative individuals. Fully 80 percent of these were cyclothymic or frankly manic-depressive.

The relevance of this pattern for women artists, however, is questionable. Kris (1952) maintained that the female creative process differs substantially from that of men in that the parturition fantasies which seem so salient to male artists would be largely irrelevant to females. Several analysts have reasoned along similar lines that female penis envy is a functional analogue to male pregnancy envy and is vital to feminine artistic production (Deutsch, 1924, 1944; Horney, 1926, 1932; Greenacre, 1960). But the existence of penis envy among female artists is not nearly as demonstrable as is pregnancy envy among their male counterparts. One quick demonstration of this involves Ghiselin's (1952) anthology of eminent artists' descriptions of their creative process. Of the fifteen male writers represented, thirteen described their work using blatant feminine reproductive terms. In contrast, although only one of the five women included used birth imagery, none of the women's descriptions seemed to this reader to contain clear phallic imagery or even adopt a "phallic" tone. As the pattern discussed here seems much more robust when applied to men, the more complex dynamics of female creativity will remain for future studies.

Idiographic Material

Eminent artists of both genders almost universally profess that androgyny is critical to artistic productivity. They assert that "every artist is androgynous. . . . It is the masculine in a woman and the feminine in a man that proves creative" (Sarton, 1973), "the great mind must be androgynous" (Coleridge), and "some collaboration has to take place in the mind between woman and man before the act of creation can be accomplished. Some marriage of opposites has to be consummated" (Woolf, 1929).

In addition to such general statements, male artists enact their feminine strivings by conceiving of and describing their creativity in terms of the birth process. A. E. Housman reported that his "embryo ideas" (a sort of "secretion") would "bubble up . . . [in] the pit of the stomach . . . Sometimes [inspiration occurred] if I took my walks in a receptive and expectant frame of mine." He maintained that poetry writing is "a laborious business" (cited in Ghiselin, 1952, p. 91). Wordsworth wrote that the male artist has more tenderness and "a more comprehensive soul, than are supposed to be common among mankind" and "rejoices more than other men in the spirit of life that is in him" (cited in Ghiselin, 1952, p. 81). In the *Prelude*, Wordsworth also hinted at hypomanic periods, "unruly times," and "unmanageable thoughts." He maintained that

> . . . there is a dark
> Inscrutable workmanship that reconciles
> Discordant elements, makes them cling together
> In one society. . . .
> . . . fits of vulgar joy. . . . that giddy bliss
> which like a tempest, works along the blood. . . .
> impregnate and . . . elevate the mind.

Incidentally, inspired by Wordsworth's lyrics, Northrup Frye (1947) wrote, "A poem is like a child, an independently living being not fully born until the navel-string has been cut" (p. 113). In an essay entitled "The Birth of a Poem," the poet Brewster Ghiselin (1952) speaks plainly of the "creative labor . . . the process of bringing forth the poem" (p. 129).[1] Referring to an early draft of a poem, he writes that "In that first form it was no more than an intimation, like an embryonic heartbeat. The poem was as yet unborn" (p. 129). Upon formulating the idea for a future novel, the depressive Henry James remarks, "but she'll [Life] strangle it in the cradle,

[1] Ghiselin's selection of male artists may be influenced by his own striking views on the procreative aspects of creative process. Nonetheless, his sample's descriptions seem consistent with those of artists not included.

even while she pretends, all so cheeringly to rock it. . . . [For James] The thing had 'come,' the flower of conception had bloomed" (cited in Ghiselin, 1952, pp. 153–155).

EMINENT-ARTIST CASE STUDIES

The admixture of mania and melancholia which presumably typifies the artist has been commented upon by Plato and Aristotle and myriad personality theorists and artists ever since. The chronology and character of this persistent association are well described elsewhere (Wittkower and Wittkower, 1963). The following writers demonstrate both gender and affective bipolarity and may be prototypical of a larger group of artists with such "ambitendencies."

The German poet Rainer Maria Rilke was seven or eight when his parents were separated, leaving him with a mother who "loved [him] only when it came to bringing [him] out in a new little dress before a few marveling acquaintences" (Rilke, 1945, letter of December 4, 1894). He "went about until school years like a little girl" (April 3, 1903) and played almost exclusively with females. As an adult, he insisted that artistic creativity was "The birth process which in a purely spiritual way the man artist enjoys, suffers, and survives" (June 12, 1909). He later asserted that such poetic maternity is not merely ephemeral:

> in the man there is motherhood, it seems to me, physical and spiritual; his procreating is also a kind of giving birth, and giving birth it is when he creates out of inmost fullness. And perhaps the sexes are more related than we think . . . [July 16, 1903].

He further explained that

> It is natural for me *to understand girls and women*; the deepest experience of the creator is feminine-: for it is [the] experience of receiving and bearing. The poet Obstfelder once wrote, when describing the face of a strange man: "it was" (when he began to speak) "as if there were a woman in him-"; it seems to me that would fit every poet who begins to speak . . . [November 20, 1904].

As both the poet's lover and a psychoanalyst, Lou Andreas-Salomé was especially well qualified to comment on Rilke's psychodynamics. She reported that the poet suffered from an "uncommunicable longing for pregnancy" and that he considered the body of his work "something ejected from himself. . . . [which] he brought forth from his internal self" (cited in Simenauer, 1954, p. 240). Rilke's chronic depression was punctuated by ecstatic hyperproductive episodes during which the poet "delivered" a plethora of poems and letters (as many as 115 a day) and could not eat nor sleep (Shahly, in press).

Another of Andreas-Salomé's admirers, Friedrich Nietzsche, wrote of the "sudden birth" of *Thus Spoke Zarathustra*. Upon calculating the length of the book's "gestation," he reported somewhat humorously that "we get eighteen months for the pregnancy. This figure of precisely eighteen months might suggest, at least to Buddhists, that I am really a female elephant" (*Ecce Homo*, p. 295). The philosopher adopts a more earnest tone in *Genealogy of Morals*:

> [The philosopher's] "maternal" instinct, the secret love of that which is growing in him, directs him toward situations in which he is relieved of the necessity of thinking *of himself*. . . .
>
> . . . As for the "chastity" of philosophers, finally, this type of spirit clearly has its fruitfulness somewhere else than in children; perhaps it also has the survival of its name elsewhere, its little immortality. . . . There is nothing in this of chastity from any kind of ascetic scruple . . . : it is rather the will of their dominating instinct, at least during their periods of great pregnancy. Every artist knows what a harmful effect intercourse has in states of great spiritual tension and preparation; those with the greatest power and surest instincts do not need to learn this by experience, by unfortunate experience—their "maternal" instinct ruthlessly disposes of all other stores and accumulations of energy, of animal vigor, for the benefit of the evolving work . . . [pp. 110-111].

Nietzsche's father died when the philosopher was only four, leaving him the only male in a household comprised of his mother, younger sister, grandmother, and two maiden aunts (Kaufmann, 1974). Subsequently, like Rilke, Nietzsche felt a special affinity with women:

> May I here venture the surmise that I *know* women? That is part of my Dionysian dowry. Who knows? Perhaps I am the first psychologist of the eternally feminine. They all love me—an old story—not counting *abortive* females, the "emancipated" who lack the stuff for children [*Ecce Homo*, p. 266].

In this context, it should be remembered that Nietzsche also authored *The Birth of Tragedy* in which he proposed the antithetical aesthetic psychology of the Dionysian-Apollinian principles. The philosopher's fascination with the Dionysian element is consistent with his feminine identification and hypomanic tendencies. Classical mythology recounts that the infant Dionysos (son of Zeus and the moon goddess Semele) was dismembered at Hera's command, but reconstituted by Zeus and reared, disguised as a girl, in the woman's quarters of a Grecian king. Because of his early trauma, he was frequently mad, generally effeminate, and prone to transform himself into a girl during his Bacchanalian revels (Graves, 1955). His surnames include (*Psendanor*, "the man without virility," and *Gynnis*, "the womanish" (Deutsch, 1969). Rosenmeyer (1968) states that "Dionysos appears to be neither woman nor man; or, better, he presents himself as woman-in-man, or man-in-woman, the unlimited personality . . ." (p. 154). For Nietzsche, Dionysos elevates "artistic power . . . to the highest gratification of the primordial unity" (*Birth of Tragedy*, p. 37). The "rapture of the Dionysian state" annihilates "the ordinary bounds and limits of existence" (*Birth of Tragedy*, p. 59).[2] Alluding to both manic and feminine tendencies, the philosopher insisted that "one must harbor chaos in oneself to give birth to a dancing star." When his creative energies were "flowing most abundantly," Nietzsche could dance or walk for several hours "without a trace of weariness" (*Ecce Homo*, pp. 302-303). Then also,

> one is altogether beside oneself, with the distinct consciousness of subtle shudders . . . ; a depth of happiness in which even what is most painful and gloomy does not seem something opposite but rather conditioned, provoked, a *necessary* color in such superabundance of light . . . [*Ecce Homo*, p. 300].

The parallels between Rilke and Nietzsche are perhaps significant. As noted above, both men courted Lou Andreas-Salomé, a woman "of masculine intellect" (Hendry, 1983, p. 23) and androgynous name, whose mother wished that she had been a sixth son rather than a sole daughter (Peters, 1962). Both Rilke and Nietzsche reported intensely conflictual relationships with "overbearing" mothers. Both lost their fathers in early childhood through divorce and death, respectively, and neither man had brothers. Both suffered from intermittent gastrointestinal distress. Nietzsche even admitted that his condition was "no organically conditioned stomach complaint" (*Ecce Homo*, p. 223) and noted that "The bad conscience is an illness, there is no doubt about that, but an illness as pregnancy is an illness" (*Genealogy of Morals*, p. 88).

The French poet-artist Jean Cocteau was the youngest child by eight years of a "perfect" mother and a purportedly homosexual father who committed suicide. The poet was only ten when his father died, but as his brother and sister were twenty-two and eighteen respectively, he alone was left to be pampered by his doting mother. Cocteau's closest childhood

[2] Countless writers have shared Nietzsche's fascination with the oppositional model. In *Death in Venice*, for example, Mann's hero Gustav von Aschenbach surrenders to a Dionysian frenzy which eradicates the tension between sexual polarity (Feder, 1980). Significantly, Mann also wrote that "all forming, creating, producing is pain, struggle and pangs of labor" (cited in Lowenfeld, 1941).

friend and cousin, Madame Singer, recalled that "Much of the time his mother kept him in bed and fussed over him. He loved to dress up in girl's clothes . . ." (cited in Steegmuller, 1986, p. 11). The similarities between Cocteau and Rilke are striking: both men had absent fathers, overprotective mothers who encouraged feminine behavior, a penchant for dressing as girls, and predominately female childhood friends. Like Rilke and Nietzsche, Cocteau described his work in terms of parturition: the work "makes itself in us and in spite of us demands to be born . . ." (cited in Ghiselin, 1952, p. 79).

> My cries followed one another more rapidly, and became a single crisis comparable to pre-delivery pains. A monstrous delivery, however. . . . Imagine parthenogenesis, a couple made up of a single body that gives birth. Finally, one night when I was thinking of suicide, the expulsion began, in the rue d'Anjou. It took seven days, during which the newcomer behaved with amazing cheek, forcing me to write against my will [cited in Steegmuller, 1986, p. 350].

Steegmuller (1986) remarks that "the newborn was a poem, *L'Ange Heurtebise*" (p. 350) and observes that Cocteau "felt obliged to invent that myth of personal closeness to Rilke" (p. 353). Apparently, Cocteau misrepresented Rilke's conveyed expression of "admiration" as one of "love" and falsely insisted that Rilke was translating Cocteau's own *Orphée* when he (Rilke) died. Steegmuller concludes that the fantasied relation with the author of *Sonnets to Orpheus* permitted Cocteau to "avoid the peripheral myth of 'the Virgin and her inexplicable pregnancy' and to write, more directly, of 'Orpheus and the inexplicable birth of poems' " (p. 354). Cocteau's frequent hypomania ("since the age of fifteen I haven't stopped for a minute," cited in Steegmuller, 1986, p. 4) alternated with suicidal depression. The poet medicated his cyclothymia with opium, saying, "I preferred an artificial harmony to no harmony at all" (cited in Sandblom, 1982, p. 36). Finally, whereas Rilke merely demonstrated disturbed relations with women (he wanted to "become" his female partners, Shahly, in press), Cocteau was the "prince of homosexuals."

In the autobiographical *Wisdom, Madness and Folly*, the writer John Custance (1952) documents a clear relationship between his manic-depressive psychosis and fluctuations in gender identity: "Everything, in fact, seems to suggest that the opposed states of manic-depression are closely related with or possibly caused by some fundamental opposition or process connected with sex" (pp. 80-81). Custance associates his "fertile" manic periods with femininity and his "barren" depressive phases with masculinity. When he is inspired, innumerable "embryo" ideas form in his mind (p. 29). Later, "slow-brained" writing (p. 30) reorganizes and refines the manic outpourings. Therefore, through artistic production, "the opposites are reconciled, the Eternal Masculine and Feminine are united and there is peace" (p. 46). Custance is especially fond of Nietzsche's Apollinian-Dionysian scheme and Wordsworth's emphasis on antithesis. Unfortunately, Custance writes under a pseudonym and provides only scant family history.

The irrepressible Thomas Wolfe wrote:

> It seemed that I had inside me, swelling and gathering all the time, a huge black cloud, and that this cloud was loaded with electricity, pregnant. . . .
>
> . . . And I was borne along with it. . . . there is a quality of intemperate excess, an almost insane hunger to devour the entire body of human experience, to attempt to include more, experience more, than the measure of one life can hold. . . .
>
> I would work furiously day after day until my creative energies were utterly exhausted, and although at the end of such a period I would have written perhaps as much as 200,000 words, enough in itself to make a very long book, I would realize with a feeling of horrible despair that what I had completed was only one small section of a single book. . . .
>
> . . . every artist must know . . . , that that power of creation which sustains us will also destroy us like a leprosy if we let it rot stillborn in our vitals. I had to get it out of me somehow [cited in Ghiselin, 1952, pp. 193-199].[3]

And indeed Wolfe, who was once heard in the streets exultantly proclaiming, "I wrote ten thousand words today" (cited in Nowell, 1960, p. 14), was subject to "black moods" when unable to work. Separated from his father at the age of six, Wolfe was reared by an extraordinarily possessive mother. He was the youngest of eight children by many years, and accordingly Mrs. Wolfe with much candor reported that

> He being the baby I kept him a baby. I think he has written it up himself that he slept with me until he was a great big boy. He wasn't weaned until he was three and a half years old. . . . [Tom] had beautiful curls, beautiful brown hair . . . I kept it curled every day. It struck him around his shoulders. He often said they called him a girl because he had curls . . . [cited in Nowell, 1960, p. 23].

Certainly, the experience had its effects: In a lovely amalgam of feminine reproductive and bipolar imagery, Wolfe asserted that when writing he

[3] Freud reportedly had similar projective inclinations. Riviere (1958) describes Freud's impatience at her reticence to publish: ". . . write it, write it . . . get it out, produce it, make something of it—*outside you*, that is, give it an existence independent of you" (p. 146).

was "pregnant with all the joy and sorrow of the human destiny" (cited in Ghiselin, 1952, p. 196).

CLINICAL ACCOUNTS

The clinical psychoanalytic literature documents numerous instances of pregnancy fantasies among men. Fast (1984) points out that all three of Freud's case studies of male patients (Little Hans, Rat Man, and Wolf Man) involved a central belief that man can give birth to babies. Indeed, Erikson (1954) has shown in his analysis of Freud's Irma dream that Freud himself experienced feminine tendencies in his transference to Fliess, "where submissiveness, dependence, receptiveness, and gestative qualities marked the creative struggles from which his psychological products emerged" (cited in Jaffe, 1968, p. 522). Remarkably, all of the substantial adult examples located by computer search, excluding Freud's, relate either directly to artistic productivity or to occupational productivity in nonartists. Most generally, in his classic *Psychoanalytic Explorations in Art,* Ernst Kris (1952) remarks that the fantasies of male artists are centered around "the conflict between active and passive tendencies. . . . the path leads from anal activity to homosexual passivity and thus another well-known meaning of creation is evoked—that of giving birth to a child" (p. 301). After a thorough investigation of the lives of several "great men," Hitschmann concurs that artistic productivity seems effeminate and "can be compared to the act of childbirth" (1956, p. 19). Edith Jacobson (1950) notes that male artists are frequently envious of woman's procreative capacity:

> In case they come for treatment, the analysis of their creative activity regularly shows intensely cathexed unconscious feminine reproductive fantasies. It appears that creative work quite normally is the main channel for sublimation of feminine reproductive wishes in men [p. 142].

The earliest detailed account is presented by Boehm in his 1930 article on "The Femininity Complex in Men." A physician patient reported:

> My achievements show a great fluctuation: slackness and passivity alternate with a capacity for pulling myself together and accomplishing a great deal, considerably more than anyone would expect of men. . . . [I felt] Like a woman who carries an invisible foetus for a long period and then surprises those about her by suddenly presenting a loudly wailing infant . . . [pp. 445-446].

Although the patient was not an artist, his hyperproductive, "manic" phases nevertheless clearly coincided with his subjective experience of strong feminine identification.

Van Leeuwen (1966) describes pregnancy envy in a "creative" male patient (occupation unidentified) with a passive father, an aggressive and overprotective mother, and only older female siblings. As he wanted both to impregnate himself and give birth, Van Leeuwen notes that the patient's urge was actually bisexual. During full expression of his parturition fantasies, the patient "became less restricted and more creative" (pp. 321-322), obsessed with "making something perfect" (p. 322). Later, fearing that the new baby's presence would betray his incestuous wishes, the patient reportedly inhibited his creativity. Van Leeuwen concludes that pregnancy envy has not only negative effects, but "may also result in greater productivity and be an added stimulus to creativity" (p. 323). Unfortunately, the precise form the patient's creativity took is never specified.

Robbins (1969) presents a similar case, this time involving a young male artist who insisted that "artistic creation was like sexual procreation: that artists are insecure people who fear for their potency and express it through their hands, the finished work being like an ejaculation or a child" (p. 246). The patient was diagnosed as having manic-depressive psychosis, and it was observed that his depression alternated with periods of elation and accelerated artistic productivity. The boy's father was killed when the boy was seven and his mother was notably domineering.

Jaffe (1968) discusses the case of a male writer who complains that he is "unproductive." His parents were divorced shortly prior to his birth and he was reared in a household of domineering women. Jaffe remarks that his patient's "Heightened feminine identification . . . accentuates the conflict over procreative wishes. . . . Further, the psychological significance of procreative function, from its cultural-historical roots, is integrally connected with femininity in all its aspects" (p. 542).

Koptagel (1972) reports the case of a male patient who discharged homosexual and transvestite tendencies in pictorial representations of himself as a woman. The patient was separated from his father at the age of three and was reared in a home dominated by females. Like Rilke and Cocteau, he wore dresses until his school years. When painting or writing, the patient was markedly enthusiastic; when nonproductive he felt "desperate and utterly dissatisfied" (p. 75).

Kubie (1974) presents a male artist patient suffering from a "symbolic work block." No achievement was enough

> until finally he discovered in analysis that what he had always wanted unconsciously was to possess at the same time not only the phallus but also the woman's breasts as part of his own body, that he craved also the ability to inseminate himself, to gestate, to produce, and to nurse his own

progeny. . . . Indeed this was precisely what the unconscious goals of his entire artistic career had been for him [p. 361].

Kubie reports a second patient with pregnancy fantasies whose possessive mother dressed his younger brother "in curls and frills" until adolescence. Although Kubie unfortunately neglects to identify the patient's occupation, he does mention that the man's crippled father was eclipsed by his domineering mother and that the man himself suffered from severe indigestion and "morning nausea." This case is particularly interesting in that it combines the three elements observed among the eminent artists: the domineering mother recalls both Rilke and Nietzsche; the confusion in gender roles recalls Rilke, Cocteau, and the transvestism of Nietzsche's alter ego Dionysos; and the digestive difficulties recall Rilke, Nietzsche, and Housman.

Similarly, Evans (1951) describes a male patient's delusional pregnancy, involving vomiting and acute stomach pains of sufficient severity to prevent employment. Although only minimal information is provided about the man's parents and siblings, Evans maintains that the patient clearly identified with his mother and only mentions sisters. Data on occupation and affect are not provided.

After intensive interviews with nationally and internationally acclaimed male artists, Rothenberg (1979) comments that his artists, especially the writers, describe an emotion akin to postpartum depression after completing a project:

> Citing a manifest analogy between the production of a novel or other artistic work and the birth of a baby, they emphasize the feelings of transitory sadness connected with the simultaneous loss and achievement of bringing forth a creation [p. 135].

Most recently, Fast (1984) describes a male patient whose inability to bear children was related to "work difficulties focusing on a sensed inability to be creative or to produce anything worthwhile" (p. 19). No information was provided regarding affect.

In a chapter on "Artistic Ability and Boyhood Femininity," Stoller (1968) observes that excessive feminine identification and remarkable artistic ability coexisted in all three of his young male transvestite patients. In each case, a masculine mother encouraged her son's overattachment and cross-dressing, while the father was emotionally passive and often physically unavailable. While Stoller concedes that the boys' urge to create may derive from an unconscious desire to have a baby, he cautions that such artistic impulses may also be motivated by a fear of death, alternatively stated as the "fear of absolute dissolution of identity" resulting from mother-child symbiosis (p. 129). Although Stoller reports marked hyperactivity among these children, no depression is evident. Perhaps this is because the young boys fully expected to be women when they grew up; none had yet been disabused of their fantasies as had been the previously cited adult patients whose depression coincided with the realization that their biologic gender was irrevocable.

SUMMARY OF IDIOGRAPHIC MATERIAL

Several generalizations emerge:

A. The group made frequent use of birth imagery as a metaphor for creativity. They generally idealized pregnancy and often sustained parturition fantasies to the extent of having intestinal bloating, cramping, and morning nausea.

B. The group experienced elevated mood states of varying intensity coincident with their distinctly feminine poetic production. They professed that creativity required profound passivity and divine inspiration, and believed their creativity was hampered by masculine-type intellectualization.

C. The group most frequently had absent fathers, domineering mothers, and no brothers (only one of ten male artists for whom such information was available had a brother at home and that brother was dressed effeminately until adolescence). This finding is consistent with empirical reports that mothers of effeminate boys are domineering (Domino, 1969) and masculine (Stoller, 1968; Green, Williams, and Goodman, 1985), and fathers are emotionally distant and more likely to be physically absent (Stoller, 1968; Green, Williams, and Goodman, 1985). Burgner's (1985) finding that father absence in particular interferes with the establishment of a masculine sexual identity in boys may explain the bisexual trends among this sample.

D. The prevalence of absent parents among both eminent artists and clinical examples was enormous: seven of the nine cases wherein such information was provided had suffered the early loss of a parent through either death or divorce. Of the remaining two, one father was notably passive and the other was crippled. In view of this, it seems significant that the artists emphasized the durability of their artwork and contrasted it with the impermanence of human life. Most maintained that their dual-gender qualities, their "primal unity" (Nietzsche), obviated the need for partnership and enabled them to generate art which transcends corporeal reality.

Perhaps the disappearance or disablement of a parent prompted these artists to seek imaginatively a reunion with the lost object via the creation of idealized muse figures and to achieve self-sufficiency via gender completeness. The drive to give birth to an immortal offspring may defend against the actual or psychological loss of an all-too-mortal parent. This reading is consistent with Pollock's (1978) belief that creative productivity enables a "working through" of early loss.

Creativity and Androgyny: Theoretical Observations

The observation that creative men "labor" under feminine strivings is perhaps so pedestrian that many authors seem content merely to state the association. Only a few attempts have been made to delineate the evolution of such contrasexual urges.

Freud and Kris believed that the passivity which the male artist experiences during inspiration is evidence of a homosexual orientation. Although the preoedipal wish for a baby was normative owing to the young boy's inevitable identification with his mother (Brunswick, 1940), persistence of parturition fantasies into adolescence indicated an oedipal reversal wherein the boy regressed from appropriate phallic strivings to anal eroticism and symbolically emasculated himself by seeking to bear his father's child. Kris (1952) further connected the intestinal disruptions which frequently accompanied artistic productivity in men to pregenital notions regarding the anal manufacture of babies. The paternal recipient of the baby = feces = artwork was, Kris felt, censored from the artwork itself (Kris's example was A. E. Housman).

Somewhat later, Edith Jacobson (1950) also noted that a boy's homosexual attachment to his father and subsequent maternal impulses are normally surrendered in the course of heterosexual gender development. She also observed, however, that if at the height of the boy's castration anxiety a sibling is born, his early identification with his mother may be reactivated and may manifest in adulthood as the desire to create lasting works of art.

Jung (1933) emphasized the feminine aspects of (male) creativity without reference to present sexual orientation and gender development:

> It makes no difference whether the poet knows that his work is begotten, grows and matures with him, or whether he supposes that by taking thought he produces it out of the void. His opinion of the matter does not change the fact that his own work outgrows him as a child its mother. The creative process has feminine quality, and the creative work arises from unconscious depths—we might say, from the realm of the mothers [p. 170].

Several analysts challenged the androcentric Freudian position, emphasizing instead man's envy of the feminine reproductive capacity. In "Flight from Womanhood" (1926), Horney attributes the greater productivity of men to their inability to give birth to babies:

> Is not the tremendous strength in men of the impulse to creative work in every field precisely due to their feeling of playing a relatively small part in the creation of living beings, which constantly impels them to an overcompensation in achievement? [p. 61].

Horney further observed that man, in his envy and dread of woman's more genuine procreative abilities, devalues pregnancy and the maternal role and overemphasizes the importance of male genitality (see also Fromm, 1943, and Zilboorg, 1944). Similarly, Boehm (1930) identified a "parturition-envy" which provided "considerable incentive to the capacity for production in men" (p. 456). He was undecided whether such envy arose simply from the narcissistic injury of being incapable of childbirth or from homosexual attachment to the father as Freud claimed.

Other work has emphasized the bisexual rather than the homosexual underpinnings of creativity. Otto Rank focused on the conjunction of feminine and masculine elements in the innovative man. He observed that the word *genius* derived from *gignere*, "to beget": "we can say of all artistic creation that the artist not only creates his art, but he also uses art in order to create" (1932, p. 7). He suggested, moreover, that the male artist projects onto his female muse, his "bisexual creative urge—of begetting and of bearing" (1932, p. 378). Similarly, Erikson (1954) specified the artistic nature as bisexual:

> every act of creation, at one stage, implies the unconscious fantasy of inspiration by a fertilizing agent of a more or less deified, more or less personified mind or spirit. This "feminine" aspect of creation causes tumultuous confusion not only because of man's intrinsic abhorrence of femininity but also because of the conflict (in really gifted individuals) of this feminine fantasy with an equally strong "masculine" endowment which is to give a new and original form to that which has been conceived and carried to fruition [pp. 48-49].

More recently, Kubie (1974) describes "the drive to become two sexes," an unconscious drive "*not* to give up the gender to which one was born but to supplement or complement it by developing side by side with it the opposite gender, thereby ending up as both . . ." (pp. 356-357).[4] He attri-

[4] The following passage by Thomas Mann (1954) beautifully captures Kubie's notion:

> Dreams of love, dreams of delight and a longing for union—I cannot name them otherwise, though they concerned not a single image but a double creature, a pair fleetingly but profoundly glimpsed, a brother and sister—representative of my own sex and of the other, the fair one. But the beauty here lay in the duality, in the charming doubleness. . . .

butes the drive to the "deepest tendencies in human nature . . . to attempt to identify with and to become both parents: with the stronger parent so as to acquire his strength, with the weaker out of sympathy and to seek and provide consolation" (p. 370). Although the drive motivates laudable creative endeavors, it also ensues in dangerously conflictual impulses:

> Gender identities are deeply ambivalent among many creative people. . . . Furthermore the effects of these conflicts and their pathogenic influence are especially serious in the arts. The arts automatically provide individuals with ways of hiding their conflicts while at the same time giving them partial gratifications. In this sense they reward the neurosis in us until we become psychotically disorganized, or commit suicide . . . [pp. 358-359].

Kubie also maintains that the drive manifests itself in alternating diurnal rhythms, becoming greatest toward evening. The parallel between this and the diurnal variation of affective illness is striking.

Fast (1978, 1984), citing the universality of bisexual figures in myth and art along with recent biological data and ample case example, rejects Freud's notion that boys and girls are functionally masculine in early childhood. Rather, Fast posits that the child initially experiences an overinclusive sense of gender. The child's interest in gender differences entails a recognition of limits; that is, the boy becomes absorbed with the maternal role in childbearing and the girl becomes preoccupied with her lack of penis. The socially required renunciation of the nonbiologic gender is associated with depression and a sense of constriction.

The formulations of Kubie and especially those of Fast suggest an explanation for the reported phasing of mania and dual-gender identification. The expansiveness and euphoria of the poet may in part be due to the recovery of lost gender attributes.[5] The sense of manic grandiosity may be related to the omnipotence of pre-gender-stereotyped childhood.

One final piece of theoretical evidence regarding the efflorescence of creativity during adolescence is consistent with the premise that the artistic impulse arises from bisexual strivings. Several investigators have described the strong bisexual identification of adolescents (e.g., Deutsch, 1944; Greenacre, 1950). The remarkably vigorous creativity of the adolescent has also been a matter of some comment. Spiegel (1958) surmises that the

> the image of the girl alone, without her fraternal complement, would never have lapped my spirit in such sweet dreams. Dreams of love, dreams that I loved precisely because—I firmly believe—they were of primal indivisibility and indeterminateness, double; which really means that only then is there a significant whole blessedly embracing what is beguilingly human in both sexes [*Felix Krull, Confidence Man*, pp. 80-81].

[5] I am indebted to Dr. Abby Wolfson for this formulation.

creativity of adolescence is "linked indirectly to cathectic oscillations" (p. 299) and so figures importantly in ego differentiation. Blos (1962) observes that creativity during this phase has the character of "giving life to a new existence" (p. 126) and further remarks that the precipitous decline in creative activity

> coincides with the emergence of a stable ego organization and the establishment of firm boundaries between self- and object-representations. In the ego organization of the artist this delineation is probably never drawn as sharply as it is in other people [p. 181].

The comparison between adolescents and artists is informative. Both lack defined ego boundaries and, perhaps subsequently, are bisexually oriented. The achievement of adult heterosexuality typically heralds an end to the richly creative period of adolescence, suggesting a causal connection between diffuse ego structure/sexual ambiguity and artistic production.

Certainly there is abundant evidence of such primitive ego development, of "ego hunger and a need for completion" (Greenacre, 1958, p. 540) in the lives of writers. Keats remarked that art

> is everything and nothing. . . . It has as much delight in conceiving an Iago as an Imogen. . . . A poet is the most unpoetical of any thing in existence, because he has no Identity—he is continually informing and filling some other body [cited in Wellek and Warren, 1977, p. 90].

Steegmuller (1986) noted that throughout his career, Cocteau

> kept changing his guise, his views, his activities; to use a word [Cocteau] liked, his life was a series of "mues"—moultings. . . . Usually he actually *was* each person whose role he was playing. . . . his only properties were his selves [p. 4].

Similarly, Rilke (1947, letter of December 2, 1922) observed, "Who knows who I am? I change and change," and Ted Hughes said of his wife:

> Sylvia Plath was a person of many masks, both in her personal life and in her writings. Some were camouflage cliché facades, defensive mechanisms, involuntary. And some were deliberate poses, attempts to find the keys to one style or another. These were the visible faces of her lesser selves, her false or provisional selves, the minor roles of her inner drama.
>
> Most of us [poets] are never more than bundles of contradictory and complementary selves [Plath, 1982, pp. xiv-xv].

Such contradictory character traits, fluctuations in gender roles, and the lack of authenticity and continuity of self recall Akhtar's (1984) description of the adult identity-diffusion syndrome.

As an aside, it is interesting to recall the vivid birth imagery employed by the male psychologists themselves (see this paper: Barron, p. 305, Jung, p. 301, and Erikson, p. 302). Freud, who suffered from depression and digestive difficulties (Fine, 1979), wrote to Fliess that "It was on November 12, 1897. The sun was in the eastern quarter; Mercury and Venus were in conjunction. . . . I gave birth to a new piece of knowledge" (1950, p. 268). In a more sober tone, he noted that the treatise on narcissism "was a difficult labor and bears all the marks of a corresponding deformation" (cited in Jones,1953-1957, 2:302). Jung insists that "the human psyche is the womb of all the sciences and arts" (p. 152) and a "pregnant chaos" (p. 160). In his introduction, Kubie (1974) describes the slow evolution of his thesis and then remarks: "Nevertheless since I have now gestated this conceptual child as far as I am able to carry it myself, it is time to set it down on paper as a foundation for future building by others" (p. 354). In his book on creativity and psychopathology, Prentky (1980) defines creativity as something "born into this world that did not exist before" (p. 22). Strikingly, the women psychologists quoted thus far have not used similar imagery.

Empirical Studies

CREATIVITY AND ANDROGYNY

Perhaps the most useful summary of empirical research on creativity and gender orientation was provided by Helson (1978):

> Recent work on masculinity and femininity in relation to creativity suggests that creative individuals do not necessarily have more characteristics of the other sex than their fellows, but that they have characteristics of both sexes in a form that (a) makes difficult a simple identification with either sex role, and (b) facilitates creative expression in a symbolic medium [p. 555].

Helson and her associates at the Institute for Personality Assessment and Research (IPAR) have conducted the most intensive inquiries of creative individuals. An early IPAR project involving male military officers found an association between originality and feminine interest patterns. Barron (1957) surmised that creative men had greater access to tabooed subjects and impulses and could

> integrate these superficially discordant phenomena into a more complex whole.
>
> Another possible explanation is that some degree of cross-sex identi-

> fication is important for creativity in men and perhaps women as well. The creative act is a kind of giving birth, and it is noteworthy that as an historical fact intellectual creativity has been conspicuously lacking in women, whose products are their children [p. 737].

However, a later IPAR study of male architects found that while creatives scored significantly higher than their less innovative counterparts on the Femininity scale of the California Personality Inventory (CPI) and the Feminine Interests scale of the Minnesota Multiphasic Personality Inventory (MMPI), they also scored higher on the typically "masculine" scales assessing aggression, autonomy, and self-assertiveness. McKinnon (1962) attributed the enhanced creativity of the study sample to "the reconciliation of these opposites of their nature" (p. 34).

Several more recent studies have verified IPAR's general statement regarding the flexible dual-gender identifications in highly creative individuals. Hammer (1964) noted that creative male high-school students, as identified by art scholarships and teacher nomination, gave more feminine responses to projective tests but also scored higher on indexes of strength, confidence, determination, ambition, and power than noncreative controls. Hammer concluded that "This integration allows the necessary sensitivity and intuition to combine with purposive action and determination. The end result is a masculine-feminine *blend* conducive to the capacity for creative artistry" (p. 414). In a study of creative potential in kindergarten-aged boys, Biller, Singer, and Fullerton (1969) found that boys with mixed sex-role patterns were significantly more creative than either rigidly masculine or feminine boys. Such sex-role *discrepancy* was postulated as broadening the child's range of experience and providing a stimulating "cognitive challenge." Similarly, Milgram, Yitzhak, and Milgram (1977) found that the simultaneous endorsement of masculine and feminine sex-role characteristics typified highly creative children. Corroborative evidence is provided by A. Ellis's (1959) and Domino's (1977) finding that overt, nondysphoric homosexuality is negatively related to creative ability.

Anastasi and Schaefer (1969) found a reversal of role model and stronger influence of the opposite-sex parent among gifted children. Sexual ambiguity may be more pronounced among the parents of creatives as well. Domino (1969) reported that mothers of creative sons score lower on femininity scales and higher on initiative and autonomy than do mothers of noncreative controls. Correspondingly, fathers were significantly more feminine on a variety of measures than were control fathers (Grant and Domino, 1976).

The empirical findings on creativity and gender orientation are generally congruent with the biographical data presented for the writers above. The men studied typically combined masculine traits and object choice with feminine reproductive urges, and were more identified with their mothers than their frequently absent fathers.

CREATIVITY AND MANIC-DEPRESSION

Exceptional creativity has been linked with madness since the pre-Hellenic period. In an often-cited quote, Schopenhauer insists that "Genius is closer to madness than is ordinary intelligence. . . . The lives of men of genius show how often, like lunatics, they are in a continual agitation" (cited in Jamison, in press; Prentky, 1980; Wittkower and Wittkower, 1963). Other early assessments, while perhaps less anecdotal, were nonetheless problematic. Difficulties with diagnostic and inclusionary criteria rendered the findings of studies by H. A. Ellis (1926) and Juda (1949) almost meaningless (Jamison, in press). Later studies were more informative. McNeil (1971), attempting to unconfound the genetic and environmental components of creativity, studied 144 Danish adoptees rated by occupation type as high, above average, or low creatives. Thirty percent of the high creatives had a psychiatric record, 40% involving affective disorder; compared with 10% among the above-average creatives. Affective disorder was manifest in 6% of the total high-creative sample compared with 2% in the remaining samples. Manic-depression occurred only among the high creatives. In biologic parents, mental disturbance was 28%, 8%, and 12%, respectively, suggesting a genetic basis for the psychopathology observed among the highly creative group. Unfortunately, creativity was not operationalized (Prentky, 1980), and the creativity of biologic and nonbiologic family members was not assessed.

Andreason and Canter (1974) compared a group of fifteen writers participating in the prestigious University of Iowa Writers' Workshop with a group of fifteen persons employed in a nonartistic field, matched for age, education, and sex. Consistent with McNeil's findings, the familial incidence of psychopathology was much greater among the creative group: the incidence of affective disorder and alcoholism was 21% among primary relatives of writers and only 4.4% among relatives of controls. Schizophrenia was much rarer than expected in writers' relatives and was absent in control relatives. The writers themselves appeared even more symptomatic than their relatives: ten of the writers (67%) met diagnostic criteria for affective disorder compared with two (13%) of the controls ($p < .02$). Two of the affectively disordered writers were bipolar versus none of the comparison group. Nine (60%) of the writers received a secondary diagnosis of affective disorder with cyclothymia compared with two (13%) of the controls ($p <$ .05). Andreason and Cantor conclude that

> Taken as a group, the writers were remarkable for their combination of significant success and achievement with symptoms and habits that would ordinarily be considered as representing significant psychopathology and perhaps incompatible with high levels of functioning. . . .
>
> Depression and alcoholism are the demons that pursue the creative writer in the twentieth century, and his underlying personality is cyclothymic rather than schizoid [pp. 127-129].

Richards (1981) cautions, however, that participation in a social event such as a workshop represents a selection bias against schizophrenia. Furthermore, although Andreason and Canter's writers were extremely heterogenous with respect to eminence, no study of its effect was made. Nonetheless, their findings are consistent with IPAR studies which identified greater psychopathology coupled with greater ego strength among high creatives generally (Barron, 1963).

Next, Andreason and Powers (1975) compared conceptual styles of presumably the same fifteen writers as measured by the Goldstein-Sheerer Object Sorting Test with those of sixteen hospitalized bipolar patients in manic phase and fifteen hospitalized schizophrenics. They found that the writers resembled manics more so than schizophrenics. Both creative writers and manics demonstrated overinclusive thinking, sorted into large groups, and used vague concepts as categorizing principles. Unlike the manics, however, writers could control their fantasies while sorting. Since it is unclear whether this writer sample was identical to Andreason and Canter's largely cyclothymic writer sample, it is uncertain whether a manic cognitive style is generally associated with creative states or whether this finding is limited to a particular cohort.

Schou (1979) questioned twenty-four bipolar artists whose disease had been prophylactically controlled with lithium regarding creative power during treatment. Twelve patients reported subjective increases in productivity, six unaffected productivity, and six decreased productivity. Schou concluded that the effect of treatment on creativity may depend on the severity of the disease and on the capacity to utilize manic episodes productively. It should be noted that many of Schou's subjects were amateurs and most were sufficiently ill to require hospitalization. Given Andreason and Canter's (1974) finding that accomplished artists could seemingly tolerate significant psychopathology with little detriment to productivity, adherence to the eminence criterion would seem important.

In contrast, in an anecdotal report of three manic-depressive artists,

Marshall, Neumann, and Robinson (1970) observed that in all cases accelerated creativity was always associated with a manic phase and nonproductivity with depressed periods. Lithium treatment resulted in a more uniform level of artistic activity.

In an as-yet-unpublished study of forty-seven acclaimed British writers and visual artists, Jamison (in press) examined rates of treatment for affective disorders, seasonal variations in affect and productivity, and the perceived role of intense mood states. Thirty-eight percent of Jamison's sample had reported seeking treatment for an affective disorder. Poets most likely received medication for their depression (33%), and only they required treatment for mania (17%). This 50% rate of significant mood disorder is especially striking when compared with lifetime prevalence rates of bipolar (1%) and unipolar major depression (8-12% for men and 20-26% for women, Boyd and Weissman, 1981). Interestingly, the biographers sampled—competent, but presumably less imaginative, writers—revealed no history of labile mood. Jamison further found that all poets, novelists, and artists; 88% of the playwrights; and merely 20% of the biographers experienced creative episodes sufficiently intense to warrant being labeled hypomanic. Half of the writers reported hyposomnia and hyperacusis, but relatively few admitted to hypersexuality, impulsive spending, loquaciousness, etc. Most of the writers believed their "moodiness" was essential (60%) or very important (30%) to their creative process. In writers with a treatment history, increased productivity either preceded or followed elevated affect, while in the nontreated group productivity coincided with elevated affect. Jamison surmised that high mood-productivity might result in less treatment seeking or that the treated group is clinically hypomanic and so experiences greater dysphoria, distractibility, and stimulus hunger which would presumably interfere with necessary work habits. This is consistent with Schou (1979) and Andreason and Canter's (1974) findings that acute hypomania disrupts the focus and control necessary for the completion of artistic projects.

In a supplemental review of eminent artists and manic-depression, Jamison (in press) reports that eight of the thirty-six (22%) twentieth-century poets included in *The New Oxford Book of American Verse* suffered from manic-depression severe enough to require at least one hospitalization. Further, five of the same eight poets (62%) committed suicide.

Given the 17-22% rate of manic-depression which Jamison observed among her subjects and major twentieth-century poets and the 60% rate of cyclothymia which Andreason and Canter found in their Writers' Workshop sample, the 80% incidence of apparent affective bipolarity in the male pregnancy-envy sample presented here strongly suggests that such artists are at even greater risk for bipolar disorders than artists generally.[6] Unfortunately, as Andreason and Canter and Jamison's reports do not address subjective gender experience, no comparative assessment can be made. It would be interesting to compare rates of bipolar illness among markedly androgynous or bisexual and "monosexual" artists.

Creativity and the Reconciliation of Opposites

In a study of hermaphrodism and creativity as evidenced in Michelangelo's *ignudi,* Oremland (1985) reports that for the homosexual sculptor, "creating and procreating are one. . . . Michelangelo repeatedly, as do many creative individuals, referred to his art as his love, at times as his wife, and to his works as his children" (p. 426). Accordingly, Oremland proposes that

> particularly in creative individuals a shifting, at times, confused sense of maleness and femaleness, often loosely termed homosexuality, should not be considered along the conventional ideas suggested by the gender-defining words "masculine" and "feminine." I suggest that the subjective sense of shifting maleness and femaleness in the creative is closely related to elemental qualities concerning continuing developmentally early, in that way primitive, fantasies of hermaphrodism, autoinsemination, and autogestation. Such primitive fantasies, a kind of *primal biunity,* have long been closely associated with creativity in literature, mythology, and psychoanalytic theory [p. 414].

Oremland further notes that the ability to shift between gender roles is closely related to the extraordinarily flexible intrapsychic capacities in artistic individuals hypothesized by Kris (1952). That the capacity to shift from male to female roles and from secondary to primary process might also be related to mood swings is suggested by Erikson (1954):

> All in all, the creative individual's typical cycle of moods and attitudes . . . probably permits him, at the height of consummation, to identify with father, mother, and newborn child all in one; to represent, in equal measure, his father's potency, his mother's fertility, and his own reborn ideal identity [p. 49].

The specific cognitive processes involved in creativity have been identified as oppositional in other respects as well. Koestler (1964) maintains that "bisociation" or the coalescence of habitually incompatible frames of ref-

[6] The brevity of the reports do not permit precise diagnoses. Consequently, admittedly liberal diagnostic criteria were employed. Mood swings were included as cyclothymic. Two cases were excluded for lack of information.

erence is vital for creativity. Similarly, Rothenberg (1979) emphasizes the importance of "Janusian thought" or the simultaneous conception of antithetical ideas or images. In support of the notion, he observes that for Coleridge the "pleasure arising from art consisted of 'the identity of two opposite elements. . . .' In *The Marriage of Heaven and Hell*, [the poet] unequivocally asserted that 'Without contraries is no progression' " (p. 144). For Robert Graves, poetry arose from "the unforseen fusion in [the poet's] . . . mind of apparently contradictory ideas" (cited in Rothenberg, 1979, p. 193). Rothenberg further notes that modern literary critics, including I. A. Richards, William Empson, Allen Tate, John Crowe Ransom, Robert Penn Warren, and Cleanth Brooks, have "all emphasized the bipolar, ambiguous, and antithetical elements in poetry and literature, Brooks particularly arguing in a famous essay that paradox is 'the language appropriate and inevitable to poetry' " (p. 193). In Rothenberg's own study on associative style, creative subjects "showed a definite and self-consistent tendency to reply with opposites" on word-association tests (p. 197).

There is also evidence that artists can shift between brain hemispheres more fluidly than nonartists. Mebert and Michel (1980) found that the incidence of left-handedness was considerably higher among visual artists than among the general population. Comparing college art students with students not studying art, Mebert and Michel discovered that 20% of the artists were left-handed as compared with only 7% of the nonartists. Twenty-seven percent of the artists were ambidextrous versus 15% of the nonartists. The results are interesting because left-handedness and ambidexterity are associated with more bilateral distribution of language functions. The researchers suggest that creativity may be enhanced when interhemispheric flexibility is maximized. Bogen and Bogen (1969) also postulate that transcollosal interhemispheric exchange facilitates verbal-visuo-spatial interaction and so is vital for creative thought. Jung's (1933) observation that "Every creative person is a duality or a synthesis of contradictory aptitudes" (p. 168) may be explained, in future research, by basic brain anatomy.

At any rate, it seems obvious that people who are capable of identifying with both gender roles or experiencing the extremes of joy and despair would produce richer, more engaging artworks. Gough (1964) maintains that "Somehow, a creative product must give a sense of reconciliation, of having resolved in an aesthetic and harmonious way the discords and disharmonies present in the original situation" (p. 6). Individuals with sexual and/or affective ambitendencies would more likely seek such a compromise, and what better medium than the plastic and fantastic realm of art wherein the dictates of a dichotomous Aristotelian reality need not be observed.

Moreover, creativity itself is purportedly a *biphasic* process, typically involving a passive inspirational phase and an active elaboration phase (Kris, 1952); it therefore demands rapid shifts between "feminine" and "masculine" cognitive styles and the associational fluency afforded by hypomanic arousal. For any of these commonsensical reasons, androgynous or cyclothymic characters might meet with more success in artistic pursuits than rigidly heterosexual or euthymic individuals. Androgynous cyclothymes might be especially suited to achieve artistic eminence. Such natural-selection criteria would presume no inherent relation between the two traits.

However, in view of the artists' accounts presented earlier and in keeping with a long psychoanalytic tradition linking male procreative envy, artistic production, and elevated mood states, it also seems reasonable to assume that androgynous and cyclothymic characters are meaningfully related with respect to creativity. Henry Miller's description of noncreative periods as "monotony and sterility" (cited in Ghiselin, 1952, p. 190) highlights the intimate relation between gender and affective experience. One explanation, discussed briefly above, involves Fast's formulation of the original gender matrix: the adoption of the poetic role for men necessarily entails a "feminization." The simultaneous experience of masculine and feminine identifications may produce a sense of grandiosity and exultation (hypomania) reminiscent of the archaic, overinclusive condition. The depression reported to follow especially creative periods (e.g., Rothenberg) would result from the return to the unisexual condition heralded by the noninspired state and would reiterate the original loss of nonbiologic gender functions.

Alternatively, a genetic predisposition to bipolar affective illness may simultaneously confer a cognitive style conducive to artistic productivity (.e.g., verbal and associational fluency, hyperacusis, hypermentation, and increased energy) and an expansive, overinclusive character prone to bisexuality as well as hypersexuality. Although such explanations are certainly not mutually inclusive, the persistent occurrence of the family configuration reported earlier—absent or passive same-sex parent, dominant other-sex parent, no same-sex siblings—would seem to argue for the primacy of the second (Fast) hypothesis: (1) the bisexual constitution of children from such homes was less likely to be discouraged, and (2) a harmonious combination of male and female elements may help compensate for the missing or inactive parent and thus be especially gratifying. The inheritance of a cyclothymic constitution (and there is good evidence that bipolarity is genetic) would then potentiate creative ability.

Yet a fourth explanation is suggested by the similarity between adolescents and adult artists. A primary defect in ego development—promoted by the lack of satisfactory same-sex role models or the eclipse of such models by especially admirable or domineering other-sex models—could engender an identity-diffusion syndrome (after Akhtar). Such a syndrome would parsimoniously explain the fluctuating mood states and gender identities of artists and is consistent with their family profile. The early disappearance of a parent through either death or divorce may prompt one to fantasize intimate and instructive spirits (muses) or seek merger with the lost object via suicide, or may disrupt ego and gender development, contribute to characterologic depression, and result finally in a maniacal obsession to form some permanent object or artwork.

In sum, androgyny and cyclothymia may co-vary independently, a primary androgyny may promote cyclothymia, a primary cyclothymia may promote androgyny, or both androgyny and cyclothymia may result from an underlying ego deficit. Selecting among these alternatives seems premature until more is known about the life histories and genotypes of artists generally. Moreover, it is doubtful whether a single formulation will explain the association; more likely, various elements will be prominent in different artists and each should be considered individually.

Given that the writers cited thus far are all moderns (several of whom were acquainted), the question arises whether a different cohort, epic poets for example, would demonstrate the same constellation of symptoms. In other words, is there a historically conditioned selection bias for cyclothymic, androgynous artists? As mania and depression have been central to the conception of artist since the classical Greek era (Wittkower and Wittkower, 1963) and feminine reproductive urges have been persistently associated with such creative individuals as Michelangelo (Oremland, 1985), it seems likely that the observed pattern is not historically dependent.

A final question which emerges from such an inquiry is whether the synthetic aspect of creative production in fact helps minimize the "discordant elements" (Wordsworth) of which artists complain. The psychotherapeutic benefit of creativity is frequently boasted by the artists themselves. Heinrich Heine wrote:

> Disease may well have been the ground
> In full for that creative urge,
> Creation was my body's purge,
> Creating I've grown sane and sound.
> [cited in Sandblom, 1982, p. 44]

Similarly, Graham Greene asserted that

> writing is a form of therapy; sometimes I wonder how all those who do not write, compose or paint can manage to escape madness, the mel-

> ancholia, the panic fear which is inherent in the human situation [cited in Sandblom, 1982, pp. 44-45].

Rilke refused psychoanalysis, saying "my work is really nothing but a self treatment" (1947, letter of January 14, 1912); however, he became progressively reclusive and suffered increasingly from dissociative episodes. Although Sylvia Plath referred to "poetry as therapy" and Virginia Woolf relied on her "art to keep [her] head sane," both women committed suicide (incidentally, Plath was cyclothymic and Woolf was manic-depressive). Indeed, artists generally—as do manic-depressives—suicide at an alarmingly high rate (Jamison, in press; Kubie, 1974). Perhaps, as Greenacre (1958) suggests, art provides an exaggerated but sporadic sense of ego integration. Similarly, Noy (1979) maintains that

> The search for "perfect form" in art . . . , is a part of the organizational effort, and it reflects the activities of the ego in ordering the disparate parts of the self, in reconciling the opposites that may threaten to tear the self apart, and in enabling the maintenance of a stable self-image [pp. 244-245].

The "partial gratifications" of art to which Kubie (1974) alludes may include transient identifications with multiple roles, each satisfying a portion of a fragmented ego. Tragically, such "role playing" cannot sustain a genuine self-consistent personality and satisfactory object relations. A sense of imposture is accompanied by intense, often morbid dysphoria. Failing to be everything, such artists opt to be nothing, a fate strangely consistent with their polar, antithetical nature. Perhaps having "borne" an enduring work of art, they elude the simple nonexistence which suicide typically entails. In addition to being both man and woman, both joyful and despairing, they are and are not simultaneously.

Summary

This paper attempts to identify a subtype of creative male personality having both bisexual gender orientation and cyclothymia. More specifically, it proposes that excessive feminine strivings in men predispose them to artistic interests as a means of discharging their pregnancy envy and engender a corresponding cyclothymic "artistic temperament." For such men, "fertile" inspired states are euphoric and "barren" nonartistic periods are depressive. Less extreme examples of such gender reversals are apparent in many writers' descriptions of their creative process; creation almost invariably connotes procreation. Four hypotheses are tendered to explain the coincidence of bisexual and cyclothymic tendencies. Finally, the importance of the reconciliation of opposites to artistic production is discussed.

REFERENCES

Akhtar, S. (1984), The syndrome of identity diffusion. *Amer. J. Psychiat.*, 141:1381-1385.

Anastasi, A., & Schaefer, C. E. (1969), Biographical correlates of artistic and literary creativity in adolescent girls. *J. Applied Psychol.*, 53:267-273.

Andreason, N. J. C. & Canter, A. (1974), The creative writer: Psychiatric symptoms and family history. *Comprehensive Psychiat.*, 15:123-131.

——— & Powers, P. S. (1975), Creativity and psychosis. *Arch. Gen. Psychiat.*, 32:70-73.

Barron, F. (1957), Originality in relation to personality and intellect. *J. Personality*, 25:730-741.

——— (1963), *Creativity and Psychological Health: Origins of Personality and Creative Freedom.* Princeton, N.J.: Van Nostrand.

Biller, H. B., Singer, D. L., & Fullerton, M. (1969), Sex-role development and creative potential in kindergarten-age boys. *Devel. Psychol.*, 1:291-296.

Blos, P. (1962), *On Adolescence.* New York: Free Press.

Boehm, F. (1930), The femininity complex in men. *Internat. J. Psycho-Anal.*, 21:444-469.

Bogen, J. E. & Bogen, G. M. (1969), The other side of the brain III: The corpus callosum and creativity. *Bull. L. A. Neurol. Societies*, 34:199-217.

Boyd, J. H. & Weissman, M. M. (1981), Epidemiology of affective disorders: A reexamination and future directions. *Arch. Gen. Psychiat.*, 38:1039-1046.

Brunswick, R. M. (1940), The preoedipal phase of the libido development. *Psychoanal. Quart.*, 9:293-319.

Burgner, M. (1985), The oedipal experience: Effects on development of an absent father. *Internat. J. Psycho-Anal.*, 66:311-320.

Custance, J. (1952), *Wisdom, Madness and Folly.* New York: Pellegrini and Cudahy.

Deutsch, H. (1924), The psychology of women in relation to the functions of reproduction. In: *Women and Analysis*, ed. J. Strouse. New York: Grossman, 1974, pp. 147-161.

——— (1944), *The Psychology of Women: A Psychoanalytic Interpretation*, vol. 1. New York: Grune & Stratton.

——— (1969), *A Psychoanalytic Study of the Myth of Dionysis and Apollo.* New York: International Universities Press.

Domino, G. (1969), Maternal personality correlates of sons' creativity. *J. Consult. & Clin. Psychol.*, 33:180-183.

——— (1977), Homosexuality and creativity. *J. of Homosexuality*, 2:261-267.

Ellis, A. (1959), Homosexuality and creativity. *J. Clin. Psychol.*, 15:576-579.

Ellis, H. A. (1926), *A Study of British Genius.* New York: Houghton Mifflin.

Erikson, E. (1954), The dream specimen of psychoanalysis. *J. Amer. Psychoanal. Assn.*, 2:5-56.

Evans, W. N. (1951), Simulated pregnancy in a male. *Psychoanal. Quart.*, 20:165-178.

Fast, I. (1978), Developments in gender identity: The original gender matrix. *Internat. Rev. Psycho-Anal.*, 5:265-273.

——— (1984), *Gender Identity: A Differentiation Model.* Hillsdale, N.J.: Analytic Press.

Feder, L. (1980), *Madness in Literature.* Princeton, N.J.: Princeton University Press.

Fine, R. (1979), *A History of Psychoanalysis.* New York: Columbia University Press.

Freud, S. (1950), Letter 66. Defense against memories. *Standard Edition*, 1:258. London: Hogarth Press, 1966.

Fromm, E. (1943), Sex and character. *Psychiat.*, 6:21-31.

Frye, N. (1947), *Fearful Symmetry.* Princeton, N.J.: Princeton University Press.

Ghiselin, B. (1952), *The Creative Process.* Berkeley: University of California Press.

Gough, H. G. (1964), Identifying the creative man. *J. Value Engineering,* 2:5-12.

Grant, T. N. & Domino, G. (1976), Masculinity-femininity in fathers of creative male adolescents. *J. Genetic Psychol.,* 129:19-27.

Graves, R. (1955), *The Greek Myths,* vol. 1. Middlesex, Eng.: Penguin Books.

Green, R., Williams, K., & Goodman, M. (1985), Masculine or feminine gender identity in boys: Developmental differences between two diverse family groups. *Sex Roles,* 12:1155-1162.

Greenacre, P. (1950), Special problems of early female sexual development. *The Psychoanalytic Study of the Child,* 5:122-138. New York: International Universities Press.

——— (1958), The relation of the imposter to the artist. *The Psychoanalytic Study of the Child,* 13:521-540. New York: International Universities Press.

——— (1960), Woman as artist. *Psychoanal. Quart.,* 29:208-227.

Hammer, E. F. (1964), Creativity and feminine ingredients in young male artists. *Perceptual & Motor Skills,* 19:414.

Heilbrun, C. G. (1964), *Toward a Recognition of Androgyny.* New York: Norton.

Helson, R. M. (1978), Creativity in women. In: *The Psychology of Women: Future Directions in Research,* ed. J. A. Sherman & F. L. Denmark. New York: Psychological Dimensions, pp. 553-604.

Hendry, J. F. (1983), *The Sacred Threshold: A Life of Rainer Maria Rilke.* Manchester, Eng.: Carcanet New Press.

Hitschmann, E. (1956), *Great Men: Psychoanalytic Studies.* New York: International Universities Press.

Horney, K. (1926), The flight from womanhood. In: *Feminine Psychology,* ed. H. Kelman. New York: Norton, 1967, pp. 54-70.

——— (1932), The dread of women. In: *Feminine Psychology,* ed. H. Kelman. New York: Norton, 1967, pp. 119-132.

Jacobson, E. (1950), Development of the wish for a child in boys. *The Psychoanalytic Study of the Child,* 5:139-153. New York: International Universities Press.

Jaffe, D. S. (1968), The masculine envy of woman's procreative function. *J. Amer. Psychoanal. Assn.,* 16:521-548.

Jamison, K. R. (in press), Manic-depressive illness and accomplishment: Creativity, leadership, and social class. In: *Manic-depressive Illness,* ed. F. K. Goodwin & K. R. Jamison. New York: Oxford University Press.

Jones, E. (1953-1957), *The Life and Work of Sigmund Freud.* 3 vols. New York: Basic Books.

Juda, A. (1949), The relationship between highest mental capacity and psychic abnormalities. *Amer. J. Psychiat.,*106:296-307.

Jung, C. G. (1933), Psychology and literature. In: *Modern Man in Search of a Soul,* trans. W. S. Dell & C. F. Baynes. San Diego: Harcourt Brace Jovanovich, pp. 152-172.

Kaufmann, W. (1974), *Nietzsche: Philosopher, Psychologist, Antichrist.* 4th ed. Princeton, N.J.: Princeton University Press.

Koestler, A. (1964), *The Act of Creation.* New York: Dell.

Koptagel, G. (1972), The pictorial expressions serving as a means of self-satisfaction for a young man with homosexual and transvestite tendencies. *Confina Psychiat.,* 5:71-76.

Kris, E. (1952), *Psychoanalytic Explorations in Art.* New York: International Universities Press.

Kubie, L. (1974), The drive to become both sexes. *Psychoanal. Quart.,* 14:349-426.

Lowenfeld, H. (1941), Psychic trauma and productive experience in the artist. *Psychoanal. Quart.,* 10:116-130.

Mann, T. (1954), *Confessions of Felix Krull, Confidence Man,* trans. D. Lindly. New York: Knopf, 1955.

Marshall, M. H., Neumann, C. P., & Robinson, M. (1970), Lithium, creativity and manic-depressive illness: Review and prospectus. *Psychosomat.,* 11:406-408.

McKinnon, D. W. (1962), The nature and nurture of creative talent. *Amer. Psychol.,* 17:484-495.

McNeil, T. F. (1971), Prebirth and postbirth influence on the relationship between creative ability and recorded mental illness. *J. Personality*, 39:391-406.
Mebert, C. J. & Michel, G. F. (1980), Handedness in artists. In: *Neuropsychology of Left-handedness*, ed. J. Herron. New York: Academic Press, pp. 273-279.
Milgram, R. M., Yitzhak, V., & Milgram, N. A. (1977), Creative activity and sex-role identity in elementary school children. *Perceptual & Motor Skills*, 45:371-376.
Nietzsche, F. (1872), The birth of tragedy. In: *The Birth of Tragedy, and the Case of Wagner*, ed. & trans. W. Kaufmann. New York: Vintage Books, 1967, pp. 15-144.
——— (1888), On the genealogy of morals. In: *On the Genealogy of Morals and Ecce Homo*, ed. & trans. W. Kaufmann. New York: Vintage Books, 1969, pp. 3-198.
——— (1908), Ecce Homo. In: *On the Genealogy of Morals and Ecce Homo*, ed. and trans. W. Kaufmann. New York: Vintage Books, 1969, pp. 201-344.
Nowell, E. (1960), *Thomas Wolfe, a Biography*. Garden City, N.Y.: Doubleday.
Noy, P. (1979), Form and creation in art: An ego-psychological approach to creativity. *Psychoanal. Quart.*, 48:229-256.
Oremland, J. D. (1985), Michelangelo's *ignudi*, hermaphrodism, and creativity. *The Psychoanalytic Study of the Child*, 40:399-433. New York: International Universities Press.
Peters, H. F. (1962), *My Sister, My Spouse: A Biography of Lou Andreas-Salomé*. New York: Norton.
Plath, S. (1982), *The Journals of Sylvia Plath*, ed. T. Hughes & F. McCullough. New York: Ballantine.
Pollock, G. (1978), On siblings, childhood sibling loss, and creativity. *This Annual*, 6:443-481. New York: International Universities Press.
Prentky, R. (1980), *Creativity and Psychopathology*. New York: Praeger.
Rank, O. (1932), *Art and Artist: Creative Urge and Personality Development*. New York: Tudor.
Richards, R. A. (1981), Relationships between creativity and psychopathology. *Genetic Psychol. Monogr.*, 103:261-324.
Rilke, R. M. (1945), *Letters of Rainer Maria Rilke 1892-1910*, ed. & trans. J. B. Greene & M. D. H. Norton. New York: Norton.
——— (1947), *Letters of Rainer Maria Rilke 1910-1926*, ed. & trans. J. B. Greene & M. D. H. Norton. New York: Norton.
Riviere, J. (1958), A character trait of Freud's. In: *Psychoanalysis and Contemporary Thought*, ed. J. D. Sutherland. London: Hogarth Press, pp. 145-149.
Robbins, M. D. (1969), On the psychology of artistic creativity. *The Psychoanalytic Study of the Child*, 24:227 251. New York: International Universities Press.
Rosenmeyer, T. G. (1968), *Tragedy and Religion: The Bacchae in Euripides*, ed. E. Segal. Englewood Cliffs, N.J.: Prentice Hall.
Rothenberg, A. (1979), *The Emerging Goddess: The Creative Process in Art, Science, and Other Fields*. Chicago: University of Chicago Press.
Sandblom, P. (1982), *Creativity and Disease*. Philadelphia: Stickley.
Sarton, M. (1973), *Journal of a Solitude*. New York: Norton.
Schou, M. (1979), Artistic productivity and Lithium prophylaxis in manic-depressive illness. *Brit. J. Psychiat.*, 135:97-103.
Shahly, V. (in press), "A Girl, Almost": Rilke's false female self. *Psychoanal. Rev.*
Simenauer, E. (1954), "Pregnancy envy" in Rainer Maria Rilke. *Amer. Imago*, 2:235-248.
Spiegel, L. A. (1958), Comments on the psychoanalytic psychology of adolescence. *The Psychoanalytic Study of the Child*, 13:296-308. New York: International Universities Press.
Steegmuller, F. (1986), *Cocteau*. Boston: Nonpareil.
Stoller, R. J. (1968), *Sex and Gender: On the Development of Masculinity and Femininity*. London: Hogarth Press.
Van Leeuwen, K. (1966), Pregnancy envy in the male. *Internat. J. Psycho-Anal.*, 47:319-324.
Wellek, R. & Warren, A. (1977), *Theory of Literature*. 3rd ed. San Diego: Harcourt Brace Jovanovich.
Wittkower, R. & Wittkower, M. (1963), *Born under Saturn*. New York: Norton.
Woolf, V. (1929), *A Room of One's Own*. San Diego: Harcourt Brace Jovanovich.

Wordsworth, W. (1850), The prelude. In: *The Norton Anthology of Poetry*, ed. A. W. Allison, H. Barrows, C. R. Blake, A. J. Carr, A. M. Eastman, & H. M. English, Jr. New York: Norton, 1975.

Zilboorg, G. (1944), Masculine and feminine. *Psychiat.*, 7:257-296.

November 1986

Kafka's The Metamorphosis: *A Contemporary Psychoanalytic Reading*

MARGRET SCHAEFER, Ph.D. (Chicago)

I. The Story

The Metamorphosis is "not just one among Kafka's stories, but an exemplary Kafkan story" (Corngold, 1970, p. 103). This "horror story" (Neider, 1948, p. 77), which Kafka himself described as "exceptionally repulsive" (Kafka, 1912, p. 117),[1] is generally considered "the most haunting and universal of all of his stories" (Corngold, 1970, p. 91), and one of his most famous.

In *The Metamorphosis*, a man wakes up one morning to find himself turned into a huge *Ungeziefer*, usually translated as "cockroach," or "insect." Kafka minutely details Gregor's and his family's reaction to his fantastic transformation with a dry, deadpan matter-of-factness for which he is famous. Gregor has been a traveling salesman living with his parents and younger sister, and has been their sole source of support. When he does not come out of his room the morning of his transformation, both his family and the chief clerk of his office reprimand him for his lateness. After Gregor does finally manage to drag himself out of bed—not without much difficulty—and comes out of his room, he cannot understand why his family and the clerk recoil in horror at him.

Gregor only slowly begins to realize that his family finds the very sight of him disgusting. The parents leave his care to the younger sister. Once, when the mother catches sight of him on the wall of his room by accident, she faints from shock, whereupon his father, suspecting him of having

[1] Translations from this and all other Kafka writings, except for *The Metamorphosis*, are my own. All page references will be to the original German editions.

perpetrated some violent act, bombards him with objects to drive him back into his room. An apple remains festering in his back.

The injured Gregor vacillates between rage and despair as his family is forced to take in three boarders for economic reasons. His sister has to give up her dream of going to the conservatory to learn the violin in order to help support the family. As she plays her instrument one evening, however, Gregor, moved by the music, ventures out of his room one last time. However, he succeeds only in terrifying the three boarders and driving them away, and in outraging his sister, who breaks down and tells the family they would be better off if Gregor were dead. Gregor accepts his death sentence and proceeds to die—peacefully—in his room. The story ends with the sister on a tram ride "stretch[ing] her young body" in the spring sunshine (Kafka, 1915, p. 453).

This puzzling story is a paradigmatic example of the macabre Kafkan vision of an irrational world in which fantastic and absurd happenings are minutely and realistically described. The story has attracted voluminous commentary and a wide range of interpretations, ranging from the psychological to the political to the metaphysical and religious. Gregor the insect has been seen as a symbol of the isolated, modern artist (Politzer, 1962); the Jew caught between a Judaism he has lost and a Christianity that he cannot reach (Weinberg, 1963); the "alienated worker, cut off from society and radically estranged from it" (Pfeiffer, 1962, p. 58); "the dissolution of the prevailing order of things such as took place under the impact of war" (Thomas, 1964, p. 77); and modern man's inability to feel at home in his world.

The image of man as insect, of course, suggests all these meanings, and more. Beneath the diversity, however, there is general agreement that Gregor is a self-representation of Kafka's, whether in the subjective, the historical, or the metaphysical dimension. The explicitly autobiographical nature of Kafka's works—Kafka (1951) once wrote about how his writing externalized his "dream-like inner life" (p. 420)—has led to attempts to understand how the figure of Gregor is grounded in Kafka's subjective experience.

Much criticism of Kafka, both literary and psychoanalytic, has followed Kafka himself and read him through the lens of his own oedipal reading of his life and works in his autobiographical "Letter to Father" (1917). The oedipal reading of Kafka sees all of his works, including *The Metamorphosis*, as allegories of Kafka's conflictual relationship to his father. In this view, the puzzling nature of Kafka's stories have to do with the peculiar nature of their "distinct oedipal content" (Levine, 1977, p. 169). *The Metamorphosis*, like many of his other works, is read as an oedipal narrative in which Kafka embeds his own experience as a guilt-ridden son seeking punishment from a castrating and rejecting father (Levine, 1977; Luke, 1964; Kaiser, 1931; Webster, 1959; White, 1967). In the words of J. White (1967, p. 194), "the motivation of Kafka's conflict ridden psyche and his works" is "the anxiety resulting from the repressed sexual desires [and] guilt feelings for the murderous intent against the father." Gregor the insect is said to be Kafka's representation of himself as guilty oedipal son; the story is a "punishment fantasy associated with an extremely primitive father image" (Luke, 1964, p. 26).

There are many details in *The Metamorphosis* that support such an oedipal reading of the story, as a survey of the criticism will make apparent. Yet I want to suggest another reading of the story, one that does not see *The Metamorphosis* primarily as an oedipal narrative in which Kafka in the guise of Gregor concretizes his relationship with a castrating, oedipal father. It seems to me that while the father-son theme is important in the story, it is not central to it; Gregor's relationship with the father neither dominates it nor is the ultimate cause of Gregor's perception of himself as vermin. The central and most elaborated relationship in the story is the one between Gregor and his younger sister, not the one between Gregor and his father. Gregor's death at the end is portrayed not as the result of (castrating) wounds inflicted by the father, as is often argued, but as a direct consequence of his final rejection by his sister. And Gregor's relationship with the sister is not described primarily in oedipal, erotic terms (i.e., the sister as a substitute for the oedipal mother), despite Gregor's fantasy of a kiss from her at one point. Instead, it is described in terms that suggest it is primarily what Kohut described as a (preoedipal) selfobject relationship.

Kafka's detailed descriptions of what it means to be a cockroach do not evoke associations relating to the competitive and erotic feelings associated with the oedipal complex. The emotions evoked by the images and descriptions of Gregor are related to issues of self-esteem and self-cohesion, i.e., humiliation, shame, low self-esteem, alienation, rage, abject helplessness, and aloneness. *The Metamorphosis* makes more sense interpreted as a paradigmatic story of a "fragmenting self" (Kohut, 1977). Gregor's is the story of a radically insecure self who desperately tries to gain an empathic response from the important others in his world and fails, experiencing himself as alien and monstrous as a result, not the story of an aggressive son guiltily submitting himself to the (deserved) punishment of a castrating father. As Heinz Kohut once suggested, Gregor can be seen as an example of modern "tragic man," a "disconnected self" (Kohut, 1977, p. 225; Wolf, 1978, p. 103) existing in an unsupportive and unidealizable world.

Kafka's descriptions of Gregor's awakening to find himself turned into a cockroach metaphorically represent the experience of someone who suddenly experiences his own body as alien and disconnected. Gregor is surprised to discover that the "hard, brown dome" he sees in front of him is his belly. He only gradually recognizes—through pain—that the thin little sticks that "wave helplessly" in the air are his own legs. He is unable to locate the exact sources of the various discomforts and pains he feels, and when he tries to scratch some itchy spots, he feels a "cold shiver" run through him at the alien sensation of his own touch. He does not recognize a scratchy, screeching sound as the sound of his own voice.

Clearly, in Gregor's experience of himself as insect, Kafka is portraying is metaphorical form experiences of depersonalization, estrangement, and derealization. Such experiences and perceptions of one's body in isolated, disconnected bits and pieces, and the difficulties in integrating various visual and tactile percepts are typical somatic expressions of what Kohut calls a state of threatened self-fragmentation. The striking focus on body parts experienced as alien and isolated from one another instead of as parts of a whole, and the associated global and unlocatable pains are typical of the hypochondriasis that Kohut describes as characteristic of such states.

Experiencing himself as awkward, uncontrolled, and helpless, Gregor desperately tries to contact others, only to be traumatically rejected every time. Neither his employers, his fellow workers, nor his family are empathic to his neediness. Every time he ventures from his room he is driven back into its loneliness. Every time he approaches them, they recoil in disgust and revulsion. Every time he speaks to them, they hear only a screech. What he wants and fails to get from them is well expressed by his plaintive wish as he tries to turn the key in his door with his mouth: "they should all have shouted encouragement to him, his father and mother too: 'Go on Gregor,' they should have called out, 'keep going' . . . (Kafka, 1915, p. 418). His father beats him with sticks and bombs him with apples, while the mother can't even bring herself to look at him, much less to feed him. It would be hard to come up with a clearer image of a self "disconnected from its needed self-objects" (Wolf, 1978, p. 107) than this one.

It has often been noted that the story begins with what is really its climax: Gregor's metamorphosis into a cockroach. This device suggests that what seem to be results are really causes: i.e., that what seem to be the *consequences* of Gregor's turning into an insect (the family's rejection of him) are really the *causes* of his doing so. The self-as-insect is a symbol of the unmirrored, rejected self. Gregor obviously does not exist in the supportive environment which he needs in order to experience himself as whole and human, and which is in the first instance a function of a maternal figure. The cockroach image expresses not the self in relation to a castrating, oedipal father but the self in relation to an unmirroring and rejecting preoedipal mother.

In fact, the image Kafka paints of Gregor on the day of his metamorphosis suggests nothing so much as a huge, helpless, and desperate baby. The emphasis on Gregor's total motoric helplessness when he awakens on that fatal day, his lying in bed unable to turn over, seeing objects in front of his eyes which he can't control and which he only gradually (and painfully) discovers are parts of his own body, evoke the image of an infant. The idea of an insect which crawls on the floor, unable to control its bodily excretions, also suggests an infant—seen unempathically. Gregor sees himself as an insect because he cannot see himself reflected in the gleam of his mother's eyes; when he looks at others, he sees not pleasure, but recoil and disgust, and therefore sees not a human image, but a stranger, a lowly cockroach.

The baby-as-insect image also has a hostile, aggressive component in it. Many commentators in fact have noted these aspects of the insect image, seeing in them the oedipal hostility of the son toward the father. When Gregor first comes out of his room he is said to "involuntarily" snap his jaws at his family. He is described as "exceptionally hungry" on the first day of his transformation, and later is portrayed as having fantasies about raiding the family's larder. There is also an aggressive note in the many references to the insect's dirtiness and filth. But the nasty, greedy, sucking, biting, dirty insect is a better image of a baby looked at without the "gleam in the mother's eye," than it is of an aggressive, oedipal son.

Also expressed in the image of the self as a biting, greedy insect is the rage of the unmothered infant whose needs are not met. Paradoxically, the transformed Gregor dominates, terrifies, and isolates his family. His fantasies indicate that he wishes to control them and to *force* them to respond to him. A clear illustration of this, for example, is his fantasy that he would use his terrifying appearance to frighten away others so that he could keep his sister in his room all to himself. Indeed, he does succeed in dominating the family, as they have to rearrange their economic and social lives around his care and concealment (Gorelick, 1976).

The self-as-insect image can be said to condense two conflicting images, that of an unmirrored and fragmenting self with that of an archaic omnipotent self. The gigantic insect can be considered an almost psychoticlike image of a threatened self that has reconstituted itself on the plane of archaic grandiosity. In fact, Kafka had once before used the insect image to represent a grandiose self that has magical control and power over others and the world. In "Wedding Preparations in the Country," written in 1907, five years before the writing of *The Metamorphosis*, the protagonist Raban imagines himself splitting into two selves, one of which has an insect shape. He fantasizes that the insect self is his "real self," and imagines it lying in front of his window, magically able to control through the power of his thoughts the traffic and the activities of the people passing outside his window. But the insect self in "Wedding Preparations in the Country" is seen as purely positive, a gentle and appealing baby, having none of the terrifying and monstrous qualities of the insect Gregor. What accounts for the negative connotation of the dung-beetle in *The Metamorphosis*? Gregor—unlike Raban in his story—fails to get the empathic and nurturing responses from his family that he needs, and he is therefore full of rage and despair even though on the surface he holds himself, not them, at fault.

It is crucial, as noted before, to notice that the primary relationship in the story is the one between Gregor and his sister, not that between Gregor and his father. In fact, the story is about first the establishment, then the gradual deterioration, of Gregor's special relationship with her. Its three major narrative episodes detail the steps in his progressively deteriorating relationship with her. The first episode, which describes Gregor's transformation and the family's reaction to it, shows her as the only person able to be empathic with him. When everyone else rejects him, it is she who feeds him, cleans his room, and is sensitive to his feelings of shame and discomfort. She becomes for him the mother of early childhood, the feeding, nurturing, mirroring, and confirming preoedipal mother, who literally and figuratively keeps him alive. There is nothing in the story to suggest that she is the erotically desirable, oedipal mother. This is even true of Gregor's fantasy that he could lock her into his room, tell her that he would fulfill her wish to go to the conservatory, and then become the recipient of her admiring gratitude and kiss. This fantasy has sexual overtones (cf. Beauty and the beast), to be sure, but these need to be seen rather as the sexualization of selfobject needs to be admired and mirrored rather than as manifestations of genuine oedipal, incestuous wishes.

The second major episode of the story describes how the sister gradually becomes less empathic with Gregor and begins to turn away from him. The climax of this is when she decides that the furniture in his room should be taken away as it isn't suitable for an insect. Convinced (partially by his mother) that this would mean acknowledging the reality of his really having become an insect, he desperately tries to retain the furniture which testifies to his human status. He fights to keep two things in particular, a picture of a woman on his wall and his "writing desk," from being taken away from him.

These attempts can both be seen as reparative efforts on Gregor's part to establish a selfobject relationship in order to maintain a sense of self. His attempt to avoid the loss of the picture by literally "sticking" to it is a striking embodiment of a wish to "hang onto" and merge with an idealized selfobject. (This episode also has a specific autobiographical dimension, which I will discuss later.) The loss of the writing desk represents the loss of the capacity for writing, i.e., for creative endeavor which can serve as a substitute selfobject able to help preserve his self-cohesion. (This reference to writing is perhaps the only autobiographical element in the story that is not fully integrated into it.) The loss of both the picture (the failure to establish a viable, idealized selfobject relationship) and the writing desk (the failure of the capacity for creative activity) represents Gregor's failed attempts at relationships and activities that would help preserve a sense of self-cohesion as his relationship with his sister begins to deteriorate.

The third major episode of the story concerns Gregor's last attempt to regain his relationship with his sister. Moved by her playing, he tries to approach her while she is playing her violin and to tell her that he is going to send her to a conservatory to study. But the result of his approach is only that she repudiates him entirely. She now angrily denounces him as nothing but an insect after all, an "it" that they must "get rid of." Until that point, Gregor had retained some sense of human connection. But with her betrayal, he sees that he no longer has any hope, and gives up: "the decision that he must disappear was one that he held to even more strongly than his sister, if that were possible . . ." (p. 449). We can interpret this as meaning that with her total rejection, Gregor can no longer maintain any sense of self. His grandiose defensive fantasy of a special relationship with her (e.g., of becoming her admired benefactor) abruptly shattered, he totally falls apart, i.e., "fragments," which is symbolized by his dying.

Yet his death is portrayed almost positively. Gregor dies peacefully, without anguish or pain. Why? Most commentators have seen Gregor's death as a self-imposed punishment for Gregor's guilty oedipal aggression against the father. For such aggression there is no evidence in the story. Others suggest that Gregor feels guilty in regard to the sister. For example, White (1967) writes that "the transformation of the sister into a mature woman after the brother's death is the expression of the reactive guilt feelings in Kafka for having hampered his sister's normal development" (p. 219). The only problem with this is that in the story's terms, it is not Gregor, but the sister who should feel guilty.

Perhaps Gregor's death is so peaceful because it expresses not so much punishment, but a wish. Through death he can merge with his sister and thus become her. The positive portrayal of the sister's rebirth at the end of the story, which has bothered many critics, is comprehensible as a rebirth or merger fantasy of Gregor's. Through his death, he becomes his sister. His suicide can be seen as a (grandiose) compensatory wish to merge with the one who is both the mirroring and idealized other.

This interpretation solves the "problem" of the ending of the story. Many have been bothered by the sister's joyful rebirth scene at the end of the story and have felt that it doesn't fit the tone of the story. Indeed, Kafka himself in later years felt that there was something inappropriate about it: in 1914, he pronounced it an "unreadable ending" (1951, January 19, 1914). If the rebirth of the sister represents the resurrection of Gregor, however, a joyful ending is appropriate.

Gregor has every reason to want to be his sister. She is, after all, the favored child, the one that the parents, in particular the mother, love, while they reject him. The portrait of the younger sister in the story, particularly in the ending, is an older sibling's portrait of how his younger sister replaced him in his parents' affection: a sort of "sibling's complaint." One way of dealing with sibling jealousy is identification with that sibling. If the ending of the story involves a fantasy of identification and merger with the sister, a different interpretation of the various images of castration in the story (e.g., the images of Gregor's legs being torn off, his bleeding from the side of his body, and the open, festering wound that the father has created by the apple that remains stuck in Gregor's back) becomes possible. These images may express a wish to become female like the sister, not in order to adopt a feminine stance toward the father, but in order to be loved by the mother.

To understand fully the centrality of the sister figure in the story, however, requires that we turn to Kafka's life. If—as Kafka maintained—*The Metamorphosis* has autobiographical roots, what circumstances, feelings, and events might have stimulated it? If Gregor is indeed a self-portrait of Kafka's, as he said it was, what might account for Kafka's experiencing himself as a cockroach at this time in his life? A wealth of biographical and autobiographical material in the form of voluminous letters to friends and family and long, daily diary entries make it possible to gain some reasonable answers to these questions. The foregrounding of the younger sister in the story suggests that Kafka's relationships with his younger sisters at the time of the writing may be important in this respect.

II. The Life

Kafka wrote *The Metamorphosis* at the age of twenty-nine, in a period of a few weeks, from November 17 to December 6, 1912. Although he was a voluminous diarist, there are no diary entries for five months after September 25, 1912, because on that day he began a series of lengthy, almost daily letters to a woman who later became his fiancée, Felice Bauer. His letters to her are the major source of biographical information concerning the writing of *The Metamorphosis*.

Franz Kafka was born in 1883 to a middle-class Jewish family in Prague, the first of six children of Herman and Julie Kafka. Two brothers, one born when Kafka was two, the other when he was four, died in infancy, the first when Kafka was three and a half, and the second when he was five. The family moved many times during Kafka's early childhood, and his mother was often absent helping in the father's fancy-goods store, leaving him in the care of successive nurses. Of his three sisters, he was closest to the youngest, Ottla, born when he was nine. She was twenty when he wrote *The Metamorphosis*. At that time he wrote to Felice that Ottla was his "best friend in Prague" (Kafka, 1912, p. 87).

At the prodding of his parents, Kafka had gone to law school after attending the university and had earned a law degree. But he had chosen to work as an official in a workmen's-compensation-insurance office instead of as an attorney, because working hours for an insurance official ended at 2:30 in the afternoon. This left him time to devote the rest of his day to his writing, which he regarded as his real work. Writing had first become centrally important to him in early adolescence, even though neither of his parents ever regarded it seriously. Kafka (1917) never forgave his father for once saying apathetically, "just put it on the bedside table" (p. 51) when Kafka gave him one of his published stories. He equally resented his mother's insistence on regarding his writing as a "recreational activity" (Kafka, 1912, p. 115). His parents did not hesitate to saddle him with demands that took him away from his writing. But although he had been at odds with his parents about this and many other things, he was still living in the parental home at the time of the writing of *The Metamorphosis*, when he was already twenty-nine.

The diaries indicate that he felt he had a writing block in the year and a half (1911–1912) before he began writing to Felice, and that he was suffering from emotional distress in the form of overt anxiety, depression, and a variety of somatic symptoms. He worried constantly about not being able to write, losing his eyesight, being sensitive to noise, and about a toe that he considered slightly deformed (1951, p. 35). There are repeated complaints about severe headaches, stomachaches, irritability, insomnia, and extreme hyperacusis. He was bitter about his family's lack of interest in his writing and about the pressure of his office work.

In the months just previous to the writing of the story (i.e., September and October 1912), his difficulties were exacerbated by a series of events that culminated in his family's insistence, in late October, that he take over the management of a family-owned asbestos factory for a period of two weeks while his brother-in-law, the usual manager, was away on a trip. This request threw him into a suicidal state.

It is true that Kafka had always particularly abhorred work in the factory. First of all, it required special travel time and cut deeply into his available writing time. Secondly, he resented being forced into being involved with his father's business interests. In his *Letter to Father,* he writes of the shame and embarrassment he felt when he had been in his father's shop as a boy, because of the tyrannical, suspicious, and unjust way he had seen his father treat his employees (Kafka, 1917, p. 34). And now he was supposed to play the manager role. Additionally, this was a dusty asbestos factory, at a time when Kafka already had some lung symptoms, later to be diagnosed as tuberculosis. He had been in a sanitorium during the summer, although his illness had not yet been diagnosed.

Yet it is difficult to understand why the family's request that he work two weeks at the factory should have precipitated the extreme emotional reaction indicated in his writing about it to his friend Max Brod. To him he wrote on October 10, 1912, that "bitterness—I don't know whether it was only gall—ran through my whole body. I understood with perfect clarity that for me there were now only two possibilities, either to jump out of the window after they've all gone to sleep or else to go every day for the next fortnight to the factory and my brother-in-law's office" (1958, p. 108). He wrote that he had actually stood at his window and seriously considered jumping, adding in a postscript: "I hate them all, every one of them, and in the next two weeks hardly expect to find words for bidding them good morning." Brod was so concerned about the seriousness of Kafka's suicide threat that he wrote to Felice: "his parents wanted him to work in the store in the afternoons. As a consequence, Franz was determined to commit suicide and even wrote me a suicide note. At the last minute . . . I succeeded in protecting him . . ." (1912, p. 115).

What could account for Kafka's exaggerated reaction to his parents' asking him to work for them in the factory—which he had done many times before without feeling suicidal about it? I suggest that it was a series of events which he experienced as abandonments, particularly a "betrayal," as he considered it, by his sister Ottla.

During the two-month period just before and during the writing of the story, Kafka suffered a whole series of losses relating to his sisters. His second-oldest sister, Valli, whom he considered the most attractive of his sisters, became engaged in September. This caused him to muse in his diary that "Love between brother and sister [is] the repetition of the love between mother and father" (1958, p. 186). And in October, two weeks before the writing of the story, his oldest sister, Elli, gave birth to a second child. This birth, Kafka (1912) wrote to Felice, made him feel "nothing but raging envy against my sister, or rather against my brother-in-law" (p. 82). Part of the reason for this was that Elli's older child, Kafka's nephew, only ten months old at the time, had come to stay with the Kafka family during the sister's confinement. Kafka reacted with jealousy and resentment to his stay, writing to Felice about how he was "forced to endure" his parents' playing with the infant. It seems obvious that the birth of his new niece and the infant nephew's usurping his parents' attention at home revived in Kafka painful feelings of exclusion and jealousy related to the birth of his sisters.

Additionally, his best friend, Max Brod, chose this time to become engaged. Brod, who idealized Kafka boundlessly, saw him as a kind of saint, and was to write more than a hundred articles, books, and reviews proselytizing for Kafka's work, obviously performed an important mirroring function for him. His engagement caused Kafka to grumble to Felice "to me he'll [now] be disengaged" (1912, p. 435). Obviously, Brod's engagement did make him temporarily less available to Kafka, thus adding to the feelings of abandonment and exclusion related to his two sisters that Kafka already felt.

On top of all this, Ottla, whom he counted on to support him against his family, "betrayed" him in the matter of the factory incident. Of his three sisters, the youngest, Ottla, born when he was nine, was Kafka's avowed favorite. In *Letter to Father* Kafka describes her with particular affection and calls her his ally against his father. He describes how she interceded for him and became his spokesman vis-à-vis the parents. Having no other place to go, they would meet in the bathroom that was between their two rooms (the layout of their apartment is the same as that described in *The Metamorphosis*), in order to discuss issues and share secrets. Ottla was the only one of his family able to comprehend and be empathic to his literary ambitions. In later life, she often went out of her way to provide him with the emotional and physical conditions he needed for writing. She let him stay in a house she once rented and took care of him even though it inconvenienced her greatly. She was empathic to and supported many of Kafka's interests that the family thought bizarre, such as, for example, his vegetarianism, and his involvement with the Yiddish theater. She was often the first person to hear his stories (e.g., *The Judgment*). Writing to Max Brod, Kafka (1958) once spoke of their relationship as a "good minor marriage" (p. 171). Elsewhere he wrote, "Ottla is literally bearing me up on her wings through the difficult world" (p. 165).

Kafka's statements about his relationship with Ottla indicate that it can be considered a kind of twinship relationship (Kohut, 1984, p. 193) which served to stabilize him. However, in the quarrel over the parental request that he work in the family factory for two weeks, Ottla did not take Kafka's side, as he counted on her to do. Instead, this once Ottla sided with his father and mother against him and urged him to help out at the factory (Kafka, 1958, p. 108). About this he wrote to Max Brod, "my youngest sister, who normally stands up for me, abandoned me to my parents with a monstrous lack of understanding" (p. 108). It was the loss of her support, the shock of Ottla's desertion, I suggest, coming on top of all the other experiences of abandonment that he was then experiencing, which accounts for his extreme reaction to working at the family factory.

Kafka's shock and bitterness at what he called Ottla's "betrayal" of him in his diary and letters suggest that she functioned for him as a necessary selfobject, whose withdrawal of support at a critical time made him feel like an unwanted insect. It is the deterioration of his relationship to Ottla, I suggest, that is reflected in the story of the deterioration of Gregor's relationship with the "younger sister" in *The Metamorphosis*. Many details of Kafka's relationship with Ottla appear in the story of Gregor and the younger sister. The younger sister is the one who mediates between Gregor and his family and takes care of Gregor's needs—just as Ottla did Kafka's. Gregor's fantasy that he is going to help his younger sister attend a conservatory reflects Kafka's wish to help Ottla to enroll in an agricultural school that she wished to attend. As Ottla mothered Kafka, so the younger sister mothered Gregor. As the younger sister takes over Gregor's feeding (literally as well as psychically), so did Ottla make Kafka's vegetarian meals for him, something his family refused to do. It is very likely that Gregor's possessive fantasy of locking his sister in his room, keeping her all to himself, telling her that he is going to send her to the conservatory, which would have the result that she "should need no constraint, she should stay with him of her own free will; she should sit beside him on the sofa . . ." (p. 445) is Kafka's fantasy regarding Ottla.

Kafka's suicidal fantasies, at times desperate behavior, depression, and worsening physical symptoms (stomach distress, headaches, insomnia, and lack of appetite) in response to the above-mentioned blows suggest that he was experiencing a threat of self-fragmentation because of the traumatic effect of the series of emotional abandonments. It is precisely this extreme anxiety that Kafka was able to concretize so effectively in the image and the story of the floundering insect Gregor. Fortunately, Gregor and not Kafka acted out the suicide threat that Kafka expressed to Brod.

Kafka was somehow able to use creative writing to keep himself from sharing Gregor's fate. What saved Kafka from suicide and made it possible for him to write about his emotional states, thereby enabling him to temporarily shore up his self-cohesion? For the year and a half before he wrote *The Judgment* and *The Metamorphosis*, he had complained about a writer's block, which caused him great anxiety. But beginning in September of 1912, he experienced a burst of creativity: he was able to write not only the two stories mentioned above, but also parts of a novel later to be called *Amerika*, and several other stories. It was, I suggest, the epistolary relationship that Kafka had just begun with Felice Bauer, whom he had met in August, that made it possible for him to write at this time. Kafka's burst of creativity began the day after he began his correspondence with her, when he wrote *The Judgment*.

Kafka began his intense, though almost entirely epistolary, relationship with Felice Bauer in September, two months before he wrote *The Metamorphosis*. Considering that he had only met her once, in August—and had after meeting her described her in his diary in very unflattering terms as having "a bony, empty face that carried its emptiness openly . . . an almost broken nose, blond, rather stiff, unappealing hair, strong chin" (Kafka, 1951, p. 178)—it is difficult to understand his intense involvement with her in realistic terms. Yet he wrote to this stranger as if his letters to her and hers to him were a kind of lifeline through which he could barely manage to cling to life. He importuned her to write him every day and tried to impress her with the depth of the anxiety, restlessness, and depression he felt whenever he did not receive a letter from her. He wrote of how he "tremble[d] with unbearable anticipation" for her letter, which seemed to him "something alive" (1912, p. 126). When he failed to get a daily letter from her—which happened sometimes as a result of the post or other reasons—his acute panic led him either to anxiously telegraph her or to write her angry letters breaking off with her. At other times—e.g., on November 24, 1912, when he failed to receive a letter—his depressive reaction was such that he could literally not bring himself to get out of bed for the whole day (p. 126).

Despite the fact that Felice clearly did not understand Kafka's emotional states or his work (as her comments on the first story, *The Judgment*, which he had dedicated and sent to her, indicate), he fantasized a complete congruence and mystical telepathic oneness between them. In the same letter quoted above (November 24, 1912), for example, he wrote, "dearest, have you noticed what an unbelievable agreement there exists between our letters, how one wants what the other one brings the next morning . . . there have been so many of such telepathic communications that I've already come to take them for granted . . ." (p. 126). An outside observer would, however, have said the exact opposite.

Clearly, his picture of Felice grew out of his need rather than from any reality. The intensity of his need, as well as the intensity of his reaction to real or imagined slights from her, suggests that she was for him an idealized selfobject, to whom he turned as the result of the loss of his other important relationships. In view of the fact that his burst of creativity at this time coincided exactly with the beginning of his epistolary relationship with her, his relationship with her can be seen as an example of that "transference of creativity" that Kohut hypothesized as necessary for some artists, who "during their most daring creativity will choose a person in the environment whom they can see as all-powerful, a figure with whom they can temporarily blend" (Kohut, 1976, p. 819). Felice was at this time Kafka's Fliess—at least for a while. Like Freud's relationship to Fliess, it was undoubtedly facilitated by the fact that she lived far away, and that he hardly knew her. Reality disappointment did not intrude very much upon his relationship with her: he could fantasize the empathic response that he needed for as long as he was not actually with her. It is not surprising that when actually confronted with the possibility of living with her, he panicked, and that the relationship ended in a series of disappointing meetings and several broken engagements.

Kafka's relationship to Felice can be explained as an effort to build compensatory psychological structure in reaction to the series of abandonments he was experiencing at that time. He turned to the distant Felice in a fantasy that she would give him the self-validation that Max Brod and his sisters, particularly Ottla, usually managed to provide for him. Felice was a replacement for Ottla.

Kafka's desperate clinging to Felice appears in *The Metamorphosis*, just as Ottla does. In one of the episodes of the story, Gregor violently attempts to "cling to" a picture of a woman he had cut out of a magazine, to keep it from being taken out of his room. It is not an accident that Kafka had on November 24, when he was writing the story, received a photograph of Felice, which he used like a talisman. Kafka (1912) wrote to Felice with profuse emotion upon receiving the picture, and told her that he carried it about with him at all times "in [my] breast pocket" (p. 127). He told her that when he took it with him on a business trip, he had looked at it constantly and at night put it on a chair next to his bed (p. 130). No doubt this picture served the same purpose for Kafka as Gregor hoped the picture of the woman would serve for him.

In the just-mentioned episode of *The Metamorphosis*, Gregor attempts to cling not only to the picture of the woman on the wall of his room, but also to his writing desk. This detail, which suggests that writing was important for Gregor's sense of identity, is not really integrated into the story (there are no other allusions to Gregor's writing) and is perhaps the only unassimilated biographical reference. Kafka was well aware of the important function that writing served for him; he knew that writing was for him an essential means of self-esteem and self-cohesion. During the composition of *The Metamorphosis*, on November 1, he wrote to Felice, "My life has always consisted of attempts to write, and mostly out of failures to succeed at it. But if I didn't write, then I would already be on the ground, worth only to be swept away" (p. 65). Being "swept away" off the ground is of course precisely what happens to Gregor, who was unable either to retain the picture of the woman on the wall (i.e., a selfobject relationship) or his writing desk (i.e., he could not use creative activity for this purpose, either).

The Metamorphosis reflects Kafka's experiences at the time of its writing to an unusual degree, and this not only in its concretization of Kafka's emotional state and perception of reality in the figure of Gregor-as-insect, but in its specific details as well. For example, the day that Kafka conceived of the idea for *The Metamorphosis* was one of those days in which he found himself depressed and unable to function because he had not yet received a letter from Felice. On November 17, he wrote to her, "I was resolved not to get out of bed before your letter came, and I didn't need much strength for this resolution, because I was so depressed I just couldn't get up" (1912, p. 101). It was while thus lying in bed that morning that he thought of a story "which occurred to me in my misery, and which disturbs me internally."

In the story, Gregor, like Kafka on the morning he outlined it in his mind, is lying in bed unable to get up. Like Kafka, Gregor has a job which he hates, which requires traveling, which he wants to quit, and for which he blames his parents. Gregor is probably expressing Kafka's exasperation about having to travel for his insurance work and additionally to the asbestos factory when he says, "Traveling about day in, day out. It's much more irritating work than doing the actual business in the office, and on top of that there's the trouble of constant traveling, or worrying about train connections . . ." (Kafka, 1915, p. 410). Kafka's writing of *The Metamorphosis* was in fact interrupted by a business trip. In the story we find that Gregor did not really need to continue to work, as his father had squirreled away money that Gregor had brought in. In life, Kafka evidently wished that his parents would support him so that he wouldn't need to work for money. Max Brod wrote to Felice at this time, "if his parents really loved and understood him, they'd give him 30,000 Gulden just as they would a daughter, so that he could quit working at the office and go somewhere to the Riviera, to some cheap place, where he could create his works" (Kafka, 1912, p. 115). Implied here is the belief that Kafka's parents were in a position to support his writing, but chose not to do so, which is similar to Gregor's finding out in the story that his father had saved money and did not really need him to go to work for him.

Kafka's feeling of not being understood by anyone around him is metaphorically and graphically portrayed in the story by Gregor's speech becoming incomprehensible because it is an insect's "scratchy" horrible voice, and by his gradual abandonment of any attempt to speak to his family at all. This not only reflects Kafka's often-stated feeling that his family did not understand him, but also refers to a concrete concern that his speech was halting and stammering. In *Letter to Father* Kafka complains that he has "not mastered the normal flowing manner of human speech" (p. 17), and he blames his father for it. He writes,

> the impossibility of calm discourse [with you] had the result that I unlearned how to talk . . . From early on, you forbade my speaking; your threat, "no back talk from you!" and your threateningly lifted fist [another detail picked up in *The Metamorphosis*, where the father is often shown in this pose] accompanied me from the beginning. I acquired in front of you . . . a hesitating, stuttering manner of speaking; even that was too much for you; finally I became silent . . . because I could neither think nor speak in front of you [pp. 17–18].

The story is faithful to Kafka's feelings toward his parents as well as to his feelings about Ottla. His "I hate them all," which he wrote to Brod (Kafka, 1912, p. 108), is integrated into the story in his portraits of them. The father in the story is portrayed as dense, hostile, uncomprehending, violent, and a fraud, just as Kafka described his own father in his *Letter to Father*, where he subjected his relationship with him to a searching analysis. This letter, written in 1917, never reached his father, since characteristically the mother had intercepted it and refused to give it to him for fear that it might upset him. It is a kind of predecessor to *Portnoy's Complaint*. In it, Kafka details his father's insensitivity and lack of understanding of him, his own futile efforts to please him, his deep fear and feelings of inferiority and helplessness vis-à-vis him, his rage at the injustice of the father's enforcing laws that he himself did not keep, and his deep disappointment in him.

Kafka characterizes his father as "strong, loud, forceful, excitable, angry and insensitive," too much for a sensitive child like himself. The father's child-rearing methods, he says, were "accusations, screaming, threats, sarcasm, and malicious laughter" (Kafka, 1917, p. 18). He speaks of the humiliations involved in comparing his own "thin, weak, small" body (p. 12) with that of his father's "gigantic, strong" one while they were both at a swimming pool, writing, "I was already made to feel inferior through the bare fact of your corporeality" (p. 11).

It is possible, of course, to understand Kafka's relationship with his father as the result of intense oedipal conflict, fear, and retreat to feminine identification, as most psychoanalytic biographers have done. But close attention to the anecdotes and incidents that Kafka recounts shows that most details can be alternatively and better understood using a self-psychological rather than an oedipal framework. The painful incidents Kafka remembers all have to do with his feelings of narcissistic injury, shame, and humiliation vis-à-vis his father. Even in the just-mentioned comparison of his own small body with his father's huge, strong one, Kafka emphasizes the narcissistic humiliation, not the competitive or hostile aspect of a typical oedipal situation. Over and over again in endless detail he recounts feelings of shame and self-debasement and complains about lack of respect and appreciation on the part of his father. A paradigm of their relationship is his account of what would happen when he came home with some small triumph in school: arriving happy, he would tell a story from his day, but his father would refuse to respond appropriately to his pleasure and instead would make sarcastic comments such as, "that and 90¢ will get you a ride on the bus" (p. 9), traumatically deflating him.

Equally painful for Kafka was the fact that early on he was forced to recognize the difference between the man his father thought himself to be (and, even more importantly, the man Kafka wanted and needed him to be) and the man he really was. He was particularly pained by what he early recognized as the unjust, capricious way in which his father treated his employees, in which he recognized how he treated him. This realization is more relevant to early traumatic failures of paternal idealization than to oedipal competition and hostility. Kafka was aware of how much he idealized his father, how he "thought he was god" and made his words into absolute law. Kafka's famous "father problem" is more a desperate need for and traumatic disappointment in an idealized father imago than oedipal rivalry and defeat.

Despite Kafka's myriad complaints, however, one senses a strong emotional connection, albeit a conflicted and disturbed one, between him and his father. By contrast, the mother is conspicuous by her almost complete absence in Kafka's account of his childhood history. It's almost as though she didn't exist. Either his feelings about his father defensively covered deeper feelings about his mother, or there was a shallow emotional connection between them. He only writes two things about her in this letter: one is that "mother unconsciously played the part of a beater during a hunt" (p. 21) by assuaging the father's anger and smoothing things over, so that he could not rebel against the father; and the second is that "she loved you [father] too much" (p. 14). At the time of the writing of the story, he complained that "her love of me is just as great as her lack of understanding" (1912, p. 111).

This characterization also fits the mother in *The Metamorphosis* who is depicted as weak and submissive to the father, and as ineffectually "loving" as Kafka felt his own mother to be. She tries to be empathic to Gregor, even to defend him against outsiders, but is too weak to be able to save him or even to be able to tolerate the sight of him. The sister has to "protect" the mother from even seeing Gregor—and when the mother does see him by accident, she faints in horror. She meekly allows the sister to take over Gregor's care, as though she just couldn't handle it herself. One might say of the mother of the story, as of the mother described in *Letter to Father*, that she is not a real emotional presence in Gregor's life.

Kafka's portrayal of his mother in his letters and diaries indicates that Kafka felt his own mother to be emotionally unavailable and unempathic. He talks a good deal about her total lack of understanding of him. Is it possible that Kafka's mother was depressed or otherwise emotionally unavailable to Kafka when he was young? Such an assumption is warranted by what we know of Kafka's childhood history. You will recall that Franz Kafka was Julie Kafka's oldest child, the first of six children. The two siblings born immediately after him both died in infancy. We can assume that the psychic stress of the death of these two infant sons must have been considerable for Julie Kafka. Her adaptation could not have been helped by the father's continual emotional and social demands on her, including the insistence that she continue helping him at his shop. In fact, she later blamed the father for making her leave the children and expressed the feeling that the lives of the two infants might have been saved had she stayed home with them (Hayman, 1982, p. 11). The impact of these deaths may further have been aggravated by the fact that she herself had been exposed to traumatic childhood loss: Margaret Mitscherlich-Nielson (1979) has pointed out that when Kafka's mother was herself three, she "lost her mother, who died of typhus, and, when she was four, her grandmother committed suicide" (p. 5). Even if Julie Kafka did not experience the profound depression in reaction to the loss of her two infants that Mitscherlich-Nielson suggests she did, a degree of emotional unavailability must have characterized her relationship to Franz Kafka, her oldest child, especially as the loss of the two children coincided historically with her frequent absences from the home in order to work in the father's shop.

The ending of the story, which I have already discussed as a rebirth fantasy in which Gregor imagines his rebirth in female form as his sister, also reflects, I think, Kafka's childhood sibling history. Kafka was the only surviving male child in the family: the first two siblings who displaced Kafka were male, and both died. The subsequent girls all lived. It must have appeared to the child that girls lived, while boys died—a circumstance that could lead a fragile, male firstborn to believe that it is dangerous and vulnerable to be a male, while to be female is to be strong and to survive—and to gain mother's love successfully. Thus the wish to be female that the ending of the story and some of its imagery suggest is related not to an oedipal feminine identification vis-à-vis the father, as has been suggested for Kafka, but to his preoedipal childhood sibling constellation.

Kafka the child might also have believed that he had killed his two male rivals with his hostile wishes, a guilty fantasy commonly found in children with a sibling who dies (Pollock, 1978). This doing away with the male siblings could be what is symbolized by the episode in which Gregor succeeds in driving away three intrusive "lodgers" who have taken over the house while he is locked away in his room. The three lodgers could represent Kafka's two brothers and Kafka himself, all the male issue of the Kafka family. At the end of the story only the sisters—collapsed symbolically into one sister—survive. The death of Gregor could reflect a self-punishment for the imagined killing of the siblings: by dying, the lonely, rejected Gregor punishes himself for his hostile wishes. On one level, Kafka's story is saying in the guise of Gregor, "I will die, too, a baby, like my brother[s]" and then, as a defense, "I will be reborn as a girl, then you will love me like you love my sister[s]."

At the deepest and most archaic level, the figure of Gregor the insect may express Kafka's guilty identification with his two dead brothers, the first one of whom was named *Georg* and died when Kafka was three and a half. Freud and Fenichel (1945) have observed that vermin and insects and other small animals often symbolize "little children," particularly siblings (Fenichel, 1945, p. 415). The names "Georg" and "Gregor" are very similar. And Kafka had even used the name "Georg" directly in his story *The Judgment*, which was written around the same time as *The Metamorphosis*, just a few months before. We know that Kafka explicitly identified with this "Georg" of *The Judgment*: first in his diary and then later to Felice he wrote at length about how the name "Georg" had the same number of letters as "Franz," his own first name (1912, p. 275; also 1951, p. 297). He seems surprised at this. The name Georg obviously had unconscious archaic reverberations for him. There is a detail which I think further demonstrates Kafka's identification with his dead brother Georg in the figure of Gregor—namely, the multitude of itchy "spots" that Kafka describes as afflicting Gregor's insect carcass. This could be an (unconscious) reference to the illness that apparently caused his brother Georg's death: measles. An archaic identification with this figure could be reactivated in later life whenever circumstances conspired to make him feel excluded and rejected—as they obviously did at the time of the writing of *The Metamorphosis*.

Such an identification would explain why the insect is depicted as a kind of huge, awful baby, as suggested above. Gregor is first of all Kafka's rival Georg, the baby who usurped his place with his mother; and then, by way of guilty identification, himself. It is likely that the suicidal fantasies which Gregor and Georg and others of Kafka's heroes act out for him and the feeling of pervasive guilt that so many of his stories embody have as much do with guilt over hostile fantasies against the brothers who died as with the much discussed guilt over aggressive wishes toward the father.

If we now ask why his dead brother Georg might have been on Kafka's mind around the time of the writing of the story, what specifically might have reawakened his memory, we can point to the already mentioned birth of a child to his sister Elli, which occurred around the time of the writing of *The Metamorphosis*. Kafka (1912), as I have already said, expressed himself quite explicitly about the rivalry he felt toward the young nephew who came to stay with the Kafkas during Elli's confinement (p. 82), and jealously compared his parents' treatment of the boy with their treatment of him (1917, p. 43). The birth of the new niece, in addition to the insult of his betrayal by Ottla, and his partial loss of Max Brod, probably reawakened the unconscious memories and feelings of the birth and death of Georg.

"All art is autobiography," said Oscar Wilde. Kafka's art, at least in *The Metamorphosis*, illustrates the truth of this statement. Kafka's genius allowed him to portray brilliantly his own loneliness and despair in the figure of Gregor, thereby shoring up the cohesiveness of his fragile self, rather than to succumb to an act of self-destruction and die like his brothers. Kafka said that his story *The Judgment* had come out of him "like a real birth, covered in filth and slime" (1951, February 11, 1923). In giving birth to Gregor through his writing in *The Metamorphosis*, Kafka identified with his mother and made reparation to her for the death of Georg, thereby giving literature a masterpiece that will never die.

REFERENCES

Corngold, S. (1970), Kafka's *Die Verwandlung*: Metamorphosis of the metaphor. *Mosaic,* 3:4, 91-107.

Fenichel, O. (1945), *The Psychoanalytic Theory of Neurosis*. New York: Norton.
Goldberg, A. (ed.) (1978), *The Psychology of the Self: A Casebook*. New York: International Universities Press.
Gorelick, K. (1976), Franz Kafka's *The Metamorphosis*: A Psycholiterary Analysis. Unpublished manuscript.
Hayman, R. (1982), *Kafka: A Biography*. New York: Oxford University Press.
Kafka, F. (1915), *The Metamorphosis*, trans. Willa and Edwin Muir. In: *Classics of Modern Fiction: Eight Short Novels*, ed. I. Howe. New York: Harcourt, Brace and World, 1957, pp. 409-453.
——— (1951), *Tagebücher 1910–1923*. New York & Frankfurt: Schocken Books.
——— (1953), *Brief an den Vater* [1917]. New York & Frankfurt: Schocken Books.
——— (1953), *Wedding Preparations in the Country*, ed. E. Kaiser & E. Wilkins [1907]. New York: Norton.
——— (1958), *Briefe 1902–1924*, ed. M. Brod. New York & Frankfurt: S Fischer Verlag.
——— (1967), *Briefe an Felice und andere Korrespondenz aus der Verlobungszeit*, ed. E. Heller & J. Born [1912], New York & Frankfurt: S. Fischer Verlag.
Kaiser, H. (1931), Franz Kafka's inferno: Eine psychologische Deutung seiner Strafphantasie. *Imago*, 17:41–104.
Kohut, H. (1971), *The Analysis of the Self*. New York: International Universities Press.
——— (1976), Creativeness, charisma, group psychology: Reflections on the self-analysis of Freud. In: *The Search for the Self*, vol. 2, ed. P. Ornstein. New York: International Universities Press, 1978, pp. 793–844.
——— (1977), *The Restoration of the Self*. New York: International Universities Press.
——— (1978), *The Search for the Self*, vol. 2, ed. P. Ornstein. New York: International Universities Press.
——— (1984), *How Does Analysis Cure?*, ed. A. Goldberg. Chicago & London: University of Chicago Press.
Levine, R. (1977), The familiar friend: A Freudian approach to Kafka's "The Judgment." *Literature and Psychology*, 27:164–173.
Luke, F. D. (1964), The Metamorphosis. In: *Franz Kafka Today*, ed. A. Flores. Madison: University of Wisconsin Press, pp. 25-44.
Mitscherlich-Nielson, M. (1979), Psychoanalytic notes on Franz Kafka: The psychobiography of a disturbed genius. *Psychocultural Rev.*, 3:1-24.
Neider, C. (1948), *The Frozen Sea*. New York: Oxford University Press.
Pfeiffer, J. (1962), The Metamorphosis, trans. R. Gray. In: *Kafka: A Collection of Critical Essays*, ed. R. Gray. Englewood Cliffs, N.J.: Prentice-Hall, pp. 53-59.
Politzer, H. (1962), *Franz Kafka: Parable and Paradox*. Ithaca, N.Y.: Yale University Press.
Pollock, G. H. (1978), On siblings, childhood sibling loss, and creativity. In: *This Annual*, 6:443-481. New York: International Universities Press.
Thomas, R. H. (1964), *Franz Kafka*. Frankfurt: S. Fischer Verlag.
Webster, P. D. (1959), Franz Kafka's "Metamorphosis" as Death and Resurrection Fantasy. *Amer. Imago*, 16:349–365.
Weinberg, Z. (1963), *Kafkas Dichtungen*. Bern-Munich: Franke Verlag.
White, J. (1967), Psyche and tuberculosis: The libido organization of Franz Kafka. *The Psychoanalytic Study of Society*, 4:185-251. New York: International Universities Press.
Wolf, E. (1978), The disconnected self. In: *Psychoanalysis, Creativity, and Literature: A French-American Inquiry*, ed. A. Roland. New York: Columbia University Press, pp. 103-117.

June 1986

Notes on Abandonment, Loss, and Vulnerability

GEORGE H. POLLOCK, M.D. (Chicago)

I

Over the years I have had, and continue to work with, patients, directly or through supervised analyses, who were actually abandoned totally and permanently for critical periods of their childhood, or adopted at birth, abandoned by a divorced parent who did not obtain custody, abandoned when one or both parents suicided when the patient was a young child, deserted by a parent, placed in an orphanage or foster home because of economic issues, suffered the institutionalization of one or both parents institutionalized for serious emotional illness, felt they were abandoners either because of giving up newborns for adoption or inducing abortion, who divorced, felt they were abandoning their elderly parents by placing them in nursing homes, gave pets up for adoption or "put them away," lived with one or both depressed parents where there was no physical separation but there was emotional abandonment or threat of it. These latter patients usually are more damaged than those who suffered an actual parent loss through death and subsequently were cared for by others who were involved and caring, widows who find they are abandoned by their friends who suddenly see them as sexual competitors (unlike attitudes toward widowers in our society), the dying patient abandoned by his or her "loved ones" in a hos-

Portions of this work were presented in New York at the November 1984 workshop on "The Significance of the Reconstruction of Trauma in Clinical Work," sponsored by the American Psychoanalytic Association.

This work was supported, in part, by the Anne Pollock Lederer Research Fund of the Institute for Psychoanalysis of Chicago.

pital, hospice, or nursing home (decathexis before death), those who "abandon themselves," e.g., the Musselmen in the concentration camps, or feel abandoned at the birth or adoption of a sibling, especially if the mother is away for a period of time, visiting the father on overseas military duty, perhaps, leaving the child with inhospitable caretakers, or the child placed in a boarding school. Because of issues of confidentiality, I am unable to give many details of these clinical experiences, but I will highlight a few. Let me say that through reconstructions in the analytic situation, the analysis of the transference situation and dreams, retrospective understandings and recollections, the traumatic constellations surrounding the abandonments became clear and could then be further investigated and in many instances "worked through."

In thinking about this broad subject, I arrived at the idea of a spectrum of abandonment—ranging from the actual total physical (outer) abandonment to the transitory intrapsychic (inner) "decathexis" or "deinvestment" that occurs in many normal relationships—for example, the exhausted mother who reaches a low point of tolerance for her demanding infant and wishes it would go to sleep or "leave me alone," and who thinks this. Transitory decathexis opens up for us newer means of understanding such phenomena as detachment, forgetting, and even denial or splitting. The temporary physical or intrapsychic abandonment may be acute or chronic, a single event or chronic oscillations, temporary or permanent, external or internal; these abandonments may be related to death, divorce, desertion by a key figure and by the resulting depression, pathological mourning, psychotic withdrawal of the significant remaining figure—e.g., James Barrie's mother after the death of her favorite son, the older brother of James; the psychosis of Charlie Chaplin's mother and his placement in the workhouse as a child; the complete desertion of Jack London by his biological father, and of Edward Dahlberg.

Do these abandonments, traumatic constellations, and events have later pathological consequences? Can they be treated psychoanalytically? Do these abandonment events result in deficits and/or internal conflicts? Does it make a difference who leaves, e.g., parents, grandparents, siblings, and/or parents, or when the abandonment occurs? Can there be massive social and emotional abandonment, as in a concentration-camp victim's experience, without consequences? When abandonment occurs, what impact, if any, do the temporary caretakers have on what occurs? Does day care, even without sexual or any other physical child abuse, help or hinder further healthy development? What about the one-parent family in terms of optimal development? We know that not all traumata are pathogenic, but some do sensitize the individual to certain events throughout the life course.

Recently, an analytic patient of mine, whose father died when he was fourteen and who subsequently had a lifelong anxiety reaction whenever an individual who is meaningful to him left even for a few days, began his session by saying, "The next week will be difficult for me . . . (pause). My son, Peter, wants to come home for Thanksgiving. (The son is in an Eastern boarding school and does not have a holiday.) He cried on the phone. I began to sob. I thought, 'What kind of image is that for him? I guess he feels abandoned' (pause . . . tears). I feel abandoned here. (Here?) You won't be here this Friday and then next Thursday—Thanksgiving. You'll probably be with your family—all together (crying). Why does this still upset me? I know it is connected to my father—but you are o.k.—you'll be back—you had better be or I'll get sore. I hate you for leaving me like this and at this time."

Another recent clinical vignette: a woman in her seventies, with whom I had worked many years ago, returned to treatment following the death of her husband from a malignant blood dyscrasia a few months before. She began her session with, "It has been a terrible time. I am so sad—alone—I am feeling so abandoned by Michael—so many of his things I have to get rid of—so many old photos—he saved everything. Now I have to go through each little item and cry over them—weekends are the worst—damn him—why did he have to die? I had a nightmare.

"Michael and I were in our living room—he was in the chair—I was lying on our couch. Suddenly he got up and said, 'What are your favorite pre-Columbian pieces?' I said, 'These,' pointing to two death masks. He went over to them and smashed them to bits. I couldn't believe what I saw and I woke up with a start. He was so alive, so angry (pause). I guess I hate him for leaving me—the old death masks—I want to smash them—get rid of them and what they cover. You'll smash them for me (long pause). You know he killed himself. (He did?) Not actually, but he took so many x-rays—he was so hypochondriacal—always x-rays—self-medication—some doctor he was—he probably induced his blood malignancy. I hate him for leaving me (starts crying). Why did he need annual GI, chest, skull, and gallbladder x-rays? We all told him he was fine. I found his personal medical diary—it is unbelievable—such an obsessive. So he killed himself trying to keep himself from dying. I was the sick one—all those years of treatment with you. I look at his picture and say, 'You God damn fool—look what you did to me and to you.' "

A third clinical example: Patient at age seven angered his father, while father was presumably drunk. The child did not know what to do. Father lunged at him, caught him, and threw him through a screen door, onto a porch. He heard the door slam and was all alone in the dark. The mother had earlier left the house in a panic. The child, shaking and cold, sat huddled in the corner all night. In the morning, a neighbor, walking her dog, saw him and took him into her house. In the analysis, his behavior initially was not intelligible. He would lie on the couch, huddled up, fearful that something would happen to him. Only in the subsequent years could we understand retrospectively his anxiety, concern, reliving, and later intense rage at this experience.

A fourth illustration: a predental student was referred to me because of intense anxiety that began in his comparative-anatomy class while dissecting a cat. He became panicky and had to leave the laboratory. An excellent student, conscientious and diligent, he went to his instructor who, after hearing about his pain, sent him to the student-health service and they referred him to me. He came from Germany and as a young adolescent was caught in a Nazi net and sent to a death camp. His father was in the same camp—he only saw his father on a few occasions and was shocked at his appearance. Not long afterward his father was killed. My patient was on a work crew that collected gold fillings from the unfortunates after they were gassed and before they went to the crematorium. He managed to escape, living in the woods, and was liberated at the end of the war and came to this country. He resolved to become a dentist—the motivation was obvious—but he was not conscious of it until his analytic treatment allowed him to see this. He felt very abandoned—by his protective father, by his German government, by his God.

Interestingly, he did get into an excellent dental school—had great anxiety in anatomy where he had to dissect the head. The next year, in physiology, he panicked at working on live dogs. In the third year, autopsies fascinated him, and yet he had nightmares which directly took him back to the Nazi camp. In the fourth year, he took an elective in head and neck and oral surgery. By this time his analysis was far advanced and he had no difficulty. One of the pivotal features of his therapeutic progress was, as he put it, "You stuck with me even in the dark days. I was not alone."

A fifth analytic example: A young pediatric resident began analysis because he found he could not comfortably enter into a meaningful relationship with a woman without becoming angry with her, even though he had no potency problems and could even feel love toward her. This pattern repeated itself so often that he recognized the problem as an internal one. Initially, he was quite open in his analytic work with me, but as time went on he had severe reactions on the weekend, when we did not meet, and when I had to be away from Chicago for meetings. I had known that his mother had died when he was a child, but the exact details emerged only in the course of his treatment. When he was three, his mother developed a life-threatening pulmonary disease. His father and mother left Chicago to go to a warmer climate so that she could recuperate. From three to five, he heard nothing from his parents, being left in the care of a harsh governess. He feared this individual, especially when she yelled and when she spanked him for trivial offenses. When the father returned, he was told his mother died, and even later he never saw her grave. He found himself very involved with helping helpless children, but knew he had a fear of dying, of being left, and of upper-respiratory illnesses. In the analysis, when I would cough, he initially would get panicky. We arrived at various understandings of his patterns and reactions to me, and gradually he was able to address other aspects of his developmental pathology—oedipal problems, fears of castration, and the like.

I also wish to describe a young woman who was adopted at birth, whose adoptive mother died when she was twelve, and who was intensely involved in reincarnation, extrasensory psychic phenomena, and astrology. She was depressed, had episodes of eating and drinking with resultant obesity that was controlled. We could reconstruct many facets of her psychological problems, how they were manifested in the here and now, and where they came from. She was quite introspective and benefitted from therapy.

Franz Kafka, in the classic work *The Metamorphosis*, details the inner feelings related to abandonment—first the abandonment of one's body and the strangeness and alienation it produces, then subsequent abandonment by key members of his family, and ultimately by life itself—a parting with no return.

Let me now turn to an illustration of another form of abandonment—the deeply grieving and melancholic mother and its impact on the surviving, growing child. I have discussed this in the case of Käthe Kollwitz (Pollock, 1978, 1982), but here I use James Barrie as my clinical example.[1]

Margaret Ogilvy, certain that her firstborn, Alec, would be a credit to her, concentrated her ambition on her second son David. He was a very bright child, and his mother was certain he would outdistance Alec and become a Doctor of Divinity, the highest reward on earth for which she could hope. The youngest son, Jamie, gave no signs during the first six years of his life of being other than an ordinary small-town Scottish lad. He was good at reading, but what Jamie liked best were games and entertainment.

Alexander did well, graduating with an M.A. with first-class honors in classics, and opened a private school in Lanarkshire in Scotland. Alexander

[1] The material on James Barrie has appeared, in slightly different form, in my 1978 paper, "On Siblings, Childhood Sibling Loss, and Creativity."

thought that David, who was now almost fourteen, should leave the small town of Kirriemuir and go off to school. Margaret Ogilvy, who had never been able to disguise the fact that David was her favorite, was intensely ambitious for him to become a minister, but was reluctant to let him go and join Alec. Finally, realizing that he would get a much better education under his brother's tutelage, she agreed. David settled down happily in his brother's school and lived with Alec and sister Mary, who was Alec's housekeeper. In January of 1867, Alexander gave his brother a pair of iceskates, and on the eve of David's fourteenth birthday he went skating with a friend. "After a few turns on the ice, David took off the skates and gave them to his friend, who strapped them on and went spinning away at great speed. In doing so he cannoned into David, causing him to fall heavily, head first, on the ice . . . David survived for a few hours (he had a badly fractured skull), but remained unconscious. While there was still some glimmer of hope, Alexander sent a telegram to his parents, telling them to come as soon as possible, but presently he had the grim task of sending a second telegram, saying David was dead" (Dunbar, 1970, p. 20).

Margaret Ogilvy never recovered from this death. Although only in her late forties, she was completely overwhelmed by her grief and seemingly was oblivious to her other children. The trauma of the brother's death was compounded by the trauma of the withdrawal and regression of the mother. The children felt rejected by her. James Barrie, and his sister Jane Ann, who was thirteen years older, apparently were most affected by this painful and unhappy situation. Jane Ann, who never married, never left her mother, but cared for her until she died, three days before her mother's death. Barrie writes: "My timid mother saw the one who was never to leave her carried unconscious from the room and she did not break down. She who used to wring her hands if her daughter was gone for a moment never asked for her again" (Barrie, 1896, p. 199). Barrie goes on, "They were buried together on my mother's seventy-sixth birthday, though there had been three days between their deaths" (p. 200). On her last day, just before she died, Margaret went through her house. When she returned to bed and became weak, she said, "Is that you, David?" She asked for the old christening robe, to which I will return in a moment.

> It was brought to her, and she unfolded it with trembling, exultant hands, and when she had made sure that it was still of virgin fairness her old arms went round it adoringly and upon her face there was the ineffable mysterious glow of motherhood. Suddenly she said, "Wha's bairn's dead? Is a bairn of mine dead?" but those watching dared not speak, and then slowly as if with an effort of memory she repeated our names aloud in the order in which we were born. Only one . . . did she omit, the one in

> the next room, but at the end, after a pause, she said her name and repeated it again and again, lingering over it as if it were the most exquisite music and this her dying song [pp. 201–202].

She then had the christening robe folded, said good-bye to all, turned her face to where her husband had lain, prayed, and died.

This moving account is from a book written shortly after the mother's death by Barrie and called *Margaret Ogilvy—By Her Son*. It was dedicated to the memory of his sister, Jane Ann. "Barrie's book about his mother, written when he was thirty-six, is our only real record of how his relationship with his mother changed after David's death. One day he was the youngest brother, noisy and carefree, not yet ready to be dreamed over but still his mother's own and separate child. The next day he was a substitute for one who could never be replaced" (Dunbar, 1970, p. 21). Perhaps the best way to describe what Barrie felt is to use his own words now.

> She had a son who was far away at school. I remember very little about him, only that he was a merry-faced boy who ran like a squirrel up a tree and shook the cherries into my lap. When he was thirteen and I was half his age the terrible news came, and I have been told the face of my mother was awful in its calmness as she set off to get between Death and her boy. We trooped with her down the brae to the wooden station, and I think I was envying her the journey in the mysterious wagon; I know we played around her, proud of our right to be there, but I do not recall it, I only speak from hearsay. Her ticket was taken, she had bidden us goodbye with that fighting face which I cannot see, and then my father came out of the telegraph-office and said huskily, "He's gone!" Then we turned very quietly and went home again up the little brae. But I speak from hearsay no longer; I knew my mother for ever now . . . [1896, pp. 5–6].
>
> She was always delicate from that hour, and for many months she was very ill. I have heard that the first thing she expressed a wish to see was the christening robe, and she looked long at it and then turned her face to the wall. That was what made me as a boy think of it always as the robe in which he was christened, but I knew later that we had all been christened in it, from the oldest of the family to the youngest, between whom stood twenty years . . . [pp. 7-8].
>
> My mother lay in bed with the christening robe beside her, and I peeped in many times at the door and then went to the stair and sat on it and sobbed. I know not if it was that first day, or many days afterwards, that there came to me my sister, the daughter my mother loved the best; yes, more I am sure even than she loved me, whose great glory she has been since I was six years old. This sister, who was then passing out of her 'teens, came to me with a very anxious face and wringing her hands, and she told me to go ben to my mother and say to her that she still had

another boy. I went ben excitedly, but the room was dark, and when I heard the door shut and no sound come from the bed I was afraid, and I stood still. I suppose I was breathing hard, or perhaps I was crying, for after a time I heard a listless voice that had never been listless before say, "Is that you?" I think the tone hurt me, for I made no answer, and then the voice said more anxiously "Is that you?" again. I thought it was the dead boy she was speaking to, and I said in a little lonely voice, "No, it's not him, it's just me." Then I heard a cry, and my mother turned in bed, and though it was dark I knew that she was holding out her arms.

After that I sat a great deal in her bed trying to make her forget him, which was my crafty way of playing physician, and if I saw any one out of doors do something that made the others laugh I immediately hastened to that dark room and did it before her. I suppose I was an odd little figure; I have been told that my anxiety to brighten her gave my face a strained look and put a tremor into the joke (I would stand on my head in the bed, my feet against the wall, and then cry excitedly, "Are you laughing, mother?")—and perhaps what made her laugh was something I was unconscious of, but she did laugh suddenly now and then, whereupon I screamed exultantly to that dear sister, who was ever in waiting, to come and see the sight, but by the time she came the soft face was wet again. Thus I was deprived of some of my glory, and I remember once only making her laugh before witnesses. I kept a record of her laughs on a piece of paper, a stroke for each, and it was my custom to show this proudly to the doctor every morning. There were five strokes the first time I slipped it into his hand, and when their meaning was explained to him he laughed so boisterously that I cried, "I wish that was one of hers!" Then he was sympathetic, and asked me if my mother had seen the paper yet, and when I shook my head he said that if I showed it to her now and told her that these were her five laughs he thought I might win another . . . [pp. 11-14].

It was doubtless that same sister who told me not to sulk when my mother lay thinking of him, but to try instead to get her to talk about him. I did not see how this could make her the merry mother she used to be, but I was told that if I could not do it nobody could, and this made me eager to begin. At first, they say, I was often jealous, stopping her fond memories with the cry, "Do you mind nothing about me?" but that did not last; its place was taken by an intense desire (again, I think, my sister must have breathed it into life) to become so like him that even my mother should not see the difference, and many and artful were the questions I put to that end. Then I practised in secret, but after a whole week had passed I was still rather like myself. He had such a cheery way of whistling, she had told me, it had always brightened her at her work to hear him whistling, and when he whistled he stood with his legs apart, and his hands in the pockets of his knickerbockers. I decided to trust to

> this, so one day after I had learned his whistle (every boy of enterprise invents a whistle of his own) from boys who had been his comrades, I secretly put on a suit of his clothes, dark grey they were, with little spots, and they fitted me many years afterwards, and thus disguised I slipped, unknown to the others, into my mother's room. Quaking, I doubt not, yet so pleased, I stood still until she saw me, and then—how it must have hurt her! "Listen!" I cried in a glow of triumph, and I stretched my legs wide apart and plunged my hands into the pockets of my knickerbockers, and began to whistle.
>
> She lived twenty-nine years after his death. . . . But I had not made her forget the bit of her that was dead; in those nine-and-twenty years he was not removed one day farther from her. Many a time she fell asleep speaking to him, and even while she slept her lips moved and she smiled as if he had come back to her, and when she woke he might vanish so suddenly that she started up bewildered and looked about her, and then said slowly, "My David's dead!" or perhaps he remained long enough to whisper why he must leave her now, and then she lay silent with filmy eyes. When I became a man and he was still a boy of thirteen, I wrote a little paper called "Dead This Twenty Years," which was about a similar tragedy in another woman's life, and it is the only thing I have written that she never spoke about, not even to that daughter she loved the best. No one ever spoke of it to her, or asked her if she had read it: one does not ask a mother if she knows that there is a little coffin in the house. She read many times the book in which it is printed, but when she came to that chapter she would put her hands to her heart or even over her ears [pp. 15–19].

In later years, Barrie still tried to amuse his mother, only now with his writing. It was Margaret who read with him after David's death, and it was Margaret who encouraged his early compositions. In fact, *Peter Pan*, Barrie's masterpiece which bore the subtitle, *The Boy Who Wouldn't Grow Up*, originally was called *Peter and Wendy*. Wendy was very much like the Margaret who as a little child was close to her father and brother David. Peter Pan, the boy who wouldn't grow up and who went to "never-never" land, might represent David in heaven. Thus the play could be said to be about David and Margaret—the children who never grew up.

II

Although some of these emphases have already been or will be stated, they bear repetition. Separation is not the same as loss or abandonment, although these terms are frequently used interchangeably. Following separation, we can get growth, further development, and individuation, even though some loss of the prior state occurs. For example, in fatherless families (see Adams, Milner, and Schrepf, 1984), there are some children who never had a father. They were abandoned even before birth.

THE CASE OF EDWARD DAHLBERG

Paul Carroll has called Dahlberg "the Job of American Letters" (1967, p. xx). His writings are lamentations and quarrels with the world and his sexuality. In his autobiography, *Because I Was Flesh* (1964), he tells us of his troubled early life. He was born in a Boston charity hospital in 1900, an illegitimate child. He grew up fatherless and conceived of himself as an outcast—a pariah from an early age. His mother had many suitors, but none was interested in him, and he viewed them all as rivals for his mother's affection. One insisted he be removed from the Kansas City house in which he and his mother lived. "At age twelve, bewildered and resentful, he was packed off to a Jewish orphanage in Cleveland" (Conger, 1984-1985, p. 54). In Kansas City, Dahlberg first experienced the isolation, the loneliness, the desolation that came first from an emotional abandonment by his mother, a total abandonment by his unknown father, and an actual later abandonment when he was sent to an orphanage in another city. He truly felt victimized, helpless. He returned from the orphanage in 1918, having been gone for six years of adolescence. He then headed west, rode freights, suffered miserably from hunger and exposure, but managed to survive. The neglect and abuse of his childhood seemed to follow him and some of his ambivalence, especially his bitterness which he in part transferred to Kansas City, a locale associated with personal suffering.

Dahlberg, in describing his mother and himself as luckless souls, notes that she "had two miserable afflictions, neither of which was she ever to overcome: her flesh—which is my own—and the world, that cursed both of us" (Carroll, 1967, p. 37).[2] He recognized that she suffered from solitude and this was the basis of sexuality—to ease her loneliness. He does not know how he came to have the Swedish name of Dahlberg, as his maternal grandfather's name was Dahlberg and the family was Jewish, coming from outside of Warsaw, Poland. His mother married at sixteen, to a furrier in New York, at the insistence of her brother. She had three children with this man, although she detested her husband. One child died, and she abandoned her two small sons, began an affair with a barber, fled to Boston, where she bore a bastard (Dahlberg's term!) in the charity hospital. "She

[2] The quotations that follow are taken from *The Edward Dahlberg Reader*. Copyright © 1967 by Edward Dahlberg. Reprinted by permission of New Directions Pub. Co.

gave me her father's name to hide the fact that I was illegitimate" (Carroll, 1967, p. 42). The barber taught her how to trim hair, moved to Dallas, Texas, where she was in great demand by her male clients. Her lover stole her money, and often he attempted to hit the infant son. She ran off to Memphis with the child. From there she went to New Orleans, Louisville, Denver, and finally came to Kansas City in 1905, where she began working in a barbershop with other young women who were also working as barbers. Lizzie, Dahlberg's mother, worked very hard under circumstances of poverty and deprivation. But, determined, she opened her own shop, which she called Star Lady Barbershop, and prospered.

Dahlberg writes that, "In April 1912, when he was eleven, [he] became an inmate of the Jewish Orphan Asylum in Cleveland. . . . No Spartan ordinances could have been more austere than the rules for the orphans" (Carroll, 1967, p. 72), who rose every morning at 5:30 A.M. The buildings were described as similar to "almshouses, reform schools and charitable penal institutions of the late Edwardian period" (p. 73). The description of the routine imposed upon the children out-Dickens Dickens's workhouse of the Victorian era, even to the point of calling each child by its assigned number instead of by its name—a diabolic, dehumanizing practice seen in the Nazi death camps. Demerits were freely given for infractions, and restrictive punishments could result from relatively slight misdemeanors. Beatings were given to boys caught talking to girls.

Edward was designated as Number 92. "Brutality was also an orphanage fetish; the smaller children were bullied by the older boys" (p. 76). Edward wrote his mother, begging her to let him return to Kansas City where he could be close to her and escape from that which frequently caused him to cry—but to no avail. The letters were strictly censored, and if a child called the institution a reform school, he or she could receive many demerits, be deprived of the infrequent picnic, or even lose the privilege of "going out walking" (p. 77). Despite all of this, the threat of expulsion and the return to "a blank, kinless city" was worse than the orphanage. A boy left the orphanage after confirmation. Dahlberg called the orphanage children "a separate race of stunted children who were clad in famine. Swollen heads lay on top of ashy uniformed orphans" (p. 82). "How little love, or hot sperm, had gone into the making of their gray-maimed bodies?" (p. 83).

Everyone had daily work assignments, but everyone still was bored, felt starved, and had various mild infections. The stronger boys tyrannized the younger and protection bribery was not uncommon. Remembering his mother was painful for Number 92. As Dahlberg writes of his world of horrors one can wonder if what appears in his descriptions of the asylum might include some of the child's anger and remorse at being abandoned by a seemingly uncaring mother who turned him over to a restrictive abusing environment from which there was no escape—in a sense the abandonment was a variant of child abuse. But finally Edward was confirmed in the class of 1917, and "a boy had died and a man had sprouted. Whatever the child had been, the man must overcome" (p. 97).

After a period of wandering Dahlberg graduated from Columbia University. He would visit his mother occasionally. After Captain Smith abandoned her (he was responsible for Lizzie sending Edward to the orphanage), her lonely life contributed to her deterioration. She did join him in New York, living in an apartment that he found for her in Queens, although there was a marked distance between Edward and his mother. Further poverty necessitated a move to a coldwater flat in a slum tenement in Manhattan. Lizzie deteriorated further, and only her resolve to stay alive seemed to keep her going. She could not part with anything; her life was rapidly coming to a close, and she was tenacious about giving up any part of it. She lived in her memories of the past and regarded the clock with hatred. Edward was unemployed, and poverty affected both mother and son as it had from the beginning of their life together. He feared her death as he would lose her image—abandonment again.

"Unable to drive out of my bones that one dirge: 'My mother will disappear,' I fled from her. . . . I saw that man was born to be deceived and that he is a wan image roaming an orbed plain in the Void. Sleep is death, and death is sleep because we are never alive" (Carroll, 1967, p. 154). Dahlberg's deep depression at his mother's final abandonment of him was very much in evidence. He wrote that both he and his mother were the unloved ones. He avoided his mother's face, did not kiss her, found it harder to recognize her. Many times when she was in the room, he neither heard nor saw her, and "so she grew fainter. When we fail to see the phantoms near us they vanish from our sight" (p. 155).

One night he dreamed,

> I saw a woman who was only two empty udders; I imagined I beheld her, but there was no mouth or chin or cheeks in her. As I grieved for her, water grew around me. It was neap tide, and my sleep was shoaly, and sour and dyspeptic, and I endeavored to walk in the water toward her to give her a filial kiss to restore the mouth, the cheeks and chin that were missing—but the waves held me back so that I could not reach her. Then I saw a cruse of water and a loaf of bread, and I awoke and moaned, "She is dead, and the bottle of water and the bread she has left me are for my hunger." I sat there on the bed, and the vision clung to me like the fog bank that gathers around one's eyes after a migraine. I looked

> about for my mother; then I hurried over to her small casket, the iron cot into which she descended every night. A skinny sheet lay awry over the pallet, but the shabby becrumbed coat was gone. I threw on a jacket and rushed out into the street, which was painted with sleet. There I saw coming toward me a woman whose back was lumped by her unforgiving hopes; she walked with unsteady feet on the ice, carrying two milk bottles under her arm. Relieved when I saw her knobby chin and the nose that fell over her deflowered mouth, I upbraided her: "O my mother, why are you so stupid? Do you wish to fall on the ice? What are you doing with those two empty udders?" Started when I heard these words, I grasped the bottles from her and ran back to the flat. The dream would not let go of me, and I tried to shape the face I could not collect. I had resolved to kiss her hands when I saw her, but as she came through the door the devils grinned at me, and I could not forgive her—but for what I did not know. I believed I saw a forsaken and palsied heap of rags go to that accursed cot and lie down [Carroll, 1967, pp. 155-156].

Dahlberg was forty years of age at this time, and was finally thinking of marriage—but he was uncertain. I might suggest, could he trust a woman not to abandon him again and leave him with two empty udders? He told his mother about the woman, and she promptly wrote her agent in Missouri to sell her houses so that her son might have the money to provide for a wife.

Dahlberg married, got a temporary job teaching at a university, and he and his wife stayed with his mother for a while. She gave him all of the money she had collected and shortly thereafter began to decline more rapidly. She realized she was dying and wanted to sign over whatever she had left to her son. Edward was immobilized and felt guilty over what he "had already stolen" from her (Carroll, 1967, p. 159). He knelt on the floor beside her bed and kissed her before going to bed. With the money he received from her, he and his wife bought an old house on Cape Cod and a secondhand car. One night they decided to leave, and they watched the old mother walk away in loneliness.

The mother wrote twice a week to her son for the next two years. On the fifteenth of February, 1946, preoccupied with his mother, Edward had a nightmare. Awakening, he shrieked, "Mother, your wicked, fallen son will come to your side; you will not die alone" (Carroll, 1967, p. 160). He said to his wife, "Let us go to my mother before she dies" (p. 160). On the eighteenth of February, another letter came from his mother, but he would not open it. On that night she died. "She was alone, and her body lay on the cot for five days before a neighbor found it" (pp. 160-161). The final abandonment—on both sides—had come to pass. "I do not go to her grave because it would do her no good" (p. 161).

In the second category, which can apply to mothers as well as fathers, we find abandonment through death, divorce, marital and physical separation that is externally imposed upon the child, illegitimacy and subsequent adoption, desertion. Adams, Milner, and Schrepf (1984) have a third category, which I believe can apply again to mothers and fathers, temporary mother or father absence due to incarceration (prison), hospitalization for medical and/or mental reasons, military duty, economic hardships, and parental detachment or psychological absence although there is no physical absence.

THE CASE OF CHARLES DICKENS

Charles Dickens was born on February 7, 1812. He had in all eight brothers and sisters, and he himself was the eldest son and second child in the family. Wilson (1983) indicates that Dickens's childhood until age eleven seems to have been "blissful." "He was well esteemed at school, read widely in his father's books, told stories graphically, entertained company with comic songs, was an ardent theatergoer, and took long country walks with his father" (p. xlv). His mother provided him with fairy stories and stimulated his imagination by making available to him the novels of Fielding, Smollett, and Sterne, as well as an opportunity for play. He was encouraged and praised, and his precocious comic abilities were very much appreciated. He won prizes and honors, but his father incurred many debts, and before Charles Dickens was twelve years old his idyllic life collapsed. The family moved to a "poky little house" in London, he no longer enjoyed the pleasures of a secure family and approving social milieu, and then "to make horror double, his father, beloved and generous, was arrested and imprisoned for debt. Soon after, Mrs. Dickens and the rest of the family, save Charles and his sister Fanny, went to join their father in Marshalsea Prison, as the families of prisoners for debt were allowed to do" (Wilson, 1984, p. xv). "Charles had to live in bleak lodgings far from his place of work, farther still from the prison which held his family" (p. xv). He was on a poverty budget, often hungry, and undoubtedly bewildered by the sudden loss of his beloved family, his admiring and admired father, his stimulating school and friends, and by his contact with "ignorant, rough boys who worked on the factory bench" (p. xv). Wilson suggests that

> . . . certainly, the two most lasting traumas that survived from those frightening months were the boy's sense of lostness in the metropolis, his unwilling emotional identification with the abandoned children of the early-Victorian city streets and underworld, and his double image of his beloved and loving father as the man whose weakness . . . has con-

> signed his young son to this lonely netherworld. In real life, the mature, successful Dickens could and did interest himself in successful, benevolent activity on behalf of lost and helpless children; he could and did wrestle with his father's continuous impecunious cadging and financial dishonesty. But only in his fiction could he face the memories and images of those boyhood months of hell. There are very few of his novels that do not contain one of these two situations, although in many strange guises [1984, pp. xv–xvi].

For example, we see this in *Oliver Twist*, his life in the workhouse and his contacts with the world of crime and prisons, and in *Nicholas Nickleby*, where Ralph Nickleby, the usurer, abandons his illegitimate son. David Copperfield's happy life with his indulging, widowed mother and benevolent, loving nurse, Peggotty, comes to a sudden close, and David is sent to a brutalizing boarding school as a prelude to his return to the blackening factory which was "more horribly seen than in real life, for David is now an orphan; abandonment and despair are total" (Wilson, 1984, p. xix). Dickens's traumas played a central role in his work—in his autobiography and in his fiction.

"After the terrible blacking-factory months, the twelve-year-old Charles was again sent to school, and remained there until he was given a job as a clerk in a lawyer's firm at the age of fifteen" (pp. xxxi-xxxii). When Dickens was seventeen he fell deeply in love with a banker's daughter. However, the social and financial differences in their status, especially when it was learned that Dickens's father had been in debtors' jail, quickly ended the relationship when Dickens was twenty-one. Wilson again indicates that, "So enduring was the memory of this failed wooing that years after his marriage, when he came in 1846 to try to write an autobiographical essay, he found that with some difficulty he could put the terrible episode of the blacking factory on paper, but the collapse of his relationship with Maria proved too painful to recall" (p. xli). This was another part of the many abandoning experiences that Dickens endured, and it was not the last. His wife's attractive seventeen-year-old sister, Mary, of whom Dickens was very fond, died in his arms. The emotional effect of this "abandonment" affected him for many years, and Dickens used this as the basis of Little Nell's death in *Oliver Twist*.

These adolescent and early-adult abandonment experiences affected Dickens and, as indicated above, found their way in his creative writing. Were his novels an attempt to complete his mourning-liberation for a lost childhood, a "lost" father, a lost beloved, and a "lost" possible substitute, Mary, for the earlier lost "Maria"? Dickens's abandonments occurred in adolescence and early-adult life, yet their impact remained, and they were dealt with creatively. Perhaps the first eleven years did allow him to withstand the terrors that came later on.

III

In adopted children we frequently find abandonment problems. Edward Albee is an example. To be certain, there is a difference between the meaning of adoption and its accompanying fantasies intrapsychically and as it affects interpersonal strife, although there may be a connection between the two. There also may be a connection between early-life abandonees who may or may not later themselves become abandoners. In psychoanalytic treatment we try to heal the wounds of abandonment. Not all adoptees have the abandonment syndrome, although I believe it is more frequently seen if the analyst keeps this possibility in mind.

In the very moving documentary film, *John*, the Robertsons show vividly the traumato-pathogenic effects on a small child who was left for nine days in a residential nursery. The devastating regressions and rage even at reunion with mother apparently still had reverberations in his later life. Traumato-pathogenic abandonment, depending upon the circumstances of the abandonment, the age of the child, prior history, and relationships, may be of importance in later outcome. Some children have a self-righting ability that makes them seem to be invulnerable. Various writers and researchers have described these phenomena in children of psychotic parents, children who survived the Nazi concentration camps, or children with severe and serious physical illness early in life. Psychological interventions are needed, may be helpful, or in some instances are not available, and yet the child develops with relatively minimal later psychological impairment.

In some instances we find the cumulative effects of abandonment producing strain trauma. In other instances these strain phenomena can organize and strengthen an ego instead of damaging it severely. Without getting into terminologic debates, one can most frequently understand the traumato-pathogenic disruption after the occurrence, as different resiliencies may protect the ego from further disruption. However, we do operate within limits, and when these are severely traversed one can assume that disequilibrium, distress, disturbance, disorder, and even disease can occur, especially if there is no preventive intervention. We are now in a better position to define the limits and identify high-risk children. In the psychoanalytic treatment situation, one may get data that confirm or refute such predictions. We are then able to distinguish between the event itself and the meaning-fantasies of the event or events and the response to these.

One also learns of the psychological homeostatic level of the internal psychic milieu and how the individual has coped to maintain this balance. The response to severe abandonment is loss, mourning, anxiety, and even deep regression requiring therapeutic intervention. Even so, we still may find later anniversary responses to the abandonment experience; the posttraumatic stress-strain syndrome can be seen even in individuals who were not in Vietnam.

At the end of World War II, one thousand child survivors of the Nazi Holocaust entered England. With the advice and counsel of Anna Freud and under the direction of Alice Goldberger, some of these children lived in a home in Surrey. At the close of the war they ranged in age from three to eleven. Sarah Moskovitz (1983) has now interviewed twenty-four of these survivors. Her follow-up interviews reveal that they still suffer from loss reactions and feelings of being outsiders. They also reveal that not one of these survivors has given up. There have been no suicides, only one of this sample has been involved with drugs, only one lives in a psychiatric hospital. The rest are actively involved in communal activities and are compassionately related to others.

Despite horrendous childhood experiences, these children survived, and their lives on outcome follow-up studies indicate that emotional disability does not necessarily follow early severe trauma. The survivors let us learn of their indestructibility, of their yearning for love, their tenacity of hope, and their human resilience and resourcefulness. The children came from Terezin, Auschwitz, several from orphanages, and from hiding.

Abandonment of pets, of the elderly, of disabled and chronically ill children, of unwanted children through starvation, which is a form of infanticide, and the ultimate child abuse, through either overtly leaving a child even for hours each day or emotionally withdrawing from the child, through abrupt weaning after periods of indulgence, through threats of death, are but a few of the external "traumata" we observe in the spectrum of abandonment. And yet some children do survive even after the harrowing circumstances. Moskovitz (1983) revealed that the child survivors of the Nazi death camps were markedly helped in their adaptation to life through the heroic help and dedication of Alice Goldberger and her staff of psychoanalysts who could undo some of the effects of the severe abandonments these innocents suffered. Through their great care and understanding, some could be restored to health. The great support of Anna Freud facilitated this rehabilitative process. As Moskovitz (1983) observes, "losses that occurred very long ago continue to reverberate deeply throughout life. . . . at every life-marking event such as their own weddings, or their children's births, bar mitzvahs, and weddings, there is for all survivors the vivid, jarring encounter with those dead who should have been there" (p. 227). But the security and certainty of belonging still eludes some survivors, even those adopted when they were quite young.

Moskovitz found some of the adoptees still struggling with the issue of feeling part of the adoptive family itself. I, too, found this to be true of non-Holocaust children adopted at birth. Some, even as adults, still do not risk their ties with the adoptive family by asking about their biological families of origin. The children Moskovitz is studying continue to deal with issues of mourning, of not living up to ideals, of feeling stigmatized, of avoiding situations that could open up painful and upsetting areas that are either partly denied, repressed, disavowed, or just not accessible to memory. The sense of loss is interwoven with feelings of abandonment, diminished sense of esteem, guilt, shame, repressed and suppressed anger; feelings of uncertainty, especially as these relate to antiSemitism, are not uncommon. Nonetheless, Moskovitz emphasizes that among her group of interviewees there is an affirmation of life. "They have a quality of stubborn durability. They keep hoping, they keep trying to make the best of their lives. Given all they have endured, . . . no one has given up" (p. 231). Enduring and surviving are fundamental and indicate the ego strength of these children. These individuals have compassion for others, wish to have families of their own, are caring and responsible parents.

Moskovitz raises fundamental questions about heretofore accepted assumptions. The first deals with the idea "that early deprivation unalterably determines the course of life" (p. 236). My own clinical experience supports Moskovitz's question and her implicit conclusion. Some outcomes are devastating; others that should be are not so. "The first five years seem not to have had the power to inoculate all alike for good or bad" (p. 237). That some vulnerabilities remain is understandable, but "resilience, strengths, charm and ability to get affectionate care from those nearby" (p. 237) may have kept these higher risks latent. Many losses, illnesses, unfortunate circumstances can increase susceptibility to later decompensations, especially if they come together en masse in time and space. Later commitment, constancy, kindness, and genuine positive feelings are protective and healing—this is seen in these children from the camps as well as in our patients and close friends and family who escaped from the direct impact of the Holocaust. Hope and faith in a future can also have ameliorative effects in facilitating integration and positive investments in the present and in the future.

Werner and Smith (1982), Kauffman, Grunebaum, Cohler, and Gamer (1979), and Adelson and Fraiberg (1980) have also written about children who, though abandoned, were able to be retrieved and restored. Let me give a few details from the Adelson and Fraiberg study as it so dramatically illustrates what can be done beneficially even with an almost impossible situation.

Adelson and Fraiberg (1980) give a treatment description of an unmarried teenage mother and her female infant "who was being starved." The mother "herself had once been a starving infant. She had been found in the streets of a war-torn country, abandoned and unfed. After an unknown period in an orphanage, she was adopted at age 2½ by an American family" (p. 222). She was pregnant before she was seventeen. The pregnancy and delivery were normal. The baby was supposed to be adopted at birth, but the young mother refused to give up her baby. Unwanted by her adoptive mother, the young mother moved into a low-cost housing facility. With her mother unable to care for herself and the new infant because of depression, the young infant seemed to recapitulate the biological mother's own past abandonment, deprivation, and terror. The baby's condition worsened, and fear was expressed for her survival. At four and a half months of age, the baby was hospitalized for more adequate feeding. The mother seldom visited. No organic basis for her malnutrition was found, and both mother and infant were referred for treatment and evaluation. Little was initially accomplished, and the recapitulation of the biological mother's own abandonment and subsequent deprivation was in evidence—"a small baby hungered and cried and no one heard, no one helped" (Adelson and Fraiberg, 1980, p. 223). There was almost a complete identification with the abandoning mother but not with the helpless little victim.

In treatment the biological mother initially was very negative toward the female therapist. By carefully acknowledging the patient's fury, disappointment, and distrust, a beginning relationship was established, although the patient made constant demands for special arrangements. The infant's condition was obviously one of great abnormality, e.g., vomiting copiously, sleeping with glassy, unclosed eyes, crying. The mother could not help the baby and so left the marasmic infant alone. As the mother's "desperation and anxiety mounted during the visits, she too deteriorated; her thinking became confused, at times bizarre" (Adelson and Fraiberg, 1980, p. 224). In treatment the mother recognized the ways in which her infant was like her. The parallels were striking, but the mother needed help in establishing the affective links within herself. The sensitive therapist assisted in this healing process through empathic listening to the outpouring of the painful, troubled recalling of her own early life and the way in which the birth of her baby elicited a repeated series of reactions as well as a wish *not* to subject her daughter to what was done to her: adoption meant abandonment. The therapist was asked to help with both the crying infant and the now crying mother. The mother, it turned out, was actively starving her baby by not feeding her with adequate food, and at that, only infrequently. Further neglect was in evidence when the mother never went to the baby when she cried and did not want anyone else to hold her. One might further suggest that the identification with the aggressor was actively being acted out in a destructive fashion against the infant—the hostility to the original mother was displaced onto the innocent baby who was abused in a most fundamental way.

The therapist helped the mother learn what the baby's signals indicated, how rhythms were established, and how satisfaction gradually resulted in pleasure. The therapist was treating both mother and infant simultaneously. The mother began to identify with the therapist in several ways—it seemed as if a new structure was in the process of developing, e.g., both mother and infant would be nurtured with food and with psychological giving. The infant began gradually to gain weight and stop vomiting. In the eleventh session, the therapy began to aim at separating the baby from her mother's conflicts. In some ways, the paradoxical and pathological symbiosis between mother and infant was becoming accessible to division—what was done to the mother had its impact on the mother; but what was being done to the infant, though similar to what occurred in the mother's early life, was an active doing to the infant by the mother herself.

By the child's first birthday, physical and psychological progress was very evident, e.g., grossly aberrant behaviors had disappeared; screaming, vomiting, and fear reactions were gone; the child could offer her mother a beautiful smile, a warm hug, and could toddle about discovering and exploring her small world. Even with these positive changes, both mother and child still remained at risk, and extended treatment continued for two more years. By the time the child was two years old she was a healthy, active toddler, and there was no physical evidence of her earlier failure to thrive. Her language was advanced and well used, and she could engage in inventive symbolic play. There was no evidence of pathological symptomatology. What was still lacking was harmonious reciprocity and pleasure between mother and child. The child was ready, but the mother still held herself back from full affection. In the following year many of the mother's feelings about separation, deprivation, failure, and abuse were dealt with, and the mother in turn became more empathic, protective, and nurturing to her child. A mutuality and reciprocity between mother and child were strengthened. At age three, the child was secure and dealing with age-appropriate issues. The child could turn to her mother for pleasure and understanding.

There are many fascinating aspects to this excellent therapy and the ongoing follow-up and change patterns. Even though abandonment can be and has been devastating for many, appropriate treatment can bring positive results to both child and mother.

I am grateful to my friend E. James Anthony for calling my attention to the work of Charles Odier (1956) on the neurosis of abandonment. Odier differentiates *real and objective* abandonment from *subjective* abandonment, in which the individual reacts as if there had been an actual abandonment, though one had occurred in reality. In some instances where the individual has actually been abandoned, the subjective coincides with the objective. Odier asserts, however, that the two concepts are radically opposed. I would differ with this assertion; the crucial elements are the meanings and fantasies associated with the objective and the subjective "abandonments." As I indicate here, there is a spectrum or continuum of abandonments—these must be understood in terms of how they affected the individual in the short term, and in the long term, and what if any personality distortions resulted from fantasied or actual abandonments.

Odier distinguishes between the fact of abandoning and the fact of being abandoned, i.e., where an actual relationship between two individuals has been broken. One of the partners has been the cause and the other the victim of this break. Odier calls the individual suffering from subjective abandonment as the "abandonee." He notes that this abandonee has not been objectively abandoned (I disagree with this definition in that it is too gross and general), although objective abandonment does not preclude such abandonment. Furthermore, Odier suggests that "the subjective reactions of an abandonee are very different from those of the objectively abandoned person" (1956, pp. 190-191).[3]

As is evident, Odier believes that an abandonee is an individual who, without any objective reasons, feels and believes himself abandoned. Thus, children who have actually been neglected, mistreated, and rejected feel abandoned, but "children who lack nothing, who despite the fact that they seem to possess everything to make them happy and serene, may show abandonism which is due more to a predisposition than to an acquisition" (p. 192). Odier relates this predisposition to a congenital or constitutional factor.

The abandonee's greatest fear is to be rejected or denied attention, and he attributes this to a lack of love. "The suffering subject wants to be absolutely sure that he is loved in order to defend himself against new traumas" (p. 193). The fragility and lability of internal security render him

[3] The quotations from C. Odier, *Anxiety and Magic Thinking*, are reprinted with the permission of the publisher, International Universities Press (1956).

vulnerable and predispose him to bitterness and recriminations as well as to sadness and anxiety. Odier indicates that an intimate relationship exists between phobias, obsessive beliefs, and abandonism. The dread or fear of being abandoned at times provokes the most painful feelings. Fears can become recriminations, and these may lead in turn to accusations that can indeed result in true abandonment. The projective aspect of this mechanism is obvious as are the hostile aggressive component and the sadomasochistic aspect of this "abandonment mechanism."

Odier suggests that one of the abandonee's most firmly rooted beliefs is "the functional overinvestment of the object" (p. 201). The subject attaches himself to the object after overinvesting and overvaluing him. The subject becomes attached to the object so that the latter becomes a love object. The abandonee sees himself as inferior and the object as the only one capable of reassuring him. The result is an unstable relationship based on very old feelings of insecurity, inferiority, and helplessness. A need for protection against abandonment is normal for the infant and child, but if it persists into adult life the overvaluation of the object and the belief in the reality of this overvaluation may give rise to later difficulties. The overvaluation of the object, Odier believes, is paralleled by a self-devaluation.

These unconscious processes can lead to (1) dissatisfaction, doubt, and worry in love, professional, social, and intellectual spheres; (2) periodic depressions; and (3) absolute dependency upon the overvalued object and what he represents, e.g., benevolent power. Since the object keeps the subject in a state of inferiority, he also becomes an instrument of valuation and devaluation—"magnifying others is to diminish oneself; overrating other persons' value diminished one's own value" (p. 203). The function of the overvalued object is to provide security and protection, not love satisfaction. The overvalued object is invested with majesty, omnipotence, power that can be benevolent or malevolent. The abandonee is fearful of losing the security-producing action of his object. The inestimable value of the latter renders him blind to the implications of the overvaluation. "He valuates himself highly only so long as he is tied to his object and so long as this superior person is interested in him" (p. 205). The fear of abandonment has its implications for religious leaders, political leaders, scientific leaders, and organizational structures, even when there may not be a single omnipotent leader. The security of the omnipotent object gives rise, as Odier notes, to the establishment of the subject's self-esteem. But the subject lives on borrowed values. "His own value is closely related to his object's value and the prestige and glory ascribed to him overshadows his real value. Dazzled by his object, the subject becomes blind to his own deficiencies; if he is conscious of his own inferiority feelings, he hardly worries about them" (p. 206). "The abandonee becomes entirely dependent upon his object, a dangerous and degrading position. In order not to suffer from this, his only resource is to confuse this dependency with the blind happiness it procures" (p. 207).

The unlimited confidence in the authority conceals the subject's total lack of self-confidence, self-security, self-esteem, feelings of inferiority and inadequacy. I believe this mechanism may be the basis for the protective function of identification with the aggressor. However, the existence of the basic insecurity remains, and if there is a loss of faith in the authority object or if the authority object withdraws from the subject, there are a loss of self-security, a feeling of abandonment, and the emergence of grief and pain—mourning, if you wish—for the irreplaceable object. Sorrow and despair appear, and the self-desperation appears to be similar to melancholia, or pathological mourning.

Odier defines the object by two propositions:

> A. *The object is the person who communicates to the abandonee the most stable and strong feelings of security and is most able to preserve them*; i.e., the most able to free the subject from insecurity and lack of self-confidence . . .
>
> B. *The object is the person who is most successful in giving the subject self-esteem*, or inversely, of freeing him from his painful feelings of inadequacy and inferiority, in a word, of nonvalue [pp. 207-208].

The parallels between Odier's ideas and those of Heinz Kohut are clear even though there are some significant differences. The Odier focus on abandonment, however, is especially relevant to this presentation and so the parallels and differences will not be discussed further at this time.

Odier notes that a disagreement on the part of the abandonee with the authority has an ominous meaning because it forbodes a break. The suffering results from insecurity. When the break in the relationship takes place, the abandonee suffers not from the actual loss of his object, but from its subjective consequences. He suffers not from the grief which the normal person experiences in such circumstances (I have described this as the normal mourning-liberation process) but from a loss of subjective security and self-esteem. The object itself is of less importance than what it means functionally. The suffering stems from the double loss of security and self-esteem—the loss of the object is confused with the loss of his functions, frequently felt as an intense depression (see p. 221). This depression is characterized by affective suffering, e.g., sadness, despondency, dull anxiety, a feeling of inadequacy, a sense of worthlessness, a loss of faith in anybody. Although "a depressive state is always an ego state . . . this does not prevent it from being determined by extrinsic causes or motives, that is, by causes foreign to the ego and independent of it" (p. 224). There is also a depression of ego origin, seen especially in various neuroses, e.g., insecurity, inferiority, and abandonment.

Odier's differentiation between true absence following direct separation from "absence in the presence" is useful. The latter is more potentially pathogenic in the abandonment syndrome. This "nonaffective" presence, seen in parents who are "not quite here," is a form of emotional abandonment. Odier describes three forms of these "nonaffective" presences:

> The "purely material presence": body care, toileting, dressing, medication, hygiene, supervision, etc.
>
> The "cold presence": wry, cold, silent, at times directly frustrating and painful (punishment, etc.).
>
> The "dutiful presence": the person is there only because it is her moral, educational and physical duty to the child. The accomplishment of this duty is the sole justification for being with the child [p. 256].

At the base of these "nonaffective" or nonpositive attitudes is complete disregard for the subject's needs, and in analytic treatment patients themselves frequently refer to these as the original sources of all of their troubles. This disregard for the child's need for security is at the basis of the neurosis of abandonment. The reactions of the abandonees of all age groups to the "false" or "nonpositive" affective presence are as varied as they are harmful. Generally, Odier finds they can be divided into active and passive reactions. Among the active forms we find the particularly harmful recrimination complex. A frequent form of the passive reaction is sulking as a way of retaliating against the object. The child withdraws into himself or herself. The presence of the object having become unbearable, he brings about separation and absence as if true insecurity were preferable to false security. The sulking and withdrawing individual prefers a true absence to a make-believe presence (p. 258).

Odier's contributions to the theory of abandonment, though overlooked by contemporary clinicians and theoreticians, have much insight and are worthy of further study in clarifying our understanding of the varied forms, characteristics, and manifestations of the abandonment syndrome.

Rochlin (1965) is another one of the few analysts to write about the "dread of abandonment." Although he does not deal with the intrapsychic effects of abandonment, he articulates in lucid fashion the possible effects of abandonment loss on damaged self-esteem, instability, and the evocation of aggression, frustration, and rage responses and the connection of the fear and the act of abandonment "in common fantasies of being lost and losing, of destruction and of aggression towards objects, [and] of grief and death" (p. 28).

IV

The temporary abandonment of children has been discussed by me elsewhere (Pollock, 1985), but in this section I wish to discuss briefly the relationship of abandonment to homicide, be it infanticide or the killing of the old. Stager and Wolff (1984) have studied new evidence that indicates that child sacrifice was an ancient practice. Its origin can be traced to the ancient Israelites who had a name, "Tophet," for a place where children were sacrificed by fire on a special altar. The prophet Jeremiah (7:30–32) describes it, but there are references in other sections of the Old Testament as well. A huge cemetery of sacrificed children has been found in Carthage, and in Sicily, Sardinia, and Tunisia—all connected with Phoenician settlements. Most of the two thousand urns were probably deposited between 400 and 200 B.C. Later burned animals were believed to be substitute sacrifices for children; however, Stager and Wolff indicate "that the demand for human infant sacrifice, as opposed to animal sacrifice, seems to increase rather than decrease with the passage of time" (1984, p. 40). Ancient writers have hypothesized that during times of crisis, massive child sacrifice was practiced to appease the gods and ward off further tragedy. The ancient Greeks did follow this custom. Stager and Wolff give evidence that this was the exception rather than the rule. Mass sacrifice was rare. The commonest reason for child sacrifice was fulfillment of a vow, and "child sacrifice at Carthage was largely an upper-class custom, at least until the third century" (Stager and Wolff, 1984, p. 45). The dedicants were the parents of the child or children whose remains have been found in urns and under monuments. I would suggest the possibility that these new findings may require us to reexamine the cultural practices among the Greeks at the time of the supposed abandonment of Oedipus by his biological parents. "Some Biblical scholars have suggested that child sacrifice was limited to first-born males" (Stager and Wolff, 1984, p. 47), but as we will see below this was not true in other cultures. Stager and Wolff's evidence refutes this link between the dedication of the first-born and its sacrifice. In the fourth century B.C. most of the children sacrificed were one to three years old. This suggests that such ritual infanticide was a means of regulating population growth. Such a means of keeping the population constant was found in later times. Flandrin and Peyronet (cited in Stager and Wolff, 1984) have shown that this was the principal means of birth control in

France before the eighteenth century. Langer (1974) notes that in 1833, 164,319 babies were abandoned in foundling hospitals in France and few survived. Infants today are still abandoned in garbage pails, hospitals, churches, etc. This abandonment is a less direct form of infanticide—though its lethal outcome seems to have been what was desired.

Fuchs (1983) found that abandoned children were found among the nineteenth-century French poor. In a study of the Florentine census of 1427 (Herlihy and Klapisch-Zuber, 1985), it was found that infanticide and abandonment were relatively common. Hospitals could no longer provide for the great increase in the abandoned children. In 1419, the Florentine commune established a special hospital for the abandoned babies of the city. Abandonment was a frequent recourse when there was a famine, plague, or special war tax raising the cost of supporting a family. Girls constituted 70 percent of the foundling population. A substantial number of the abandoned babies were offspring of liaisons between a master and his slave. If the illegitimate child was a boy, the father was more inclined to retain him and rear him in his own household. Among the poor, systematic infanticide or secret abandonment was the practice of disposing of unwanted children. Since deserted infants frequently died, this was a form of disguised or delayed infanticide.

Wagatsuma (1981) found abandonment to be more frequent than child abuse or neglect in Japan. The age of the deserted children ranged from one day old to three years. The "trash can" children found in the United States today are usually very young infants or newborns.

Abandonment of children, of the elderly, of the seriously ill, especially of those with chronic disabilities, is a form of homicide. These homicidal abandonments may take the form of exposure to the elements, drowning, starvation, strangulation, poisoning, or suffocation. Stager and Wolff (1984) suggest that infanticide was preferable to abortion because it was less harmful to the mother physically. They note that "as early as 787 A.D. the first foundling home was established in Milan, followed by hospitals in Rome, Florence, and other cities. . . . at the end of the 12th century, Pope Innocent III established the Hospital of the Santo Spirito in Rome 'because so many women were throwing their children into the Tiber.' London, Paris and St. Petersburg had well-known children's hospitals" (p. 51). Many of the children died during the first few weeks, and few reached the age of six. In London, by the mid-eighteenth century, it was impossible to deal with the great number of unwanted children, and the institutions became houses for the dead.

The abandonment dread of the young child—or of the adult—even though it is repressed, may represent at its base the fear of being killed by those who should care and give life.

V

Jay Katz (1984), in an eloquent and very significant volume, discusses the feeling of abandonment that patients have when their physicians do not communicate or interact with them. This is especially seen when a "silent world" is experienced by a seriously ill or dying patient. There is a sense of isolation, depression, anger that is unexpressed—hopelessness, helplessness, feelings of estrangement, especially when the caretakers retreat to a position of abandonment and withdrawal. We see this in the current care of AIDS patients. Katz notes that patients feel unimportant, frightened, disregarded, ignored, patronized, dismissed from life, and untrusted (1984, p. 210). Even in instances of cautious prognosis, faith, hope, support, and communication can help reduce the abandonment that the sick individual feels. One might ask if the "silent world of the doctor and patient" exists only with very physically ill patients in hospitals. There are others who feel alienated and like outsiders. The physician can be an abandoning figure, too. Perhaps unwittingly we ourselves participate in this process.

VI

How can one conclude a paper which in some ways is only a beginning? Although some of the ideas and work had been ongoing for some time, it was only when I was a patient in the intensive-care unit that I realized the unifying thread in the themes presented above. A diagnosis had not yet been made, this was my first major hospitalization, and the concerns of all who were and are very close to me were in evidence. I, too, was very concerned, felt "my body was abandoning me," and that, as a result, I was in jeopardy. My caretakers were and are excellent, but the central ideas I have tried to develop kept returning. Paying close attention to my dreams, I realized that I was "in touch" with aspects of me that existed before conscious memory or willing recollection. Very shortly after my birth, my mother developed a serious, septic breast abscess. She and I were separated as it was feared that I, too, might become very ill from contact with her. I was entrusted to unwilling relatives who, in retrospect, were incompetent to deal with and care for a newborn infant. During my hospitalization, which culminated in a coronary-bypass operation, old archaic feelings unlinked to conscious events appeared. By working at them and the accompanying dreams, I could interpret with great value to me what these meant, where they came from, and how the past was resurrected by the "present" catastrophic crisis.

The idea of temporary abandonment and noncaring caretakers came together with what I had been trying to put into appropriate perspective. Clinical data from my work with patients, supervisees, colleagues, "fit," and so I pursued the lines of scientific association wherever they led. By using literary figures and biographical data in the public domain, no data about patients has been revealed, although information and levels of understanding derived from my clinical work are abundant throughout. I have shared a fragment of my own autobiography because I believe knowing how something begins, what was in the mind of the conceiver, can be useful in understanding the product that ensues. Reconstructing the history of the psychological lives of creative individuals has and will be the subject of much discussion. Facts alone do not tell us the story. Patterns which are repeated by the individual themselves and which have similarities in different individuals can open areas for further study. Even with the concerns of methodological issues, there is value in seeing biography as outcome studies with attempts to identify some contributing antecedents.

Stambolian (1972) points out that one is able to recognize various themes, images, and patterns of expression that characterize an author's particular view of reality. Proust calls these phase-types and asserts that understanding an artist's unique characteristics, their ongoing similarity enables a reader to appreciate the writer further. But the task of reconstructing involves knowing the special view of reality that is peculiar to a particular writer (see Stambolian, 1972, p. 2). This we get from attempting to find evidence about the inner structure of a writer's creative personality and from the ways in which the writer's experiences in life (external and internal) were transformed into a work of art. Stambolian devotes his book to a study of Proust, but his insights can be applied to many other creative individuals as well. Submerged past comes into the present; memory, impressions, reminiscences, and reconstructions occur; and patterns emerge. This allows us to get "new truths" which allow us to move further—have new insights, eliminate gaps in the continuity of our understanding, and explain the interests, motives, and outcomes of ourselves and others. This "psychoanalytic process" can occur in a psychoanalytic treatment setting, in a self-induced psychoanalytic encounter where one feels, experiences, and then observes what is or has emerged, and in the study of other lives. Insight can be the creative outcome.

I wish to close by returning to my central theme: abandonment as seen from the point of view of the abandoned has many different facets. The impact will depend on various factors, e.g., when the abandonment occurred, the prior emotional organization of the individual, the circumstances of the abandonment, the "replacements" for the abandoner or abandoners. How can this be handled preventively? Not always easily—preparation, replacement, continuity of contact with a familiar person, facilitating discharge of feelings—be they fear, rage, despair, and recognition and awareness of the caretakers of the turmoil that is ongoing. Man is involved in many experiences where he or she may feel abandoned. In some instances, however, these experiences are of such severity, chronicity, quality, suddenness, or persistence that they render the individual vulnerable to such events in later life. It is by understanding their meaning that we can then intervene therapeutically.

REFERENCES

Adams, P. L., Milner, J. R., & Schrepf, N. A. (1984), *Fatherless Children*. New York: Wiley.

Adelson, E. & Fraiberg, S. (1980), An abandoned mother, an abandoned baby. In: *Clinical Studies in Infant Mental Health*, ed. S. Fraiberg. New York: Basic Books, pp. 221-241.

Barrie, J. M. (1896), *Margaret Ogilvy: By Her Son*. London: Hodder & Stoughton.

Carroll, P. (ed.) (1967), *Edward Dahlberg Reader*. New York: New Directions.

Conger, B., Jr. (1984-1985), Edward Dahlberg and Kansas City. *New Letters*, 51:52-62.

Dahlberg, E. (1964), *Because I Was Flesh*. New York: New Directions.

Dunbar, J., & Dunbar, J. (1970), *J. M. Barrie: The Man behind the Image*. Boston: Houghton Mifflin.

Fuchs, R. G. (1983), *Abandoned Children: Foundlings and Child Welfare in Nineteenth-Century France*. Albany: State of New York Press.

Herlihy, D. & Klapisch-Zuber, C. (1985), *Tuscans and Their Families: A Study of the Florentine Catasto of 1427*. New Haven: Yale University Press.

Katz, J. (1984), *The Silent World of Doctor and Patient*. New York: Free Press.

Kauffman, C., Grunebaum, H., Cohler, B., & Gamer, E. (1979), Superkids: Competent children of psychotic mothers. *Amer. J. Psychiat.*, 136:1398-1402.

Langer, W. (1974), Infanticide: A historical survey. *Hist. Childhood Quart.*, 1:353-365.

Moskovitz, S. (1983), *Love Despite Hate: Child Survivors of the Holocaust and Their Adult Lives*. New York: Schocken Books.

Odier, C. (1956), *Anxiety and Magic Thinking*. New York: International Universities Press.

Pollock, G. H. (1978), On siblings, childhood sibling loss, and creativity. *This Annual*, 6:443-481. New York: International Universities Press.

——— (1982), The mourning-liberation process and creativity: The case of Käthe Kollwitz. *This Annual*, 10:333-353. New York: International Universities Press.

——— (1985), Abandoning parents and abusing caretakers. In: *Parental Influences: In Health and Disease*, ed. E. J. Anthony & G. H. Pollock. Boston: Little, Brown, pp. 349-400.

Robertson, J. & Robertson, J. (producers) (1968), *John, 17 months, for nine days in a residential nursery* (film). London: Tavistock Child Development Research Unit.

Rochlin, G. (1965), *Grief and Discontents*. Boston: Little, Brown.

Stager, L. E. & Wolff, S. R. (1984), Child sacrifice at Carnage. Religious rite or population control? *Biblical Archaeol. Rev.*, 10:30-51.

Stambolian, G. (1972), *Marcel Proust and the Creative Encounter*. Chicago: University of Chicago Press.

Wagatsuma, H. (1981), Child abandonment and infanticide: A Japanese case. In: *Child Abuse and Neglect: Cross-Cultural Perspectives*, ed. J. E. Korbin. Berkeley & Los Angeles: University of California Press, pp. 100-138.
Werner, E. E. & Smith, R. S. (1982), *Vulnerable But Invincible: A Study of Resilient Children*. New York: McGraw-Hill.
Wilson, A. (ed.) (1983), *The Portable Dickens*. New York: Viking Press & Penguin Books.

July 1986

INDEX